DATE			

MEN WANTED FOR THE __U.S. ARMY

AMERICA'S EXPERIENCE WITH AN ALL-VOLUNTEER ARMY BETWEEN THE WORLD WARS

Robert K. Griffith, Jr.

CONTRIBUTIONS IN MILITARY HISTORY, NUMBER 27

Greenwood Press
Westport, Connecticut • London, England

Library of Congress Cataloging in Publication Data

Griffith, Robert K.
    Men wanted for the U.S. Army.

    (Contributions in military history, ISSN 0084-9251;
no. 27)
    Bibliography: p.
    Includes index.
    1. Military service, Voluntary—United States—His-
tory—20th century. 2. United States. Army—Recruitment, enlistment, etc.—History—20th century. I. Title.
UB323.G74   355.2' 2362' 0973   81-6686
ISBN 0-313-22546-X (lib. bdg.)   AACR2

Library of Congress Catalog Card Number: 81-6686
ISBN: 0-313-22546-X
ISSN: 0084-9251

First published in 1982

Greenwood Press
A division of Congressional Information Service, Inc.
88 Post Road West, Westport, Connecticut 06881

Printed in the United States of America

10 9 8 7 6 5 4 3 2 1

For my daughter,
Katharine Harley Griffith,
In Loving Memory

CONTENTS

TABLES

ABBREVIATIONS

ACS	Assistant Chief of Staff
AEFU	American Expeditionary Force University
AFL	American Federation of Labor
AG	Adjutant General
AGO	Adjutant General's Office
AMA	American Medical Association
ANJ	*Army and Navy Journal*
AWC	Army War College
CA	Corps Area
CCC	Civilian Conservation Corps
CG	Commanding General
CIO	Congress of Industrial Equality
CS	Chief of Staff
G1	Assistant Chief of Staff, Director of Personnel
GPO	Government Printing Office
HQ	Headquarters
KAOWC	Keep America Out of War Congress
MHI	U.S. Army Military History Institute
MHRC	Military History Research Collection
MTCA	Military Training Camps Association
NA	National Archives
NCO	noncommissioned officer
NEC	National Emergency Committee
NRA	National Recovery Act
NYT	*New York Times*
OSS	Office of Strategic Services
RG	Record Group
ROA	Reserve Officers' Association
ROTC	Reserve Officer Training Corps
SG	*Report of the Surgeon General*
UMT	universal military training
USARS	U.S. Army Recruiting Service
USMA	United States Military Academy
WDPC	War Department Pay Commission
WPA	Works Progress Administration
WPD	War Plans Division
YMCA	Young Men's Christian Association

PREFACE

Peacetime conscription ended in the United States at midnight June 30, 1973. Ever since, the debate over the success or failure of maintaining the standing forces through volunteerism has gone on more or less constantly. Opponents of the all-volunteer system argue that it is too expensive, brings a disproportionately large number of minorities into the ranks, and undermines the reserve system. They take great pleasure in pointing out recruiting abuses, shortfalls, and low intelligence-test scores by recruits as proof of the services' inability to meet their own standards.[1] Supporters of the volunteer system are equally zealous in their defense of the effort. In 1975, the Department of Defense, while conceding that the current recession might be stimulating enlistments, declared the volunteer force a success, and in September 1977, the Rand Corporation ratified DOD's official optimism. The Rand study argued that the armed forces were not a refuge for blacks and other low-income minorities but continued "to be viewed as an alternative employment option for a very broad cross section of American society. . . ." High costs of recruitment, which Rand conceded, resulted from outdated policies carried over from selective service days.[2]

Both critics and supporters of the volunteer system begin by referring to the President's Commission on an All-Volunteer Armed Force. The Gates Commission, proceeding from its charge by President Nixon in 1969 to develop "a comprehensive plan for eliminating conscription and moving toward an all-volunteer armed force," recommended a prompt end of selective service and transition to the volunteer system.[3] The main inducements offered to volunteers were higher pay, more attractive terms of service, and more relevant practical training.

Although the Gates Commission purported to examine the feasibility of an all-volunteer force for the United States, in fact the report did little more than ratify the conventional American wisdom that more money and better working conditions would insure a steady supply of "labor" for the armed forces. The commission paid scant attention to America's historical experience. The only references to the past were a summary of opposition to conscription in America and a study of methods used to raise forces during wars and national emergencies.[4]

Perhaps the failure to examine America's previous experience with the all-volunteer concept in peacetime is appropriate. David Donald, professor of history at Harvard University, concluded in 1977 that because the United States has passed from an era of abundance to one of limited resources, "the 'lessons' taught by the American past are today not merely irrelevant but dangerous."[5] But if social critics do not even know what the experience of the past was, they can never judge whether or not it is relevant. This study seeks to fill a gap in our knowledge of all-volunteer forces in peacetime and to explore the place of the military in American society during the interwar years, 1919–1940.

In the recent past America's experience with an all-volunteer armed force is indeed rich. Though small by contemporary standards, the interwar army was the largest peacetime force ever maintained by the United States. At the beginning of the period, Americans debated and rejected proposals to substitute universal military training for the volunteer principle as the basis for raising and maintaining an adequate peacetime force. During the relative prosperity of the 1920s, recruiters struggled to keep the army's ranks filled. Familiar slogans like "earn while you learn" and "quality not quantity" are legacies of the recruiting programs of the 1920s. Throughout the decade the War Department, hobbled by the parsimony of the Republican administrations, tried to maintain an adequate force. It labored to improve service attractiveness, and, cognizant of the role of pay as an inducement to enlist, it pleaded (to no avail) for a pay raise in 1928 and 1929. Despite these efforts, enlistments lagged. Commanders complained of poor-quality recruits. Recruiters countered that commanders did not do enough to reenlist good men. The volunteer army was in serious trouble by 1929.

The 1929 stock market crash and ensuing Great Depression caused a swift reversal of the all-volunteer army's fortunes. For a time the high unemployment of the early 1930s greatly enhanced the quality and quantity of enlistments. During the New Deal, however, the volunteer army again experienced difficulties. Annual appropriations remained low, and emergency relief and unemployment programs competed with recruiters for military-age males. Deteriorating world conditions leading to gradual rearmament and expansion of the army beginning in 1936 brought renewed criticism of the volunteer army. By 1939 rearmament required such a rapid expansion of the army that concerned citizens feared the volunteer system was inadequate; it was supplemented with selective service in 1940.

After World War II the draft, uninterrupted except for a brief hiatus in 1947, continued to supply new men to the armed forces until dissatisfaction with the Vietnam War forced a thorough reevaluation of American foreign and military policy. Americans had forgotten that volunteer armies were the norm in peacetime. But when the volunteer army was resurrected in 1973, the problems associated with it had also been forgotten.

This study is divided into four parts: the post–World War I period, which included demobilization and army reorganization; the 1920s to the onset of the Great Depression; the depression years, 1930–1936; and rearmament. Each part consists of two chapters. The first chapter examines events, attitudes, and legislation that affected the army during the period. Legislation, especially the annual appropriation bills, establishes the place of the army in American society, for it is the power of the purse that most effectively influences the armed forces. The second chapter of each part examines the experience of the volunteer army under the changing conditions of American society—what policies governed enlistments and reenlistments, how the army sought to attract and retain enlisted men, and how those policies succeeded during reorganization, prosperity, depression, and rearmament. The primary focus is military manpower procurement. But in examining how the United States raised and maintained its army "to provide for the common defense" during the interwar years the study also seeks to clarify the place and role of the peacetime army in American society.

I incurred many debts in the course of this study since it began on a much smaller scale as a seminar project in 1973. As a teacher Dr. James T. Patterson of Brown University is without peer. It was he who introduced me to recent American history. He always made himself available with ideas and suggestions to guide my research, and his ubiquitous red pencil insured a much improved manuscript. Dr. Howard P. Chudacoff of Brown was also very generous with his time and assistance.

The bulk of the primary sources on the subject are located in the Old Military and Naval Records branch of the National Archives and the U.S. Army Military History Research Collection of the Military History Institute, Carlisle Barracks, Pennsylvania. Of the many people who helped me at the archives, Dr. Timothy K. Nenninger deserves special mention. His tireless efforts at tracking down obscure references when I was ready to give up kept me going on more than one occasion. Col. James Agnew, Director of MHI when I was doing my research, gave me free run of the old Army War College papers and the institute's excellent library. Dr. Richard Sommers, the archivist at MHI, was eager to assist and brought several items to my attention that I might otherwise have overlooked, and Mr. John Slonaker's knowledge of interwar writings on the old volunteer army proved invaluable.

I completed a good deal of my work while a member of the history faculty at West Point. Col. Thomas E. Griess, chairman of the department, and Col. James L. Abrahamson, director of the American history division, gave frequent and valuable advice and constantly encouraged me to keep at it when duties intervened and my spirits flagged. The Association of Graduates, USMA, provided a timely grant that allowed me to continue my research in 1976. Dr. Edward M. Coffman, visiting professor of military history at West Point in 1977–1978, read an earlier manuscript and offered sound criticism and advice. The staff of the Cadet Library, under the direction of Egon Weiss, gave fully of their time. The assistance of Robert Schnare, Irene Veith, and Charlotte Snyder was especially helpful.

My colleagues at the Combat Studies Institute, U.S. Army Command and General Staff College, saw the manuscript through its final revision.

Col. William A. Stofft, director of CSI, and Lt. Col. David Glantz, chief of the teaching committee, gave me the support I needed to keep reading and writing while trying to break into a new job and field. Dr. Ira Gruber, Morrison Professor from 1979 to 1980, helped me over some rough spots in the revision. Dr. D. Clayton James, Morrison Professor in 1980–1981, read the entire final manuscript and suggested some very helpful last-minute changes.

Miss Deborah Bittle of Highland Falls, New York, typed the final manuscript. But she did more than type. Debbie possesses a keen editorial eye, and she saved me from many copy errors. She also reads what she types and, on more than one occasion, offered constructive ideas on organization and content.

I also want to thank the editors and staff at Greenwood Press for their interest and tolerance. Without either of these qualities this manuscript would still be a manuscript in search of a publisher. I especially would like to thank Marie Smith and Arlyne Dorn at Greenwood.

Through it all my family remained a constant source of inspiration and support. My parents, brother, sisters, and in-laws were always asking "How's the book coming?" It was great tonic. My wife Johana finds it hard to remember when this project—surely the "other woman"—was not part of her life. She did double duty as research assistant, proofreader, and copy editor while she pursued her own career and kept our children, dog, and cat away from my desk. She knows more about the interwar army than anyone would reasonably want to know. My debts to her cannot be calculated. Our children were born and are growing up never knowing a time when their father was not working on his book. Yet their presence, more often than not a distraction, was essential.

To all of these and many others not named but not forgotten, my thanks. All the errors contained herein are mine alone. The views expressed are my own and do not necessarily represent those of the Department of the Army or Department of Defense.

RKG
December 1980
Fort Leavenworth, Kansas

NOTES

1. See, for example, "Signs that the Volunteer Army May Come Up Short," *U.S. News and World Report,* May 28, 1973, p. 54; "A Year Without the Draft—How Volunteer System is Working," *U.S. News and World Report,* April 1, 1974, pp. 47–48; "Unemployed Answer U.S. Army's Call," *Washington Post,* January 6, 1975, p. A20; "Army is Disturbed by Recruit Quality," *New York Times,* (hereafter, *NYT*) January 11, 1977, pp. 1, 15; Morris Janowitz, "A New Role for

Military Forces: Toward an All-Volunteer Military Force," *Current* 141 (June 1972): 39–48; Morris Janowitz, "All-Volunteer Military as a Sociopolitical Problem," *Social Problems* 22 (February 1975): 432–49; Alan N. Sabrosky, "The First Years of the Modern Volunteer Army: A Preliminary Assessment," in *American Defense Policy,* 4th ed., ed. John E. Endicott and Roy W. Stafford, Jr. (Baltimore, Md.: Johns Hopkins University Press, 1977) pp. 456–67; Warren Rogers, "Volunteer Army—Is It Working?" *Boston Sunday Globe,* July 27, 1978, pp. A1, A4; Drew Middleton, "The Volunteer Army, Is It Enough?" *NYT,* August 2, 1978, p. A8; David Syrette and Richard H. Kohn, "The Dangers of an All-Volunteer Army," *Military Review,* 52, no. 6 (June 1972): 70–79; Thomas H. Etzold, "Our Diminishing Manpower Reserves," *Army,* 30, no. 1 (January 1980): 10–14; Robin Beard, "The All-Volunteer Army: Hard Facts and Hard Choices," *Strategic Review,* 7, no. 3 (Summary 1979): 42–46.

2. Examples of the opposite view are found in John T. Wheeler, "New Volunteer U.S. Army is Called 'The Best Ever'," *Providence Sunday Journal,* April 27, 1975, p. F12; "Volunteer Army Called Success," *NYT,* February 14, 1975, p. 9; "Volunteer Army Called Success; Pay and Pension Overhaul Urged," *NYT,* September 26, 1977, pp. 1, 15; Richard V. L. Cooper, "The All Volunteer Force: Five Years Later," *International Security* 2 (Spring 1978): 61–131; "All Recruiting Goals for August Met," *NYT,* September 24, 1980, p. B4.

3. *Report of the President's Commission on an All-Volunteer Armed Force* (New York: Macmillan Co., 1970), frontpiece, n.p.

4. Ibid., pp. 157–64; John L. Rafuse, "United States' Experience with Volunteer and Conscript Forces," in *Studies Prepared for The President's Commission on all All-Volunteer Armed Force,* vol. 3, pt. 3 (Washington, D.C.: GPO, 1970), pp. 1–46.

5. David Donald, "Our Irrelevant History," *NYT,* September 8, 1977, p. 27.

MEN WANTED
FOR THE
U.S. ARMY

1

REORGANIZATION AND REFORM, 1919–1920

The volunteer army of the interwar years was the product of the National Defense Act of 1920, which reorganized the army after World War I. The act concluded nearly two decades of a reform effort that attempted to define the role of the army in American society. Reformers within the army and their civilian supporters attempted to create a new kind of army for the United States, one which, in their view, would serve both the social and the military needs of the nation. They envisioned a relatively small standing professional army that would work closely with a larger citizen force to ensure that the United States would have a well-trained and equipped military establishment in peacetime and thus be prepared for all contingencies in the future. But the new army of the postwar era would benefit society in many more ways than merely assure an adequate armed force. Military training for all American males would make them better citizens—physically, mentally, and morally— and would better equip them to be more productive, efficient members of a modern, industrial state.

Several forces frustrated efforts to reform the army. The army, itself a largely conservative hierarchy, showed little inclination for new departures from established concepts. More important, however, Americans in general were apathetic. Anxious to demobilize rapidly, as they had done after every war, Americans in 1919 and 1920 were repeatedly shocked by events at home and abroad that suggested the dangers of reform or radical change. The Bolshevik Revolution continued in Russia and threatened to spread into Western Europe. At home a wave of strikes and a few terrorist bombings seemed to indicate that the revolution might even reach America. The idealism of the war effort, which might have sustained reform of the military, gave way to cynicism in 1919 as Americans watched the Treaty of Versailles take shape. By 1920 many Americans clearly sought a return to quieter times and more traditional values, which, as applied to the army, meant a small, inexpensive force composed of volunteers that was far from the sight and mind of the general public. When the army reorganization plan came before Congress in the spring of 1920, it fell victim to what would shortly be called "normalcy." In its final form the National Defense Act of 1920 did reorganize the army but on a more

1

limited scale than intended and in so doing created many of the problems that would plague the volunteer army for the next two decades.

World War I had only interrupted a reform effort within the army that had had its origins in the chaotic performance of the military establishment during the Spanish-American War.[1] Beginning in 1899 the army underwent a significant organizational change. Under the visionary guidance of Secretary of War Elihu Root the military began a slow and often painful process of reorganization designed to bring it into better harmony with the nation's new position in the world.

In November 1900 Root reported that the strength of the regular army at the close of the current fiscal year would be 2,447 officers and 29,025 enlisted men.[2] At that strength the regular army performed several functions. It garrisoned the southwest border, manned the coastal defenses, provided a ground force supposedly capable of fighting in an emergency until a sufficient volunteer army could be raised, and acted as the nucleus around which that volunteer army could be raised and trained.[3] At that time the army was also engaged in Philippine Insurrection operations. Root complained that the size of the regular army did not reflect the new burdens placed upon it "as our country has grown in wealth and variety of interests, and as more intimate contact with the other nations of the earth has resulted from the natural extension of our trade. . . ."[4] Congress, after prodding from Root, increased the maximum enlisted strength of the regular army to 100,000.[5] Root also pressed for and succeeded in establishing a war college to develop plans and provide information and advice to the commander in chief, and a general staff to enable centralized direction of War Department activities. In response to a broad range of problems with the state militia, revealed by the war with Spain, the reserve system was improved by the Militia Act of 1903. Under this law, known as the Dick Act, the states retained control of their militia, but the federal government assured itself of a better reserve for the regular army by providing arms and equipment at no cost to the National Guard (the organized units of the state militia), by requiring a minimum number of training days for guard units annually, by supplying regular army officers to instruct and train guard units, and by scheduling periodic inspections of the units by regular officers.[6]

One student of the institutional development of the army noted that Root's reforms served "principally as a foundation for continued future improvement."[7] The heart of the nation's ground force, the regular army, remained in many respects the isolated frontier constabulary it had been in peacetime. Although larger than before the Spanish-American War, the regular army remained scattered throughout the United States in small units at small posts dating from the Indian wars and after 1899 in Cuba and the Philippines. Root, his successor Henry L. Stimson, and Chief of Staff Leonard Wood, sought to eliminate many of the army's far-flung units by concentrating them into larger, more centralized organizations. But the numerous posts and forts, then as now, were too important to too many congressmen to be eliminated. Although more centrally organized at the top, the field army continued to display the problems that plagued it in 1898. A test mobilization of a regular army division in 1911, for example, required ninety days to assemble 13,000 troops near San Antonio.[8]

When the European war erupted in August 1914, observers in the United States, already critical of the army's ability to respond to sudden military emergencies, nervously watched the smooth mobilization of Germany and France. During the preparedness campaign that preceded American entry into World War I the very nature and purpose of the regular army were called into question. The debate that ensued focused on a question that would underlie many arguments after 1919: Should the United States have a small professional army that could be expanded with volunteers or conscripts to meet emergencies, or should it rely on an army of citizens trained in peacetime and called forth in an emergency?

Most professional military men harbored a long-standing dislike of citizen soldiers. The militia, they noted, was a citizen force, under the control of the states and was understrength, irregularly equipped, and badly trained. It was also the second line of defense behind the regular army, and the regulars felt that they deserved a more dependable backup. The most articulate spokesman for this view before 1900 had been Emory Upton. A graduate of the Military Academy, Upton served with distinction in the Civil War, rising to the rank of brevet major general. In 1867 he revised the army's infantry tactics, gaining recognition of the commanding general of the army, William T. Sherman, in the process. Sherman appointed Upton commandant of cadets at West Point, where he also acted as the instructor in tactics. In 1876 Upton headed a commission that toured Europe and Asia to observe foreign armies. He was greatly impressed by the German army, which had so recently triumphed over Austria and France. Upton particularly noted the German cadre system whereby the units of the professional standing army could expand, divide, and expand further with trained reservists when mobilized. Remembering with horror the carnage of the Civil War, which he attributed to the use of poorly trained militia and volunteer units, Upton proposed a similar expandable army system for the United States. He advanced his recommendations first in *The Armies of Asia and Europe* in 1878 and then in an expanded version in *The Military Policy of the United States from 1775*, published posthumously in 1904. Upton's expandable army became the goal of the professionals who despaired of ever achieving a reliable potential for mobilization through the militia.[9]

By 1914 the European armies that so impressed Upton had grown to monstrous size. The development strengthened the resolve of Upton's followers, who doubted that they could ever create a similar American army if they had to depend on a reserve composed of state militia. The crux of the problem lay in the quality of the citizen soldier. In Upton's opinion, a view still shared by most military professionals, civilians required extensive and repetitive military training before they could constitute an effective reserve. European armies depended on peacetime conscription, service of two or three years in the active army, and long-term service in the reserves to accomplish this task. The problem facing Upton's followers, however, was that such a program was clearly unacceptable to Americans, who cherished their "minuteman" heritage of the citizen in arms springing to the nation's defense after war was declared, and harbored traditional fears of a large standing army and professional military elite.

Fear of a large army and the celebration of the virtues of an armed citizenry dated from the origins of the republic. Cultural memories of Cromwell's New Model Army that dominated England for a decade following the English Revolution and of British regulars controlled by the crown enforcing royal prerogatives in the American colonies led the leaders of the American Revolution to insist on civilian control of the military as one of their major goals. As American military policy evolved after the Revolution, those concerned with assuring civilian supremacy found that one of the best ways to limit the influence of the military was to restrict its size. The state militia, also a vestige of the colonial experience and mobilized only in wartime or domestic emergency, was celebrated in American history as the true military strength of the nation.[10]

The Uptonians challenged the validity of the militia myth. The small professional army backed by irregularly trained state militia, they argued, no longer served the best interests of the nation. If forced to confront a modern military machine like Germany, the small regular army would be overwhelmed before the militia, in the form of the National Guard and citizen volunteers, could be mobilized. To remedy the situation, Uptonians urged the creation of a large standing army of long-service professionals, which would form the core of an expandable wartime force. They envisioned a regular army of between 250,000 to 500,000 men, which could expand to an emergency force of 750,000 to 1.5 million men if necessary. Upton's followers assumed that the manpower necessary for such an expansion would be volunteers but did not rule out conscription.[11]

While professional soldiers worried over the inability of the United States to build an army according to Uptonian principles, an alternative solution gradually emerged under the sponsorship of Leonard Wood, undoubtedly the most unconventional chief of staff the army ever had. A graduate of Harvard Medical School, Wood entered the upper echelon of the army politically. He did distinguish himself as a contract surgeon during the Indian wars, but it was his friendship with Republican politicians that secured him the command of the Rough Riders in 1898. Wood's

Republican connections, especially his friendship with Theodore Roosevelt and shared convictions regarding the role of the United States in world affairs, eventually led to his appointment as chief of staff in 1910.[12]

Wood rejected Upton's proposals for building an American army on European lines. Citizen soldiers, he argued, did not require long service in the regular army but could be trained in six months. The problem was not the citizen but state control of the militia. His ideas appeared in a supplement to the Annual Report of the Secretary of War for 1912. Secretary Stimson and Wood gave close attention to the young general staff captain, John McAuley Palmer, who prepared the report.[13] Palmer found the expandable army concept unworkable for the United States:

> When I assumed a peacetime nucleus big enough to make a real foundation for effective expansion for a great war, I found that the American people would be saddled with a big standing army in time of peace. When I assumed a peacetime nucleus small enough to give any chance of acceptance by Congress, it would result in too small a war army—unless I also assumed a rate of expansion that would be obviously absurd.[14]

Palmer proposed an army in being, a full-strength force containing all the arms and organizations necessary to fight at the beginning of hostilities, not one that required expansion before it could fight effectively. The mission of such an army, the regular army, would be to fight in the early stages of a war while the citizen army mobilized behind it. To circumvent the problems inherent in state control of the National Guard and emergency volunteers, Palmer favored the creation of a regular army reserve. Such a force would be raised by extending the regular army enlistment contract from three to six years. Enlistees would serve on active duty for three years and have the option of being furloughed to the reserve for the final three years of their contract. Designed to become effective over a number of years, the regular army reserve would provide a replacement pool of trained soldiers for the regular army during an emergency. The proposed plan envisioned ''an effective force of 460,000 mobile troops and 42,000 Coast Artillery'' as the ''minimum number of first-line troops necessary . . . at the outbreak of a war with a first class power . . .'' compared to the existing force of 92,121 in the regular army and the unknown quality of the militia whose strength averaged 100,000.[15] Later Palmer modified his plan. He abandoned the idea of raising the regular army reserve through long-term enlistments and suggested instead that all able-bodied males in the country receive military training in peacetime and be assigned to reserve units that could be called into federal service only in times of declared war.[16]

Like their civilian counterparts. Palmer and other reform-minded army officers of the Progressive Era were seeking to restructure institutions of society to cope with the changing world around them. Reorganizing the army in such a way as to make the regular army the instructor of a larger citizen army would make the military establishment more efficient and therefore more capable of serving the military interests of the nation. But the regular army as a school for citizen soldiers had broader possibilities. Military training and service in the reserves could be used to improve and uplift the entire nation. Beyond that, some spokesmen suggested that the army could be used to teach citizenship and self-discipline and in so doing serve as a vehicle for the Americanization of the nation's increasingly heterogeneous population.[17] The reforms of Palmer and his followers were the military manifestations of the efficiency-minded progressivism of pre–World War I America.

As the preparedness campaign heated up, Leonard Wood, though no longer chief of staff, took up the cudgels. His first effort on behalf of preparedness was the "Plattsburg Idea." As originally conceived in 1913, while Wood was still chief of staff, the plan involved summer training for college students. The purpose of military training summer camps was to increase the number of trained men in the citizenry who might be called upon to serve as officers in a national emergency.[18] The War Department operated two camps on an experimental basis in 1913 and authorized limited funds for more camps in 1914. After the outbreak of the war in Europe the camps attracted the attention and support of an influential group of New York businessmen led by Grenville Clark, a law partner of Elihu Root's son. Clark and his associates formed the Military Training Camps Association (MTCA), an organization that, in an often stormy alliance with Wood, became a key pressure group in the effort to reform the army.[19]

The "Plattsburg Idea" involved training educated young men to be officers. But the army also needed soldiers. In pressing his advocacy for a citizen army, Wood next called for conscription. "The voluntary system," he declared in 1915, "has failed us in the past and will again fail us in the future."[20] Wood was hardly the first military leader to consider conscription necessary in future American wars. Army planners assumed by 1915 that some form of compulsory service would be necessary in a future war involving the United States and a major power. Wood found influential support from Stimson, his former boss, and from Stimson's predecessor, Root. Both men became members of the advisory board to the National Association for Universal Military Training, one of a host of preparedness organizations that blossomed after the beginning of the war in Europe.[21]

President Wilson resisted the preparedness campaign as long as possible. Wilson feared that military preparations by the United States would detract from his efforts to mediate the European war. But several developments in 1915–1916—a vociferous lobby for preparedness, the threat of war with Mexico, growing tensions with Germany—finally led him to act. Under the direction of Secretary of War Lindley M. Garrison, the general staff prepared a prescription for the nation's military shortcomings. The "Statement of a Proper Military Policy for the United States" made concessions to the concept of the citizen soldier but clearly reflected the Uptonians disdain for the militia. Translated into legislative proposals, the plan called for the creation of a Continental army of 400,000 citizens to be recruited over three years. The Continental army in effect bypassed the National Guard as the second line of defense because, like Palmer's regular army reserve, it was to be under federal control at all times.[22]

Garrison's plan won little support. The preparedness campaigners divided over the proposal. The MTCA supported the Continental army scheme in return for official recognition of the "Plattsburg Idea." More extreme advocates of preparedness including Leonard Wood continued to demand conscription in the form of universal military training in peacetime and service in an emergency. But the real opposition came from the National Guard and states' rights congressmen. Under the leadership of Virginia Democrat James Hay, chairman of the House Military Affairs Committee, an alternative emerged. It aimed at strengthening the National Guard by improving its responsiveness to the federal government. Garrison adamantly opposed any compromise and resigned. Wilson replaced him with Newton D. Baker, formerly the progressive mayor of Cleveland.[23]

Baker and Hay cooperated, and the House soon approved a plan approximating Hay's proposals. The Senate, more responsive to preparedness pressure, stuck with the Continental army plan. The deadlock that ensued was broken not by events in Europe but by a flare-up on the Mexican border.

In March 1916 General Francisco "Pancho" Villa led a raid into New Mexico burning the town of Columbus and killing nineteen citizens in an effort to discredit the new government of his rival, Venustiano Carranza. Washington responded by ordering Brigadier General John J. Pershing across the border in pursuit of Villa. Pershing's 5,000-man expedition virtually denuded the Southwest of regular troops as it plunged into northern Mexico. Secretary of War Baker frantically tried to recruit the regular army up to strength and, in response to nervous pleas from governors in the region, called out the National Guard of the southwestern states to guard the border. Recruiting lagged and the states' militia revealed themselves to be woefully understrength and inadequately equipped and trained. In this atmosphere Congress compromised on the army legislation before it.[24]

The result was the National Defense Act of June 3, 1916. It provided for an increase in the peacetime strength of the regular army from 94,000 to 175,000 over five years. Following Upton's formula, this regular force was designed to expand, through use of trained reservists, to a maximum strength of 286,000 in wartime. The act increased the National Guard from 123,000 to 457,000 and created a reserve corps to be manned by former regular army enlisted men and officers commissioned under a Reserve Officers Training Corps (ROTC) program at various colleges throughout the country. The act also permitted the president to federalize the guard with the consent of Congress. Although affirming a universal obligation of "all able-bodied male citizens" between the age of eighteen and forty-five, service in all components of the military establishment remained voluntary.[25]

The act came under harsh criticism from extreme preparedness advocates who, pointing to the mass armies then locked in trench warfare in Europe, argued that it did not go nearly far enough toward giving the United States an adequate capability for mobilization. Events on the Mexican border soon buttressed their contentions.

President Wilson called the National Guard into federal service almost immediately after signing the new National Defense Act. At that time the enlisted strength of the regular army was 94,000 and that of the National Guard about 123,000. Secretary Baker continued to recruit for the regular army and in addition began seeking men for the guard. But inducements were poor, and volunteers responded slowly. In ten months the enlisted strengths of the two forces increased by only 27,197 and 50,600 respectively. On the southwestern border, meanwhile, the usual problems continued to plague the federalized National Guard units. Critics of the new defense policy felt vindicated. The guard remained inefficient, and reliance on volunteers in time of emergency appeared to be inadequate to meet the demands of modern mobilization and warfare. In view of what they considered to be the obvious failure of half-steps toward reform, preparedness advocates demanded universal military training.[26]

During the short session of Congress following the elections of 1916 Oregon Senator George Chamberlain, head of the Senate Military Affairs Committee, introduced a universal military training (UMT) bill, and the general staff began work on a version of its own. With the support of the Chamber of Commerce, the National Education Association, the Union League, and most of the urban press (efficiency-minded groups that favored "rational" solutions to the problems of society and the abandonment of traditional values that impeded progress), the advocates of UMT sensed that victory was at hand. It was not. Rapid deterioration of relations with Germany following the resumption of unrestricted submarine warfare in February 1917 eventually led America into the war. Schemes for long-term military reform gave way to more immediate considerations.[27]

When Woodrow Wilson asked Congress for a declaration of war against Germany on April 2, 1917, he also requested that the manpower necessary for the undertaking "be chosen upon the principle of universal liability to service. . . ."[28] In February, Wilson, convinced by Baker that voluntary enlistments would be insufficient if war came, had already ordered the War Department to prepare a conscription bill. The bill received quick congressional attention after the declaration of war and became the Selective Service Act on May 18, 1917.

Initially, men could still volunteer for the regulars or the guard provided they had not been ordered to report for induction in the newly organized national army, which was to be raised wholly by conscription. The regular army continued to accept volunteers until December 15, 1917, when all men of registration age were prohibited from enlisting. Thereafter the regular army continued to accept qualified volunteers not eligible for selective service until the War Department suspended all enlistments in August 1918. Between April 1917 and August 1918, a total of 883,519 men volunteered and were accepted for service in all components of the ground forces; 2,666,867 men entered all components of the service under the provisions of the Selective Service Act.[29]

Although the Selective Service Act called for a separate regular army, national guard, and national army, the demands of war quickly resulted in a blending of components as men were transferred back and forth to different units. By January 31, 1918, the regular army and National Guard contained some 51,000 drafted men.[30] On August 7, 1918, the amalgamation of the army received official recognition when the War Department issued a general order abolishing the distinction between components and created the Army of the United States.[31] The Selective Service Act also stipulated that the service of all men entering the Army after April 1917, whether as draftees or volunteers, should expire four months after the end of the war.[32] The consequences of the merger of army components and the "service for the duration" clause of the Selective Service Act did not become apparent until just before the armistice.

By 1919 only a few thousand men who had enlisted prior to April 1917, when the "service for the duration" clause went into effect, and thus were still bound by their enlistment contract to a full three years of service, remained in the army. The draft ceased with the armistice, and with voluntary enlistments suspended the army suddenly found itself faced with a manpower crisis. Most Americans considered the armistice as good as the end of the war, and pressure mounted to "bring the boys home." The amalgamation of army components during the war further complicated the problem. Few regular army units existed with enough men, whose terms of service did not expire within four months, to remain effective. The Siberian and Murmansk-Archangel Expeditionary Forces, an occupation army for the American sector on the Rhine, bases in France, and the prewar duties of the regular army required the continued presence of soldiers on duty. In order to alleviate the critical shortage of men in the regular army units and speed demobilization, Secretary Baker asked Congress to fund an interim army of 509,909 enlisted men until such time as the United States could determine the shape of the postwar world and formulate new policies accordingly.[33] This appeal forced a renewed debate over the nature of America's peacetime army. This debate, unlike that of the prewar years, settled the question of what size the army should be and whether the force should be strictly voluntary or supported by universal military training.

During the preparation of Baker's interim army bill the general staff, which had prepared a universal military training bill for Senator Chamberlain's committee prior to American entry into the war, again considered including a proposal for UMT. But Peyton C. March, who became chief of staff in March 1918, was an Uptonian and adamantly opposed any form of UMT. March firmly believed in an expandable standing army in peacetime supported by conscription in case of war or an emergency.[34] He refused to permit the inclusion of a UMT plan in the bill. The National Guard received no mention either, because March believed that the National Defense Act of 1916 adequately covered guard operations.[35]

In presenting a bill requesting a 500,000-man army with no mention of either UMT or the National Guard, the War Department offended virtually every interest group concerned with military affairs. The National Guard could not support legislation that did not assure its postwar status. UMT advocates also objected to being ignored. During hearings Baker avoided questions about universal training saying he did "not believe it wise to decide upon a policy until the peace terms are settled."[36] Baker ran into greater trouble over the large strength figure, which received a cool reception from representatives traditionally hostile to a large standing army and from those elements of Congress who reflected growing public concern over the size of federal expenditures. Representative Otis Wingo of Arkansas noted that an army of 100,000 had been sufficient before the war, and he saw no reason why it should be increased.[37] Percy Quin of Mississippi asked, "Why should we need 500,000 men after we have just won the great war, and the President over yonder around the peace table proposing a league to prevent war?" He went on to the applause of the House:

Across the seas are still two millions of men. We may need some there, but the greater part of that great number . . . should be transported back across the Atlantic Ocean and put out into the fields. Old Bossy and old Muley are calling for them. The bobwhites out in the cornfield are calling for the boys back on the farm, and here we are proposing to keep two millions of men standing about in idleness, drawing salaries, and wasting money, and to have 500,000 more in this country. What are the people going to think about it? I will tell you what they are going to think. They are going to talk in 1920. They are going to talk at the ballot box.[38]

It soon became evident that the bill would not pass during the current session. In order to provide troops for the army, the House agreed to consider a Senate bill authorizing the resumption of enlistments for the regular army under the provisions of the National Defense Act of 1916.

When finally approved on February 22, 1919, the bill restricted enlistments, thus holding maximum strength of the army at 175,000.[39] Discussion of further army reform was postponed until the new Congress, scheduled to meet in special session beginning in May 1919, took up the army appropriation bill for 1920.

Undaunted by the reversal of his plans in February, March prepared to push the same bill before the new Sixty-sixth Congress in June. It became known in May 1919 that the War Department planned to press for the same strength of 529,000 officers and men when the appropriations bill was reintroduced.[40]

This issue—of army size—was complicated by a simultaneous debate over UMT. Shortly after American entry into the war two preparedness lobbies, the National Security League and the Army League, had vowed to continue their efforts to educate the public and Congress of the necessity for a permanent UMT program.[41] They gained support in June 1918 when the American Medical Association (AMA) and the Rotarians endorsed UMT at their conventions. The AMA, for example, applauded "the wonderful mental and physical benefits which have been manifested in the young manhood of America through intensive military training [during the war]." The association urged the swift adoption of UMT in peacetime "for all young men before the right of suffrage is granted them. . . ." Other groups that continued to support UMT included the YMCA and leading educators led by the presidents of Columbia and Harvard universities.[42] The Military Training Camps Association, too, believed that UMT was necessary. Its support represented the logical extension of the "Plattsburg Idea," for while reserve officers were trained at the summer camps and the newly created ROTC, no provisions yet existed to secure trained enlisted men on a large scale. To this end the MTCA now lent its full support to UMT and added the declaration "Devoted to the Cause of Universal Military Training" to the masthead of its journal.[43] The crusade for UMT reflects both the efficiency-conscious progressivism of prewar America and the war-induced power of professional and corporate groups who hoped that UMT would make possible a more trained, disciplined, and productive work force. Business's search for more efficient labor through UMT was but one aspect of its pursuit of that illusive quarry. Before the war, American businessmen had been fascinated by the disciplined German work force. When Henry Ford adapted Frederick Taylor's time and motion studies to mass production, the drive for greater efficiency through standardization and worker conformity acquired even greater urgency.[44] If UMT, which implied the melding of undisciplined youths into soldiers, could contribute to business's needs, so much the better!

After the armistice the UMT groups stepped up their efforts. On November 19, 1918, H. H. Sheets, secretary of the National Association for Universal Military Training, declared, "Universal Military Training in time of peace and equal national service in time of war . . . is the lesson

500,000 enlisted men in peacetime. A big army, congressmen argued, would be expensive—costing $798,660,000 annually. The cost for the two years prior to entry into the war averaged $240 million. General March estimated an additional outlay of $94 million for the three-month training program.[59] More than cost was at issue. Senator Hiram Johnson of California expressed the feelings of many Americans when he asked March why, after having just concluded the war to end all wars, "where we are facing an era of universal peace, we should have an Army many times larger than we have ever had in our history before?" Responding for March, Baker replied that the League of Nations, and American participation in it, was not a settled issue. Should the league not be formed, Baker warned, an army of 500,000 would be too small.[60]

The National Guard also opposed the Baker-March bill. Major General John F. O'Ryan, the only National Guard officer to command a division throughout the war, declared the regular army "an obsolete institution," expensive to maintain, and "out of harmony with efforts to establish world peace. . . . The creation and maintenance of a large Regular Army will make our protestations of peaceful intentions seem insincere to the rest of the world," he warned. O'Ryan suggested retaining a 100,000- to 120,000-man force of professionals to train a larger citizen army formed by merging the remaining components of the regular army, National Guard, and reserves.[61] Another faction of guard officers supported a plan that envisioned a smaller regular army and a more independent national guard. Speaking for the National Guard Association, Colonel Ransome Gillette of the New York guard said, "the dependence of the United States for its Army forces . . . must rest upon the citizenship and not upon a professional-paid army." The National Guard Association presented its own bill, sponsored by Senator Joseph Frelinghuysen of New Jersey, that advocated UMT as "a necessary step toward adequate national preparedness . . . that . . . can best be developed in conjunction with the National Guard."[62]

The Military Training Camps Association also expressed dissatisfaction with the War Department's plan. Ostensibly testifying on behalf of the MTCA bill, Leonard Wood took every opportunity to undercut the big army provisions of the Baker-March bill. The former chief of staff argued that a 500,000-man army was too big and too expensive for peacetime America. Furthermore, the period of training proposed by the army was too short; six months would be more appropriate. Wood then extolled the benefits that would accrue to the nation under UMT. His words captured nicely the efficiency consciousness of the UMT advocates and their supporters in the business community:

The man comes out of the training camp . . . better physically. He comes out with a better coordinated mind and muscle; he has learned habits of promptness, personal neatness, respect for authority, respect for the law, respect for the rights of other people; he has learned to do things when he is told and as told and to do them with promptness and exactness. . . . I think it is one of the strongest forces for Americanization we have.[63]

Wood was supported by former Secretary of War Henry L. Stimson, who considered the 500,000-man army "a larger size than I had thought necessary and I am quite clear that under any method of recruiting, which has been in force since I have been acquainted with the War Department, it would be impossible to raise such an army upon anything like the pay which the Army is now receiving." He supported an army of 300,000 men and universal military training for six months.[64]

The Baker-March bill drew sharp criticism from outside interests like the UMT groups and the National Guard, but in terms of interest group opposition, elements within the army itself scuttled the bill. On October 19, 1919, John McAuley Palmer, now a colonel, appeared before Senator Wadsworth's committee. Palmer had served as Pershing's chief of operations for a time in France and later as a brigade commander in the Argonne. Shortly after the armistice Palmer returned to general staff duty as a deputy in the War Plans Division, where he had unsuccessfully objected to March's ideas and domination of the reorganization plans. Nevertheless, Palmer got the opportunity to testify.[65] His views were well known in army circles, and the hearing room was crowded with officers.

Palmer began by stating that the Baker-March bill was out of harmony with American institutions. He emphasized the need for greater citizen participation in the military. By organizing the citizen army and maintaining only a small regular army on active service in peacetime, costs could be held to a minimum. Furthermore, he added, "as all our great wars have been fought in the main by citizen armies, the proposal for an organized citizen army in time of peace is merely a proposal for perfecting a traditional national institution to meet modern requirements which no longer permit extemporization after the outbreak of war." He recommended a standing regular army of 280,000 enlisted men—not an expandable force following Uptonian principles, but a force in being that would maintain the military facilities of the nation and provide a ready force for the early stages of an emergency. "The main feature of the military establishment of the United States," he said, "should be a trained citizen army. . . ." Initially that army should be composed of veterans of the war, and then universal military training would provide replacements for the veterans. The task of the regular army was to provide training cadre and administration necessary for the citizen army's maintenance. Palmer so impressed the committee that Wadsworth requested his services as an adviser.[66]

Palmer's testimony, which was similar in most respects to that of Wood and Stimson, hurt the War Department badly, but the *coup de grace* came from Pershing. The general of the armies' feelings on the size and role of the postwar army remained a mystery, but it was known that he had devoted considerable thought to the subject. Pershing was acquainted with Palmer and his ideas, and he followed the testimony of all witnesses carefully. His appearance on October 31, 1919, before a joint session of the House and Senate Military Committees ended the mystery. At the outset it was clear that he did not support March. Instead, he too endorsed a citizens' army. "It is my belief," Pershing told the congressmen, "that if America had been adequately prepared [at the beginning of the war,] our rights would never have been violated; our institutions would never have been threatened." He went on to outline what he felt was necessary:

As a military policy we should have, first a permanent Military Establishment large enough to provide against sudden attack; second, a small force sufficient for expeditionary purposes to meet our international obligations, particularly on the American continent; third, such force as may be necessary to meet our internal requirements; fourth, a trained citizen reserve organized to meet the emergency of war.

Following Palmer, he favored a standing army of 275,000 to 300,000 backed up by a federalized National Guard and an organized reserve force manned by citizens trained for a minimum of six months according to a universal program.[67]

After Pershing's testimony the Baker-March bill was clearly a dead issue. On November 16, 1919, the Senate Committee on Military Affairs announced its intention to draft its own bill. Colonel Palmer would assist in preparing the new legislative proposals.[68]

The successful opposition to the big army proposals contained in the War Department appropriation requests of January and June 1919 and in the Baker-March bill rested less on the objections of army opponents than on grass-roots hostility to large armies. Judging from newspaper editorials across the country, there was clearly little support for the 500,000-man force. The Springfield *Republican* declared, "Opposition in Congress to a standing army of that size is natural and wholesome." The *Literary Digest,* commenting on Senator Chamberlain's remark that the Baker-March bill was "Militarism Gone Mad," observed that opposition to the bill came from many quarters including those usually supportive of the army. Senator Arthur Capper wrote in his Topeka *Capper's Weekly,* "I believe we should have a small de-Prussianized regular army to do police duty and to train a larger National Guard of citizen soldiers." The *New York Times,* which generally supported army reorganization, cautioned, "Rational economy in the administration of the Government is expected by the people, and they will not tolerate an inflated military establishment." The *Times* applauded what it called a "frankness and wisdom [which] Congress has never heard from the army before," concerning testimony on the Baker-March bill. John McAuley Palmer came in for special praise. The *Times* approved of his selection by the Wadsworth committee to draft the new bill because, "No one else has given the subject so much study or has been so tremendously earnest about realizing the plan of a people's army."[69]

While the critics of the Baker-March bill opposed a large standing army, many favored UMT. Senator Chamberlain, for example, directed his outrage at March when he called the big army bill a "preposterous scheme." Chamberlain remained a staunch advocate of UMT. Major General John O'Ryan, commander of the New York National Guard, who vigorously condemned the Baker-March bill during Senate hearings, also favored UMT. "All the leaders of the movement for real preparedness," O'Ryan said, "have urged the organization of an army like those of Switzerland and Australia," which served as the models for Palmer's ideas. The *New York Times,* while refraining from a flat endorsement of UMT at the time, spoke warmly of Palmer's ideas and suggested that if Congress followed his advice, it would shortly "give the country a mobile force of several million men who could be rapidly mobilized."[70]

The year 1919 did not bring total defeat to Newton Baker. Universal military training, a program Baker now wholly supported, came through the hearings relatively unchallenged and remained a real possibility in the minds of its advocates. Baker also realized a personal victory in 1919 when Congress approved funds to sustain a program of educational and vocational training for soldiers. The program had begun simply enough during the war. In February 1918 Baker had ordered the creation of a Committee on Education and Special Training. The committee, headed by Colonel Hugh Johnson, was directed "to study the needs of the . . . service for skilled men and technicians, [and] to determine how such needs shall be met. . . ." In May 1918 the army ordered 80,000 men sent to educational institutions and industrial establishments for special training.[71] During the war educational and vocational training served primarily military needs and interests. As the end of the war became apparent, it assumed a new role. In October 1918 Brigadier General R. I. Rees, the new chairman of the committee, approached the chief of staff with a proposal that soldiers waiting to be discharged be offered "training along educational lines to better prepare [them] for re-entrance into civilian life."[72] The plan was approved, and Rees was sent to France to implement it. In January 1919 he established the American Expeditionary Force University at Beaune. A faculty composed of professional teachers already in the army and civilians brought from the United States was recruited and classes began on March 15.[73]

Before he left for France, Rees expressed the opinion that the educational and vocational program need not be temporary. In December 1918 the *Army and Navy Journal* reported on his ideas for making the army a

national school. Rees advocated "productive preparedness." He proposed an army of a million men of which only 250,000 would be engaged
strictly in military activities. The remaining 750,000 would serve for a
year, and during that time they would receive "practical education . . . in
which the soldier would be taught to become a civilian of greatly increased
earning power after his period of public service. . . ."[74] The idea was not
entirely new. Before the war army and nonarmy progressives had talked
of using military service to uplift the nation. Moreover, it appealed to
UMT advocates and others eager to promote a well-disciplined, productive
nation. The idea struck a positive note with Newton Baker. In May the
New York Times reported that Baker would shortly announce plans to use
"the military establishment as a medium for training the youth of the
nation. . . ."[75] A modest version of the program was incorporated into the
army's appropriation request for the fiscal year beginning July 1, 1919.
Baker proposed the establishment of schools at all major army installations
in the United States and overseas. The measure survived congressional
hostility to the big army provisions of the bill. Congress voted $2 million,
mainly for teachers' salaries and texts, to get the program started.[76]

Baker's ready acceptance of the concept of using the army to uplift the
educational level of the nation clearly reflected his progressive background. But the plan also demonstrated a practical side of the secretary of
war. The draft ended with the armistice. The army needed men. As Baker
explained later, there were three ways to get men into a peacetime army.
The first method was by compulsion. He dismissed conscription saying,
"the American spirit would not sustain an application of the draft . . . in
peacetime." Baker also dismissed raising soldiers' pay. Such a step would
"bring the Army as an occupation into competition with civil pursuits."
Not only would increased pay be expensive, but it would lower the service
to the level of a mere job, "and [deprive] it of the patriotic
impulse . . . which is one of the ennobling features of being a soldier. . . ."
The remaining alternative lay in making the army "so inherently attractive
that young men will seek to get into the army because of the advantages
it offers." By offering educational and vocational training, the army would
"become a place in which a young man serving the state and getting an
enlargement of mind and spirit which comes from service of the state,
receives also new capacities for civilian usefulness, a new outlook on life,
new educational and vocational advantages."[77] Furthermore, although he
never said so directly, Baker could not help but see the vocational training
scheme as but another way to obtain business support for his other army
reforms.

Baker prevailed over conservative opponents of the plan within the
army. On September 5, 1919, he ordered the creation of an Educational
and Recreation Branch of the War Plans Division, general staff, to admin-
ister the program. In addition to the $2 million approved by Congress, the

program received the facilities, equipment, and unexpended funds left over from the wartime program. The army became a national school.[78]

With the educational and vocational question settled, Congress now resumed its discussion of UMT, which became the center of attention in early 1920. Supporters of universal training rallied to the cause. At its first national convention the new American Legion, organized in France shortly after the end of the war by Colonel Theodore Roosevelt, Jr., and several other Plattsburg alumni, endorsed universal military training.[79] Major Richard Stockton presented the case for UMT in a dispassionate article in the *North American Review*. Responding to critics who claimed large armies and compulsory training were unnecessary after the "war to end all wars," Stockton said, "With or without a League of Nations, the day of war has not passed." He went on to point out that since opposition to a large army forced the United States to maintain a small standing force, it must be "supplemented by a large, efficient citizen soldiery."[80] The MTCA, cooperating closely with the American Legion and National Security League, launched a massive publicity campaign through the winter of 1919–1920 in support of UMT, and worked closely with Colonel Palmer and Senator Wadsworth on preparation of the Senate bill.[81]

Wadsworth's committee reported its bill on January 26, 1920. The bill provided for a standing regular army of 280,000 men, a federalized National Guard, a reserve army of citizens raised by a compulsory military training program, and standby draft authority for the president. The citizen reserve could be called to duty only in time of declared national emergency. The cost of the program totaled $500 million, but was expected to decline after three years.[82] The *New York Times*, whose assistant publisher Julius Ochs Adler was a member of the MTCA, hailed the bill saying, "The Country should have for its protection an available citizen army, and unless young men are trained to be a reserve to the Regular Army, the second line of defense, the first being the navy, will surely dwindle and deteriorate."[83] Other supporters of UMT quickly added their praise of the bill. General O'Ryan, whose influence in the National Guard was significant, called it the "biggest thing that has been proposed in the line of military legislation since the beginning of our country."[84]

Before long, however, it became evident that UMT was doomed. Perhaps blinded by their enthusiasm for the program, its supporters underestimated the opposition to the measure centered in the West and South. While the white majority in the South traditionally was promilitary, southern military loyalties lay with a strong National Guard under state control rather than with a larger regular army that responded to the federal government. Furthermore, UMT raised the specter of arming and training blacks, a notion that white southerners could not tolerate. Opposition to UMT from antimilitarist, labor, and farm organizations was well known. During hearings in both houses in the autumn of 1919, the committees had heard additional evidence of grass-roots opposition to UMT. For example, Orlando Holway, adjutant general of the Wisconsin National Guard, told the Wadsworth committee in December, that while employers and other prominent men from his region favored UMT, ". . . The farmer and the employed men [do] not, and they are in the majority." John Hipp, a Denver lawyer, wrote to the committee noting ". . . with regret that the military authorities are still clamoring for and seeking to enforce universal military training." He urged the committee to reject the measure, adding that his views "represent those of a large majority of the people whom I meet in church and lodge and in social circles in my daily intercourse. . . ."[85]

Opponents of UMT reacted swiftly to the Wadsworth bill. The *Pittsburgh Sun* called it "another Prussianized Proposal." The *Des Moines Register* agreed, calling the Senate bill "precisely the program Bismarck persuaded Germany to adopt. . . ." Others concurred. The *Jacksonville Times-Union* said, "Congress knows that the people are for peace, not war, and the protests of the regulars and the ammunition makers will not be sufficient to cause the placing of an unnecessary burden on the country at this time."[86] These expressions represent the traditional American fear of standing armies and compulsory service. There were fears, too, of more sinister motives attributed to UMT. Summarizing the UMT and standby draft provisions of the Wadsworth bill, William Chenery wrote in *The Survey*, "Whatever the arguments for universal military training and for conscription were prior to the World War it is certainly obvious that no foreign enemy has either the resources or the will to invade America at the present time or in the immediate future." Chenery concluded that the only possible purpose for such policies "lies in the domestic rather than in the foreign field," perhaps for the suppression of "any expression of the grievances of workers."[87] His statement reflected the feeling of many groups—ethnic, labor, farmers—that UMT aimed at stamping out dissent and keeping the working classes in line.

Taking heart from such opposition, congressional figures joined in the assault in 1920. On February 1, 1920, William E. Borah of Idaho declared, "universal military training and conscription in time of peace are the taproots of militarism." UMT, Borah charged, would cost the taxpayer between $700 million and $1 billion a year. "Only the most imminent necessity would justify adding this additional expense," he concluded.[88] Many of Borah's colleagues concurred in this questioning of Wadsworth's estimate of the cost of UMT.

Opposition to universal training was even more evident in the House of Representatives. The military affairs subcommittee dealing with army reorganization, chaired by Daniel R. Anthony of Kansas, noted the mood of the country and prepared a bill without provisions for UMT. When the bill was reported in February 1920, supporters of UMT threatened to carry the issue to the floor. But on February 9 a Democratic caucus voted 106 to 17 against inclusion of any provisions for military training in the reorganization bill.[89]

Faced with the obvious fact that the House would not approve compulsory training, Senate proponents of the measure sought to save some form of the idea by offering to substitute voluntary military training for universal training. Hastily worked out by Palmer and introduced as an amendment to the Wadsworth bill by Senator Frelinghuysen of New Jersey, the voluntary training plan was approved by a vote of 46 to 9 in the Senate. It offered four months of military training to civilians between the ages of eighteen and twenty-eight who volunteered for the program. When the bill went to conference, House members successfully demanded elimination of even voluntary training. The proposed standby draft authority for the president was also struck from the final bill.[90]

Opponents of universal military training were, of course, pleased with the outcome. Oswald Garrison Villard, editor of *The Nation,* and an avowed pacifist and outspoken foe of the military establishment, summed up the antimilitarist view. Villard considered the elimination of standby draft legislation a "triumph for publicity" and declared the defeat of UMT "almost equally gratifying." But he took little solace in the victory, because, as he pointed out, the act increased the strength of the regular army to its greatest peacetime level in history "after the war to end war and to safeguard democracy."[91]

President Wilson, still suffering from the effects of his collapse the previous September, considered a veto. Wilson privately supported UMT although he had steadfastly refrained from endorsing it, first because he feared it would becloud the peace talks and later because he wanted to avoid creating a partisan issue. Newton Baker agreed with Wilson that the absence of UMT was a mistake. The bill, he said, was "far less excellent than it was as reported by the Senate Committee, and in its present form shows that there are, unhappily, many things which this war has taught us but which we have not learned." Nevertheless, he urged Wilson to sign the bill. There were parts of the legislation that warranted approval. Furthermore, Baker counseled, a veto "will leave the Army in a rather critical state, with uncertainty affecting its organization and nothing to guide us but the old legislation." Wilson signed on June 4, 1920.[92]

The National Defense Act of 1920, as the legislation came to be called, clearly marked a step forward in military policy making. For the first time after a war, Congress debated at length the peacetime role and organization of the army. For the first time in peace the army was organized into tactical formations capable of a logically planned response to an emergency. In another departure the general staff received the task of preparing mobilization plans and revising them as necessary. Professional soldiers and preparedness advocates, although obviously disappointed at the failure to secure UMT, hailed the beginning of a new era of defense policy. Military professionals believed that the public had finally accepted both them and an adequate armed force as necessary in peace as well as in war. Colonel William A. Ganoe, a professor of military history at West Point, later echoed the initial feelings of most army officers when he called the National Defense Act of 1920 "by all odds the greatest provision for the efficient control of war ever enacted by the Congress." Even March, who, like Palmer, had seen his visions for a postwar army dashed, agreed that the legislation "afforded a definite basis for proceeding with the reorganization of the Army."[93]

The act increased the peacetime strength of the regular army from a maximum of 175,000 to 280,000 enlisted men. The troops were organized into a fully operational force, not an expandable army according to Uptonian principles, and given specific missions. The regular army retained sole responsibility for overseas areas such as the Philippines. Regulars in the United States were organized into combat divisions, which could quickly serve as an emergency force. The National Guard, which regained some autonomy, and the Reserve Corps, established in 1916, were also organized into divisions. Reflecting John McAuley Palmer's philosophy and handiwork, the act provided for close cooperation between regular and civilian components. The final and, in Palmer's opinion, the most important task of the peacetime regular army, was to assist in the training of the civilian components in each of nine new geographically ordered corps areas.[94]

But in its final form the new defense legislation enacted the rhetoric of greater civilian participation and preparedness without providing the means. It reflected in part the feelings of antimilitarism and anticentralization that grew in postwar America, not the heady, efficiency consciousness of progressivism and of the war years. The overseas missions, the force in being, the corps area divisions, and the civilian training role all had assumed that UMT would provide a steady flow of new men through the army annually. Under the compromise legislation, service in all components remained voluntary. The regular army, as well as the guard and reserve, would have to keep its ranks filled without any assistance from compulsory training. The regular army had never exceeded a peacetime strength of 100,000 enlisted men before. Whether it could recruit enough men to maintain a force in being of 280,000 remained to be seen. For the next two decades the army struggled to find enough men to make workable a volunteer army plan that many experts and interests—in and out of the military—had not much wanted or anticipated.

NOTES

1. The best survey history of the United States Army is Russell Weigley's *History of the United States Army* (New York: Macmillan Co., 1967); see chapter

14 for an introduction to the reforms following the Spanish-American War. An older survey that is still useful for pre–World War I reforms and for a brief contemporary view of post–World War I developments is William Addleman Ganoe, *The History of the United States Army* (New York: D. Appleton-Century Co., 1942). For a closer look at the army during and immediately after the Spanish-American War, see Graham A. Cosmas, *An Army for Empire: The United States Army in the Spanish-American War* (Columbia, Mo.: University of Missouri Press, 1971).

2. Report of the Secretary of War, in *Annual Reports of the War Department of the Year Ending June 20, 1900,* vol. 1 (Washington, D.C.: GPO, 1900), p. 50. Hereafter, *Annual Report, 1900.*

3. *Annual Report, 1900, SW, 1900,* p. 51.

4. Ibid., *SW, 1900,* p. 50.

5. *Annual Report, 1919,* p. 53.

6. Weigley, *History of the U.S. Army,* pp. 316–22, passim.

7. Ibid., p. 322.

8. Ibid., p. 334.

9. Upton deserves more than a paragraph summary. Russell Weigley devotes a chapter to him in *Towards an American Army: Military Thought from Washington to Marshall* (New York: Columbia University Press, 1962), pp. 100–26. See also Stephen Ambrose, *Upton and the Army* (Baton Rouge, La.: Louisiana State University Press, 1964), and Upton's own writings *The Armies of Asia and Europe* (New York: Appleton, 1878) and *The Military Policy of the United States from 1775* (Washington, D.C.: GPO, 1904).

10. Allan R. Millett, "The American Political System and Civilian Control of the Military: A Historical Perspective," An unpublished study for the NSIA Division, The President's Reorganization Project, Nov. 1978, pp. 1–3, 7–11.

11. Weigley, *Towards an American Army,* pp. 136–61; Edward M. Coffman, *The Hilt of the Sword: The Career of Peyton C. March* (Madison, Wisc.: University of Wisconsin Press, 1966), pp. 175–81.

12. Weigley, *History of the U.S. Army,* pp. 327–28. For a biography of Wood, see Jack C. Lane, *Armed Progressive: General Leonard Wood* (San Rafael, Calif.: Presidio Press, 1978).

13. Weigley, *History of the U.S. Army,* pp. 336–39.

14. John McAuley Palmer, *America in Arms* (New Haven, Conn.: Yale University Press, 1941), p. 136.

15. *Annual Report,* 1912, pp. 94, 126–27; Weigley, *History of the U.S. Army,* p. 340.

16. Universal military training (UMT) did not originate with Palmer. He was not in Washington when the concept took form. Palmer's advocacy of UMT came later, after the war when he returned to the general staff and synthesized the philosophies opposing Upton.

17. See, for example, Captain Merch B. Stewart, "The Army as a Factor in the Upbuilding of Society," *Journal of the Military Service Institute* 36, No. 135 (May–June 1905): 391–404; Lieutenant Ron Winton, "The Problem of Patriotism," *Infantry Journal* 9, No. 6 (May–June 1913): 773–77; General Leonard Wood, "Heat Up the Melting Pot," *The Independent* 87 (July 3, 1916): 15; and General Hugh L. Scott, *Annual Report, 1916,* pp. 161–62. For an analysis of these

and other examples of ideas for using the army to uplift society, see Richard C. Brown, "Social Attitudes of American Generals, 1898–1940," (Ph.D. diss., University of Wisconsin, 1951), chapter 3, pp. 78–124.

18. John Garry Clifford, *The Citizen Soldiers: The Plattsburg Training Camps Movement, 1913–1920* (Lexington Ky.: University Press of Kentucky, 1972), pp. 1–29.

19. Ibid., pp. 95–115.

20. Leonard Wood, *The Military Obligation of Citizenship* (Princeton, N.J.: Princeton University Press, 1915), pp. 344–45.

21. Weigley, *History of the U.S. Army,* p. 343.

22. *Statement of a Proper Military Policy for the United States* (Washington, D.C.: GPO, 1916), pp. 1–21; C. Joseph Bernardo and Eugene H. Bacon, *American Military Policy* (Harrisburg, Pa.: Stackpole Books, 1961), pp. 340–44. For a detailed analysis of the preparedness campaign, see John Patrick Finnegan, *Against the Specter of a Dragon* (Westport, Conn.: Greenwood Press, 1974).

23. Ibid., pp. 73–90.

24. A good account of the Mexican situation leading up to the Villa raid is found in Arthur S. Link, *Woodrow Wilson and the Progressive Era: 1910–1917* (New York: Harper & Row, 1954), pp. 107–44. For details of the effect of the raid on the congressional deadlock over the army bill, see Finnegan, *Against the Specter of a Dragon,* pp. 139–57.

25. Weigley, *History of the U.S. Army,* pp. 348–50; Bernardo and Bacon, *American Military Policy,* pp. 345–46; U.S. *Statutes at Large,* vol. 39, pt. 2, pp. 166–217. For a contemporary account of this legislation, see John Dickinson, *The Building of an Army* (New York: The Century Company, 1920), pp. 29–56.

26. Weigley, *History of the U.S. Army,* pp. 350–52; Bernardo and Bacon, *American Military Policy,* pp. 345–46; Clifford, *The Citizen Soldiers,* pp. 147–49; Finnegan, *Against the Specter of a Dragon,* pp. 165–71.

27. Finnegan, *Against the Specter of a Dragon,* pp. 173–83; Clifford, *The Citizen Soldiers,* pp. 203–15.

28. *New York Times,* (hereafter, *NYT*), April 3, 1917, p. 1.

29. Dickinson, *The Building of an Army,* pp. 88–92. Dickinson goes into considerable detail in analyzing the effects of selective service on voluntary enlistments. He notes that the navy continued to accept volunteers after December 1915 and enjoyed a significant increase in volunteers after that date. Many of these, he concludes, were undoubtedly motivated by the draft.

30. Dickinson, *The Building of an Army,* p. 85, n. 1.

31. General Order No. 73, 1918, in U.S. War Department, *General Orders, Special Orders, Bulletins and Circulars, 1918* (Washington, D.C.: GPO, 1919). Hereafter General Order, No., Year; *Annual Report, 1919,* p. 56.

32. U.S. *Statutes at Large,* vol. 40, pt. 1, p. 76.

33. Dickinson, *The Building of an Army,* p. 324.

34. Coffman, *The Hilt of the Swords,* p. 181.

35. Ibid., p. 183.

36. *NYT,* January 4, 1919, p. 10.

37. U.S., House, *Congressional Record,* 65th Cong., 3rd sess., p. 3207.

38. U.S., House, *Congressional Record,* 65th Cong., 3rd sess., p. 3287. The complete debate is recorded on pp. 3197–244, 3278–93.

39. U.S., House, *Congressional Record,* 65th Cong., 3rd sess., p. 3287; Dickinson, *The Building of an Army,* p. 327.

40. *NYT,* May 10, 1919, p. 14.

41. *NYT,* April 19, 1917, p. 3; June 17, 1919, p. 13.

42. *NYT,* April 19, 1917, p. 3; June 17, 1917, p. 13; February 17, 1918, sec. 5, p. 2; February 11, 1918, p. 7; February 16, 1919, p. 10.

43. Clifford, *The Citizen Soldiers,* pp. 263–64.

44. John D. Hicks, *Republican Ascendancy, 1921–1933* (New York: Harper Torchbooks, 1963), p. 4; Burton I. Kaufman, "The Organizational Dimension of United States Economic Foreign Policy, 1900–1920," *Business History Review* 46 (Spring 1972); 22–28; William E. Leuchtenburg, *The Perils of Prosperity, 1914–1932* (Chicago: University of Chicago Press, 1958), p. 179.

45. The full statement appears in *Infantry Journal* 15, No. 7 (January 1919): 537–40.

46. Clifford, *The Citizen Soldiers,* pp. 365–70, 373–74.

47. Clifford, *The Citizen Soldiers,* p. 274. For the complete text of the bills, see U.S., Congress, Senate, Subcommittee of the Committee on Military Affairs, *Hearings on the Reorganization of the Army* (hereafter, *Senate Reorganization Hearings),* 66th Cong., 1st sess., 1919, pp. 8–16, and U.S., Congress, House, Committee on Military Affairs, *Army Reorganization Hearings* (hereafter, *House Reorganization Hearings*), 66th Cong., 1st sess., pp. 6–13.

48. For an excellent description of these opposing forces in the prewar fight over conscription, see John Whiteclay Chambers, II, "Conscripting for Colossus: The Progressive Era and the Origin of the Modern Military Draft in the United States in World War I," in *The Military in America: Essays and Documents,* ed. Peter Karsten (New York: The Free Press, 1980), pp. 275–96, as well as Finnegan, *The Specter of a Dragon.*

49. Henry Litchfield West, "Universal Military Training," and Charles T. Hallinan, "Compulsory Military Training: The Negative," *The Arbitrator* 1 (February 1919): 3–13.

50. Arthur A. Ekirch, *The Civilian and the Military: A History of the Antimilitarist Tradition* (Colorado Springs, Colo.: Ralph Myles, Publisher, 1972), p. 200.

51. "Our Military System as It Appears to America's Citizen Soldiers," *Infantry Journal* 15, no. 10 (April 1919): 771–87; "American Militarism Waning," *The Nation,* 108, no. 2816 (June 21, 1919): 973.

52. Ibid.

53. Clifford, *The Citizen Soldiers,* p. 274.

54. Newton D. Baker, "A Permanent Military Policy for the United States," *Saturday Evening Post,* 191 (May 31, 1919): 30.

55. *Senate Reorganization Hearings,* p. 45.

56. Ibid., pp. 16–27; *NYT,* August 5, 1919, p. 1; Coffman, *The Hilt of the Sword,* pp. 197–98; Dickinson, *The Building of an Army,* pp. 330–34.

57. Clifford, *The Citizen Soldiers,* p. 275. The best biography of Wadsworth is Martin L. Fausold, *James W. Wadsworth, Jr., The Gentleman from New York* (Syracuse, N.Y.: Syracuse University Press, 1975). Wadsworth came from a family with a long tradition of military service. He was a friend of Elihu Root and succeeded him in the Senate in 1914. An early supporter of preparedness, he was appointed to the Committee on Military Affairs in 1917 where he was considered

a staunch friend of the army. For his early views on UMT, see Fausold, *James W. Wadsworth, Jr.*, pp. 114–15.

58. Baker summarized his argument in his annual report for 1919; see *Annual Report, 1919*, pp. 58–59. For Baker's testimony to the Senate subcommittee, see *Senate Reorganization Hearings*, pp. 147–214.

59. *Senate Reorganization Hearings*, pp. 48–49.

60. Ibid., p. 55; Coffman, *The Hilt of the Sword*, p. 198.

61. *Senate Reorganization Hearings*, pp. 513–19; Coffman, *The Hilt of the Sword*, p. 182.

62. *Senate Reorganization Hearings*, pp. 1835–40; Coffman, *The Hilt of the Sword*, p. 198. For an overview of the National Guard as a pressure group, see Martha Derthick, *The National Guard in Politics* (Cambridge, Mass.: Harvard University Press, 1965).

63. *Reorganization Hearings*, pp. 619–35.

64. Ibid., pp. 1233–54.

65. Palmer, *America in Arms*, pp. 165–67. Neither Baker or March objected to officers with dissenting opinions testifying. Coffman, *The Hilt of the Sword*, p. 303, n. 58.

66. *Senate Reorganization Hearings*, pp. 1173–232; Palmer, *America in Arms*, pp. 168–69.

67. U.S. Congress, House *Reorganization Hearings*, p. 1436. Pershing's complete testimony is contained in pp. 1435–568.

68. *NYT*, November 17, 1919, p. 2; Palmer, *America in Arms*, p. 169.

69. *Literary Digest* 62, no. 13 (September 27, 1919): 9–10; *NYT*, June 27, 1919, p. 14; November 22, 1919, p. 12.

70. *Literary Digest* 62, No. 13 (September 27, 1919): 9–10; *NYT*, November 22, 1919, p. 12.

71. Memo, SW to AG, February 5, 1919, Chief of Staff Files, 1918–1921, file no. 428, Box 55, National Archives, Washington, D.C.; Memo, CS to AG, May 6, 1918, Chief of Staff Files, 1918–1921, file no. 428, Box 55, NA.

72. Memo, Brig. Gen. Rees to CS, October 28, 1918, Chief of Staff Files, 1918–1921, File no. 428, Box 55, NA.

73. American Expeditionary Force University Bulletin 91, *The Catalogue*, Part 1 (Beaune, Côte d'Or, France: Headquarters AEFU, May 16, 1919), pp. 4, 15. This publication is located at the U.S. Army Military History Institute, Carlisle Barracks, Pa. (hereafter, MHI.)

74. *Army and Navy Journal* (hereafter, *ANJ*), December 14, 1918, p. 540.

75. *NYT*, May 17, 1919, p. 8.

76. *The Educational System of the United States Army: The Army as a National School* (Washington, D.C.: The Adjutant General of the Army, 1920), p. 1., MHI.

77. Digest of a Conference held in Room 247, State, War, and Navy Building, Washington, D.C., January 5, 1920, War College Division, General Staff File no. 8213-95, Box 260, NA.

78. *Educational System of the U.S. Army*, p. 1.

79. Roscoe Baker, *The American Legion and American Foreign Policy* (Westport, Conn.: Greenwood Press, 1974), pp. 12, 115.

80. Richard Stockton, "The Army We Need," *North American Review* 210 (November 1919): 645–55.

81. Clifford, *The Citizen Soldiers,* pp. 284–85.

82. *NYT,* January 27, 1920, p. 8.

83. *NYT,* January 28, 1920, p. 10.

84. *Senate Reorganization Hearings,* pp. 1948, 2041–42.

85. *NYT,* February 1, 1920, pt. 2, p. 1; Dickinson, *The Building of an Army,* p. 363.

86. "Compulsory Military Training," *The Literary Digest* 64, no. 7 (February 14, 1920): 19–20.

87. William L. Chenery, "Conscription in Peace Time," *The Survey* 43 (February 14, 1920): 575–76.

88. *NYT,* February 2, 1920, p. 28.

89. *NYT,* February 10, 1920, p. 1.

90. *NYT,* April 9, 1920, p. 9; April 10, p. 17; Palmer, *America in Arms,* p. 182; Dickinson, *The Building of an Army,* p. 373.

91. *The Nation* 110, no. 2866 (June 5, 1920): 742.

92. Coffman, *The Hilt of the Sword,* p. 211; Clifford, *The Citizen Soldiers,* pp. 290–92; Palmer, *America in Arms,* pp. 183–84; Newton D. Baker to Woodrow Wilson, June 3, 4, 1920, Baker Papers, Box 13, Library of Congress, Washington, D.C.

93. Ganoe, *History of the U.S. Army,* p. 481; March in *Annual Report, 1921,* p. 162.

94. U.S., *Statutes at Large,* vol. 41, pp. 759–812.

2

THE ARMY IN 1920

Between the armistice and the passage of the National Defense Act of 1920 the army operated in a sort of limbo. While Congress considered the numerous reorganization bills, debated and rejected the 500,000-man regular army and universal military training, and finally crafted its own legislation, the army attempted to settle into a peacetime routine with little guidance. The readjustments involved in demobilization produced considerable turbulence, especially in terms of manpower. Except for an occupation force of some 18,000 men in Germany and the Siberian and Murmansk-Archangel Expeditionary Forces, numbering about 8,000, the massive army in Europe came home.[1] Training camps closed, and the army began to redistribute the men who were still on active duty to garrisons and units in the United States, Panama, and the Philippines, which had been stripped of all available personnel during the war. The lack of a clear-cut policy on the size and method for raising the postwar army complicated demobilization and made it difficult for army personnel managers to reestablish an effective recruiting program. Thus, when the Army resumed recruiting in 1919, it did so on an *ad hoc* basis. With no idea of how many men it would have in the future or what kind of inducements it could offer recruits on a long-term basis, the army entered the postwar era on shaky ground.

Initially, the army gave demobilization top priority. Between November 15, 1918, and November 15, 1919, the army discharged more than 3 million enlisted men. Actual enlisted strength dropped from 2,442,647 to 763,441 between January and June 1919; by the end of fiscal year 1920 it was down to 177,974.[2] This was approximately two times the prewar strength, but well below the number the army thought it needed and below the 280,000 it would be authorized in the National Defense Act of 1920.

With the draft suspended and universal training an unresolved issue, Congress had authorized a resumption of recruiting for the regular army in February 1919. Initially, Congress set a ceiling of 175,000 on the number of enlisted men in the regular army. In May 1919 in its annual appropriations for fiscal year 1920, Congress authorized enough funds to pay for an average of 325,000 enlisted men during the year. Army planners estimated that after demobilization was complete, they could maintain as many as 225,000 men a month with that authorization.

The army faced a formidable recruiting problem in 1919 and 1920. By law, all soldiers who entered the army after April 1917 had to be released. By official estimate, only about 50,000 men, who had enlisted prior to April 1917, remained in the army. Thus, even if all prewar soldiers remained, the army needed to recruit approximately 125,000 new men (more than its total prewar strength).[3]

Before the war the army had obtained most of its enlisted men through a General Recruiting Service which, operating under the direction of the adjutant general, maintained recruiting offices throughout the country. The number of officers and men on duty as recruiters varied according to the army's needs. In July 1916, for example, 126 officers and 1,077 enlisted men were on recruiting duty at 189 stations. After Congress raised the enlisted strength of the army from 97,284 to 122,693 in response to the Mexican emergency, the adjutant general increased the number of recruiters and opened more offices. By the end of the fiscal year (June 30, 1917), the General Recruiting Service had expanded to 188 officers and 2,087 enlisted men at 401 stations.[4]

In the summer of 1918 the General Staff expected the war to last well into 1919. Consequently, when voluntary recruiting ceased altogether in August 1918, the adjutant general decided to close down the General Recruiting Service. In September, the adjutant general directed the service to close all recruiting stations, cancel leases, box their records, and ship them to Washington. Men on recruiting duty were reassigned.[5] The sudden end of the war found the army with no recruiting machinery. Without it, no voluntary army could develop.

Congress expressed doubt concerning the army's ability to recruit enough men annually to fill the ranks of the peacetime regular army to even the stopgap force of 175,000 authorized in February 1919. Secretary of War Baker harbored no such doubts. Representative Richard Olney of Massachusetts, a member of the House Committee on Military Affairs, asked Baker how it would be possible to raise a large peacetime force voluntarily when industry paid higher wages than the army. The secretary had an answer: "My judgment is that we would be able to raise it for the present for the reason that a very large number of men have now had military experience and like the military life. They like the out-of-door, open life, and I think it will not be difficult to raise that size army."[6]

Unimpressed, the army prepared to go back into the recruiting business. On February 12, 1919, the chief of staff directed the adjutant general to prepare for the resumption of recruiting. March ordered the adjutant general "to inaugurate a vigorous recruiting campaign immediately upon the enactment of the enlistment law. . . ." The directive emphasized urgency: "It is necessary that a great many recruits be secured. . . . Nothing must be delayed in the organization of recruiting districts and in the planning of a recruiting campaign. . . ."[7] Drawing on prewar precedent, the adjutant general reestablished the General Recruiting Service and divided the country into 56 recruiting districts with 513 stations. The War Department also authorized units, posts, camps, and stations to recruit locally. Men obtained by this method would be assigned directly to the unit that recruited them; men enlisting through the General Recruiting Service were assigned where needed. The adjutant general expected cooperation between local recruiters and the service.[8]

In an informal letter to new recruiters the adjutant general likened them to salesmen for a large commercial firm. The letter cautioned recruiters against being "discourteous to a civilian or applicant. . . . No one ever sold anything by impolite or discourteous treatment." Officers assigned to district recruiting headquarters also received advice: "It is impossible to maintain sub-stations in all the towns in the territory, therefore, in order to work these places canvassing parties should be sent out to stop at the different towns and canvass the recruits." Officers were instructed to seek free publicity whenever possible. One recommended method was to announce the departure of canvassing parties. Newspapers, the instructions advised, also provided possible sources of recruits. For example: "If a factory has just closed down in some town in the district, at once rush a canvassing party there. . . ." Other good places to look for recruits included farmers' markets and summer fairs.[9]

Recruiters also recognized the potential of paid advertising. Colonel J. T. Conrad, chief of the Recruiting Publicity Bureau, urged the adjutant general to consider an ad campaign in conjunction with the reopening of enlistments. "The general public is *not* informed regarding terms of enlistment," Conrad wrote. "Advertising of the kind used by big business concerns has never been tried by the Army." Conrad's request for $250,000 for the purpose was so unprecedented that it went all the way to the secretary of war, who approved an expenditure of $185,000. A typical ad, run in the "help wanted" section of major newspapers, read:

Men Wanted for Enlistment in the U.S. Army from 18–40 yrs. of age for a 3 yr. period with every Opportunity to Earn, Learn & Travel.[10]

On March 1, 1919, voluntary enlistments for the regular army resumed. For the most part Congress simply approved prewar standards for enlistment: "Any male citizen [between the ages of eighteen and forty], able-bodied, free from disease, of good character and temperate habits, may be enlisted or accepted for reenlistment. . . ." The enlistment or reenlistment of married men was discouraged lest their dependents become a burden on the service. Departing from prewar standards, Congress authorized the recruiting and enlistment of illiterates—partly, undoubtedly, in deference to Newton Baker's plans to demonstrate the social utility of the army as a national school and partly to expand the pool of men from which it could recruit. Over the objections of the War Department Congress also created

a one-year enlistment option, which it hoped would encourage returning
or discharged veterans to reenlist. The army argued unsuccessfully that
the one-year enlistment was inefficient. The same time and expense necessary to recruit, process, assign, and train a three-year man was required
for a one-year enlistment, but the return on the investment was considerably smaller. Congress prevailed and stipulated that at least one-third of
all enlistments be for one-year terms.[11]

The enlistment of "Colored Men" did not resume in 1919. The army,
reflecting the social norms of its day, was strictly segregated. Nearly half
of the 367,000 blacks who served in World War I went to France; most
were assigned to service battalions, but approximately 40,000 served in
units that saw action. The subject of blacks in combat provoked much
controversy, and after the war the army was quick to be rid of a potential
problem. The black units came home, paraded through Harlem, and were
disbanded. After demobilization only about 10,000 blacks remained on
active duty, more than enough to fill up the four black regiments. Reenlistments were high in the black units, and black recruits, simply not
needed, [12] were not accepted in 1919.

Initially the recruiting effort centered on the demobilization centers.
The results appeared to justify Newton Baker's optimistic predictions.
When the army announced in mid-March that it needed volunteers for
France, men rushed to recruiting offices. Even before the district recruiting
officers received their quotas, exsoldiers began calling for information,
according to Major William B. Cochran, in charge of the New York City
district. The majority of men inquiring about enlistment, Cochran said,
were exsoldiers and out of work. By mid-April the War Department
announced that enlistments nationwide averaged 3,000 weekly.[13]

The army offered every reasonable inducement to bring in recruits.
Former soldiers could enlist at their wartime rank; volunteers got their
choice of unit, branch, or place of assignment; soldiers reenlisting for their
own vacancies got a month's furlough; soldiers on leave or furlough who
successfully encouraged a civilian to enlist got an additional furlough.[14]

Between March 1919 and June 1919 recruiting continued at a brisk pace.
Colonel Charles W. Martin, chief of the Recruiting Division of the Adjutant
General's Office, reported in June 1919 that enlistments during the late
spring and early summer ran ahead of prewar averages. Between February
28 and June 30, 1919, a total of 69,933 men signed up at an average of more
than 4,000 per week. But the total number and high weekly rate of enlistments were deceiving. Nearly half of the men who enlisted between February and June 1919 did so for only one year. Furthermore, two-thirds of
the enlistments during the period were made at posts, camps or stations,
suggesting that many of the "new men" were actually reenlistments or
former servicemen reentering the army after demobilization. The General
Recruiting Service recruited only about 32,000 men before the close of

fiscal year 1919. This trend continued well into the summer. In July, Major General Peter C. Harris, the adjutant general, reported 9,635 enlistments in twenty days.[15] Who enlisted, and why?

General Harris believed that most of the recruits were drawn to the army by the new educational and vocational training opportunities that it offered. Colonel Martin agreed. In June 1919 Martin told the *New York Times* that the army attracted men who wanted to get ahead. "Our appeal is not to the skilled workman," he said, "but to the young man who has been unable to complete his education."[16] Recruiting officers from the New York City area told a *New York Times* reporter who visited their office on Whitehall in lower Manhattan that volunteers were willing to serve anywhere in any branch of the army because of the offer by the service to teach them a trade or vocation. Major C. B. Howard reported that branches that stressed educational opportunities received the largest number of applicants. Two recruits interviewed at the Whitehall station represented " 'the desires of the majority of the men who have applied for enlistment in this district,' said Major Howard." Albert Hite, a thirty-nine-year-old garage worker from New York City, saw the educational and vocational training program as a chance to learn about gasoline engines. Joseph Axelrod, age twenty-one, of Waterbury, Connecticut, quit his $21-a-week job as a press hand to join the army at $30 a month and learn something.[17] Though it is impossible to quantify the motives of the enlistees, it appears that the allure of educational or vocational training was of vital importance.

The War Department worked hard to ensure that its highly touted educational and vocational training program lived up to its promise. During fiscal year 1920, the first year of the program, the army offered courses at every post, camp, and station in the continental United States. By the end of the fiscal year Baker happily reported some 86,000 men, mostly new enlistees, enrolled in about 3,335 classes. Reflecting the concern for national homogeneity that was characteristic of the turbulent postwar years, Baker especially praised the Americanization efforts of the courses. "These courses vary from agriculture and practical farming through the mechanical arts to the purely formal and academic subjects," Baker described, and he added:

In all of them . . . certain basis requirements are insisted upon with a view to giving every soldier such a course in American institutions and history as will develop in him a knowledge of more affection[sic] for the country which he serves. . . .[18]

Participation by enlisted men in the educational and vocational training program was voluntary except for illiterates. Once a man enrolled in a course, however, completion was mandatory. Soldiers in the program attended classes five days a week for an average of three hours a day. The army required illiterates and non-English-speaking enlistees to attend a special recruit training program that included English courses. In April 1920 the War Department reported that 5,390 illiterates (representing forty-five national groups) were enrolled in the special program.[19]

Determining who enlisted is more difficult than establishing what attracted volunteers to the army. War Departments reports on enlistments are not as detailed for the immediate postwar period as they become later in the 1920s. Much must be inferred from later data.[20] In fiscal year 1922, the first year for which such information is available, for example, 46,538 men enlisted or reenlisted in the regular army. Of these men, 4,379 (9.4 percent) were foreign born, 1,764 (3.8 percent) were "Colored" (by then, some space was available), and 1,166 (2.5 percent) were listed as "other," a category that included Puerto Ricans, Mexicans, and other racial groups.[21] Information regarding religion, ethnic background, and age is unavailable, and data on education and previous employment are fragmentary. Two reports on enlistments processed by the main recruiting office in Chicago for December 1922 and January 1923 suggest that most recruits there were of urban backgrounds and had some previous employment as either semiskilled or unskilled workers. Compared to the population at large, they were not badly educated: the majority (250) of the 382 recruits had between five and eight years of school; 124 had completed the eighth grade, 106 reported some high school, and 9 had attended college. Only forty of the Chicago enlistees were farmers, but this low figure probably tells little about nationwide patterns of recruitment in small cities and towns. The largest occupational group (130) was "laborer." Some possessed skills: eleven electricians, five telegraphers, three draftsmen. There were also recruits with office skills (forty-one clerks, two mail clerks, and one bookkeeper) and mechanical skills (thirty-eight mechanics and twenty-three chauffeurs) and assorted tradesmen and craftsmen.[22]

The army that these men joined after World War I represented an improvement over the one that prewar Regulars remembered. Recruits in 1919 received $30 a month (reduced to $21 in 1922). This compared to the $15 a month they had gotten in 1915, and to the $27.66 a week that unskilled manufacturing workers received in 1919. They also got uniforms and a monthly uniform allowance, medical treatment at no expense, meals, and lodging in barracks. The typical daily routine was not considered demanding. After reveille at 6 o'clock, soldiers participated in calisthenics followed by breakfast, barracks cleanup, and inspection. Mornings were devoted to drill and military instruction. After the noon meal the troops attended educational or vocational training classes or took part in organized athletics. At 5 o'clock the day's scheduled activities came to an end at a retreat ceremony. Evenings were free until taps at 11 o'clock. Wednesday and Saturday afternoons and Sundays were normally free time. Soldiers could expect their share of fatigue duty such as KP, post cleanup, and labor details on an equitable basis, but assignment to such jobs was not to interfere with military training, education or recreation, or free time.[23]

The army went to great lengths to make service life attractive to enlisted men. In addition to offering educational and vocational training after the war, the War Department developed an extensive recreation program for the soldiers. During the war various religious and civic welfare groups had donated large quantities of athletic equipment to the army, organized and run athletic programs at training centers and encampments, and operated canteens, clubs, and libraries for enlisted men. Impressed by the apparent effects of such services on troop morale, the War Department took over the activities after the armistice. The army established a school at Camp Benning, Georgia, to train physical education instructors, surplus athletic equipment was returned from France and distributed to camps in the United States, and Congress appropriated additional funds to procure new equipment and continue other recreational services.

In addition to organized athletics the army provided for the soldiers' leisure-time activities. Beginning in October 1919, the War Department obtained, distributed, and presented motion pictures to posts in the United States. By the end of 1919 the motion picture service reached 184 camps and attendance approached the half-million mark. The army also operated libraries and servicemen's clubs. The clubs featured lectures, dances, musical entertainment, and shows and provided reading and writing rooms. The Education and Recreation Branch of the War Plans Division, which managed the educational and vocational training program, coordinated all of the army's recreational activities.[24]

This description of postwar army enlisted life sounds almost like that of a summer camp for boys, as recruiters undoubtedly intended it to. But there was a less appealing side to the army. The enlisted men occupied the lowest position in a rigid caste system that separated officers from noncomissioned officers and common soldiers. Enlisted men rarely spoke directly to officers. When enlisted men or noncommissioned officers addressed an officer, it was commonplace for them to use the third person. Officers and noncoms called soldiers by their last names until they were promoted to corporal (which often took between six and ten years). Soldiers performed all of the army's menial labor. Noncommissioned officers supervised work crews, but according to an officer's manual of the period, "a custom as old as the army itself is the one which exempts non-commissioned officers from performing manual labor when on fatigue."[25]

The daily routine, though not overly burdensome, could be boring. For most soldiers military training meant drill and marksmanship. In the cavalry, for example, soldiers routinely exercised their horses ten miles a day five days a week, stood mounted inspections on Saturday, and spent hours grooming their beasts on Sunday. In addition to equitation, cavalrymen of the interwar years drilled and trained with the pistol, rifle, and saber, and took annual qualification tests with each weapon. Precision in weaponry, the army believed, could only be achieved through thorough familiarity with one's arms; repetition was the key.[26] Organized athletics, servicemen's clubs, and motion pictures undoubtedly relieved some of the tedium of enlisted life, but soldiers frequently sought and found other diversions off the post.

In the communities surrounding army bases soldiers were usually treated like pariahs. They were welcome by local townsmen for their money until it ran out (usually the night after payday). Drunkenness, fights between soldiers and between soldiers and civilians, and venereal disease were the common results of an enlisted man's trip to town. Company commanders and their first sergeants usually spent the morning after payday transferring men from local jails to the post stockade. Disciplinary action inevitably followed. A soldier could be fined, reduced in grade, or even court–martialed for drunkenness. In 1920, 195 enlisted men were convicted by general courts–martial for offenses related to drinking.[27]

The army took a no-nonsense view toward soldiers who could not perform their duty due to drunkenness. Time spent in the stockade "drying out" or awaiting trial was considered "bad time" and was added to a soldier's term of enlistment. And the service was officially puritanical about venereal disease. During the war venereal disease reached epidemic proportions in the army. In 1920 the surgeon general reported that 149.6 of every thousand soldiers had venereal disease during the war. A Venereal Disease Control Division was established shortly after the war in an effort to control the problem. Soldiers were required to submit to frequent inspections, had to attend venereal disease lectures, and could be court–martialed for failing to use prophylaxis after exposure. In 1920 army general courts went so far as to convict ten enlisted men of "contracting venereal disease."[28]

The army believed that the high incidence of venereal disease and off-duty drinking by soldiers were related and vigorously enforced prohibition when it became law. Throughout the interwar years the army continued to warn soldiers of the twin evils of alcohol and loose women. In a handbook for enlisted men, written in the form of discussion between an experienced noncommissioned officer and recruits, the proverbial "old sergeant" painted a grim picture of the consequences of falling in with "bad company":

After everyone is pretty well moistened up, someone suggests that they go down the line. You hesitate. Right here the old devil comes up, touches you on the shoulder and says, "Come on buddy, don't be a piker." Back home you did not do this stuff. Decent fellows didn't do it. . . . But the gang's going and you are part of it. You have not the moral courage to fall out.

At the joint where you head in, a couple more drinks find their way to you. A yellow-haired damsel climbs up on you and parks her feet in your lap. The devil is standing behind you saying, ''She's all right buddy, take her.'' You book her for the night. You sneak out early the next morning and beat it back to the post for reveille. When you get there, you find yourself again broke. And that's not half of it. You've got somethin' you've brought back with you.[29]

Thus, even as elements of the larger society experienced something of a moral revolution in the 1920s, the interwar army continued to equate continence and temperance with high moral character and attempted to influence the conduct of its men even in their off-duty time.

The less attractive aspects of the army were relatively unknown to recruits, and with free education as a drawing card and genuine improvements in service life to induce men to enlist and remain in the service, the future of the volunteer army should have been bright. But manpower problems persisted. While it is true that the postwar army attracted new men in record numbers in 1919, it also lost men at a very high rate. Between July 1, 1919, and June 30, 1920, 718,346 men left the army. Demobilization accounted for most of the loss until December 1919, and indeed the army had to lose these men in order to contract to its maximum authorized strength of 175,000 by the end of the fiscal year. But by January 1920 it became evident that strength was declining too rapidly. Monthly gains did not balance losses. After the initial surge of volunteers in the spring and summer of 1919 (when enlistments averaged over 4,000 a week), enthusiasm for the new army died down. By the winter of 1919–1920 total enlistments settled down to an average of about 9,000 a month. Reenlistments and enlistments by former servicemen declined from nearly 18,000 in July to an average of about 3,000 a month by the spring of 1920. Moreover, by March 1920, 31,903 one-year enlistments, which the army had objected to the year before, began to expire. A crisis loomed, and to combat it the army once again tried an *ad hoc* solution.

Hoping to avoid a shortage of personnel, the War Department launched a major recruiting campaign at the end of March. The campaign, patterned after wartime bond rallies, sought to combine patriotism with the functional benefits of army service. In a telegram to all recruiters General Harris said that the campaign would ''insure immediate recognition that the Regular Army is not only in theory but in fact a part of the Nation and not a thing apart,'' and that the result ''will make not only for the welfare of the Army's lasting benefit, but for the welfare of the nation as a whole.'' All other military activities were subordinated to the campaign, and commanders at every level were directed to furnish additional officers and men to the local recruiting effort.[30] Secretary Baker wrote to every state governor asking for a public endorsement of the campaign ''as a means of furthering this patriotic purpose and building a 'background' for more intensive recruiting. . . .''[31]

Baker successfully courted organized labor, too. Samuel Gompers, in a reply to the secretary's appeal for support, publicly praised educational and vocational training saying, "When the American Army should have co-ordinated its system of military training with a well-developed policy of supplemental instruction in educational and vocational subjects . . . it will have solved the problem of its future status in the broader field of practical usefulness to the country in time of peace."[32] Clergymen throughout the country were asked to declare February 22 "Army Sunday" and appeal to the young men of their congregations to join up. The army assigned every regular army unit to a geographical locality in the country hoping to stimulate interest in the "home town outfit."[33]

With characteristic zeal Newton Baker even involved children. On January 14 he announced a national school essay contest on the subject "What Are the Benefits of an Enlistment in the United States Army?" Every recruiting district awarded prizes, and medals were presented to the three best essays. Donald L. Campbell, a fifteen-year-old from Clinton, Iowa, won first prize. Paraphrasing Horace Greeley, Donald urged, "Young man join the army! It is the big opportunity of the age." Donald, like Baker, stressed the educational and vocational opportunities of the army.[34]

The great campaign fizzled. Only 23,640 men signed up by the end of March, 28.1 percent of the goal. Despite all the promotional activities and effort, monthly enlistments during the campaign hardly increased at all; the average for January–March, 1920 was 6,000 original enlistments.[35] Not one recruiting district secured its quota. The big cities of the East made the poorest showing: New York City, 1,510 of a 7,833 quota; Boston, 291 of 2,145; Philadelphia, only 283 out of 1,980. The *Army and Navy Journal* concluded that the drive failed because "the industrial centers of the population present too strong an attraction to young men at the present time for the Army to compete with."[36]

The *Journal* was probably correct. A private in 1920 received $30 per month; a private first class got $35 monthly. These two enlisted grades constituted the unskilled labor of the army. Privates and privates first class with skills received specialty pay (a maximum of 30 percent of all army privates and privates first class could be classified as specialists). A private first class in the top specialty grade received $60 a month, the maximum possible for "skilled labor" in the army. Full-time "lower skilled" labor in manufacturing industries averaged $25.98 a week in 1920. Laborers and helpers in the building trades received $44.80 for a full week's work. Skilled labor fared better. Journeymen in the building trades made $51.20 weekly, and skilled production workers earned $34.10 a week.[37] To the prospective recruit civilian wages undoubtedly looked better than army pay.

Although the winter recruiting drive in 1920 failed, the army learned some lessons. Patriotic appeals and statements from public figures carried little weight in peacetime. Service benefits would have to be the big attraction. Colonel Martin, still in charge of the Recruiting Service, shuffled his personnel, requested and got more men on recruiting duty, and renewed the effort. Many of the innovations tried during the campaign remained, such as efforts to drum up civilian interest through direct contact. From June to October 1920 teams of soldiers toured the country on the Chautauqua circuits. These units, known as "Americans All" detachments, were composed of immigrant soldiers trained in English after enlisting. They appeared as proof that the army provided opportunities for enlistees.[38] First Lieutenant Sam McCullough, in charge of an Americans All detachment, reported on a typical stop in August 1920:

Dekoven, Ky.—Arrived here at about 9 A.M. This is a mining town and the people who brought the Chautauqua to town were the workers, the mine owner was strongly against it to the end causing quite a bit of friction. Our program was liked the best of any of the three days and it is not surprising as classical music such as given in the first two days of the Chautauqua is not appreciated by this class of people. Sent in the name of one recruit and talked to a number of others who were badly off as far as education was concerned and who were interested.[39]

Recruiting officers toured their districts addressing high school assemblies, American Legion meetings, picnics, and any other gathering that would have them. One officer on the lecture circuit compared the "New Peace Army" to the "Old Army":

No longer do we have just outside of our camps the dreadful menace of booze. No longer does a father warn his daughter against associating with soldiers or his son against contemplating joining the ranks. In the old days you knew few soldiers, more often none, and you believed every unkind thing you heard about them.

He summarized the educational opportunities and benefits of clean living and proclaimed ". . . this new Army is a bigger better organization. A new day has dawned for the army." The officer, Captain Lester Harris, assistant recruiting officer in Springfield, Missouri, reported that his lectures were well received, that "the better element of citizenship in each place sought further information, and that recruiting in these towns has been accelerated and opposition squelched."[40]

Essentially Colonel Martin continued the recruiting drive on a lower key. The War Department helped with more realistic quotas. Martin also instilled the fear of God or at least of Charles Martin in the Recruiting Service. He did it with the help of one man. Late in 1920, Colonel Martin sent First Lieutenant Harry G. Dowdall, a former journalist from California, on a confidential inspection of the Recruiting Service. Posing as an unemployed drifter, Dowdall visited thirty-five districts and allowed himself to be approached and recruited thirty-eight times. His weekly reports, sent directly to Martin, provided the Recruiting chief with a unique assessment of the effectiveness of recruiters and the army's recruiting program. Dowdall's reports minced no words. He named names at all levels when he found slovenly or rude recruiters or lazy and incompetent district officers. On November 19, 1920, Dowdall was in Boston. He waited in the main station for half an hour before being approached. In his report he suggested that perhaps the Boston recruiters had an "off" day. Dowdall "enlisted" in Boston with the help of a sergeant who faked his eye examination correcting his 20/200 vision to the acceptable 20/70 without glasses. A few days later, Dowdall arrived in Providence, Rhode Island. He observed many unemployed men but few recruiters on the job. "I soon learned," he reported, "that it was next to the impossible thing to attract [a recruiter's] attention by any action. . . ."[41] With Dowdall's help Martin eliminated considerable deadwood.

By the end of the fiscal year the adjutant general was able to report improvement in the recruiting situation. General Harris observed, "During the fiscal year ended June 30, 1920, a total of 117,783 applicants for enlistment at general recruiting stations were accepted for enlistment. . . . The total number of enlistments (including regular posts and bases) during the same period amounted to 151,513. . . ." That figure represented an increase in 124,759 over fiscal year 1916, the last normal recruiting year before the war.[42] Harris attributed the success to good publicity, the local recruiting effort, and patriotism. Newton Baker believed that the tremendous increase in enlistments was "due to the educational and recreational program which has made service in the Army an opportunity to acquire education both of the hand and head and has relieved Army service of its tedium and monotony. . . ."[43]

At the end of June 1920 the enlisted strength of the army stood at 177,974, well short of the new legislative ceiling of 280,000 provided in the National Defense Act of June 4, 1920. Still, army leaders remained confident. Despite the failure of the winter drive, men were enlisting in high numbers. The General Recruiting Service looked forward to the challenge. Colonel Martin told his recruiters, "It will be the General Recruiting Service on whom the chief burden of maintaining the New Army will fall. It's a man-sized job, but I am certain it will be accomplished. . . ."[44]

While the adjutant general and Colonel Martin busied themselves with building an effective recruiting system for obtaining the higher number of volunteers that the postwar army needed, others in the War Department considered what to do about enlisted losses. During fiscal year 1920 the army's total losses numbered 718,358.

Most of the men discharged in fiscal year 1920 were emergency troops who left the army as a result of demobilization. By November 1919 demobilization was virtually completed, and by January 1920 the number of men leaving the army each month approached a peacetime level. The

Table 2.1 *Enlisted Losses, Fiscal Year 1920*

Retired	543
Relieved from active duty	1,197
Discharged	672,687
Furloughed to reserve	29,265
Died	2,244
Deserted	12,422
	718,358

Source: Report of the Adjutant General, in *War Department Annual Reports,* 1920, Vol. 1, p. 280.

army's goal in managing enlisted strength was to balance losses and gains in order to maintain itself at the authorized average strength. In order to ease the burden on the General Recruiting Service and presumably allow it to pick from the best men available, the army sought to cut down on losses. Securing a high number of reenlistments from the men leaving the army at the end of their enlistment was seen as the best way to reduce losses. The army viewed every honorably discharged soldier as a potential reenlistment, and every man who reenlisted saved the army the expense of recruiting and training a new volunteer. During fiscal year 1920 reenlistments and enlistments by former soldiers accounted for 54.4 percent of total enlistments. That figure compares more than favorably with prewar reenlistments. In fiscal year 1916 reenlistments accounted for only about 17 percent of total enlistments.[45]

High reenlistments in 1920 encouraged the army, but the large number of desertions during the same period suggested that the new volunteer army still had problems. Desertions had plagued the prewar army. The desertion rate averaged 4.53 percent of enlisted strength per year between 1906 and 1915.[46] The army never was certain how many men deserted during World War I and the demobilization period. Accurate figures for the postwar period begin with July 1919. Computed by the official method, the desertion rate for fiscal year 1920 was 1.37 percent, but the figure is meaningless because of the large number of emergency soldiers still on the rolls during the period.[47] Actually desertions were high in fiscal 1920, higher than in prewar years. More than 12,000 men deserted between July 1919 and June 1920.

Traditionally the army relied on two measures to combat the desertion problem: bounties to encourage civilian assistance and stiff punishments for convicted offenders. From 1920 to 1932 any civilian law enforcement official who tracked down and turned in a deserter received $50 ''at the discretion of the Secretary of War.'' In 1933 the amount was reduced to $25 as an economy measure; Congress discontinued the practice altogether in 1938.[48] During the 1920s about 5,000 deserters were returned to army control annually. Of these about 3,500 faced general courts–martial each year. The conviction rate for men charged with desertion averaged 78 percent.[49]

But in the years after World War I, as the army sought new ways to attract men to peacetime service, the War Department began to search for positive means to deal with deserters. What really caused concern at the War Department was the knowledge that nearly 10,000 deserters were among the total of 69,000 new men who had enlisted since March 1919. Such a high number of deserters from the new army, with its multitude of opportunities and benefits, raised serious doubts concerning attractiveness and general morale in the service.

Matters of morale were the specialty of Colonel Edward L. Munson of the Medical Corps. During the war Colonel Munson had become interested in developing ways to prepare soldiers psychologically to fight. Many soldiers, he said, "do not have a clear idea of the cause for which they are fighting. . . ." He recommended "the creation of a special section in the military service whose sole function should be to create the 'fighting edge'. . . ."[50] Munson's plan caught fire, and a separate division of the General Staff known as the Morale Branch was created in June 1918. Munson served in the Morale Branch for the rest of the war and became its chief early in 1919.[51]

Army commanders are traditionally charged with two general responsibilities: accomplishment of the mission, and providing for the welfare of their troops. Munson concerned himself with the latter. He believed that "the United States has been too materialistic where the military service is concerned." The nation, Munson said, equated money and the latest expensive equipment with good soldiers and an efficient army. When it came to the welfare of the troops, Munson said, the nation applied "the old idea of 'the greatest good for the greatest number'." Munson disagreed, arguing instead that good morale depended on "endeavoring to secure the greatest good for everyone." As chief of the Morale Branch, Colonel Munson sought to put his philosophy to practice and to find the "greatest good for everyone."[52]

In 1919 Congress prepared to readjust service pay back to prewar levels. Munson and his Morale Branch led the fight to retain the pay increase enacted during the war as part of the Selective Service Act of 1917. Comparing living costs of 1919 with those of 1908, the year of the last peacetime military pay increase, Munson demonstrated that even with the wartime pay increases, purchasing power, especially that of lower-ranking enlisted men and officers, was lower than before the war. Largely on the strength of Munson's study and vigorous testimony, Congress agreed to retain the wartime increases, with minor revisions, as part of the National Defense Act of 1920 until a more complete study could be conducted.[53]

For Munson the fight to maintain pay at wartime levels represented a holding action. He knew that it took more than adequate monthly remuneration to retain men in the army. Munson identified seven general causes of manpower loss: discharges without reenlistment, discharges by courts–martial, discharges by order, desertions, disability discharges, retirement, and death. The last three he considered legitimate; the first four could be affected by morale. Improve the morale of the service, Munson said, and reenlistments would go up, and desertions, courts–martial, and directed discharges would go down.[54]

In 1920 Munson ordered a study of the desertion problem. The study, completed in September, was prepared by Major Edward N. Woodbury. A reflection of Munson's views, it ranged well beyond the problem of desertions and showed the intimate relationship between the army and the society at large. Woodbury's study reviewed the desertion experience of the army since 1828 and identified conditions in the army and society that appeared to affect desertions. The significant causes of desertion within the army's control, Woodbury noted, included the length of the enlistment period, increases or decreases of strength, and pay. An increase in the enlistment contract, such as occurred in 1838 and 1912, or a decrease in pay, as in 1871, produced coincident rises in desertions. The converse occurred after pay increases and enlistment term decreases. Any abrupt change in the size of the army, Woodbury found, produced an increase in desertions. During a reduction in strength men scheduled to be released frequently deserted rather than waiting to be discharged, especially if they felt the process was taking too long. Periods of rapid increases in strength required large numbers of recruits. Woodbury found that "nearly 72 percent of all deserters have deserted during their first two years of service," and concluded that the large-scale introduction of "new men" into the service brought a natural increase in desertions.[55] Coincidentally, the army had just ended a period of rapid strength reduction and was engaged in recruiting large numbers of new men in an effort to meet a higher peacetime strength authorization.

The most significant outside influence on desertions, according to Woodbury, was the economy. He used the terms "panic" and "prosperity." Woodbury discovered that desertions decreased sharply during every panic in American history: in 1873, a 46 percent drop; 1893, 21 percent; 1907, 32 percent. The converse, he found, was also true. When employment was high, desertions rose and reenlistments declined.[56]

Woodbury considered outside influences beyond the army's ability to affect. He concentrated on the internal influences. Most deserters, he noted, were young and serving their first enlistment. Beyond pay, length of enlistment, and size of the army, conditions of army life affected soldiers most. These conditions included comfortable barracks, good food, lenient pass and furlough privileges, adequate recreational facilities, and an absence of excessive guard and fatigue duties. All the conditions named,

Woodbury said, fell under the control of the local commander. The commander who looked after his soldiers' health, welfare, and living and working conditions was the key to keeping desertions down.[57]

Major Woodbury also explored the relationship between desertions and enlistments and reenlistments. Not surprisingly, he concluded that the economy affected all three. "It is believed," he said, "that both desertion and enlistment depend a great deal on the employment conditions and that national panic may be expected to increase enlistment in the same manner that it has been shown . . . to decrease desertion." Reenlistments, he found, varied inversely with desertions because "the causes which produce lack of contentment with the service undoubtedly increase desertion and prevent reenlistment."[58]

While he agreed that service attractiveness affected desertions and reenlistments, Woodbury did not believe it influenced recruiting. He based his conclusion on a survey of 236 recruits assigned to the Seventh Division between January and May 1920. Only six indicated that they had enlisted to improve themselves. The most frequent reason for enlisting was "to see what the army is like," (117). Other reasons given included: to get away from home (27), to see the country (36), desire for army service inspired by the war (21). About 25 percent of the recruits surveyed were out of work when they joined. Most indicated that they knew little about the army or the opportunities it offered until they enlisted.[59]

Woodbury's survey and the conclusions he drew from it directly contradicted the arguments of recruiters and War Department officials, who claimed that the opportunities of the "new army," especially educational and vocational training, attracted recruits. Although his sample was small, Woodbury's findings were probably closer to the truth than the public-relations-inspired boasts of the Recruiting Publicity Bureau. Most men who enlisted had little knowledge of the army and of army life. Thus many became dissatisfied. The most dissatisfied deserted; other served out their enlistment and failed to reenlist.

Woodbury offered no immediate recommendations. The significance of his study, the most far-reaching of its kind, lay in the wide circulation it received. Every general officer and regimental commander in the army received a copy and was asked to comment. The replies provide an insight into the attitudes and ideas of the army's command structure toward enlisted men in general and the problem of manpower procurement and maintenance in particular.

To some officers the problem and solution were simple. Lieutenant Colonel T. S. Moorman, commanding the Fifty-fifth Infantry, believed that the major cause of dissatisfaction in the army was Newton Baker's educational and vocational training program. "A good many men attend the Educational and Vocational Schools for the purpose of 'beating' fatigue and kitchen police," Moorman wrote. Eliminate the frills and get back to basics, he argued. The so-called "opportunities" tended to attract the wrong kind of man who could never soldier and subsequently deserted.[60] A few other officers agreed with Moorman, but those who blamed the army's problems on frills and claimed that the army was going soft were in a definite minority.

A significant number of replies did, however, go along with Moorman's contention that the army was getting the wrong kind of recruit. Brigadier General Henry Jervey, the assistant chief of staff for operations, noted that "the Army is striving to secure for itself such general high opinion throughout the country that worthy Christian families will be glad to allow their boys to enter the Army because of the mental, physical and moral benefits to be derived from service in the Army." This is an impossible goal, he declared. "We cannot expect to enlist supermen or a set of Sunday School boys, and average men of reasonable self-respect are to be considered highly satisfactory." The problem in Jervey's mind lay in the fact that the army was taking in men from the "undesirable class." This group included the

mentally deficient or ignorant, irresponsible, young, unstable or easily influenced, addictive to drugs or excessive use of intoxicants, physically weak, ill, or physically deficient, degenerate or weak character, of known bad or criminal civil record, discontented or disgruntled, given to excessive association with or victims of immoral women.

Jervey added to this list "certain men apparently neither vicious, depraved nor mentally deficient, [who] possess the fault of character of being what might be called 'rolling stones'." Tighten recruiting requirements to weed out the undesirables even if it means accepting fewer men, Jervey recommended. Above all end recruiting drives, which induce recruiters to accept the dregs in order to meet quotas. "Whenever recruiting drives are initiated, the increased demand for recruits causes the acceptance of some undesirables who would not have been accepted under ordinary conditions."[61]

Jervey's comments and recommendations reflected the feelings of a considerable segment of the army's leaders. Any problem having to do with enlisted men, such as desertions, was considered to be the result of poor recruits and thus poor recruiting. Of the 156 comments on Woodbury's study received by the War Department, fully half mentioned recruits and recruiting as a major factor of the desertion problem.[62] Major General Charles P. Summerall, commander of the First Division, felt that "the fundamental cause of desertion is instability of character, a thing that is, I think, beyond the power of the Military to remove." Summerall, a future chief of staff, suggested an additional study of individual deserters to identify better and then eliminate potential deserters. Like Jervey, he felt the best way to reduce desertion was to keep potential deserters from enlisting.[63] Brigadier General Douglas MacArthur agreed with Summerall, whom he would succeed as chief of staff in 1930. MacArthur, then superintendent of the Military Academy at West Point, praised Woodbury's study highly. He agreed with most of Woodbury's points and added an observation. The army could do more than simply prevent potential deserters from enlisting. Desertions were also a function of dissatisfaction. Rather than eliminate sources of discontent, MacArthur urged that misfits be discharged. "In all business enterprises, except that of the military or naval establishment," MacArthur wrote, "men who do not fit the positions for which they are hired are discharged almost immediately." MacArthur was only one of the more eloquent who thus blamed the recruit, the enlisted man, or the Recruiting Service for the army's problems.[64]

Another group of officers blamed the army for desertions. Leonard Wood, one of the leaders of the prewar reform effort, best summed up the opinions of those who felt that army policies needed changing. Wood conceded that "unfavorable local conditions, the attractions of greater opportunity for advancement outside the service, opportunities stimulating the imagination, such as the opening of gold mines, booms in certain sections, high wages, etc., all have their influence. . . ." But the root cause of desertion is poor morale, and poor morale stems from "the failure on the part of officers to keep in sufficiently close touch with their men and see to it that N.C.O.'s are of the right type and understand how to treat men coming under their control." Wood urged even-handed and fair discipline, elimination of "hard-boiled" noncommissioned officers, and closer contact between officers and enlisted men. Above all, the former chief of staff stressed, "if we are to reduce desertions those in command of men must . . . have enough human interest in them to try to find out what is going wrong and to correct bad conditions."[65]

In addition to citing failures of leadership, many respondents believed army personnel policy created unrest that led to a high desertion rate. Brigadier General Malin Craig, commander of Camp Jones, Arizona, included overbearing or inexperienced officers, uneven discipline, and poor working conditions in his reply. But the man who would replace MacArthur as chief of staff in 1935 considered "rapid change of personnel" arising from the frequent reassignment of officers in troop-leading positions and one-year enlistments as the key to the desertion problem. "Reasonable continuity of personnel is essential," Craig wrote. Without personnel stability officers could never get to know their men and address the morale problems of their commands.[66]

Most of the officers replying to Woodbury's study listed causes and conditions within the army that affected desertions. The question of outside factors received scant treatment. Most officers, if they mentioned society as a factor in the desertion problem at all, simply acknowledged it as beyond the army's means to affect. The conclusion was correct insofar as the army was too small to move or change the larger society it served, but there remained the obvious connection between the economy and enlistments, reenlistments, and desertions. One officer, Major C. W. Harlow, commander of the Tenth Field Artillery at Camp Pike, Arkansas, recognized the economic factor and addressed it candidly. Harlow felt that the brunt of the blame for high desertion rates fell on poor recruits. Although he did not hold the army or the Recruiting Service blameless, he believed

that all these causes simmer down to one. Protracted peace produces genuine economic prosperity which in turn by increasing the pay of industrial workers relatively reduced the pay of the soldier, whereupon the recruiting service, compelled to fill the Army, accepts men below a good standard. . . .

It is in periods of depression that the army gets good men, Harlow said. "Industry's extremity thus becomes the Army's opportunity." Harlow recommended that the army cease recruiting drives in good times and concentrate on picking up good men in bad times. Depressions, he said, are the times when the "Army gains material for its non-commissioned officers."[67]

Woodbury compiled the comments on his study and made his recommendations in April 1921, He found that the respondents divided almost equally in placing the blame for high desertions, and parenthetically other losses including failure to reenlist, on poor quality recruits or on poor treatment of enlisted men. Each view was valid, although hard evidence to support either is difficult to find. Officially the army insisted that the "new army" was better than ever in terms of both the men it attracted and the conditions of army life. General Recruiting Service news releases for the period suggested that postwar recruits represented a cross section of society. But Harry Dowdall found it necessary to pose as an unemployed drifter to attract recruiters as he went from city to city inspecting the General Recruiting Service for Colonel Martin. Similarly, the army went to extremes in advertising the benefits and comforts of the "new peace army" in 1919 and 1920. Yet at the same time, Newton Baker admonished commanders at all levels of "the vital necessity for a considerate and thoughtful treatment of . . . newly enlisted men. . . ." Baker specifically warned against abusive training methods, bullying, and threats of dire punishment. Clearly the secretary of war wanted the reorganized army to succeed, and was worried that "old army" elements might endanger the experiment by adhering to traditional practices.[68]

To improve recruiting, Woodbury recommended the careful screening and training of men selected for the duty, and the development and institution of tests to determine the intelligence and stability of applicants, "that no man be enlisted in the Army unless he be able to produce evidence of good character by some responsible person known to the Recruiting

Officer,'' and the prohibition of enlisting men with former service or allowing reenlistment of men with less than "Excellent" character ratings. While he agreed that improved recruiting practices would help, Woodbury also believed that much could be done to improve service attractiveness beyond offering benefits such as educational and vocational training and recreation programs. He urged more liberal furlough and transfer policies for deserving soldiers, that unit commanders at all levels receive more frequent instruction in "leadership, disciplinary policy, and customs of the service," longer assignments for officers with troops so that they could become more familiar with their men and their problems, and that a clear-cut policy of encouraging "the enlisted man to confer with his Company Commander on troubles real or fancied both of a military and a personal nature," with "a certain *definite* period be laid aside each day for the hearing of grievances. . . ."[69]

By the time Woodbury completed his report and presented his recommendations, events had passed him by. The army was reeling from reductions in appropriations. There is no evidence that the chief of staff ever saw the final report. None of its recommendations was immediately adopted. Nevertheless, the study and the replies are significant. During the next twenty years the army was to encounter many of the problems that the study addressed. The desertion problem continued until 1930, when, as Major Harlow suggested, the depression resolved it. The army continued to grapple with the issue of recruiting and internal improvements. Studies on the subjects of quality recruiting, high losses, reenlistments, and morale begin with Woodbury and either update his statistics or echo his findings and recommendations.[70] The Morale Branch was gone by the end of 1921, a casualty of economy measures. But Woodbury and men like him who had been influenced by Munson continued to address the problems of service attractiveness, morale, and other aspects of manpower procurement and retention.

The close of fiscal year 1920 brought the army to the end of the postwar reorganization period. The National Defense Act of 1920 supposedly laid the groundwork for the future. The General Recruiting Service, rebuilt and reorganized, was bringing in men in record numbers. Despite vexing losses, it appeared that enough men were being recruited to maintain strength, and Baker was optimistic that the new, higher authorized strength of 280,000 could be achieved shortly. More important, the War Department had seriously begun to investigate the sources of its high peacetime losses.

Mid-1920 marked a high point for the peacetime volunteer army. No longer a separate entity, the army seemed to be better accepted as a permanent part of society. The usual pattern of postwar retrenchment, neglect, and decay had apparently not occurred to quite the same degree as in the past. Newspapers and periodicals carried frequent stories about the new army. Newton Baker's educational and vocational training program received widespread attention and praise. Officers were welcome on the lecture circuit. Recruiters toured the Chautauqua. Wherever its activities brought it into contact with the people, the army made every effort to be accommodating.[71] But it was not to be. Even as the army hailed the National Defense Act of 1920 and complimented itself on its new recruiting records, the value of the educational and vocational training program, and all the other features of the "New Peace Army," the winds of reaction were blowing. The signs of change were visible from the start, but in its efforts to court society the army did not seem to notice.

NOTES

1. Report of the Adjutant General in *Annual Reports of the War Department for the year ending June 30, 1920,* Vol. 1 (Washington, D.C.: 1920), Table C, facing p. 282. Hereafter *Annual Report, 1920.*

2. Ibid.

3. A brief contemporary description of the problems associated with demobilization and concurrent maintenance of the army and the legislation authorizing resumption of voluntary enlistments is found in the Report of the Chief of Staff, contained in *Annual Report, 1920,* Vol. I, p. 156.

4. *A Study of Voluntary Enlistments, Army of the United States, 1775–1945* (Army War College, September 1945), p. 18. MHI.

5. *Annual Report, 1919,* Vol. 1, p. 518.

6. *Historical Documents Relating to the Reorganization Plans of the War Department and the Present National Defense Act* (Washington, D.C.: GPO, 1927), p. 261.

7. Memo, Assistant Chief of Staff, Director of Operations (G3) to the Adjutant General (AG), February 12, 1919, AGO 341.6 (2-12-19), RG 407, Box 792, NA.

8. *Annual Report, 1919,* Vol. 1, p. 519.

9. "A Suggestion of Methods for Conduct of Recruiting, Et cetera" (mimeographed), February 1919, MHI.

10. Memo, Publicity Bureau—USARS to AG, April 25, 1919; Memo, G1 to AG, May 27, 1919; Memo, James Totten, AG to All General Recruiting Officers, June 18, 1919, AGO 341.01, RG 407, Box 785, NA.

11. *Regulations for the Army of the United States,* 1913, corrected to April 15, 1917 (Washington, D.C.: GPO, 1918), Article 66, par. 846, 849, p. 174; "Instructions Governing Voluntary Enlistments," War Department Circular No. 113, March 6, 1919, in *Compilation of General Orders, Bulletins; Circulars, and General Recruiting Service Circular Letters Relating to Recruiting; October 1, 1918 to June 30, 1919* (Washington, D.C.: GPO, 1919), p. 18, MHI.

12. Very little has been written about blacks in the interwar army. The assumption that governed policy was that blacks were inferior, for the most part required white officers to lead them, and should be organized in segregated units. For summaries of army attitudes and policy regarding blacks, see Richard M. Dalfiume, *Desegregation of the U.S. Armed Forces* (Columbia, Mo.: University of Missouri Press, 1969), pp. 5–24; L. D. Reddick, "The Negro Policy of the United States

Army, 1775–1945," *Journal of Negro History* 38, no. 1 (January 1949): 9–29. Statistics on service by blacks in World War I and on demobilization are found in Dalfiume, *Desegregation of the U.S. Armed Forces,* p. 13; Reddick, "The Negro Policy of the United States Army," p. 22; *Report of the Surgeon General for 1920* (Washington, D.C.: GPO, 1921), p. 536. Hereafter *SG, 1920.*

13. *NYT,* March 30, 1919, p. 19; April 18, p. 6.

14. *Annual Report, 1920,* Vol. 1, p. 170.

15. *NYT,* June 19, 1919, p. 28; July 28, p. 24; *Annual Report, 1919,* Vol. 1, p. 520.

16. *NYT,* June 19, 1919, p. 28; July, 28, p. 24

17. *NYT,* June 19, 1919, p. 28.

18. Report of the Secretary of War, in *Annual Report, 1920,* Vol. 1, pp. 16–17, 29.

19. Ibid., pp. 29, 303–4.

20. Beginning in 1922 the adjutant general reported monthly recruiting results by corps area. Once recruiting of blacks resumed, racial characteristics of recruits were given. Information such as religion, educational level, previous employment, ethnic group, or rural or urban residence is not available except in scattered reports, and to the best of my knowledge was not routinely recorded for statistical purposes. Information of that nature is contained in individual army personnel records, which are protected by the Privacy Act. The files of the regular army enlisted men of the 1920s and 1930s are stored at the National Archives Regional Depository in St. Louis, Missouri, and were partially destroyed in a fire in 1974.

21. *Annual Report, 1922,* p. 200.

22. Compiled from consecutive reports on enlistments for Chicago published in *U.S. Army Recruiting News,* January 15, 1923, p. 17, and March 1, 1923, p. 17. *Recruiting News* was the official publication of the General Recruiting Service. It was put out byweekly or monthly by the Recruiting Publicity Bureau, located in New York City.

23. Summarized from *The United States Army as a Career,* an information book published by the Adjutant General's Office for recruiters and recruits (Washington, D.C.: GPO, 1929), pp. 25–27; U.S., Department of Commerce, Bureau of the Census, *Historical Statistics of the United States, Colonial Times to 1957* (Washington, D.C.: GPO, 1960), p. 91.

24. *Annual Report, 1920,* pp. 305–8.

25. *The Officers' Guide* (Washington, D.C.: The National Service Publishing Co., 1930), pp. 124–25.

26. Based on an interview with Gen. Robert G. Porter, U.S. Army (Ret.) at West Point, N.Y., January 19, 1978. General Porter was commissioned in the cavalry in 1930. His observations of life in the Fourth Cavalry from July 1930 to June 1933 are typical of service conditions in that branch throughout the interwar years.

27. Interview with General Porter; Report of the Judge Advocate General, 1920, contained in *Annual Report, 1920,* p. 371.

28. *SG, 1920,* pp. 611, 678–79; *Annual Report, 1920,* p. 371.

29. William H. Waldron, *The Old Sergeant's Conferences* (Washington, D.C.: National Service Publishing Company, 1930), pp. 19–20.

30. Telegram "Union One," AG to Recruiting Officer, Portland, Ore., Jan. 8,

1920. Central files of the Adjutant General's Office, No. 341.1, Record Group 407, Box 786, National Archive. Hereafter AGO 341.1, RG 407, N.A.

31. Letter, Newton Baker to Governor Smith of New York, Jan. 24, 1920, AGO 341.1, RG 407, Box 785, NA.

32. Samuel Gompers to Newton Baker, April 2, 1920, as reported in *Recruiting News* 2 (April 10, 1920), p. 2.

33. *Army and Navy Journal* (hereafter, *ANJ*), Jan. 31, 1920, p. 675.

34. *NYT,* Jan. 15, 1920, p.10; April 19, p. 6.

35. *AG, 1920,* p. 281.

36. *ANJ,* April 17, 1920, p. 998.

37. Pay of enlisted men is based on that established by the National Defense Act of 1920. See War Department General Orders No. 44, July 20, 1920, in *War Department General Orders and Bulletins* (Washington, D.C.: GPO, 1920); civilian pay is derived from *Historical Statistics of the United States,* pp. 91, 94. For a more complete discussion of army pay and allowances, see Ibid. pp. 116–119, and appendix C.

38. Memo, General Haan to AG, April 20, 1920, AGO 341.01, RG 407, Box 783, NA.

39. From report of 1st Lt. Samuel McCullough, Circuit "E" Chautauqua, week ending Aug. 17, 1920, AGO 341.01, RG 407, Box 783, NA.

40. Letters, Col. A. E. Williams to AG summarizing a memo about the lectures of Cpt. Lester J. Harris, AGO 341.01, RG 407, Box 783, NA.

41. Excerpts of the Report of 1st Lt. Harry G. Dowdall, Boston, Mass., Nov. 19, 1920, pp. 1, 4; Providence, R.I., Dec. 7, 1920, p. 1, AGO 341.1 (Confidential), RG 407, Box 786, NA.

42. *Annual Report, 1920,* p. 280.

43. Ibid., p. 14.

44. C. H. Martin, "A Word to Recruiters on the New Army Law," *Recruiting News,* June 12, 1920, p. 1.

45. Reenlistment statistics are derived from the *Annual Reports.* Figures for fiscal year 1920 are found in *Annual Report, 1920,* p. 281. Prewar data is contained in a special report on recruiting between March 1919 and January 1921. AGO 341.1, RG 407, Box 786, NA. This study is discussed further in chapter 4.

46. The War Department calculated the desertion rate by taking total desertions as a percentage of total enlistment contracts in force during the year. Total enlistment contracts were obtained by adding total losses to the end of year enlisted strength. For example, the desertion rate for FY 1920 was calculated as follows: Total enlisted losses, FY 1920 (724,634) plus enlisted strength, June 30, 1920 (184,848) divided into desertions (12,432) equaled the desertion rate (.0137). *Annual Report, 1920,* p. 282.

47. *Annual Report, 1920,* p. 282.

48. War Department Bulletin No. 28, June 23, 1920, p. 14; Bulletin No. 5, March 16, 1933, p. 6; Circular 80, December 30, 1938, Section 2. Prior to World War I annual reports gave detailed analyses of desertion statistics including the number returned under the bounty system. These reports and statistics disappeared during the war and did not resume thereafter.

49. Figures are based on an analysis of desertion and court–martial rates for 1921–1929 as reported in *Annual Reports.*

50. Memo, Assistant Chief of Staff to CS, May 10, 1919, Records of the Chief of Staff, 1918–1921, file 428, Box 55, NA. Hereafter CS, 1918–1921, 428. This memo quotes from Munson's original proposal written sometime in February 1918.

51. Edward L. Munson, *The Management of Men* (New York: Henry Holt & Co., 1921), p. v.

52. Ibid., pp. 9, 15.

53. *Annual Report, 1920,* p. 212; Statement of Colonel E. L. Munson before Senate Subcommittee on Military Affairs, October 27, 1919, in U.S., Congress, Senate, *Reorganization of the Army: Hearings Before the Subcommittee of the Committee on Military Affairs,* 66th Cong., 3rd sess., pp. 1459–77; General Order No. 44, July 20, 1920. "Pay Provisions of the National Defense Act Approved July 4, 1920," *Extracts of General Orders and Bulletins, 1919–1921.* (Washington, D.C.: GPO, 1922).

54. Munson, *The Management of Men,* pp. 564–65.

55. E. N. Woodbury, "A Study of Desertions in the Army," (mimeographed), Morale Branch, General Staff, Washington, D.C.: 1920, pp. 2–4.

56. Ibid., p. 5.

57. Ibid., pp. 47–49.

58. Ibid., p. 19.

59. Ibid.

60. Letter, Lt. Col. T. S. Moorman to AG, Jan. 15, 1921, AGO 251.1 (10-12-20) Bulky, RG 407, Box 1709, NA. Hereafter, Replies.

61. Memo, Brig. Gen. Jervey to AG, Dec. 13, 1920, Replies.

62. Letter, Maj. Woodbury to Chief of Morale Branch, April 21, 1921, Replies. Woodbury reviewed and compiled the replies and wrote a cover letter for them.

63. Letter, Maj. Gen. C. P. Summerall to AG, Jan. 25, 1921, Replies.

64. Letter, Brig. Gen. Douglas MacArthur to AG, Nov. 17, 1920, Replies.

65. Letter, Maj. Gen. Leonard Wood to AG, Dec. 13, 1920, Replies.

66. Letter, Brig. Gen. Malin Craig to AG, Nov. 28, 1920, Replies.

67. Letter, Maj. C. W. Harlow to AG, Dec. 13, 1920, Replies.

68. Letter, Newton Baker to CS, Feb. 18, 1920, published as General Order No. 12, Section 4, Feb. 28, 1920, in *War Department General Orders and Bulletins, 1920* (Washington, D.C.: GPO, 1921).

69. Letters, Maj. E. N. Woodbury to Chief of Morale Branch, April 13, 1921, "Review of Comments on 'Study of Desertions,'" pp. 10–19, Replies.

70. The list of reports, studies, and articles on the continuing desertion problem, recruiting practices, treatment of enlisted men, and other problems is too long to list here. These studies are cited throughout this book as they become relevant.

71. Samuel P. Huntington, *The Soldier and the State* (New York: Vintage Books, 1964), pp. 282–88.

3

THE ARMY RETURNS TO NORMALCY

In June 1920, after the final passage of the National Defense Act, military professionals looked forward to an era of peace unlike those they had experienced in the past. They were soon disappointed. By the end of 1920 interest in army reorganization had already waned. The new issue of the day became economy and the army that Colonel Palmer envisioned became one of the first victims of a drive to reduce government spending. The number of men in the army and the cost of their upkeep quickly attracted the attention of the economizers, but all army programs suffered during the "prosperity decade." Throughout the 1920s while army leaders and preparedness advocates complained and worried about declining military strength, the public, for the most part, showed little interest. Only when military issues took on the dimensions of a human interest story or confrontation between competing interests, as in the Mobilization Day debate in 1924, the court–martial of Billy Mitchell in 1925, or the military housing controversy in 1926–1927, did segments of the public respond. As far as the American people were concerned, the volunteer army was out of sight and out of mind.

Analyzing the decline of the army during the 1920s, the military historian Russell Weigley observed that the peacetime structure established by "the National Defense Act of 1920 was allowed to atrophy."[1] In fact it never existed except on paper. Enlisted strength never reached the 280,000-man level established by the act of 1920. Cuts in strength and appropriations, which began even as Congress debated the reorganization bills, wrecked Palmer's plans to bring the regular army into more intimate contact with the civilian components. Exponents of Emory Upton's ideas favoring an expandable professional force prevailed. As enlisted strength shrank, the number of units in the regular force remained constant. Rather than maintain fewer units, each at full strength, as Palmer urged, the General Staff reverted to the old school and cut units to peacetime strength while planning to expand them in an emergency. Corps area training centers, designed to bring the professional and civilian soldiers together, closed and sent their personnel back to shrinking regular army units. The National Guard and newly formed organized reserve units also suffered; by the end of the decade no effective reserve system existed. In response to the neglect, which represented an apparent change of heart concerning national defense, the regular army turned inward and concentrated on its own problems. The buoyant spirit with which the army greeted the decade gave way to pessimism and frustration.

Two forces contributed to the deterioration of army fortunes during the decade: the demand for economy in government and the search for world peace. The influence of the former is more obvious. A succession of budget cuts was justified as necessary to reduce government spending after the war, and the sharp postwar recession of 1919–1921 added impetus to the desire to cut costs. The military establishment, which accounted for a major share of annual federal expenditures then as now, was an obvious target for economy-minded politicians and officials.

The effect on the army of American participation in the continuing quest for peace was more subtle. Pacifists and antimilitarists continually condemned the army in the 1920s. These elements had little direct influence, but the efforts of more moderate peace advocates and isolationists did. The cumulative effect of the Washington Naval Conference of 1921–1922, the Treaty of Locarno in 1925, renewed disarmament discussions in 1927, and finally the Kellogg-Briand Pact in 1928, combined with a growing revulsion against war stemming from disillusion with American participation in World War I to make it all the easier to ignore the army.

Spearheading the drive for economy were conservative businessmen who dominated the government between 1921 and 1930. These powerful spokesmen for small government wanted an end to governmental meddling in domestic private enterprise, protection from competition abroad and threats to its hegemony from labor at home, and a reduction in taxes on corporate and personal incomes.[2]

No one exemplified the business ethos and its influence on government policy in the 1920s better than banker Andrew W. Mellon, who served as secretary of the treasury from 1921 to 1932. Mellon believed that government must be run like a business. Sound business principles demand debt reduction and a balanced budget. Both could be achieved by reducing expenditures. Once spending was brought under control, Mellon could turn his attention to his primary goal of cutting taxes.[3]

The Harding administration moved swiftly to reduce expenditures. With congressional approval the president created a Bureau of the Budget in the Treasury Department. Henceforth all government agencies were required to submit annual appropriation requests to the Budget Bureau for approval before passing them to Congress. Harding appointed Charles Dawes, another banker, to the post of budget director and committed his administration to "a period of economy in government." He declared, "there is not a menace in the world today like that of growing public indebtedness and mounting public expenditures." Following Harding's directions, Dawes prepared a federal budget for fiscal year 1923 of $3.5

billion, nearly $2 billion less than expenditures the year the Republicans returned to the White House.[4] For the remainder of the decade government spending remained at the level Dawes established for fiscal year 1923. This policy of economy is government, more than any other development during the decades, affected the volunteer army.

America-firsters added to the antimilitary mood of the 1920s. The United States, despite its rejection of the Treaty of Versailles, did not abandon the search for a permanent peace in the 1920s. Convinced that American intervention had been a costly mistake, most Americans after 1919 were probably opposed to future involvement in European wars. But Americans were not allowed to forget the war. Popular novels of the period including Erich Remarque's *All Quiet on the Western Front,* John Dos Passos' *Three Soldiers,* the play and movie *What Price Glory,* and later Ernest Hemingway's *A Farewell to Arms* kept the memory and horror of the war fresh in the public mind and added to its disillusion.[5]

Groups committed to the establishment of a permanent peace, the reduction of armaments, and the abolition of war educated the public and encouraged the government to take part in the continuing search for peace. The American peace movement contained both conservative and radical groups. The conservatives, part of the Wilsonian Internationalist tradition, advocated American membership in the League of Nations and the World Court and participation in disarmament conferences. The Carnegie Endowment for International Peace led these groups. Dr. Nicholas Murray Butler of Columbia University was president of the Carnegie Endowment and was assisted by Professor James T. Shotwell, director of the endowment's Division of Economics and History. Butler and Shotwell traveled endlessly on behalf of peace in the 1920s. Other groups like the Carnegie Endowment included the World Peace Foundation, the American Foundation, which sponsored a peace plan award, the World Alliance for International Friendship through the Churches, and the Commission on International Justice and Goodwill, sponsored by the Federal Council of Churches of Christ.[6]

The more radical peace organizations generally agreed with the conservatives on membership in international bodies but devoted most of their attention to crusading attacks on the means of war. Groups like the National Council for the Prevention of War, run by Frederick J. Libby; the American branch of the Women's International League for Peace and Freedom; the National Committee on the Cause and Cure of War; and Samuel O. Levinson's American Committee for the Outlawry of War, constantly attacked the twin evils of armaments and militarism.[7] The army was a frequent object of the radicals' scorn. In the early years of the decade the military budget and peacetime strength drew considerable attention from the pacifists and antimilitarists. By the mid-1920s, although still dissatisfied with the size and expense of the armed forces, the peace organizations directed their efforts toward new issues. In 1924, for example, they tried to prevent a test of the army's mobilization plans. Another major target was ROTC. Thoughout the interwar years a coalition of antimilitary groups known as the Committee on Militarism in Education worked to eliminate compulsory military training from the nation's colleges, universities, and secondary schools.[8]

The army did not lack supporters. Those who had lobbied for universal military training, army reform and reorganization, and other forms of preparedness could count on the significant voice of the American Legion. The National Guard Association and groups associated with UMT like the Military Training Camps Association also continued to function and support the army. These voices, however, became increasingly muted as the years passed and the American Legion grew in size and influence.[9] A particularly vocal ally was the *Army and Navy Journal,* founded in 1863 by William Conant Church as an unofficial spokesman for the nation's military interests. Church published and edited the weekly until his death in 1917. His theme—peace through preparedness—was continued into the interwar years when retired Brigadier General Henry J. Reilly acquired the paper.

The *Journal* reached a wide audience. Army and navy officers and enlisted men considered it a "hometown paper" because it provided news on athletic, professional, and social activities for all of the services besides reporting on events and legislation. It also presented weekly summaries of the opinions on military issues of leading politicians, citizens, and newspapers. Outside the army and navy many members of Congress and public figures read the *Journal* and quoted it frequently on military matters.[10]

Other newspapers continued to advocate preparedness during the 1920s, notably the *New York Times.* The *Time's* support came from Julius Ochs Adler, nephew of publisher Adolph S. Ochs. Adler graduated from Plattsburg in 1915 and remained an active supporter of civilian military training until his death in 1955. He served in France during World War I and retained his reserve commission after the war, eventually rising to the rank of major general. During the interwar years he was an assistant publisher and editor of the *Times.* After his uncle's death in 1935, Adler became general manager. His interest in military affairs ensured that the *Times* would be an important spokesman for a responsible defense program.[11]

The army also could, and frequently did, speak for itself. Every reduced budget request met with protest. Usually, however, the chiefs of staff and General Staff officers were careful not to object too loudly or too long lest they appear to transgress the acceptable limits of civilian supremacy.[12] As a civilian the secretary of war knew no such bounds, and the secretaries of the interwar period frequently protested the small budgets and warned of the consequences of "false economy." Military men also wrote articles in the professional journals and popular periodicals of the day discussing the effects and dangers of reduced military spending.[13] None of these efforts, however, seemed to have any influence on the dominant trend of the 1920s—economy in government. The shift to reduced federal spending predated Harding's election. The Republicans dominated Congress after the election of 1918, and they offered many hints of the future of American government in the sessions of the Sixty-sixth Congress. Army appropriations for fiscal year 1921, which began on July 1, 1920, clearly anticipated the return to normalcy and what lay in store for the volunteer army in the 1920s.

During the interwar years, as today, the real business of Congress was carried on by committees. Each committee, according to a student of the legislative process "is the repository of . . . expertise within its jurisdiction, [and] committee decisions are usually accepted by the other members of the chamber. . . ." Furthermore, committee chairmen "can (and usually do) wield a great deal of influence over their committees."[14] During the postwar reorganization of the army, legislative initiative lay in the Military Affairs Committees of both houses. But as the demand for economy in government gained momentum, the appropriations committees came to wield increasing influence over military policy. In order to deal better with the large number of bills handled annually, both the House and Senate Committees on Appropriations divided themselves into subcommittees. Before 1949 both bodies maintained separate subcommittees for military and naval appropriations. Throughout the interwar period the full committees in both houses rarely overruled their subcommittees. Thus, as a historian of military spending in the 1930s observed, "the subcommittees [were] Congress as far as appropriations are concerned."[15]

Daniel R. Anthony, Jr., a Republican from Leavenworth, Kansas, chaired the House Subcommittee on Army Appropriations. Anthony opposed a large peacetime army. He had vigorously objected to the Baker-March bill in 1919 and UMT in 1920. Although he supported the army reorganization bill without UMT, he considered the 280,000-man ceiling unnecessarily high. A smaller army could be maintained, he argued, by eliminating the occupation force in Germany and reducing the number of troops stationed in Panama, Hawaii, and the Philippines. He also considered Colonel Palmer's plan for maintaining nine full-strength divisions in the United States "an unnecessary waste and expense." Anthony received bipartisan support for his views from Thomas U. Sisson of Mississippi, the ranking Democrat on the Military Appropriations Subcommittee. Both men preferred to maintain a strong National Guard, under state control, to an enlarged regular army. In so doing Anthony and Sisson neatly personified the traditional moods of the rural Midwest and South concerning both big government and a large standing army in peacetime.[16]

In the spring of 1920, while debate continued on army reorganization, the House began work on the military appropriations bill. The War Department request totaled nearly $1 billion, including funds to pay 576,000 men. In short order the appropriations subcommittee reduced the request to $377 million, largely by cutting the amount authorized for pay to enough money to provide for only 175,000 enlisted men.[17] From the end of April until June 3, 1920, when both houses approved the bill, these figures remained virtually unchanged.[18] The enlisted strength that the bill provided for directly conflicted with the figure of 280,000 men approved in the National Defense Act, which was proceeding through Congress in its final form at the same time. In the final flurry of activity associated with the reorganization bill, nobody seemed to notice or question the obvious difference between the strength figures of the new defense legislation and annual enabling act. In retrospect it seems clear that the larger figure represented a ceiling and that Congress never intended to maintain a 280,000-man army in peacetime. The House Appropriations Committee report best expressed the mood of Congress. "The Committee," wrote its chairman, "felt that at this time it is necessary to practice rigid economy."[19]

The differing enlisted strength figures led to a fierce struggle between the War Department and Congress. Newton Baker declared that the 280,000-man figure provided for in the National Defense Act and approved after the appropriations bill would be met. Baker announced a massive recruiting campaign to bring the regular army up to full authorized strength. By December 1920 enlisted strength topped 200,000, up from 177,974 at the end of June. On December 10 the Committee on Military Affairs called Baker before it and demanded an explanation. Baker declared that the National Defense Act gave him the authority to recruit to a strength of 280,000. Julius Kahn, chairman of the committee, pointed out that recruiting to the higher level would create a deficit of $160 million, and worried that such a cost might lead the public to demand a further reduction of the army. Baker replied, "The people know, and if they don't you and I know, and they should be appraised of the fact that armies are more expensive now than ever before." Baker refused to stop recruiting.[20]

After the Christmas recess Congress responded to Baker's continued recruiting. In a joint resolution Congress ordered the secretary of war to suspend all recruiting until attrition reduced enlisted strength to the 175,000 men authorized. President Wilson, embittered by previous legislative reversals from the Sixty-sixth Congress and stung by the Democrats' defeat in November 1920, stood by his secretary of war. He declared, "I am not able to see the condition of the world at large or in the needs of the United States any such change as would justify the reduction upon that minimum which is proposed by the House joint resolution," and vetoed the measure. Congress viewed Wilson's veto as a challenge to its authority to raise and maintain the armed forces, and by a vote of 271 to 16 in the

House and 67 to 1 in the Senate, promptly overrode the veto. On February 7, 1921, Baker ordered all recruiting halted.[21] Opponents of the large standing peacetime army expressed delight. *The Nation,* which considered the current strength of 175,000 men "still absurdly large," declared that passage of the resolution halting enlistments "indicates that the views of the harassed public are making some slight impression on their representatives in Congress."[22]

Baker's haughty attitude toward Congress over the recruiting issue in late 1920 did little to further the interests of the army. Congressional insistence that the regular army not go beyond the 175,000-man limit was only the beginning of an economy-conscious crusade.

Even as Baker was quarreling with Congress over recruiting, Anthony's subcommittee took up the army's request for funds for fiscal year 1922. Initially the subcommittee maintained army strength at 175,000, but when President-elect Harding told Julius Kahn and other members of the House concerned with military affairs that he favored reducing "the present Army of 218,000 men . . . to 175,000 at the earliest possible time, and that a little later another reduction, bringing it down to 150,000 should be made," Anthony's subcommittee responded almost immediately and reported a draft bill that cut enlisted strength to 150,000. Anthony declared that Congress was responding to the public's demand for an end "to waste and extravagance that have characterized the military establishment for the last few years."[23]

James W. Wadsworth, author of the National Defense Act, chaired the Senate subcommittee on military appropriations.[24] Wadsworth had accepted the necessity for a reduction in army strength to 175,000 men the year before, but was adamantly opposed to a further cut. The Senate subcommittee prepared a bill that maintained 175,000 as the enlisted strength for 1922.[25]

The issue of the size of the peacetime army carried into the first session of the Sixty-seventh Congress. The subcommittees in the new Congress remained essentially the same. Anthony's subcommittee again reported a bill reducing the army to 150,000 men, and Wadsworth continued to demand 175,000.

Foes of the 175,000-man peacetime army grounded their arguments on the necessity for economy. Few openly expressed antimilitarism, but some opponents of the larger army clearly reflected traditional fears of standing armies. Senator William E. Borah of Idaho insisted that the reduction was necessary for the "morale of the country," adding that citizenship was the best protection against unknown foes. Senator John Williams of Mississippi called "an army of 170,000 men at this time . . . a form of insanity, if not idiocy. . . . In some of the finest years of our history the United States progressed most satisfactorily with an army of 25,000 men."[26]

Supporters of the larger army protested in vain against the cuts. The new secretary of war John W. Weeks, a former congressman and banker from Massachusetts, argued that the 25,000 more men were essential for the additional missions outlined by the National Defense Act. He promised to practice strict economy in other areas in order to pay for the additional soldiers.[27] General Pershing, the new chief of staff, told the Senate that a strength reduction "to 150,00 will compel the War Department to put an end to many combat organizations, or reduce them to a strength which will destroy their value as a nucleus around which to build fighting organizations in an emergency." "Such a reduction," warned the chief of staff, "goes far toward defeating one of the principal features of the national defense act. . . ."[28]

Despite such arguments, the economy-conscious supporters of a reduced army prevailed. The Senate had originally supported Wadsworth's bill, but on June 8, 1921, Borah, one of the leaders in the drive to cut the army, brought the issue to a second vote. Support for the army came largely from the eastern and industrial states. But western Republicans joined most Democrats in opposing the larger force, and by a vote of 36 to 32 the Senate approved a reduction of strength to 150,000. Democratic opposition to a larger standing army was traditional and partisan. Like Republicans from the rural Midwest and West, Democrats continued to echo eighteenth- and nineteenth-century fears of standing armies and loss of local control over the militia. Eastern support centered in cities and the growing industrial belt and was linked to notions of nationalism such as prestige, world responsibilities, and economic interest that had gelled around the turn of the century. This pattern remained unchanged for the rest of the decade.[29]

President Harding, who had earlier supported a smaller, less expensive army, expressed concern over the swiftness of the reduction. The appropriation bill mandated that the army meet the lower level by October 1921 even if the action required dismissing men before their enlistment terms ended. Nevertheless, Harding signed the bill after a White House parlay on June 28, during which Borah reportedly threatened a further reduction to 100,000 if the president withheld approval of the swift reduction.[30]

Enlistment cuts were not the only losses the army suffered in the prolonged appropriations battle of 1921. Educational and vocational training, a key part of Newton Baker's plan to give the army social utility in peacetime, came under attack. The program, which had received broad support when inaugurated in 1919, seemed counterproductive to many in 1921. During House hearings on the appropriations bill, Frank Green of Vermont, in questioning the educational program, declared, "the army is organized for fighting, not for going to school." Joseph Walsh of Massachusetts felt that the program hurt the army because, by teaching soldiers a trade, it encouraged them to leave the army for civilian jobs. Requests for educational and vocational training were cut to $1.2 million, down $3 million from the previous year.[31] In an army still very dependent on foot mobility, horses remained important, but only \$200,100 was appropriated for the purchase of horses in 1922, a reduction from \$1.5 million the year before. Congress also reduced funds for the continued development and maintenance of the Air Service from \$33 to \$19.2 million. The National Guard also suffered cutbacks. Money for the purchase of equipment, arms, and supplies for field training, an important part of the closer relationship between the regular army and civilian components envisioned by John McAuley Palmer and other framers of the National Defense Act, dropped from \$8 to \$5.5 million.[32]

The constraints imposed by the new appropriations required strict economy. In adjusting to the restrictions, the army took steps that touched the entire rank and file. The reduction in strength necessitated the most drastic measures.

New enlistments had already ceased in February after Congress ordered Baker to halt recruiting until attrition reduced strength to 175,000. The new appropriation required a further cut to 150,000 by October. In order to comply, Secretary of War Weeks ordered the involuntary separation of all enlisted men under the age of eighteen upon the request of their parents or guardians and the discharge of any other enlisted men stationed in the United States at their own application.[33] By August the reduction was largely completed, ahead of schedule. The army discharged 48,902 men in July and another 19,726 in August; normal monthly discharges, which included men leaving at the end of their enlistments and discharges for disability and by order of courts-martial, averaged between 5,000 and 6,000 during 1921–1922. Discharges for "other causes" such as men released for fraudulent enlistment (under age or having dependents) generally numbered between 1,000 and 1,300 a month. Thus, of the 68,000 men discharged between July 1 and October 31, 1921, about 54,000 left under the "early out" program.[34] Involuntary discharges of men over twenty-one proved unnecessary.

The reduction in strength also affected officers. Over the next two years Congress cut the maximum number of officers permitted to serve on active duty in the regular army from 16,000 to 12,000. Many older officers chose to retire early when offered special annuities, but over 1,000 regular officers had to be forcibly discharged by January 1, 1920.[35]

The sudden reduction in strength affected those who remained in the regular army more than those who left. A smaller army required fewer noncommissioned officers. Since most of the men discharged left from the lower ranks, the result was a top-heavy rank structure. Furthermore, the National Defense Act set limits on the number of men in each grade based on the total enlisted strength of the army. The reduction in strength dictated reductions in grade. At first the War Department simply froze promotions, assuming that retirements and discharges would eliminate the excess soldiers in the higher grades, but the forced reduction to 150,000 by October necessitated demoting some soldiers. In July the army announced that surplus noncommissioned officers would be reduced one grade. The army defined as "surplus" all noncommissioned officers above the statutory number authorized for each rank for whom no specific job or assignment existed. The adjutant general made efforts to transfer excess NCOs and absorb the surplus. The army based its decision on individual cuts in grade on seniority and "value to the service" and tried to take into account any personal hardship the demotion might cause. Wholesale reductions did not take place until 1923, as the army attempted to stall while it sought relief legislation from Congress. Some 800 officers also accepted grade reductions in order to keep their commissions and remain on active duty.[36]

Economy measures also cut deeply into the regular army. The War Department eliminated some 21,000 civilian jobs, a reduction of about 25 percent. Uniformed personnel filled many of the civilian vacancies, thereby further cutting effective strength. The army increased overseas tours of duty (normally two to three years in length) by one year to save the cost of transfers. Other reductions included cuts in allowances for travel, transportation of goods, telephone and telegraph services, and fuel. During the winter of 1921–1922 the War Department ordered units to ration coal and consolidate facilities in order to conserve fuel and electricity. Services traditionally free to enlisted men, such as laundry, repair of shoes, hats, and clothing, and dry cleaning were eliminated on October 1, 1921.[37]

The army responded to the swift reduction and strict economy during 1922 with mixed reactions. Officially, the army demonstrated grim resolve to make the adjustments. In his year-end report Secretary Weeks noted that for the first time in its history the United States in 1920 established a military policy that "combines the experience of the present with the teachings of the past." Weeks recognized that "the close of the war left us . . . burdened with financial difficulties that are . . . disagreeably felt by the country," and he accepted the reduced strength and appropriations as "characteristic of the wisdom of our councils. . . ." But the cuts made it impossible for the army to accomplish its missions. "Just as soon as the financial situation of our Government makes it reasonable," Weeks pleaded, "we should . . . revert to a steady and uniform plan of development of the defense project as contemplated in the defense act of June 4, 1920." Pershing was more blunt. In reviewing the strength cuts, he concluded, "It is my conviction that our Regular force is cut too much for safety, and that a strength of at least 150,000 enlisted men . . . should be permanently fixed as the minimum."[38] Privately Pershing and other army leaders expressed deeper concern. In a letter to General James Harbord, deputy chief of staff, Pershing confided that he feared that the army had deteriorated to a condition worse than that of prewar years.[39]

For a military man trained to plan for every contingency, Pershing's uneasiness was hardly unjustified. But advocates of economy persisted. Shortly after approval of the 1922 appropriations, proponents of further reductions publicly turned their attention to 1923. In August 1921 Senator Borah proposed a reduction to 100,000 enlisted men.[40] Hearings began in January 1922, and it soon became clear that if the army hoped to maintain its strength, other military programs would have to be cut. During House hearings, John McKenzie of Illinois expressed the sentiment of Congress when he said, "We have either got to cut down the expense, . . . or else the size of the army . . . [is] going to be cut." One area that McKenzie suggested was schools. Pershing defended the schools at Forts Benning, Leavenworth, and elsewhere devoted to military training, but he sacrificed educational and vocational training without a wink, saying brusquely, "I am opposed to this vocational training stuff."[41] Later in the hearings even the costs of recreational services for soldiers, like the motion picture services, libraries, and servicemen's clubs, were questioned. Thomas Sisson of Mississippi declared, "I must confess that all these Government activities smack of bolshevism and German socialism."[42]

The hearings, which coincided with the Washington conference limiting naval tonnage, attracted the attention of several interests traditionally concerned with military spending. Frederick Libby, secretary of the National Council for the Reduction of Armaments, issued a bulletin on February 22, 1922, demanding a 50 percent cut in both the army and navy. Libby argued that "the 5-5-3 ratio [of capital ships] is a minimum not a maximum," and he added that the money thus saved could be spent elsewhere. "Businessmen want taxes reduced and the money liberated for business uses, and farmers, labor, educators and organized women have been seeking money from Congress in vain for constructive uses of peace." The next day the *New York Times* replied to Libby in an editorial: "Preparedness is still a duty," declared the *Times,* as it condemned the council's proposal and the activities of "pseudo-economists" in Congress who "call themselves anti-militarists as soon as the last shot in a war has been fired and they can breathe freely." But still others refuted the *Times.* One newspaper, urging "less strut, more work," observed that "with reductions of armies and navies now in sight . . . a big reduction in the ranks of army and navy men goes along with it, which is a mighty good thing. We will now have less strutting like a turkey gobbler and more honest and productive work."[43]

On March 2, the House Appropriations Committee voted to reduce enlisted strength to 115,000. Opponents of further cuts reacted swiftly. The next day, after a visit from General Pershing, President Harding called the committee to the White House and advised the members that he opposed a reduction below 130,000.[44] Preparedness advocates campaigned against the proposed cut. The *San Antonio Light* accused Congress of buying votes in the name of economy at the expense of the general welfare. The *New York Times* and *Tribune,* the *Boston Transcript, Washington Post, Chicago Tribune,* the Hearst papers, and others all opposed the reduction.[45] The House was not deterred. On March 14, the Committee on Appropriations reported its bill, drafted by Daniel Anthony, calling for an army of 115,000 enlisted men. The bill trimmed $46 million from the War Department's request for $311 million, which had already been cut by the new Bureau of the Budget.[46] During the floor debate supporters of a reduced army dominated the discussion. Anthony and Sisson managed the bill jointly. Anthony justified the proposed reduction to 115,000 men on the grounds that the War Department's desires to maintain full-strength divisions in Panama and Hawaii were excessive. He suggested that Congress eliminate all unnecessary overseas garrisons and in so doing reduce the strength of the regular army without cutting it "below the safety point for our internal protection in this country. . . ." Sisson observed that the large number of veterans in the country made a large army unnecessary and, in a reference to the swollen deficit caused by the war, justified a reduction to 100,000 men "when the condition of the country is so bad financially." Opponents of a smaller army offered little in reply. The 115,000-man figure went virtually unchallenged. As in the Senate, support for reduction of the army came from mid-western Republicans and Democrats. Those favoring a larger regular army came mainly from both parties in the urban-industrial states.[47]

While the Senate considered the House bill for further reductions in the army, the debate mounted. The National League of Women Voters opened its annual meeting on April 25, 1922, with a proposal that the army be cut to its prewar level of 100,000 men. The Women's Constitutional League of Maryland and the Massachusetts Public Interests League responded by denouncing women's organizations that urged military reductions as "sinister" and "Bolshevist in principle."[48] The *New York Times* and other leading daily newspapers across the country urged maintenance of the 150,000-man figure. The *Times* on May 2 pointed to the civil war in China as evidence that peace remained an elusive goal and warned that unsettled conditions in China and elsewhere required a posture of readiness.[49] While the Senate Committee on Appropriations considered the bill, the *Army and Navy Journal* published summaries of press comments on the proposed reduction in strength. The *Journal,* which actively supported a large army, printed an impressive list of every favorable editorial it could find.

Most of the editorials followed the argument of the Cleveland *Plain Dealer,* which said:

When the National Defense Act of 1920 was passed it was accepted by the country as embodying a permanent and carefully conceived military policy. It contemplated the coordination of Army regulars, the National Guard forces, and

Organized Reserves in a fashion that seemed to preclude a repetition of the conditions that obtained when the United States entered the great war. But before that coordination has become an actuality a group in Congress that has ever belittled the true importance of military preparedness attempts to disrupt the entire plan by rigidly reducing the Army appropriation.[50]

The Senate committee, reflecting Wadsworth's support of a larger army, approved funds for a maximum strength of 140,000 men. But when the bill reached the full Senate, opponents of a big army questioned the larger figure. Gilbert Hitchcock of Nebraska, for example, observed that the previous reduction to 150,000 had reflected the will of the people, and that despite predictions of gloom from the army and its supporters,

The ruin has not come; war has not been provoked, the Military Establishment has not been disjointed, and I am morally certain in my own mind that if we make a still further reduction we shall find at the end of the year that the Military Establishment will still be here.

Senator Henry Myers of Montana objected. He accused those urging reductions of pandering to the voters' desire for economy and of playing on fears of a large standing army. "I know that it meets with much popular favor; there is always a hue and cry against any standing army," he said. He thought the 140,000-man ceiling was "entirely within the bounds of reason. . . ."

The Senate approved the 140,000 man strength by a vote of 49 to 21. Almost all opposition to the larger figure came from the West and South.[51] In conference the House insisted on a more substantial reduction, and in meetings that were reported as "heated," forced a compromise average strength of 125,000 enlisted men. Appropriations for all military activities totaled $275 million, down about $79 million from fiscal year 1922.[52]

Once the appropriations bill passed, newspaper interest in the issue of army strength evaporated. In reality it seems there had been little such interest outside the editorial pages. Those who wanted the reduction did not cheer, and those who opposed it did not complain. Few outside of the army were directly affected, and the public apparently did not care. The *Army and Navy Journal* tried unsuccessfully to make defense reductions an issue in the 1922 elections. The service-oriented weekly openly campaigned against Daniel R. Anthony in particular. In an editorial printed on the eve of the election the *Journal* called Anthony "a consistent, persistent, determined enemy of the Army [who during his reelection campaign] has not hesitated to do everything that he could to stir up ill-will and hatred between the Regular forces and National Guard [in Kansas]." Despite the *Journal's* effort, Anthony was reelected. He remained in Congress and continued as chairman of the Military Appropriations Subcommittee until March 1929.[53]

In response to the budget cut the War Department issued another round of bulletins ordering rigid economy. The army lost several combat units. The field artillery, for example, reduced its two heavy regiments by two battalions each, the cavalry lost all of its training center troops, and the coast artillery deactivated the defenses at Key West, Galveston, and San Diego.[54]

The reduction in strength for 1923 did not necessitate wholesale discharges, but it did take a human toll. Cuts in enlisted strength meant adjusting the grade structure again. By midyear it was obvious that demotions could no longer be delayed. A total of 1,600 NCO's faced demotion as a result of the appropriations. Reduction in grade involved more than a loss of rank; it represented a pay cut, too. For instance, a sergeant first class with twenty years of service demoted one grade to staff sergeant lost $11.20 a month in pay, a 15 percent drop. A sergeant with ten years of active duty reduced to the rank of corporal could expect a 20 percent cut in pay. The result meant hardships for families as well as individuals. For one, the threatened demotion proved too much to bear. On November 2, 1922, Sergeant Major B. H. Nelson, slated to lose his rank on December 13, shot his wife and then himself in their quarters at the Presidio of San Francisco.[55]

In an effort to prevent NCO reductions Julius Kahn, chairman of the House Military Affairs Committee, introduced a bill to maintain grade structure at its present level. Eventually added as a rider to the appropriations bill for fiscal year 1924, the measure was blocked in the Appropriations Committee by a group of "small army" supporters. The reductions took place after a three-month delay on March 13, 1923. Though the War Department placed the demoted NCOs at the head of the promotion list, promotions remained frozen.[56]

Congress seemed to add insult to injury in 1922 by revising the army's pay across the board. A hodgepodge of legislation governed the military finance system. Before World War I the Pay Act of 1908 established how much soldiers received; the Selective Service Act of 1917 temporarily raised it, and due to the efforts of Colonel Munson and the Morale Branch, the National Defense Act of 1920 continued the world war increases for the most part. But there was more to the system than "pay." An elaborate system that considered rank, special skills, and number of years of service determined soldiers total monthly remuneration. Seven basic pay grades, grade seven being the lowest, identified rank. Basic pay increased with continuous service even if rank did not. The army termed these raises "longevity increases." In addition to base pay for his grade, a soldier in the two lowest grades could receive specialty pay depending on his job skill and training. Soldiers on foreign service received additional pay. Various bonuses were added for skill in marksmanship for qualified soldiers in the combat branches. All enlisted men received a monthly clothing allowance for uniform maintenance, and some soldiers also received allowances for quarters and meals under special circumstances. Married enlisted men (only those in the top three grades were normally permitted to marry) received a rental allowance for quarters if government housing was not available and a subsistence allowance for meals not taken in a mess hall.[57]

Each piece of legislation since 1908 changed allowances, specialty pay rates, and the formula for longevity pay. Furthermore, separate legislation established pay for the other services. In 1921 Congress sought to end the constant tinkering with service pay and put the uniformed services under a single system. A joint congressional committee declared that "service morale demanded increases in compensation if the several services were to present attractive careers," but added that, "owing to economic conditions a savings in appropriations had to be effected."[58] The new pay package distinguished between career and noncareer personnel. Thus for the army, base pay was increased for the higher grades and decreased for the lower grades. The legislation changed the longevity pay formula again in order to cut the continuous service pay rate. Specialty pay and bonuses continued at the same or slightly higher rates. Allowances were to be readjusted annually according to living costs as directed by the president. The Pay Readjustment Act of June 10, 1922, remained the basis for army pay until 1940.[59]

Taken by itself the Pay Readjustment Act appeared admirably logical and generous. Career enlisted men received raises. The base pay of a sergeant first class (grade 2) rose from $53 to $84 a month. Noncareer personnel (the two lowest enlisted grades, who for the most part lived in barracks and took all their meals in the mess halls) received pay cuts. The act cut the pay of a private first class (grade 6) from $35 to $30 monthly. Furthermore, the act saved money because the lowest pay grades constituted three-quarters of the army's payroll. But the act contained two significant flaws.

First, while the revised pay rates for the top enlisted grades kept up with inflation, they did not consider the impact of reductions in strength on grade structure. Between 1913 (the earliest year of continuous statistics) and 1920 the cost of goods and services in the United States doubled.[60] In 1921 when the joint congressional committee began to consider pay changes, the adjutant general compiled a report on the effects that inflation and pay readjustments were having on enlisted men. Major General Clarence R. Edwards, commander of the First Corps Area with headquarters at Boston, surveyed his command and sent the adjutant general a detailed reply. All of Edwards's subordinates reported that the continuation of wartime increases were essential. An extract from a letter from a Colonel Hearn summed up the situation:

Most of those in grades 1 to 3 have from 10 to 25 years service and could not afford to sacrifice the prospect of retirement [after 30 years service], nor can they expect to successfully compete with younger men who are more skilled in civil pursuits.

Nevertheless many state that if the extra pay is not made permanent they will be forced to leave the service. Others pathetically state that though they will be unable to properly provide for their families, they have been too long in the service to sacrifice their future retirement by seeking discharge. Such a condition would not be far from peonage.[61]

The permanent increases for the top enlisted grades just matched the rises in prices since 1908. The pay rises for the middle grades did not quite keep up with inflation. But the pay commissioners did not consider the effect that reductions in strength would have on noncommissioned officers remaining in the service. Many senior NCOs found themselves back in grade 3 or 4 after the demotions began in 1923. Some of these men had attained emergency commissions during the war and thus suffered more than one reduction in rank. Loss in rank meant a drop in pay. Peter Peterson reached the rank of captain during the war. After demobilization when temporary ranks were abolished, he returned to his former noncommissioned rank and prewar assignment to find a younger man filling his position. "We old timers are now surplus in grade and . . . will be demoted . . . while the younger men that filled our old positions will be retained and become permanent in their present grades," he complained bitterly. "That means that the majority of the old timers and those that have given most of their lives to the Service . . . will have to quit and enter civil life like a recruit . . . as it will be utterly impossible to support a family."[62] Peterson's case was extreme, but his experience was common enough to sour morale among older noncoms.

The second flaw in the Pay Readjustment Act resulted from the deliberate reduction of pay for the two lowest grades. The army considered privates and privates first class noncareer enlisted men. Low pay for those grades was in part designed to discourage men of those ranks from remaining in the service if they did not get promoted. But promotions were frozen because of the strength reductions, and demoted NCOs filled vacancies in the middle grades that otherwise might have been given to deserving privates and corporals. Furthermore, the pay of civilian workers rose steadily after 1922. In 1922 the average weekly earnings of production workers stood at $21.51, the monthly pay of a private. By 1929 the workers' pay rose to $25.03 a week. The private still received $21 a month, and many who enlisted in 1922 and stayed in the army were probably still privates in 1929.[63] With unchanging wages and the demise of educational and vocational training the army offered little by way of incentive.

The appropriations act for fiscal year 1922 and the Pay Readjustment Act firmly established Congress's approach to military policy for the remainder of the decade and for much of the 1930s. Although the National Defense Act of 1920 established peacetime military policy, Congress, in fact, modified and limited army activities through its control of the purse. Between 1923 and 1926 Congress provided an average of $260 million for military activities. Authorized strength remained 280,000 men (set by the National Defense Act), but actual strength, controlled by congressional appropriations for paying the army, was considerably less. Beginning in 1923 and continuing through the remainder of the decade, Congress never appropriated enough money to pay even the 125,000 men it had agreed upon in 1922. The army attempted to compensate for the deficiency by reducing its strength through attrition in the winter months and bringing in more men in the summer when most units conducted their field training and benefited most from the higher strength. In 1925 Congress again reduced its appropriation for the pay of the army and provided for an average strength of only 118,750 men.[64]

Table 3.1 *Appropriations for Pay and Average Enlisted Strength of the Regular Army, 1920–1929*

FISCAL YEAR	APPROPRIATIONS FOR PAY	APPROPRIATION STRENGTH	ACTUAL AVERAGE STRENGTH
1920	327,944,262	175,000	177,918
1921	np	175,000	np
1922	156,844,262	125,000	125,272
1923	128,122,081	125,000	111,341
1924	122,939,514	125,000	121,108
1925	121,532,700	118,750	115,177
1926	121,304,067	117,691	112,901
1927	120,580,598	118,750	113,066
1928	124,688,704	118,750	114,785
1929	130,334,373	118,750	117,725

Source: Compiled from *Annual Report of the Secretary of War, 1920–1929* and "A Study of Voluntary Enlistments, Army of the United States (1775–1945)," Historical Section, Army War College, September 1945. No annual report was issued during 1921. Appropriation and strength figures are not available for that year.

More than strength declined. The entire physical plant .of the army deteriorated. In 1924 Weeks reported that "shortages of funds for repairs to existing structures and utilities and the conditions under which officers and enlisted men live . . . tends seriously to reduce the morale and efficiency of both . . . " The following year Dwight F. Davis, Weeks's successor, pointed out that appropriations for the maintenance of army installations amounted to only 1.15 percent of their total value. Before the war, Davis went on, maintenance funds approximated 4.75 percent of the value of the army's holdings. "Such a comparison," he concluded, "is of itself sufficient to indicate that our plant is running down at the expense, ultimately, of true economy."[65]

A few public voices raised protests in support of Weeks and Davis. The veterans' organizations could always be counted on to demand increased strength and appropriations. The *New York Times* remained a steadfast supporter. In March 1924 the *Times* ran a feature article on the state of the army. Herbert B. Mayer, a former regular army lieutenant, reported

that army posts at present are rapidly deteriorating through the niggardliness of Congressional appropriations, that men, with pay reduced from $30 to $21 . . . are declining to enlist, and . . . that the whole military establishment is suffering from false economy to such an extent as to be hampered in its efficiency.

The seacoast defenses of New York and the rest of the United States, Mayer said, suffered from disrepair and were drastically understrength. On the West Coast, "face to face with Japan, we have all told only 2,500 men or 500 less than one war strength regiment," he reported. Nor could the army be counted upon in a domestic emergency, Mayer added. "For example, a few nights ago more than 15,000 Communist sympathizers gathered at Madison Square Garden to mourn the passing of Lenin. In the gravest possible emergency in New York City the two regiments assigned to this territory . . . could not muster more than 1,600 rifles all told."[66]

The *Times's* and other accounts of the deterioration of the army drew little public reaction. The Washington conference of 1921–1922, which resulted in widely publicized naval cutbacks, may have convinced many that the reductions were appropriate. Indeed, military contingency plans during the 1920s reflected the absence of any serious threats to the United States. Broadly speaking, army and navy strategists looked on the maintenance of the Monroe Doctrine and the Open Door in China and the avoidance of entangling alliances as their guides for formulating mobilization and war plans. Based on these principles, military theorists expected the United States to fight alone against an enemy or combination of enemies seeking economic advantages in either South America or the Far East. After World War I only two countries remained strong enough to constitute a threat, however remote, in either area: Great Britain and Japan.[67]

Contingency plans for a war with Japan had existed since 1904, and the services took the possibility of war with that nation seriously. The basic plan (called Orange) between 1924 and 1938 assumed that war would begin with an attack by Japan on United States holdings in the Pacific. The American response, according to Plan Orange, would be largely in the form of a naval offensive to recover territory and open sea lanes. The army's task would be to hold or reinforce such possessions as the Philippines.

Military thinkers considered war with Great Britain extremely unlikely, but they did have a plan (Red) for such an occasion. The army and navy also had a plan for a war with both Japan and Great Britain (Red-Orange). Neither service considered either situation even remotely possible. The navy labeled a Red-Orange plan of the era "highly improbable." Both situations envisioned limited roles for the army. The navy, it was expected, would fight to keep the sea lanes open, destroy enemy battle fleets, and repulse invasion forces. The army might be used as an expeditionary force against landings in South America or as a mobile defensive force to counter landings on the North American coast or attacks from Canada.[68]

With American war planners conjuring up such theoretical visions as a war with Great Britain and invasion from Canada in the 1920s, it is not surprising that so few in Congress or society gave much attention to military preparedness. Furthermore, many of those who opposed cuts in army strength and appropriations stated their objections in terms that probably made it difficult for citizens to support the military establishment. The *Army and Navy Journal* adopted the habit of accusing anyone who supported lower defense spending for whatever reason of being a pacifist. Headlines like "What Pacifism Has Done to the Regular Army" implied that anyone who did not support the War Department to the hilt on its budget requests was somehow an enemy of the state. In 1922, for example, the *Journal* attacked "the pacifist campaign for reducing the Army and Navy, . . . " and accused Congress of "yielding to demands from pacifist elements whose ideas can only lead to an unnecessarily long list of dead and wounded in the next war."[69] R. M. Whitney, director of the Washington Bureau of the American Defense Society, went further. In April 1923 Whitney charged that attacks on preparedness by the National Council for the Prevention of War and the Women's International League for Peace and Freedom were directed by Moscow. He urged the American Legion to join in an effort to prevent the pacifist menace and its Russian allies from undermining the United States.[70] The *Army and Navy Journal* also conducted a "smear campaign" designed to associate those supporting lower defense spending with pacifism, communism, and socialism. Later in the decade the *Journal* ran a series of articles by Fred R. Marvin, editor of the *New York Commercial,* that linked "the present day movement against the Army, Navy, preparedness, the R.O.T.C.'s, and military training in the schools and colleges . . . [to] a socialist or Communist [plot] . . . to overthrow the government of the United States and build on the ruins a Co-Operative Commonwealth. . . . "[71]

Marvin's article and the *Army and Navy Journal's* editorial policy offer revealing examples of how the army defended itself against antimilitary attacks in the 1920s and 1930s. Top military leaders understood that any direct confrontation between servicemen and antimilitarists would merely be turned against them as proof positive that the soldiers were out of control. Thus it became official army policy to rely on civilian allies in any public debate over military affairs. Behind the scenes the War Department provided assistance to its surrogates. For example, professors of military science on college campuses were encouraged to feed information on pacifist activities to local patriotic societies. In one instance an officer in the army's Intelligence Division referred a request for information on the pacifist Women's International League for Peace and Freedom to the Daughters of the American Revolution. Throughout the interwar years the Intelligence Division kept close tabs on pacifist and antimilitary organizations.[72]

When officers expressed their opinions on pacifist and antimilitary attacks on the army in public, they did so in a variety of ways. Some tried to be balanced. For example, when Major General Sherman Miles wrote a fourteen-page analysis of pacifism for the *North American Review*, he hardly mentioned specific organizations by name. Miles praised the pacifists' intentions and efforts, but he accused them of being unrealistic and likened them to the prohibitionists. Efforts to abolish war, like laws to compel abstinence, depended on willing obedience. Miles also observed that the peace societies lacked a coordinated program and leadership. To have a real impact, he advised, they would have to "study and plan and work in unison. . . . "[73]

Other officers tried to counter pacifist arguments point for point. When Norman Thomas addressed the student body at Rutgers College on the subject of "Christian Pacifism" as part of a campaign by the Fellowship of Youth for Peace to enroll members, Colonel S. E. Smiley, professor of military science and training at Rutgers, wrote an article in rebuttal. The *Infantry Journal* published the article with the suggestion that "other officers of the Army who are faced with the same situation may have information readily available with which to combat this line of destructive propaganda." To the fellowship's assertion that "war is self-defeating, involving greater evils than it can remove," Smiley asked:

Was the Revolutionary War self-defeating and did it involve greater evils than it removed? The achievement of our independence and the establishment of our republic are sufficient answers.

Was the Civil War self-defeating, and did it involve greater evils than removed? The preservation of the Union and the settlement of the slavery question are sufficient answers.[74]

At least one officer went to extreme lengths to deal with pacifism. Brigadier General Amos A. Fries, head of the Chemical Warfare Service in the 1920s, earnestly believed that the use of gas offered a humane alternative to the violent destruction of more conventional war methods. Convinced that the Communists were behind pacifist efforts to eliminate his organization, Fries devised a chart that linked the American pacifist movement to international socialism. The so-called "spider web chart" stirred up a furious protest from the peace groups, and Fries was censured for his excesses by the secretary of war. After his retirement in 1929 Fries continued to speak out violently against the pacifists. He represented, as one historian of military thought concluded, "the lunatic fringe of our military leaders," but because of his outspokenness and the threat his views represented to the peace movement, it is easy to see why pacifists tended to see Fries as representative of the military mind.[75]

The peace societies replied to extreme attacks in kind. In 1924 when the War Department announced plans for a major test of mobilization to include calling out the National Guard and organized reserves, peace groups across the country objected vociferously. Frederick J. Libby, executive secretary of the National Council for the Prevention of War, labeled the test "a radical innovation in our national policy . . . " that had a "militarizing tendency . . . particularly [in] its influence on our youth. It is calculated to stir our nation's war spirit . . . quite unnecessarily." In July, the Women's Peace Society of New York toured the city with a float demanding "No More War Day!" Governors Blaine of Wisconsin and Sweat of Colorado declared the test unnecessary and refused to order their states' forces to participate. Church groups roundly condemned the mobilization. The Unitarian organ *The Christian Register* declared the test "the worst exhibition of bristling war spirit that we have heard since Wilhelm rushed in madness from maneuver to maneuver, from Wiesbaden to Posen, in the decade immediately preceding the World War." Oswald Garrison Villard's *The Nation* demanded, "It ought to be stopped, and we believe that the common-sense of the American people . . . will put an end to it."[76]

Nothing of the sort happened. Patriotic groups rallied to the cause and pledged their support. Laura Haines Cook, president general of the Daughters of the American Revolution, announced on August 2 that twenty-six groups, including the United Confederate Veterans, the Daughters of 1812, the United Spanish-American War Veterans, and the American Legion, promised full cooperation and support of Mobilization Day. Throughout the summer pacifists and patriots traded insults. The *New York Times* dismissed the furor as "more heat than light."[77]

During the controversy President Coolidge stood firmly behind the War Department. The test took place as scheduled on September 12, 1924. The mobilization exercise required all National Guard and organized reserve units to assemble their personnel for a day of training and exercises. Local commanders decided on the activities of their units. It was like a colonial militia muster, and that is how most states conducted their part of the mobilization. The units gathered their ranks, took and reported roll to Washington, and paraded through the cities and towns. Secretary Weeks announced that the mobilization assembled 92,581 regulars, 167,633 National Guardsmen, and 59,168 reservists. According to War Department figures, 16,792,981 citizens in 6,500 communities observed the demonstration. The reaction to Mobilization Day and the public participation in observing the "national muster" symbolized traditional American ambivalence toward the military. Amidst familiar expressions of antimilitarism many people still turned out to observe the army's demonstration of preparedness.[78]

The mobilization of 1924 probably hurt the army more than it helped it. While numerous patriotic and preparedness groups supported the test, their defense of the army served only to polarize further the debate over a proper level of readiness for the United States. Furthermore, when Secretary of War Weeks declared that Mobilization Day "demonstrated that in any emergency . . . contemplated in the National Defense Act, our country will be able to take full advantage of the initiative and resourcefulness of its citizens and communities and secure the maximum benefit of that aid . . . ,"[79] he seemed to contradict complaints about the effect of retarded strength, low budgets, and false economy on readiness. Surprisingly, opponents of military spending failed to take advantage of the contradiction.

Congressional attitudes toward the army began to change in the mid-1920s. Apparently the deterioration of the physical state of the army began to be noticeable. In 1925 the army asked Congress for $280 million for fiscal year 1927. The estimate included a plea for money to improve or replace barracks and quarters for both officers and enlisted men. Initially the Bureau of the Budget reduced the request for fiscal year 1927 by $7 million to around $261 million. The War Department expressed concern that another round of strength and grade reductions would be necessary. Though President Coolidge dismissed the talk as army propaganda, Secretary of War Dwight F. Davis, who took over that office in October 1925, refused to give in without a fight.[80] Throughout the hearings he hammered on the seriousness of the army's situation, demanding more money for troops and maintenance. In the end Congress appropriated nearly $270 million, an increase of nearly $9 million over appropriations for the previous fiscal year. Congress did not appropriate money for the desired troop increase, but it earmarked most of the increase for military housing.

Poor housing was a major concern to the army. Since 1924, when Secretary of War Weeks put housing near the top of his list of problems in his annual report, the War Department had regularly approached Congress for funds. Permanent barracks and quarters for soldiers dated from before the war. The postwar army was nearly 30,000 men larger than the prewar establishment. The absence of new barracks required the army to put soldiers in temporary structures built to house the wartime army. Those buildings, constructed on pilings, often with green lumber, were blazing hot in the summer and freezing, drafty places in winter. Weeks reported that in 1924, 40,000 soldiers were unsuitably housed; "some under canvass summer and winter for many years." Many troops and families of married officers and noncommissioned officers lived in world war barracks that, due to the meager appropriations for maintenance, "are rapidly becoming uninhabitable." On some posts, Weeks reported, "it is necessary that families use community bathhouses and toilets." Weeks felt that "A decent housing arrangement should be made for the Army," but in deference to congressional insistence on economy he proposed "a construction program extending over several years. . . . "[81] Congress responded stingily with appropriations for the construction of barracks at Fort Benning and a storehouse in the Canal Zone.[82]

In 1925, Weeks's successor, Dwight F. Davis, restated the request for improved housing. He called the continued delay false economy and added that "conditions . . . have grown materially worse." Davis reported that "hundreds of thousands of dollars have been expended in the years since the World War in an attempt to make partially livable quarters . . . which in reality cannot be made livable."[83] The army began an active effort to include meaningful appropriations for housing in the budget for 1927.

In December 1925 the *Infantry Journal* published a major article on housing conditions. Its author, E. B. Johns, who was the Washington correspondent of the *Army and Navy Journal*, produced an exposé of what was undoubtedly the worst example of military housing. Johns reported that enlisted men of the Second Division in Texas lived in temporary barracks unpainted since the war. He told of noncommissioned officers and their families occupying abandoned black laborers' shacks at Fort Benning and of officers resigning rather than accepting the uninhabitable quarters offered them. The caption accompanying a photo of a West Virginia coal town read: "This indicates how private enterprise values the contentment of its employees. This invites comparison with the manner in which the U.S. Government is providing for 40,000 officers and men of its Regular Army." Johns repeated the false economy charge. "The living conditions of the Army," he said, "have actually increased the cost of maintaining the authorized strength of the enlisted men of the Army. The large turnover [of enlisted men], . . . due to desertion and failure of men to reenlist, is adding millions to the expense of the Army and decreasing its efficiency."[84]

Johns's article was timed to coincide with Secretary of War Davis's appearance before the House Military Affairs Committee in January 1926. Testifying before the committee, Davis told the congressmen that the army needed $110 million in addition to regular appropriations to fund a comprehensive building program over a ten-year period. He proposed a scheme whereby the army would sell surplus land and use the receipts for housing construction. Congress budged and authorized the secretary to submit "a comprehensive plan for necessary permanent construction at military posts . . . based on using funds received from the sale of surplus War Department real estate . . . " at the next session.[85] The *New York Times* called the move "good news for the army," and when Congress authorized $7 million for housing as part of the 1927 appropriation later in the year, Davis observed that "the appreciative consideration by Congress . . . has had a distinctly beneficial effect on the moral of the troops of the Regular Army."[86] The spending for housing, though modest and long overdue, represented congressional response to obvious need. It offered a glimmer of hope in an economy-minded decade.

Early in 1927 Congress seemed to offer still greater grounds for optimism, by approving $282 million for fiscal year 1928. As in the previous year most of the increase went to a specific program, this time the Air Corps.

Since the world war military aviation enthusiasts had been demanding the creation of an independent air service for the United States. Brigadier General "Billy" Mitchell, who commanded the army's combat air element during the offensives in 1918, emerged as the leading spokesman for the expansion and independence of American military aviation. Mitchell openly criticized a report in 1923 that recommended the continued subordination of combat air forces to the ground armies they supported. Mitchell's subsequent court martial and suspension from the army for insubordination provoked considerable public discussion and prompted President Coolidge to appoint a commission to study the subject of an independent air force.[87]

The Morrow Board, named for its chairman, Dwight W. Morrow, a New York banker, working closely with the Special Aircraft Committee of the House of Representatives and the House Military Affairs Committee, held extensive hearings in 1926 and finally submitted a report that upheld War Department opposition to an independent air army. The report also recommended improvements in the existing Army Air Service, which were ratified by Congress in the Air Corps Act of July 2, 1926. The act provided for an expansion of the Air Service, redesignated the Air Corps, to 1,800 planes, 1,650 officers, and 15,000 enlisted men over a period of five years, the addition of an assistant secretary of war to oversee army aviation, two assistants to the chief of staff, and the creation of air sections in each of the major General Staff divisions.[88]

Congress appropriated $20 million for the Air Corps in 1928, 7.1 percent of the entire army appropriation, as the first installment on the five-year plan laid down by the Air Corps Act. Virtually the entire amount went for the purchase of aircraft and new construction projects.[89] Congress, having approved of the expansion the year before, authorized the funds for 1928 with little debate. The appropriation bill passed both houses by wide margins. Aviation devotees hailed the act as a major step in the direction of modernizing the army. More generally, preparedness advocates, who did not have much to smile about in the 1920s, saw the Air Corps Act as evidence that the long decline was ending.

Actually the modest increases in appropriations in fiscal years 1927 and 1928 for material improvements did not change the personnel situation of the regular army. In fiscal 1927 even as it increased overall appropriations, Congress reduced the amount authorized to pay the army. The cut forced the War Department to reduce again the number of noncommissioned officers and specialists in the regular army. The army eliminated 1,471 NCO positions, 1,496 privates first class, and 1,380 specialists by freezing promotions until losses reduced the ranks to the new limits for each grade.[90]

The Air Corps Act and the increased appropriations for fiscal 1928 that provided enabling legislation for the improved Air Corps, also created personnel problems for the army. In 1928 Congress set regular army strength at an average of 118,750 men and provided pay for that many soldiers. Congress also ordered the army to begin implementing the Air Corps Act of 1926. With its strength fixed, the only place the army could get the 1,248 noncommissioned officers and enlisted men for the first increment of the five-year planned increase was from the other branches. Furthermore, the technical nature of aviation dictated that the Air Corps receive a larger number of enlisted specialists than the other branches. The proportion of specialty ratings remained fixed for each grade because it was determined by overall authorized strength. Thus, the effect of the increase of the Air Corps on the rest of the army was a further reduction of strength and grades.[91] The Air Corps Act reduced the regular army's overall efficiency even as it improved army aviation. By 1930 the secretary of war reported that the scheduled transfers of enlisted men to the Air Corps resulted in the deactivation of five infantry battalions and a regiment of artillery. "If the policy of building up the enlisted strength of the Air Corps by transfers from the other arms is continued," the secretary of war concluded, "the Army will soon be unable to perform its many missions."[92]

In 1929 the nation watched the inauguration of a new president who promised continued peace and prosperity. The Kellogg-Briand Pact, signed the year before, outlawed war. Even though President Hoover's predecessor declined to reduce the army and navy as a result of the pact, declaring that the nation's standing forces were of a purely defensive nature, peace groups considered the army an anachronism. But as army leaders and preparedness advocates continued to complain and worry about declining strength, reduced spending, and deteriorating readiness, the public, for the most part, expressed little interest.

By the end of the decade the pacifists seemed to have the upper hand in the debate. In the continental United States the regular army forces available for the formation of an emergency force capable of field operations numbered only 54,000 men,[93] a far cry from the emergency field army of 150,000 envisioned by the National Defense Act of 1920. Opponents of the military nonetheless argued accurately that both regular army strength and appropriations exceeded prewar levels and demanded further cuts. Chief of Staff General Charles P. Summerall responded to the critics by noting that all of the increases were for programs that did not exist before the war. Summerall reiterated the warning that the army was incapable of fulfilling its missions under the National Defense Act. In his final report as chief of staff, General Summerall concluded on a note that suggests the mood of the army at the end of the first decade of peace. "It is possible, of course, to take the view that developments in the international situation in the past 10 years have been so favorable that the state of readiness implied in the maintenance of a Regular Army of 280,000 men . . . is no longer necessary." The retiring chief of staff, with perhaps a sigh of resignation, added, "the judgment as to whether such a situation exists is the function of the Federal Government and the Congress of the United States."[94]

Not all military spokesmen shared the chief of staff's refusal to pass judgment on congressional and executive parsimony. Major General Fox Connor, writing in the *North American Review* in 1928, summarized the deterioration of the military and its inability to meet the requirements of the National Defense Act. The immediate fault, he implied, lay with Congress, but public opinion influenced Congress. "The great body of the American People want adequate defense," Connor wrote, "but the enemies of such preparation are . . . inertia, false slogans, and lack of information. . . . Stop! Look! Listen!" Connor pleaded to the public as he urged his readers to demand a proper defense system.[95]

Henry J. Reilly, who had sold the *Army and Navy Journal* in 1925 but remained active in the debate on defense, blamed the budget and committee systems of the executive branch and Congress for the failure to provide an adequate army. These systems, he claimed, operated in secret and denied the public its right to open hearings and all the facts on the defense issues. Reilly also blamed "professional pacifists" for "deceiving the public" about the size of military expenditures.[96] Reilly had frequently made this charge in his weekly paper, and it remained a popular one with advocates of preparedness and patriotic societies.[97]

Pacifism, public apathy, congressional secrecy, and false economy were easy scapegoats for professional military men. It became their conventional wisdom that the public, misled by a cabal of pacifists (and maybe even a few bolsheviks), had turned its back on the army in the mistaken belief that World War I really had been the "war to end all wars," and that America, having been lured abroad in 1917, would be less likely to do so again if its military was unable to participate in foreign "adventures."

In fact, the public and Congress were well informed. For those who cared to read them, newspapers and periodicals carried frequent reports and articles airing the views of the preparedness advocates and military professionals. The public, however, seemed uninterested in helping the army. Rather, it supported economy in government and noninvolvement in foreign affairs. Congress responded accordingly by pressing for economy. In so doing Congress acted as it had in other times of peace throughout United States history. A full-strength regular army, National Guard, and organized reserve represented a very expensive proposition at any time between world wars. No emergency threatened. The United States in the 1920s simply did not need what the National Defense Act of 1920 had called for. In approving measures to expand the Air Corps in 1926, Congress belatedly demonstrated its appreciation of future military needs. Neither the public nor Congress was ready to live up to the demands of the National Defense Act. As a statement of military policy the act was more an expression of military idealism than of reality. In the 1920s there was simply no need, and the army, as its spokesmen frequently reminded themselves, went begging.

NOTES

1. Russell F. Weigley, *Towards an American Army: Military Thought from Washington to Marshall* (Washington, D.C.: Department of the Army, 1950), p. 240.

2. For a full discussion of business attitudes and their influence on government policies in the 1920s, see James Warren Prothro, *The Dollar Decade, Business Ideas in the 1920's* (Baton Rouge, La.: Louisiana State University Press, 1954).

3. Arthur M. Schlesinger, Jr., *The Crisis of the Old Order* (Boston: Houghton Mifflin Company, 1957), p. 62. Mellon expressed his philosophy in *Taxation: The People's Business* (New York: Macmillan Co., 1924).

4. Harding quote and budget figures are from Mark Sullivan, *Our Times, The United States, 1900–1925*, vol. 65 *The Twenties* (New York: Charles Scribner's Sons, 1935), p. 209.

5. Sullivan, *The Twenties*, pp. 372–79.

6. Robert H. Ferrell, *Peace in Their Time, The Origins of the Kellogg-Briand Pact* (New York: W. W. Norton & Company, 1969), pp. 21–26.

7. Ferrell, *Peace in Their Time*, pp. 26–31.

8. The campaign to halt the 1924 mobilization test is discussed later in this chapter. The Committee on Militarism in Education's effort against ROTC was one of the more successful antimilitary projects of the interwar years. For a good treatment of the subject see Arthur A. Ekirch, Jr., *The Civilian and the Military: A History of the Antimilitarist Tradition* (Colorado Springs, Colo.: Ralph Myles, Publisher, 1972), pp. 217–33.

9. Roscoe Baker, *The American Legion and American Foreign Policy* (Westport, Conn.: Greenwood Press, 1974), pp. 113–30; John Garry Clifford, *The Citizen Soldiers: The Plattsburg Training Camp Movement, 1913–1920* (Lexington, Ky.: University Press of Kentucky, 1972), pp. 296–303; Martha Derthick, *The National Guard in Politics* (Cambridge, Mass.: Harvard University Press, 1965), pp. 45–71.

10. Donald N. Bigelow, *William Conant Church and the Army and Navy Journal* (New York: Columbia University Press, 1952) covers the founding of the *Army*

and Navy Journal and Church's lasting influence. See pp. 133–36, 243–48. Information on later publishers is sketchy. For Reilly, see his obituary in the *New York Times,* (hereafter *NYT*), December 14, 1963, p. 27.

11. *NYT,* October 4, 1955, pp. 1, 28. This is Adler's obituary.

12. I base this judgment on an analysis of public statements and writings of the chiefs of staff and other general staff officers of the 1920s. All made similar pleas for higher appropriations in their congressional testimony. But few went beyond that. Mitchell's efforts on behalf of an independent Air Corps and Summerall's public condemnation of the army housing situation (both are covered later in this chapter and in chapter 4) were exceptions that proved the rule.

13. All annual reports of the chiefs of staff and secretaries of war protested the spending cuts and warned of the consequences. Articles on national defense are too numerous to list here and will be referenced when appropriate throughout this and later chapters. Pershing authorized open expression in General Order No. 20, May 15, 1922, in U.S. War Department, *General Orders, Bulletins and Circulars, 1922* (Washington, D.C.: GPO, 1923). Hereafter *General Orders, 1922.*

14. Richard F. Fenno, Jr., *Congressmen in Committees* (Boston: Little, Brown and Co., 1973), p. xiii.

15. Elias Huzar, *The Purse and the Sword: Control of the Army by Congress Through Military Appropriations, 1933–1950* (Ithaca, N.Y.: Cornell University Press, 1950), pp. 26–29.

16. U.S., House, *Congressional Record,* 66th Cong., 2nd sess., 59, pts. 4, 6, 7, pp. 4025, 5688, 7304, 7305; U.S., Congress, *House Reports,* 66th Cong., 3rd sess., 1, Report 1264, p. 2.

17. *ANJ,* April 17, 1920, p. 1001.

18. Ibid., June 5, 1920, p. 1233.

19. Ibid., April 17, 1920, p. 1001.

20. Ibid. December 18, 1920, p. 458; U.S., Congress, House *Recruiting: Hearings before the Committee on Military Affairs,* 66th Cong., 3rd sess., pp. 3–30.

21. *ANJ,* February 12, 1921, p. 670; *NYT,* February 6, 1921, p. 1, and February 8, p. 1.

22. *The Nation* 112, no. 2902 (February 16, 1921): 251.

23. Kahn reporting on a conference with Harding on January 7, 1921, as quoted in *ANJ,* January 15, 1921, p. 561; *ANJ,* January 29, 1921, p. 622; *NYT,* February 2, 1921, p. 2.

24. Wadsworth was still chairman of the Senate Military Affairs Committee. It was normal, before 1949, for members of the Senate Military Affairs Committee to sit on the Military Appropriations Subcommittee. See Huzar, *The Purse and the Sword,* pp. 26–29.

25. *NYT,* February 23, 1921, p. 1; February 27, p. 4.

26. Ibid., June 8, 1921, p. 16; June 9, p. 17.

27. Ibid., May 16, 1921, p. 14.

28. Report of the Chief of Staff in War Department Annual Reports for Year Ending June 30, 1921 (Washington, D.C.: 1921) pp. 23–29. Hereafter, *Annual Report.*

29. For a complete discussion of the congressional maneuvering on this issue, see *NYT,* May 1, 1921, p. 5; June 6, p. 3; June 8, p. 19; June 9, p. 17; Martin L.

Fausold, *James W. Wadsworth, Jr., The Gentleman from New York* (Syracuse, N.Y.: Syracuse University Press, 1975), p. 145. The vote in the Senate on June 8 to reduce the army to 150,000 men was as follows:

YEAS [for 175,000 men] 32

Ball (R), Del.	Lodge (R), Mass.
Brandegee (R), Conn.	McCormick (R), Ill.
Bursum (R), N. Mex.	McKinley (R), Ill.
Cameron (R), Ariz.	Myers (D), Mont.
Cummins (R), Iowa	Nelson (R), Minn.
Curtis (R), Kan.	Nicholson (R), Colo.
Dillingham (R), Vt.	Phipps (R), Colo.
Elkins (R), W. Va.	Poindexter (R), Wash.
Fernald (R), Maine	Shortridge (R), Calif.
Fletcher (D), Fla.	Spencer (R), Mo.
Frelinghuysen (R), N.J.	Stirling (R), S. Dak.
Hale (R), Maine	Sutherland (R), W. Va.
Kellogg (R), Minn.	Wadsworth (R), N.Y.
Keyes (R), N.H.	Warren (R), Wyo.
Knox (R), Pa.	Watson (R), Ind.
Lenroot (R), Wisc.	Weller (R), Md.

NAYS [for 150,000 men] 36

Ashurst (D), Ariz.	Overman (D), N.C.
Borah (R), Idaho	Pomerene (D), Ohio
Broussard (D), La.	Reed (D), Mo.
Capper (R), Kan.	Sheppard (D), Tex.
Dial (D), S.C.	Simmons (D), N.C.
Gerry (D), R.I.	Smith (D), S.C.
Gooding (R), Idaho	Stanfield (R), Ore.
Haneld (R), Okla.	Stanley (D), Ky.
Hanis (D), Ga.	Swanson (D), Va.
Harrison (D), Miss.	Townsend (R), Mich.
Jones (D), N. Mex.	Trammell (D), Fla.
Jones (R), Wash.	Underwood (D), Ala.
Kendrick (D), Wyo.	Walsh (D), Mont.
King (D), Utah	Watson (D), Ga.
Ladd (R), N. Dak.	Williams (D), Miss.
LaFollette (R), Wisc.	Willis (R), Ohio
McNary (R), Ore.	Wolcott (D), Del.
Norris (R), Neb.	

U.S., Senate, *Congressional Record,* 67th Cong., 1st sess., 61, pt. 3, p. 2255.

30. *NYT,* June 16, 1921, p. 18; June 18, p. 2; June 29, p. 24; *ANJ,* July 2, 1921, p. 182.

31. *ANJ,* May 14, 1921, p. 1006; June 25, p. 1158.

32. Figures are taken from extracts of the respective appropriations acts as published in War Department Bulletin No. 28, June 23, 1920, in *General Orders, 1920,* and Bulletin No. 13, July 26, 1921 in *General Orders, 1921.*

33. War Department Bulletin No. 13, July 26, 1921.

34. *Annual Report, 1922,* Table B, facing p. 168. The adjutant general did not enumerate the sources or number of "other causes" discharges or report the length of service of the early dischargees.

35. William A. Ganoe, *A History of the United States Army* (New York: D. Appleton-Century Company, Inc., 1942), pp. 483–84.

36. Report of the chief of staff in *Annual Report, 1921,* pp. 21, 22; Extracts from the Annual Report of the Chief of the Personnel Division, General Staff (hereafter G-1), Report of the Secretary of War in *Annual Report, 1921,* War Department Circular No. 86, March 29, 1921; *General Orders, 1921,* Circular No. 58, June 16, 1921; Ganoe, *History of the U.S. Army,* p. 484.

37. *Annual Report, 1921,* pp. 16–18; *General Orders, 1922,* War Department Circular No. 80, April 14, 1922; *General Orders, 1921,* Circular No. 245, September 16, 1921.

38. *Annual Report, 1922,* pp. 9–13, 115.

39. C. Joseph Bernardo and Eugene H. Bacon, *American Military Policy: Its Development Since 1775* (Harrisurg, Pa.: The Stackpole Co., 1961) p. 387.

40. *ANJ,* August 13, 1921, p. 1328.

41. U.S., Congress, House, Military Subcommittee of the Committee on Appropriations, *Hearings on the War Department Appropriations Bill, 1923,* (hereafter, House, *Appropriations, 1923*), 67th Cong., 2nd sess., January 9, 1922, pp. 10, 27. Pershing made his remarks concerning vocational training to the House Military Affairs Committee, which was holding hearings about the same time. He was quoted in the *Army and Navy Register,* a Washington-based competitor of the *ANJ,* on January 21, 1921, pp. 1, 50, 65.

42. House, *Appropriations, 1923,* p. 1441.

43. *NYT,* February 27, 1922, p. 12; February 28, p. 18; *ANJ,* March 18, 1922, p. 687.

44. *NYT,* March 4, 1922, p. 18.

45. *ANJ,* March 4, 1922; p. 635; *Literary Digest* 72, No. 11 (March 18, 1922): 10.

46. *ANJ,* March 18, 1922, p. 678.

47. U.S. House, *Congressional Record,* 67th Cong., 2nd sess., vol. 62, pts. 4, 5, pp. 3863–89, 4733.

48. *NYT,* April 25, 1922, p. 21; April 25, p. 3.

49. *NYT,* May 2, 1922, p. 18.

50. As quoted in the *ANJ,* March 25, 1922, p. 698. Other examples are found in *ANJ,* March 25, 1922, pp. 698, 707, and April 18, p. 746. The excerpts included the *Boston Transcript, St. Louis Globe-Democrat, San Francisco Chronicle, Baltimore Sun, Chicago Daily News, Portland Oregonian, New York Tribune, Detroit Free Press, Kansas City Times,* and *Charleston* (S.C.) *News and Courier.*

51. U.S., Senate, *Congressional Record,* 67th Cong., 2nd sess., vol. 62, pt. 8, pp. 8025–32; *ANJ,* May 20, 1922, p. 894; June 10, p. 978.

52. *ANJ,* June 17, 1922, p. 1001; June 24, p. 1029; July 1, pp. 1057, 1058; *SW, 1923,* pp. 32–43.

53. Ibid., November 4, 1922, p. 229.

54. Ibid., July 15, 1922, p. 1115; July 22, pp. 1144, 1145.

55. Ibid., September 9, 1922, p. 35; November 25, p. 294. See Appendix C for pay tables.

56. *ANJ,* November 25, 1922, p. 298; March 10, 1923, p. 679; April 28, 1923, p. 841. Similar provisions were made for officers forced to take grade reductions.

57. This summary of the military pay system prior to 1922 was compiled from a review of the various acts governing the pay of the army beginning with the act of May 11, 1908, reprinted in War Department General Order No. 80, May 15, 1908, and including those portions of the Selective Service Act of 1917 and the National Defense Act of 1920 pertaining to pay, reprinted in Bulletin No. 32, May 24, 1917, and General Order No. 44, July 20, 1920, respectively.

58. The background of the Pay Readjustment Act of 1922 is contained in a General Staff brief for the War Department Pay Commission of 1937, entitled "Extract, Initial Report, War Department Pay Commission (WDPC), 1937, Annex 1, Vol. I (History)" AGO 240 (1-1-26), RG 94, Box 1182, National Archives, Washington, D.C.

59. War Department Bulletin No. 9, June 10, 1922. See Appendix C. The Pay Readjustment Act also affected officers' pay. Generals received raises and second lieutenants lost $200 annually.

60. U.S., Department of Commerce, Bureau of the Census, *Historical Statistics of the United States, Colonial Times to 1957* (Washington, D.C.: GPO 1960), Consumer Price Indexes, Series E113–139, pp. 125–26.

61. Inc. 18 to Reply from Maj. Gen. C. R. Edwards, CG, 1st CA to AG, August 31, 1921, Subject: Information Relative to Adjustment of Pay, AGO 240 (7-12-21), RG 407, Box 497, NA.

62. *ANJ,* November 4, 1922, p. 228.

63. *Historical Statistics,* Hours and Earnings for Production Workers in Manufacturing: 1909 to 1957, p. 92.

64. *SW, 1924,* p. 134.

65. Ibid., p. 3; *SW, 1925,* p. 16.

66. *NYT,* March 9, 1924, sec. 9, p. 10.

67. Fred Greene, "The Military View of American National Policy, 1904–1940," *American Historical Review* 66, no. 2 (January 1961): 33–39.

68. Louis Morton, "Germany First: The Basic Concept of Allied Strategy in World War II," in *Command Decisions,* ed. Kent Roberts Greenfield (Washington, D.C.: Department of the Army, 1960), pp. 12–18.

69. *ANJ,* March 25, 1922, pp. 698, 707.

70. *NYT,* April 5, 1923, p. 21; April 26, p. 3.

71. Fred R. Marvin, "Pacifists Poison Students' Minds," *ANJ,* May 22, 1926, p. 908.

72. Ronald Schaffer, "The War Department's Defense of ROTC," *Wisconsin Magazine of History* 53, no 2 (Winter 1969–1970): 111, 114. For a summary of the army's intelligence-gathering activities, see Joan M. Jensen, "Military Surveillance of Civilians in America," University Programs Modular Studies (Morristown, N.J.: General Learning Press, 1975).

73. Sherman Miles, "The Problem of the Pacifist," *North American Review,* 217, no. 3 (March 1923): 320–22, 325.

74. S. E. Smiley, "Pacifist Propaganda," *Infantry Journal* 24, no. 5 (May 1924): 627, 628.

75. Charles Chatfield, *For Peace and Justice: Pacifism in America, 1914–1941* (Knoxville, Tenn.: University of Tennessee Press, 1971), pp. 156–57; Richard C.

Brown, "Social Attitudes of American Generals, 1898–1940," (Ph.D. diss. University of Wisconsin, 1951), p. 262.

76. *NYT,* May 15, 1924, p. 32; July 27, pp. 1, 10; July 31, p. 15; *The Literary Digest* 82, no. 6 (August 9, 1924): 30, 31; *The Nation* 119, no. 3084 (August 13, 1924): 115.

77. *NYT,* August 3, 1924, p. 5; August 11, p. 12.

78. Ibid., September 14, 1924, p. 18.

79. Ibid.

80. Ibid., August 25, 1925, p. 1; August 26, p. 1.

81. Secretary of War in *Annual Report, 1924,* pp. 16, 17.

82. Ibid., p. 17.

83. Ibid.

84. E. B. Johns, "The Housing of the Regular Army, " *Infantry Journal* 26, no. 6 (December 1925): 689, 696.

85. *Annual Report, 1926,* p. 35.

86. *NYT,* January 8, 1926, p. 18; *Annual Report, 1926,* p. 25.

87. Russell F. Weigley, *History of the United States Army* (New York: Macmillan, 1967), pp. 412–13.

88. Ibid., p. 413; *Annual Report, 1926,* pp. 33–35. For a more lengthy discussion of the Air Corps and Military aviation policy during this period, see James L. Cate and Wesley F. Craven, "The Army Air Arm Between the Wars, 1919–1939," in *The Army Air Forces in World War II,* vol. 1, ed. Wesley F. Craven and James L. Cate (Chicago: University of Chicago Press, 1948), pp. 17–74.

89. Secretary of War in *Annual Report, 1928,* pp. 68–69, 93.

90. *ANJ,* January 9, 1926, p. 445.

91. Ibid., September 1, 1928, p. 5; Secretary of War in *Annual Report, 1928,* p. 5.

92. Secretary of War in *Annual Report, 1930,* p. 3.

93. Chief of Staff in *Annual Report, 1930,* p. 95.

94. Ibid., p. 96.

95. Fox Connor, "The National Defense," *North American Review* 225, no. 889 (January 1928): 1,11.

96. Henry J. Reilly, "Our Crumbling National Defense," *The Century Mazagine* 113, no. 6 (April 1927): 748–56.

97. See for example, "What Pacifism Has Done to the Regular Army," *ANJ,* October 6, 1921, p. 112; "Pacifism Poisons Students' Minds, *ANJ,* May 22, 1926, p. 908; "Pacifist Activities Aired in Congress," *ANJ,* June 19, 1926, pp. 1001, 1004.

4

MAINTAINING THE VOLUNTEER ARMY DURING PEACE AND PROSPERITY

In 1920 army reformers prematurely proclaimed that the military in the United States had entered a new era. The National Defense Act assured that the peacetime force would, for the first time in American history, have clearly defined roles. Furthermore, the newly established educational and vocational training program gave promise that the army would serve a positive social function as well as the more traditional military ones. But the new era of the 1920s did not include the army. The economy-conscious congresses and administrations of the decade refused to provide the necessary funds to sustain the programs envisioned by army progressives, and a war-weary society turned hostile or indifferent to the military.

While army leaders and their supporters struggled to preserve the National Defense Act of 1920, the month-to-month task of maintaining the existing army continued. The retrenchment of the early 1920s cut deeply into the volunteer army. Reductions in funds and personnel affected morale and, as a result, both recruiting and reenlistments suffered. War Department efforts to overcome these handicaps and preserve authorized strength fell into two broad categories, procurement and retention. During the first half of the decade the army concentrated on procurement and attempted to establish, in the General Recruiting Service, a system capable of securing replacements as they were needed. By the middle of the period, however, personnel managers began to focus their attention on reducing losses in order to cut down on the number of necessary recruits. The army sought to increase personnel retention by improving service attractiveness and establishing policies that would identify and eliminate misfits before they became liabilities. The successes and failures of these efforts reveal much not only about the army in the 1920s, but also about attitudes toward peacetime military service in the United States.

At the beginning of the decade procurement presented no problem at all. In 1920, using educational and vocational training to attract men, recruiters broke all previous peacetime records. The success was short-lived. Newton Baker's controversy with Congress over the authorized

strength of the army and the swift reductions in strength ordered by
Congress between February and June 1921 resulted in the cessation of all
recruiting.

War Department personnel managers estimated that the reduction of
the regular army from 213,000 to 175,000 men ordered in February 1921
would take nine months. When Congress began talking about a reduction
to 150,000, army planners projected the necessary halt in recruiting into
1922. Since it appeared that there would be no recruiting for possibly a
year, the General Recruiting Service seemed superfluous, and it was disbanded in February as an economy measure.[1]

While the Recruiting Service went through the process of terminating
leases, shipping records to Washington, and reassigning personnel, the
chief of staff ordered a study of recruiting activities. Brigadier General
Henry Jervey, assistant chief of staff, directed the adjutant general to
prepare a report "for use in the study of Army recruiting policies." The
report, "based on practical recruiting problems," was to recommend the
proper organization for future recruiting efforts.[2] Major I. J. Phillipson,
an infantry officer assigned to the Adjutant General's Office, prepared the
study. Phillipson's lengthy report summarized recruiting activity since
1915 with emphasis on the postwar period. Phillipson recommended that,
in the future, the General Recruiting Service "be sufficiently elastic to
meet the procurement requirements . . ." under any conditions. He
warned against tailoring the procurement machinery to specific conditions
that would render it "not capable of expansion sufficient to meet maximum
demands it might be required to face under peace or war conditions. . . ."[3]
Phillipson devoted a considerable portion of his study to the relationship
of publicity to recruiting. Though "the results in recruits actually obtained
through indirect publicity are small," he observed, "the cultivation of
community relations and the extension of general Army publicity . . ."
should continue to be emphasized. He especially recommended the maintenance of the Recruiting Publicity Bureau.[4] Publicity aside, Phillipson
insisted that "the trained Canvasser has always been the least expensive
and most efficient source of procurement. . . ." He determined that the
correct ratio of General Recruiting Service enlisted men to regular army
strength was 1 to 100 and that "any reduction below established limits is
believed unsafe."[5]

In a section titled "Problems which are peculiar to certain Recruiting
Districts," Phillipson revealed the lengths to which the army had gone
since the war to understand the society from which it drew its manpower.
The section contained a narrative description of each of the fifty-six
recruiting districts in the United States. The report analyzed the recruiting
potential and identified problems recruiters could expect in the districts.
Phillipson's report provides a revealing portrait of the nation through the
eyes of the army, and suggests the kinds of recruits the army was obtaining

in the early 1920s. The Atlanta district, for example, which included most of Georgia, naturally divided into mountainous and agricultural sections. Few recruits were obtained in the mountains, the inhabitants being "pure Anglo-Saxons who are noted for their simplicity and ignorance." Most recruits from Georgia came from "a belt about 60 mi. wide beginning on a line through Albany and Thomasville and extending northeast and then north through Dublin, Macon, Atlanta and Athens. . . . Recruiting officers found it profitable to watch cotton mill strikes and suspensions in work." In the upper Midwest the Aberdeen, South Dakota, district, consisting of North and South Dakota, was another likely source for recruits. "This district is very largely agricultural," the report noted. "In the harvesting season, thousands of young men follow the harvesters up from the south. . . . Many of these young men, at the end of the . . . season, find themselves many miles from home, out of employment with little or no money and, if properly approached, conclude that the Army offers the best solution to their difficulties."

The Pacific Northwest was not considered a lucrative area for recruits. Phillipson's comments on the Seattle district warned, "Generally, the people are hardy and industrious. They are not amenable to discipline and the Service has no lure for them." Boston was considered "friendly, but the local administration declines to permit the use of the historic Boston Common. . . . The District is a fertile field for recruiting activities. Canvassers with a knowledge of Italian, French, German, Polish, and Russian were found valuable. . . ." The Providence, Rhode Island, district was also considered productive. "The large turn over and wage fluctuation notably affects recruiting in this district," observed Phillipson.[6]

The inescapable impression one gets from Phillipson's report is that despite its publicity about the benefits that army service held for young men, few civilians joined except as a last resort. The army depended on the unemployment line for recruits. Furthermore, the report suggests that the army wanted men who adapted easily to the routine and discipline of service life rather than recruits with initiative. Carter B. Magruder, who was a lieutenant in the Sixth Field Artillery in the 1920s, recalled, "The soldier was mostly forced into the army by economic conditions, so we got a fairly low grade of recruit. . . . Not many came into the army because they looked on it as a desirable career."[7]

Raymond Alvord, who enlisted on March 5, 1924, considered himself a typical recruit of the mid-1920s. Alvord completed eight years of school before he ran away from home at age sixteen. He worked as a roustabout for Ringling Brothers Circus before enlisting. "I enlisted," he remembered, "because I was hungry; I got tired of fighting for three meals a day. I was walking down the street in Camden and a recruiter was coming the other way. I said, 'you're the fellow I'm looking for,' and he said, 'No, you're the fellow I'm looking for.'"[8]

Although Major Phillipson devoted most of his study to the procurement of new enlistments, he was conscious of the other half of the manpower equation, retention. He reminded his reader, "After enlistment, control of the soldiers passes from the recruiting service to the Army. It is at their hands, largely that the satisfied customer is made or lost. . . . Unless the promises made by the recruiting service are fulfilled by the Army, repeat orders are lost and the entire recruiting system rests upon unstable foundations."[9]

Phillipson sent his report through the adjutant general to the chief of staff. No one attached comments to the report at any level. There is no indication that the chief of staff ever read it and no sign that recruiting underwent any significant changes in operation. Like Woodbury's report on desertions, Phillipson's study arrived just as the army shifted gears in the area of manpower procurement, and the report failed to receive the attention it deserved.

By July 1921 it was apparent that the reduction to 150,000 enlisted men would be accomplished ahead of schedule. Since February, when recruiting offices closed, the army had permitted the reenlistment of highly rated soldiers only. In order to comply with the congressionally mandated reduction in strength, the War Department virtually let go of every soldier who wanted to get out of the army even before his three-year term was up. Unfortunately, no reports record what categories of men took advantage of this "early out" opportunity. Probably most were first-term enlistees who had been drawn into the army by the educational and vocational training offers of the recruiting campaigns of 1919, 1920, and early 1921 and found the service not to their liking.

At the beginning of August 1921 enlisted strength totaled 139,201—below the authorized level. Anticipating orders, the adjutant general proposed a three-phase plan for the resumption of recruiting. The first two phases dealt with unit and installation recruiting, and the third with the reestablishment of the General Recruiting Service. The adjutant general proposed that all phases being simultaneously.[10] Early in September recruiting resumed, but not according to the adjutant general's plan. Because of the strict economy measures then in effect, the War Department decided to try to recruit without a General Recruiting Service. Only posts, camps, and stations were authorized to seek recruits. The only funds permitted for recruiting were for transportation of recruiting parties to and from the installations and nearby localities. Applicants for enlistment could apply only at military posts and were required to furnish their own transportation and pay for meals until accepted and sworn in. Recruiting officers were advised "to insure that they ascertain the true age of each applicant for enlistment, and that they enlist no men who are not of good moral character and sufficient education to give promise of making good soldiers without the necessity for educational instruction normally given in public schools."[11] These instructions revealed that the army had abandoned, at least for the time being, the social role that Newton Baker and other progressives had envisioned for the army in peacetime. Without funds to educate illiterates the War Department wished to avoid recruiting the least acculturated and lowest classes in the population. It hoped for a minimum of internal turmoil.

The economy plan for recruiting did not work. Local recruiting simply did not bring in enough replacements. In September 1921, 1,400 men enlisted, but total regular army losses that month numbered 6,671. In October, losses were 4,684; enlistments (including reenlistments) improved to 2,720 as the local recruiting program became fully operational. In November and December losses again ran ahead of enlistments, 12,666 to 10,657. The monthly losses recorded in the autumn of 1921, after the mandated reduction in strength was completed, were typical of normal interwar months (see table 4.1).

The army did not report the rank or years of service of discharged soldiers. Most, undoubtedly, were from the lowest grades and left after their first or second enlistment. First enlistments could be made for one- or three-year terms; all subsequent enlistments were for three years. Thus men serving in their third enlistment began it with four or six years of service. Promotions in the peacetime army were slow even under the best of circumstances. A soldier could expect to spend his first three-year enlistment as a private. During his second enlistment the soldier probably was promoted to private first class. Only in his third enlistment could a man reasonably aspire to corporal's chevrons, and then only if the promotion, demotion, discharge, retirement, or death of someone above him created a vacancy.[12] Once a soldier made corporal, he was considered a career enlisted man, and it was unlikely that he would fail to reenlist.

Losses continued to exceed gains throughout fiscal year 1922. The army was losing ground daily. *Recruiting News* reported that "line organizations are clamoring for good men and they need good men to fill the blank files and to cheer those loyal ones who stayed with the army during the reduction."[13] In response to requests from the field for replacements the adjutant general began to press for more funds and men for recruiting duty. Gradually, but not officially, the General Recruiting Service was reestablished. At first recruiting stations reopened only in cities of proven potential. Recruiting officers could not lease office space but had to secure free space in federal office buildings. Congress appropriated no funds to cover recruiting costs in 1922. There was no paid advertising. In November, the chief of staff scraped up $100,000 to cover "transportation incidental to recruiting activities."[14] That was all the money recruiters got in fiscal year 1922.

New problems soon developed to complicate recruiting. Units in less densely populated regions of the country fell far short of their replacement needs. Corps areas in the Northeast and on the West Coast, the urban industrial regions of the country, which managed to fill their own needs,

Table 4.1 Enlistment Gains and Losses, Autumn 1921

	DISCHARGED				LOSSES					GAINS		
Month	ETS[1]	Disability	Court Martial	Other[2]	Died	Relieved from Duty	Retired	Deserted	Total	Enlisted	Reenlisted[3]	Net Loss
Sept.	3,019	246	295	2,381	45	3	50	560	6,671	209	1,089	5,373
Oct.	2,660	226	309	791	57	3	32	569	4,648	965	1,755	1,928
Nov.	4,109	232	287	1,040	33	2	37	475	6,215	2,120	2,224	1,871
Dec.	4,079	218	371	1,197	52	2	41	491	6,451	3,202	3,111	138
Total	13,867	922	1,262	5,409	187	10	160	2,095	23,985	6,496	3,179	9,310

Source: War Department Annual Reports, 1922, Losses, Table B, facing p. 168, Gains, p. 201.

Notes:

[1]ETS—End Term of Service
[2]Other causes included discharges to accept commissions, ineptness, minority or dependency, purchase, etc.
[3]Includes enlistment of men with former service.

90

were ordered to supply recruits to fill the quotas of the less productive areas. This suggests that more recruits came from urban than from rural backgrounds. Overseas units needed replacements, too. To save money, corps areas nearest to the port of debarkation for the overseas area received additional quotas for foreign recruits.[15]

The need for coordination of activities led the adjutant general to reestablish the framework of the General Recruiting Service by December 1921. Without any formally appropriated funds the service existed on a hand-to-mouth basis for the remainder of the fiscal year. By December recruiters were bringing in just enough men monthly to balance losses, but the overall strength remained below the 150,000 men authorized. Late in January 1922, when Congress was debating a further reduction in strength, the assistant chief of staff for personnel suggested to Pershing that since the reduction was probably inevitable, recruiting be halted until the outcome was known. When asked for his opinion, Colonel Charles Martin, the recruiting chief, noted that it had taken ninety days to resume effective recruiting in September. "It is very easy to stop the recruiting machine, but most difficult to start it up again," Martin argued. "Stop now and the Army would . . . run down below the strength authorized and the loss could not be made up."[16] Recruiting continued but at a level designed only to keep pace with monthly losses.

The army began fiscal year 1923 at its new authorized strength of 125,000 enlisted men. The recruiting service was assigned 900 men to secure 4,500 enlistments monthly. Even at the lower strength level the recruiting service failed to meet the mark. By the end of the year the army was 13,559 men short of its allowed strength. During the year monthly gains exceeded losses only once.[17]

Several forces combined to frustrate recruiters' efforts in 1922–1923. The Pay Reorganization Act of June 10, 1922, which reduced the pay of privates from $30 to $21 a month, went into effect at the beginning of the fiscal year. At the same time the country began coming out of the postwar recession. The employment picture improved, and blue-collar wages increased. In addition, the army's other big attraction to potential recruits, educational and vocational training, virtually disappeared. The large-scale educational and vocational training program begun in 1919 under the auspices of Newton Baker fell victim to economy measures in 1922. Congress made a last contribution of $1.2 million to the program in the appropriation for fiscal year 1922. The Educational and Vocational Training Division of the Education and Recreation Branch of the General Staff was abolished in December 1921.[18] Thereafter qualified enlisted men received technical training only in conjunction with their duties and assignments, although the army continued to proclaim itself as a vehicle upward for ambitious young men seeking to acquire a vocation or skill.

The impact of these changes was felt quickly. By October 1922 the army was 7,000 men below its new authorized strength of 125,000. An energetic drive for recruits began on November 1.[19] More recruits were obtained, but the service never reached the goal of 6,000 men needed monthly to make up losses. In the Boston district, Colonel Alfred Aloe, the district recruiting officer, attempted to determine the cause of the poor results. After querying his canvassers, Aloe summarized his findings in a letter to his boss. "It is consistently brought to our attention that the men object to enlisting for $21 per month," Aloe reported. "It has been said to me personally and daily to the canvassers, 'Why should we enlist for $21 a month or 70¢ a day when the Government at the Army Base and employers are offering 70¢ an hour for fatigue duty.'"[20] Aloe's observations reached Washington, but he did not get a sympathetic hearing. In commenting on the report, the adjutant general noted, "The situation in the First Corps Area is being watched and no apprehension is felt. Should the present Corps Area Recruiting Officer fail he will be relieved. He has already been informed that these conditions which cannot be changed, having been noted, should be ignored. . . ."[21]

In 1923 the army tried to overcome procurement deficiencies with local recruiting drives and cash incentives. In January, for example, the entire Sixteenth Infantry Regiment, based at Governor's Island in New York harbor, moved into the city for a week of recruiting. The *Infantry Journal* and *U.S. Army Recruiting News* offered cash prizes to the canvassers who brought in the most recruits in February.[22] The number of recruits increased but never made up for losses. In reporting on the recruiting situation at the end of the fiscal year, the adjutant general blamed "The small pay of the recruit and the remarkably high wages paid for labor of all kinds throughout the United States . . . [for] greatly discouraged enlistments. . . ."[23]

Inability to maintain authorized strength in 1923 compounded a new situation facing the army at the beginning of fiscal year 1924. Newton Baker's prodigious recruiting drive between June 1920 and January 1921, which raised enlisted strength to 213,000 before Congress stepped in, came back to haunt recruiters. About 60,000 three-year enlistments, products of Baker's drive, expired between August 1923 and February 1924. The adjutant general estimated that the army needed approximately 77,000 enlistments during the year to compensate for losses and bring the army back to full authorized strength.[24]

To meet the challenge, the War Department added 271 sergeants to the Recruiting Service, bringing its strength to 1,171 enlisted men. By the end of the year another 300 enlisted men were placed on full-time recruiting duty.[25] The adjutant general, Major General Robert C. Davis, urged corps area commanders to make a special appeal to the Officers Reserve Corps in their regions for help in the recruiting effort. Davis noted that the shortage of enlisted men would severely hamper the regular army during the summer months when it devoted most of its efforts to training National Guard units and the organized reserves.[26] In August 1923 General Pershing wrote to the commanders of the corps areas reminding them that recruiting was the responsibility of the whole army. "The present actual strength of the army," he said, "is about 113,000, and the recruiting service is obtaining about 4,000 men per month." That was not enough, the chief of staff continued, and he ordered his subordinates to increase efforts through the use of additional canvassers at the unit and post level.[27]

Congress placed an additional burden on army recruiting in 1924 by adding an amendment to the appropriation act for that year prohibiting the enlistment of men under the age of twenty-one without written consent of their parents or guardians. Furthermore, applicants over age twenty-one were required to present proof of their age before the army could accept them. Secretary of War Weeks vigorously protested the provision to no avail. The proof of age requirements remained in effect throughout the year.[28]

Despite the obstacles the army accomplished the task. A total of 77,696 enlistments were obtained during the fiscal year; losses totaled 75,868.[29] The War Department spent over $4 million, 1.7 percent of its budget, on recruiting to meet the demand.[30] Procurement peaked in January 1924 with 9,831 enlistments, and averaged about 6,000 for the remaining months of the fiscal year. By summer enlisted strength approached the authorized ceiling, and in July the War Department called a halt to new enlistments.[31] The *New York Times* praised General Davis and the adjutant general's department for its "uphill work . . . to obtain replacements during the Winter and Spring." But the *Times* also suggested that the downturn in employment during the year contributed to the recruiting success.[32] A comparison of monthly enlistments with employment supports the *Times*'s argument.

Table 4.2 *Recruiting and Employment, Fiscal Year 1924*

MONTH	*ENLISTMENTS*	*EMPLOYMENT INDEX*	*ENLISTED STRENGTH*
July 1923	4,332	105.9	110,397
August	5,197	105.1	108,397
September	5,207	104.0	107,766
October	6,803	103.4	107,435
November	7,744	103.2	108,493
December	8,906	102.0	109,862
January 1924	9,831	101.8	111,265
February	6,740	101.8	113,410
March	5,780	101.1	116,221
April	5,245	99.6	117,575
May	5,601	96.9	119,768
June	6,310	94.3	121,108

Sources: Enlistments and Strength: *Annual Report, 1924*, p. 160. Employment Index: *Statistical Abstract of the United States, 1935*, Table 349, p. 315. (Index and Employment in Manufacturing Industries, Monthly Average, 1923–1925 = 100.)

The enlisted strength column of table 4.2 suggests another point concerning the successful 1924 recruiting record. At no time did the army reach its authorized maximum of 125,000 men. Beginning with fiscal year 1925 Congress began appropriating funds for the pay of the army based on an average of 118,750 men; the ceiling remained 125,000. Although it is not stated in any policy paper before 1926, the army recognized that if it exceeded a strength of 120,000 for very long, it would run out of funds for pay before the end of the year. No effort was made to recruit the army up to 125,000 enlisted men in 1924; thus the task of the recruiting service was eased by nearly 4,000 men.

For the remainder of the decade the overall recruiting picture changed little from that of 1924. Congress appropriated pay for an average strength of 118,750 enlisted men. The War Department, "in order to permit all organizations utilized in summer training to enter the camps with a complete quota of trained men," purposely maintained the army understrength for the first half of each fiscal year and then ordered the Recruiting Service to obtain "an equal amount overstrength for the last half of the year." When a reduction was necessary or when quotas were filled, recruiting ceased, but the General Recruiting Service remained intact. The experience of 1919 and 1921 indicated that "disbanding the permanent Recruiting Service for a short period is one of the most uneconomical moves the War Department can make."[33] The problem of enlisted procurement in peacetime seemed to be settled.

After 1924 the army turned its attention to maintaining enlisted strength. Desertions rose to alarming proportions during the first half of the decade, reaching a peak of 7.39 percent of total enlisted strength in 1925. Coincidentally the number of honorably discharged men declining to reenlist was also high, as Woodbury's study of desertions, done in 1920, had suggested.[34]

The Army and Navy Journal considered the army's unacceptable desertion rate and low percentage of reenlistments as indicators of poor service morale. The Journal blamed "poor quarters and the reduction in pay, with better prospects in civil life . . . for the numerous desertions and the alarming lack of re-enlistments." Other causes of low morale included excessive fatigue duty involved in the maintenance of posts and the long summer training periods with the civilian components.[35]

Enlisted life in the army during the interwar years could be exceedingly routine and dull. For the eight hundred men of the Fourth Cavalry at Fort Meade, South Dakota, a typical line unit, the year was filled with training and horse exercise. The regiment consisted of two active squadrons of three troops each, a machine gun troop, and the regimental headquarters troop. About one hundred men were assigned to each troop. In garrison the men worked five and a half days a week. Every morning they groomed and walked their horses. Then, while one troop performed post maintenance (police, garbage pickup, building repair, and so on), the rest of the regiment trained. Training in the cavalry consisted of two broad areas: marksmanship and equine skills. The weather on the Great Plains affected the annual cycle considerably. From October to May most of the men spent most of their day attending classes on map reading and patrolling techniques and practiced weaponry in the basements of the barracks. Winter training in pistol, saber, and rifle skills consisted of endless drills focusing on proper position and trigger squeeze. The men also practiced on twenty-two-caliber ranges set up in attics or spare rooms until ammunition was exhausted.

As weather improved, the men moved outside and began to practice scouting and patrolling on horseback. In May they took an annual test in pistol and saber skills, and in June, which offered the longest hours of daylight of the year, each troop moved to the target ranges to qualify with their rifles. The men started firing as soon as it was light enough to see the targets and continued all day. Officers and noncommissioned officers stressed marksmanship above all else in training. High individual and unit qualification scores were considered to be the most accurate measure of a troop's level of readiness.

The annual training cycle reached its climax in July with field maneuvers. After examinations on scouting and patrolling, the entire regiment left Fort Meade for a 200-mile march. They returned late in August and spent September repairing equipment, evaluating the summer's activities, and preparing for the next training year.[36]

The army did little to alter the routine of enlisted life to make it more interesting or exciting for soldiers. Instead the War Department equated service attractiveness with creature comforts and focused its attention on improving the living standards of enlisted men. In the 1920s, as is frequently the case today, army leaders viewed the problem of enlisted losses solely in economic terms. Better barracks, a more palatable diet, and more pay, they believed, would reverse the trends of rising desertions and declining reenlistments.

Preparedness advocates and army leaders seeking to pry more money out of Congress frequently focused attention on the effects of the strength and pay reductions on army morale and used the desertion figures to support their claims. The best example of this approach was the housing issue of the mid-1920s.

When, in January 1927, Congress approved only $5 million for housing improvements in fiscal year 1928, the *Infantry Journal* sourly observed that at that rate "some twenty-odd years will be required before the Army will be able to rid itself of the nightmare of the rotting war-time cantonments."[37]

In October 1927 Chief of Staff General Charles P. Summerall, tired of polite requests, took the army's case to the public. Appearing before the

San Diego, California, Chamber of Commerce, during an inspection tour of the corps areas, Summerall pronounced "the housing situation of the Army . . . a disgrace," and told his audience "it is high time that the American people awaken and do something, for it is up to them."[38] The *New York Times* picked up the story and supported Summerall saying, "The country knows General Summerall and can trust him. It should see that Congress heeds his complaints, which are rising in bitterness."[39] Summerall was recalled from his tour by the White House, and the story became front-page news. The president defended the administration's record on army housing. Coolidge claimed that since 1925 $22 million had been authorized for housing improvements. On this point he was correct, but the president also admitted that only $8 million had actually been appropriated.[40] In an effort to close the issue the White House announced that Summerall's recall had nothing to do with his statements and that he had been misquoted in the press.[41] But the issue would not die. The *New York Times,* the *Chicago Evening Post, Washington Post, Baltimore Sun,* and other leading papers brought editorial support to bear. The *Literary Digest* suggested that "The 'Summerall Incident' may be closed, as a White House statement declares, but out of it . . . will come . . . a searching investigation into the Army housing situation."[42] At the next session Congress approved $25 million for permanent construction of barracks, houses, and hospitals, and by the end of the fiscal year Secretary of War Davis reported that the program was proceeding smoothly. By 1932 the housing program had provided new barracks for 28,652 soldiers, and quarters for 1,443 noncommissioned officers and 1,534 officers.[43]

While the struggle to upgrade housing occasionally drew headlines, the army successfully waged another battle in the name of morale to increase the rations allowance for soldiers. The value of the ration, set annually by executive order, was paid to units on a per capita basis to defray the costs of food served in mess halls. Normally the ration value fluctuated according to food costs averaged annually. Beginning in 1922, however, the ration became fixed at thirty cents per soldier per day. By mid-1925 food costs had risen to 36.12 cents. In December 1925 the *Infantry Journal,* in an article equating ration allowances with desertions, suggested that the difference between the authorized ration and food costs resulted in poor meals and lower morale.[44]

Food costs remained higher through 1926, and in the autumn the army requested more money to cover the difference. The request carried over to the hearings on appropriations for fiscal year 1928. In January 1927 the House Appropriations Committee agreed to raise the ration to about forty-one cents daily per man.[45] The army, however, asked that the ration be made equal to that of the navy and Marine Corps, which currently came to fifty-two and forty-nine cents respectively and in which the quality of the foods that made up the ration was higher. The secretary of war and chief of staff considered the ration issue to be so important that both personally supported it in testimony before Congress. "The fact that we have a very low ration," Secretary Davis told the House Military Affairs Committee, "has a bad effect on the morale. The situation is unfortunate in having a different ration for the Army from the Navy and Marine Corps . . . [because] the soldier feels he is discriminated against if he sees the men in the other service getting a very much better ration than he has." General Summerall declared that he believed raising the army ration would "bring an abundant return in reducing desertions, in increased morale and discipline and in efficiency." Daniel Garrett of Texas asked if the army's request implied that soldiers were being underfed by the current ration. Major General Frank Cheatham, the quartermaster general, replied:

> The question of underfed is a rather difficult one. They would not have starved. The components of the ration have a certain definite number of calories which will keep you in good health, but there is not the variety, there is not the standards in the standards of living [sic] which the rest of the country has built up to, and the ration is not satisfactory; it is not pleasing to the palate.[46]

The army's quest for a ration increase never attracted the attention that the housing issue generated, although the *New York Times* did raise its voice on behalf of an improved soldier's ration in January 1927.[47] Determined lobbying by the army's top leaders convinced the House, and it approved the increase without opposition. In the Senate some fiscal conservatives found the proposal too costly, whereupon the president, who according to the *Army and Navy Journal* "had constantly declared for a well fed Army," raised the ration to fifty cents daily by executive order.[48] Summerall later called the increase "one of the most important measures that have been taken for the betterment of the living conditions of the enlisted men. . . ." He added that the improvement of enlisted living conditions, especially of housing and the ration, was instrumental in reducing desertions and increasing reenlistments during the decade of the 1920s.[49] A comparison of desertions and the number of honorably discharged soldiers failing to reenlist at the beginning of the decade, when enlisted strength stabilized, and at the end of the period at first would seem to support the chief of staff's conclusion.

General Summerall, however, probably gave the army more credit than it deserved for the decrease in the number of soldiers deserting or failing to reenlist. As Irving Bernstein has shown, a significant labor surplus in the 1920s contributed to low turnover in jobs.[50] The army simply could have been mirroring society. Furthermore, most of the enlisted men in the regular army had been recruited since the world war, a large majority of them during the big campaigns of 1919 and 1920. Those who disliked the army had already moved on by 1924. The higher reenlistment rates of the

Table 4.3 *Desertions and Failures to Reenlist, Fiscal Years 1923–1929*

YEAR	DESERTIONS	PERCENTAGE OF TOTAL ENLISTMENTS	DISCHARGED SOLDIERS FAILING TO REENLIST	PERCENTAGE OF DISCHARGED SOLDIERS
1923	12,423	6.40	21,459	62.5
1924	14,406	7.03	18,983	51.9
1925	13,752	7.39	10,190	44.5
1926	13,644	7.26	8,674	35.5
1927	11,580	6.07	11,766	35.9
1928	10,467	5.81	6,740	30.3
1929	9,691	5.20	5,601	23.3

Sources: Desertions, Discharge and Reenlistment figures are compiled from the *Annual Report of the Secretary of War* for the respective years shown; Desertion percentages are from *Annual Report of the Secretary of War, 1941*, p. 116.

late 1920s represent the reestablishment of a corps of professional enlisted men characteristic of the prewar army.

Improvements in housing and rations marked the only successful attempts to improve service attractiveness in the 1920s. A similar effort to increase military pay failed. The pay question, like housing and rations, arose early in the decade, almost immediately after passage of the Pay Readjustment Act of 1922. The pay act was especially galling to recruiters who found that prospective civilians were aware of the cut in recruits' pay from $30 to $21 a month. In 1923 the adjutant general commented on the effect of low pay in his annual report. "In view of the high rates of pay offered by industrial and commercial concerns, as compared with those provided by law for enlisted men," General Harris wrote, "the problem of securing enlistments in sufficient numbers becomes a serious one."[51]

Problems of pay affected all services, and in 1929, at the invitation of the secretary of the navy, the uniformed services formed the Interdepartmental Pay Board to study the situation and make joint recommendations to Congress. The board conducted a comprehensive study of living conditions. Between 1908 and 1929 living costs increased 104 percent. Pointing to "very material increases in compensation in private life and in other (nonmilitary) public services as evidence of the trend to keep compensation in proper adjustment to costs of living," the board presented its recommendations for an increase in service pay.[52] The report of the Pay Board met with considerable support. The *Nashville Tennesseean,* for example, approved of the proposed increases saying, "It may be true that the American Army is the best paid Army in the world, but it is equally true that this country is one of the most expensive on earth in which to live. . . . We hope that Congress will give the consideration to this report which its importance deserves."[53]

The request for pay raises could not have come at a more inauspicious time. Just before the board released its recommendations, President Hoover, in a statement timed with the final ratification of the Kellogg-Briand Pact, announced plans for a tax reduction to be achieved through defense economizing.[54] Although the administration planned no strength reduction, it clearly did not envision any budget increases to cover a pay raise. Hoover sent the Pay Board's report to the Bureau of the Budget. The bureau questioned the validity of the report's assumptions linking pay increases to living costs and reported that the proposed pay increases would raise the War Department budget nearly 31 percent. The president then forwarded the Pay Board report to Congress with no comment.[55]

In December 1929 despite the mounting financial panic that began in the autumn, Congress established a joint committee to study the pay situation. The *Army and Navy Journal,* in familiar fashion, launched a major effort to gain support for the services' campaign for a raise. Naturally, the American Legion, National Guard Association, and various reserve organizations supported the increase, but additionally, it seemed that everybody else did, too. The *Journal* ran a special column reprinting editorials and endorsements in favor of the raise. Supporters included the American Federation of Labor, numerous chambers of commerce and business groups, newspapers from around the country, and even several municipalities. The Chamber of Commerce of the State of New York conducted a thorough study of the Interdepartmental Pay Board's report and declared the pay of the uniformed services "is inadequate and unfair" . . . that the Government because of this condition loses many of the best men, who leave the service to take positions in civil life, and that remedial legislation should be provided by the Congress. . . ."[56]

Appearing before the joint congressional committee early in 1930, the services, notably the army and the navy, cut each other's throats. The supposed unanimity of the Interdepartmental Pay Board disintegrated over conflicting views linking promotion policy to pay increases. Congress ordered the Pay Board to prepare new recommendations and present them to the next session. When the board presented its new proposals in October 1930, support for the pay raise had waned. A service pay increase during the depression was a dead issue and remained so for the next six years. The *Army and Navy Journal* philosophically observed, "In view of the extreme business depression, the administration economy drive and the important measures that will confront Congress at its next session, there is little likelihood of any speedy favorable action."[57]

Increasing service attractiveness by improving housing conditions and raising pay and rations allowances represented only part of the War Department's effort to reduce enlisted losses during the 1920s. General Staff and War College studies of the problem often referred to the attractions of the economy and suggested methods of overcoming them. Three

General Staff studies, in 1923, 1924, and 1926, addressed the relationship between the national economy and the purchase of discharges, a little-known policy of allowing enlisted men to buy their way out of the army after one year's service for $120.[58] "Discharge by purchase" had been authorized during peacetime since 1890. Corps area commanders and the chiefs of such technical branches as the Corps of Engineers, Air Corps, and Finance Corps repeatedly complained that skilled enlisted men were purchasing discharges after completing specialized training program. Recommendations from the technical services proposed raising the purchase price and prohibiting men from purchasing discharges for six months to a year after completion of a course. Like desertions, purchase discharges showed a marked increase during the 1920s.

Table 4.4 *Discharge by Purchase Compared to Index of Average Weekly Earnings in Manufacturing Industries*

YEAR	PURCHASE DISCHARGES	EARNINGS INDEX
1923	6,864	99.1
1924	8,590	99.5
1925	10,016	101.4
1926	9,345	102.5
1927	9,610	102.9
1928	8,538	103.9
1929	9,606	104.1

Sources: Purchase Discharges, *Annual Report of the Secretary of War,* respective years; Earnings Index, *Statistical Abstract of the United States,* 1941, Table 395, p. 370. 1923–1925 averages = 100.

Furthermore, as the 1926 study showed, 8 percent of enlisted graduates of special service schools purchased their discharges after completion of their courses.[59] Although the chiefs of branches overwhelmingly favored changes in the purchase law, the War Department opposed any modification. Brigadier General Charles Martin, the former chief of the General Recruiting Service, expressed the General Staff's opinion in 1923. Martin advised against allowing termination of enlistments at will, but warned that restriction of the existing purchase law would produce a "very unfavorable reaction." Furthermore, he wrote, restricting purchase discharges would hurt the army more than it would help. "To make graduates of service schools ineligible for discharge by purchase would tend to make intelligent and ambitious enlisted men avoid attendance at the service schools." Martin concluded that "when an enlisted man has a real opportunity to better his condition by leaving the Army, little is gained by keeping him in. . . . [He] will be a 'knocker,' discouraging other men from enlisting."[60] Martin's advice withstood repeated efforts to change the purchase law. It remained in effect until suspended in 1940.[61]

The purchase discharge rate, though vexing, was accepted as a necessary evil of the voluntary principle. Desertions were another matter. Although the War Department recognized, as in a 1926 War College study, that "high wages, ease of employment, . . . [and] public indifference to the offense of desertion . . . [were] causes generally . . . beyond the control of the military authorities,"[62] it continued to search for a solution to the problem. Those who studied army losses increasingly pointed to the need for more selective recruiting as a means of eliminating potential deserters or unsuitable soldiers. In 1927 the commanding general of the Sixth Corps Area wrote to the adjutant general complaining about recruits. The adjutant general replied that "the demand for labor in civilian activities" made it "necessary to accept every man who could be included under the most liberal interpretation of the regulations." He assured the general that the Recruiting Service was making "every effort . . . to secure the highest type of enlisted man obtainable under existing conditions. . . ."[63]

Articles written by recruiting officers during the period reiterated this problem of securing suitable enlisted men and recruiters' frustration at the charges of poor quality. Captain Reyburn Engles, writing in the *Quartermaster Review,* complained of minors who concealed their age and who, when detected, were subsequently discharged at great expense to the army and blame to the recruiters. "Certainly every Recruiting Officer likes to get as great a number of enlistments as he possibly can," Engles wrote, but ". . . no Recruiting Officer will knowingly make a practice of enlisting minors." Engles proposed that stiff penalties be imposed on men who misrepresented their age when enlisting.[64] The debate over who was to blame for poor soldiers, recruiters or the army itself, an issue raised before in the responses to Woodbury's 1920 study of desertions, resurfaced in a 1927 article by Captain W. J. Gilbert, recruiting officer at Providence, Rhode Island. Gilbert complained bitterly about charges of poor quality recruits and asked his readers in the line units what they were doing to decrease losses. Most men enlisted to soldier, Gilbert said. "The line is the factory which produces the goods the sales force has advertised and sold to the people." Unpleasant service experiences send the discharged soldier "away with bitter memories, so he can be a stumbling block in the way of some good man who might enlist." He urged line officers to remember "'The day to start re-enlisting a man is the day he takes the oath of enlistment.'"[65]

Attempts to reduce fraudulent enlistments and identify potential misfits through selective recruiting began in the 1920s. In an effort to cut down on the enlistment of minors the War Department required recruiters to secure notarized proof of age for applicants between the ages of eighteen and twenty-one and written notarized consent from parents or guardians of applicants under age eighteen. The army also began taking fingerprints of all applicants and checking them against discharge files and Justice Department records in an effort to prevent criminals and former soldiers discharged under other than honorable circumstances from entering or reentering the service.[66]

These efforts never proved wholly successful. Because continuing economy restrictions dictated that all correspondence with Washington be done by mail or night letter, a considerable delay resulted in processing queries on prior service records, fingerprints, or requests to enlist minors. Often rather than allow a potential recruit slip away during the wait, the recruiter took a chance. As Captain Engles observed, ". . . men must be obtained. To obtain them a certain price must be paid, and we continue to pay. . . ."[67]

In 1924, Major Edgar King, an army doctor working at the Department of Psychiatry and Sociology, United States Disciplinary Barracks, Fort Leavenworth, Kansas, proposed the establishment of screening boards to examine "every enlisted man thought to be 'possibly not fit'" for service. Recruits considered wholly unfit were to be discharged immediately. King further proposed the establishment of "special school companies" to train recruits deemed capable of development. Inauguration of the plan would result in a "marked reduction in the number of desertions and other delinquencies, with consequent reduction in court martial trials. . . ." The General Staff studied King's plan but rejected the special school companies as too expensive. A further objection surfaced over the possible stigma attached to recruits sent to the special companies. The adjutant general feared that "many recruits would be stamped as 'inferior' at the beginning of their Army careers. . . . This would lower their morale and militate against their ever becoming effective soldiers."[68]

Major King continued to work at the Disciplinary Barracks on a method for the early identification and elimination of misfits. In 1925 he developed a series of tests including a modified Simon-Binet test and what he termed a minimum mental examination. King administered the tests to inmates at the Fort Leavenworth prison and presented his findings to the surgeon general. Use of the test, surprisingly like that conceptualized by Woodbury in his 1920 study, at recruiting offices, King said, would aid recruiters in detecting men of low intelligence or criminal minds. This time the General Staff accepted King's plan. In September 1926 each corps area was directed to select one recruiting district to try out the system. All applicants for original enlistment were tested. Recruiting personnel administered the first test designed to measure general intelligence. A mental age of ten years or below was considered grounds for rejection, but if the recruiting officer felt "that the applicant will make a good soldier on account of other outstanding points in his favor," he could enlist the applicant. The second phase of the test, to be administered by medical officers only, "aims at discovering the several forms of psychosis, character defects, extreme youth and gross deficiency of moral training of the applicant.'' An applicant failing the minimum mental exam could not enlist under any circumstances.[69]

The trial use of King's intelligence and mental tests lasted for a year, and then the War Department ordered testing of all applicants for original enlistment. In implementing the testing army-wide, the War Department continued to use a mental age of ten years as the minimum standard for enlistment.[70] Its faith in such methods, which spread throughout United States society in the 1920s, revealed that the army was not attempting to serve as a haven for society's misfits but aspired to obtain and hold adequate personnel. Stability, not social work, was its goal.

The introduction of intelligence and mental testing of applicants for enlistment represented the last major innovation in recruiting during the interwar period. Army-wide testing began on October 1, 1927, and continued with few modifications until World War II. The War Department kept records of the number of applicants for enlistment rejected for failure to pass the tests until March 1938. A compilation of the reports from October 1927 to December 1929 reveals that only 4,055 of 88,254 applicants were rejected because of intelligence test scores. Another 38,241 failed to enlist for other unspecified reasons.[71] As desertions declined and the number of honorably discharged soldiers reenlisting began to rise in the late 1920s, War Department analysts pointed with pride to the apparent success of the intelligence tests and the selective recruiting program. But, as with General Summerall's praise for the positive effects of the higher ration allowance and improved housing during the same period, the army may have overstated its case. Clearly the changing trends in desertions and reenlistments reflected some improvement in the attractiveness of the army and in recruiting practices, but outside trends also played a part. While wages continued to rise after 1923, unemployment rose somewhat after 1926. Furthermore, the higher wages were paid to regularly employed skilled and semiskilled workers. Deserters were unlikely to find their way into such jobs. These outside influences, which had affected desertions and reenlistments in the past, undoubtedly combined with army improvements to reduce desertions and encourage reenlistments in the late 1920s.

By the end of the decade the army seemed to have its manpower problems under control. The General Recruiting Service was able to secure enough recruits to replace losses and maintain authorized strength. The army, with acknowledged assistance from a still parsimonious Congress, upgraded creature comforts sufficiently to overcome some of the more glaring sources of poor morale. Unacceptably high enlisted losses had been reduced. While expressing satisfaction over the improvement, the War Department did not rest on its laurels. Line commanders still complained about recruits, and recruiters still replied that the army did not do enough to hold good men after they enlisted. Articles and studies on manpower problems written between 1927 and 1930 stressed the need to recruit "quality" enlisted men and further improve service conditions in order to retain good soldiers.

Coinciding with the introduction of intelligence testing, the Recruiting Service adopted the slogan "Quality not Quantity." Articles in *Recruiting News,* the official publication of the Recruiting Service, stressed two themes. "How to do it" articles told how successful recruiters met their quotas and got good men at the same time. Another frequent theme, "earn while you learn," aimed directly at prospective recruits. A typical example reported on John L. Hunter, an Irish immigrant who enlisted in 1919. Hunter became a plumber in the army. After serving two enlistments in that capacity, he passed the Illinois state examination for a license as a journeyman plumber, purchased his discharge, and went to work in Chicago earning union wages.[72]

When Charles Lindbergh soloed across the Atlantic, army recruiters had a field day. The cover of the June 1, 1927, *Recruiting News* featured a photo of Lindbergh with the caption "Trained at Army Flying Schools." The cover story claimed, "Again the Army Succeeds Where Others Fail!" Altogether *Recruiting News* carried five stories on Lindbergh.[73]

The Air Corps hardly needed selling in the 1920s. The glamour of aviation ensured that quotas were always filled and caused the army some problems. Every recruit for the Air Corps wanted to be a pilot. Yet the pressures to recruit created problems here. In 1928, Harry G. Dowdall, still a first lieutenant eight years after his undercover recruiting work for Charles Martin, wrote a short article for *Recruiting News* reminding recruiters of the need to advise applicants for the Air Corps that few enlisted men became pilots. "They can be guaranteed no opportunity whatsoever to learn to fly unless they have at least 2 years of college education or can pass an examination covering such work," warned Dowdall.[74] A good example of the problem Dowdall referred to occurred in 1930. In October 1930 Henry Olson, justice of the peace at Lindsborg, Kansas, wrote to the adjutant general on behalf of the parents of Paul Willman, Ralph Anderson, and Carrol Ahlstedt, charging that Corporal Claud Kendall and Captain George Lockhart of the Salina Recruiting Office enlisted the young men of Lindsborg in the Air Corps under false pretenses. Subsequent investigation concluded,

Corporal Claud Kendall did not make any promises to any of these applicants that they would enter a ground school within six months; would be promoted after six months service or would fly "solo" within two years. However it is apparent that Corporal Kendall knew these young men had an ambition to become aviators; he knew that they were under the impression they were enlisting to become flyers; he knew they did not possess the necessary educational qualifications for appointment as flying cadets; he knew they did not fully understand the duties of enlisted men, Air Corps. Yet in spite of this he induced them to enlist in the Air Corps, Panama Department.

On November 6, 1930, the commanders of the Twenty-fifth Bombardment Squadron and the Twenty-fourth Pursuit Squadron, both at France Field, Balboa, Panama, received orders to release Willman, Anderson, and Ahlstedt "for discharge for convenience of Government on account of Erroneous enlistment."[75]

Despite the "quality not quantity" and "earn while you learn" campaigns, statistics that showed declining desertions and rising reenlistments, and reports of satisfaction with the system in annual reports, one is left with the lingering suspicion that all was not well with the volunteer army. A series of studies and articles in 1929–1930 reviewed the army's recruiting experience since 1920, criticized the recruiting system and its ability to meet the army's needs, and cast doubts on the claims of success for selective recruiting and the results of improved service morale. Major Albert E. Brown, in a War College study, declared, "If the small peacetime army authorized by Congress is to perform its [missions,] . . . it must be composed of type [sic] soldiers representative of efficient American manhood." Brown charged that the present recruiting system relied on the procurement of "drifters" who threatened the efficiency of the army.[76] Brown's charge is impossible to verify, since neither he nor the army provided data on who enlisted, but as a contemporary observer of the interwar army his subjective opinion cannot be discounted. Harry Dowdall also lamented the uncertain relationship between recruiting and the national economy. "That the Army Recruiting Service should depend almost entirely upon the labor market surplus for its replacements shows two weaknesses in the recruiting system," Dowdall wrote in the January 1930 *Infantry Journal*. "[F]irst, the ever present uncertainty of obtaining replacements when needed; and second, the position of being a refuge open to young men who cannot secure employment at a living wage."[77] Captain W. H. McKee, also writing in the *Infantry Journal,* analyzed the recruiters versus commanders debate and found merit on both sides. Recruiters, he said, did the best they could, but suffered from the quota system, which pressured them to enlist men regardless of quality and "has resulted in lowering standards." The units compound the problem because "low pay, fatigue, surroundings, unusual character of service, unbalanced training, and lack of recreational facilities . . . militate against the probability that the average recruit will complete the term of his enlistment."[78]

Every article and study proposed ways in which the army could improve its attractiveness to recruits after they entered the service. The most common suggestions involved raising service pay and reducing fatigue duty. The inescapable common denominator of all the studies is the recognition that maintenance of army manpower still depended on conditions largely beyond the institution's control. A General Staff report on desertion prepared late in 1930 summarized the experience of the 1920s, concluding that "the major conditions within the Army which cause desertions . . . have received and are receiving serious consideration. . . ."

Other causes attributed to social conditions, such as the economy and the public's attitude toward military service in peacetime, were dismissed as beyond ability to affect.[79] The General Staff seemed content to accept the situation as it stood.

Other officers felt that the army could improve the recruiting situation. Brown and Dowdall both wrote early in 1930 before the effects of the stock market crash of 1929 really became evident. Brown stressed the economic aspects of the recruiting. His study, which compared civilian and military wage rates, was intended to lend support to the still active bid for a service pay increase. Even when adding the value of additional benefits such as medical services, rations, and housing to soldiers' pay, Brown found that military compensation fell below that of civilian labor. Thus, Brown concluded, the army recruited its men from the unemployed of the nation. Anticipating the depression, Brown observed, "This unemployment pool is, however, variable. . . . As it increases the number available for recruitment, as well as the quality of the prospective recruit increases." Brown's message was that the better material was already employed. The only way to obtain better recruits in prosperous times was to pay for them.[80] In a few months the question was moot.

Harry Dowdall's experience as a recruiting officer and a "recruit" convinced him that the army had to do more than simply compete with the private sector for recruits. Attacking the adage that "Army methods are the result of many years of experience," Dowdall accused the recruiting service of "simply carrying on hoping for a better era. . . ." Pointing out that some 1 million young men turned eighteen annually, "and that among these are necessarily many thousands who have no prospects of a favorable career ahead of them," Dowdall declared, "it is quite obvious that the Army should have no trouble in recruiting the comparatively small number needed as replacements to keep the Army at authorized strength." The problem, he said, was public prejudice against army service. The image of the army grew out of ignorance and misunderstanding on the part of the public and complacency on the part of the army. In a tone reminiscent of Newton Baker championing educational and vocational training a decade earlier, Dowdall declared "the Army stands before the country as one of the greatest institutions in the world to aid the youth who needs help to get started in life." He urged a vigorous program to educate the public to the true virtues and benefits of military service in peacetime.[81]

Dowdall overstated his case. The recruiting service never ceased to promote the army as a preparatory school for life during the 1920s. But the suggestion that the army had become complacent in response to public indifference was not invalid. Army leaders learned to live with the strength and appropriations cuts of the early 1920s. Preparedness advocates never ceased to protest, but by the middle of the decade it was clear to them that few Americans were concerned about defense, and the army began to accept its low profile. Only when new manpower cuts threatened or when conditions affecting retention became intolerable, as in the housing and ration issues, did the War Department assert itself. No one threatened to resign over low budgets or inadequate strength.

The army clearly saw itself as a servant, and not as a policy-making agency. Summerall's effort to take the housing issue to the public is the exception that proves the rule. This attitude carried over into recruiting. As long as losses could be kept below embarrassing levels and strength maintained, officials did not complain. Men directly involved in recruiting, like Brown and Dowdall, criticized the system and proposed solutions that were "beyond the control of the army to affect." Only an emergency would alter the system. When the emergency came in the form of the Great Depression instead of a military crisis, the system functioned efficiently. The changes proposed in the late 1920s were forgotten until the 1970s.

NOTES

1. *Army and Navy Journal* (hereafter, *ANJ*), February 12, 1921, p. 670; Memo, AG to CS, April 26, 1926, AGO 341.1, RG 94, NA.

2. Memo, ACS to AG, February 9, 1921, AGO 341.1, RG 407, Box 786, NA.

3. Major I. J. Phillipson, "Report on Recruiting," AGO 341.1, RG 407, Box 786, NA, p. 10. No date is given on the report. It is attached to the initiating directive cited in n. 2.

4. Phillipson, "Report on Recruiting," pp. 35–49.

5. Ibid., p. 51.

6. "Problems Which are Peculiar to Certain Recruiting Districts," attached to "Report on Recruiting," n.p.

7. The Carter B. Magruder Papers: Recollections and Reflections. Transcripts of the Debriefing of General Magruder by Colonel Tucker, 1972. MHI, Carlisle Barracks, Pa.

8. Interview with Raymond Alvord at West Point, N.Y., February 6, 1975. Alvord served thirty-one years, eighteen days and retired as first sergeant in 1955. He died in 1978.

9. Phillipson, "Report on Recruiting," p. 51.

10. "Proposed Plan for Resumption of Active Recruiting," Memo, AG to CS, July 18, 1921, AGO 341.1, RG 407, NA.

11. "Policy for Resumption of Recruiting," Memo, ACS, G-1 to AG, September 3, 1921, AGO 341.2, RG 407, NA.

12. Information on enlisted promotions is very sketchy. The army did not report enlisted promotion rates, and few officers left impressions of them. It is common knowledge that promotions were slow; beyond that there is little to go on. This summary of enlisted promotions in the 1920s applies equally to any peacetime period between the Civil War and World War II, and is based on discussions with Professor Edward M. Coffman of the University of Wisconsin, who is currently researching a social history of the army in peacetime, while he was visiting pro-

fessor of military history at the U.S. Military Academy, West Point, N.Y., in 1977–1978.

13. *Recruiting News* 3, no. 22 (November 1, 1921) 8.

14. Memo, ACS to AG, November 10, 1921; Memo, Chief of Finance to ACS, November 25, 1921; Memo, AG to Quartermaster General thru Chief of Finance, November 29, 1921, all under file marked "Funds for Recruiting Activities," AGO 341.1, RG 407, NA.

15. *U.S. War Department Annual Reports for Year Ending June 30, 1922* (Washington, D.C.: GPO, 1922), pp. 198–99. Hereafter *Annual Report, 1922.*

16. "Suspension of Recruiting for the Regular Army," Memo, ACS, G1, to CS, January 27, 1922; Brig. Gen. Charles Martin to AG, January 30, 1922, AGO 341.1, RG 407, NA.

17. *Annual Report, 1922,* Table B, facing p. 132, p. 151.

18. Ibid., p. 36; War Department Bulletin No. 22, December 31, 1921, in *U.S. War Department General Orders and Bulletins, 1921* (Washington, D.C.: GPO, 1922).

19. "Recruiting Campaign for the Regular Army," Letter, AG to all Corps Areas, October 30, 1922, AGO 341.1, RG 407, NA.

20. Memo, Col. Alfred Aloe to Recruiting Officer First Corps Area, November 10, 1922, AGO 341, RG 407, NA.

21. Memo, AG to ACS, G-4, December 4, 1922, AGO 341, RG 407, NA.

22. *New York Times* (hereafter, *NYT*), January 3, 1923, p. 19; *ANJ,* February 3, 1923, p. 556; *Recruiting News* 5 (February 1, 1923), back cover.

23. "Extracts from Adjutant General's Report," *Recruiting News* 5 (November 15, 1923): 3.

24. *ANJ,* July 28, 1923, p. 1150.

25. Letter, AG to Commanders, All Corps Areas, July 20, 1923, AGO 220.62, RG 407, NA; Memo, AG to CS, April 26, 1926, AGO 341.1, RG 94, NA.

26. Letter, AG to Commanders, all Corps Areas, July 20, 1923.

27. *NYT,* August 19, 1923, Sec. 33, p. 9.

28. *ANJ,* January 27, 1923, p. 534; *Annual Report, 1923,* p. 26.

29. *Annual Report, 1924,* pp. 134, 160.

30. "Cost of Recruiting—Fiscal Year 1924," Special Report No. 182, October 9, 1924, Statistical Branch, General Staff. MHI file 198A. This file contains recruiting costs beginning with FY 1924 thru 1940; FY 1925 and 1932 are missing.

31. *NYT,* July 16, 1924, p. 19.

32. Ibid., July 17, 1924, p. 14.

33. Memo, AG to CS, April 26, 1926, AGO 341.1, RG 94, NA.

34. *Annual Report, 1941,* p. 116.

35. *ANJ,* October 27, 1923, p. 204.

36. Interview with General Robert Porter (Ret.) at West Point, N.Y., January 19, 1978. General Porter was commissioned in 1930 and joined the Fourth Cavalry that year. His impressions of life in the cavalry are that the training described was typical of the interwar period until about 1940 when rearmament and rapid expansion of the army forced the development of new training methods.

37. *Infantry Journal* 30, no. 2 (February 1927): 189.

38. *NYT,* October 12, 1927, p. 23.

39. Ibid., October 13, 1927, p. 24.

40. Ibid., October 15, 1927, p. 1.

41. Ibid., October 19, 1927, p. 27.

42. "Army Housing a 'National Disgrace'," *The Literary Digest* 95, no. 6 (November 5, 1927): 10.

43. Compiled from *Annual Report, 1928*, p. 5; *Annual Report, 1930*, pp. 379–80.

44. "Ration Allowances and Desertions," *Infantry Journal* 27, no. 6 (December 1925): 722.

45. *ANJ*, January 15, 1927, p. 457.

46. Ibid., January 15, 1927, p. 470.

47. *NYT*, January 12, 1927, p. 24.

48. *ANJ*, February 26, 1927, p. 608.

49. *Annual Report, 1930*, p. 145.

50. Irving Bernstein, *The Lean Years: A History of the American Worker, 1920–1933* (Boston: Houghton Mifflin, 1960), p. 62.

51. "Report of the Adjutant General for the Fiscal Year ending June 30, 1923," as reported in *ANJ*, November 17, 1923, p. 265.

52. *Initial Report, War Department Pay Commission, 1939*, Annex No. 1, "History of the Pay System," G1 Guide Books, vol. 1, See 2a, AGO 240, RG 94, NA. Hereafter, *Initial Report, WDPC*.

53. *ANJ*, August 10, 1929, p. 1026. Other newspapers supporting the pay increase included the *San Antonio Express, Buffalo Courier Express,* and *Washington Evening Star.*

54. *ANJ*, July 27, 1929, p. 977.

55. *Initial Report, WDPC, 1939.*

56. *ANJ*, March 1, 1930, p. 601, 602; March 8, pp. 625–26; March 15, pp. 649–50; March 22, pp. 673–74; March 29, pp. 697–98; April 5, pp. 721–22; N.Y. Chamber of Commerce resolution quoted in *ANJ*, April 12, 1930, pp. 745–46.

57. *ANJ*, October 25, 1930, p. 169.

58. Memo, ACS, G1 to CS, "Discharges by Purchase," August 1, 1923, AGO 220.814, RG 407, NA.

59. Memo, ACS, G1, "Discharges by Purchase," October 5, 1926, AGO 220.84, RG 94, NA.

60. Memo, ACS, G1, August 14, 1923, AGO 220.84, RG 94, NA.

61. War Department Circular No. 119, October 22, 1940, in *General Orders, Bulletins and Circulars, 1940* (Washington, D.C.: GPO, 1941).

62. Maj. H. K. Loughry, "Present Desertion Rates," Memo for Director, G1 Division, Army War College, October 16, 1926, File 331A-45, Military History Research Collection, MHI.

63. Letter, AG to CG, VI Corps Area, August 8, 1927, AGO 341, RG 94, NA.

64. Cpt. Reyburn Engles, "Recruiting Problems and Possibilities," *Quartermaster Review* 6, no. 4 (Jan.–Feb. 1927): 30.

65. Cpt. W. J. Gilbert, "The Grand Old Army of the Future," *Coast Artillery Journal* 66, no. 6 (June 1927): 531–36.

66. Engles, "Recruiting Problems and Possibilities," pp. 29–31.

67. Ibid., p. 30.

68. Memo, G1 to CS, June 30, 1924, AGO 220.8, RG 407, NA.

69. Letter, AG to CGs, all Corps Areas, September 21, 1926, AGO 319.12, RG 407, NA.

70. Letter, AG to CGs, all Corps Areas, September 20, 1927, AGO 319.12, RG 407, NA.

71. Data on the number of applicants for original enlistment and the number of applicants rejected for failure to meet intelligence test minimums are located in two adjutant general files. Each corps area submitted quarterly reports titled "Report on Results Connection Intelligence Tests for Applicants for Enlistment." The reports for October 1927 thru June 1931 are in file no. AGO 319.12, RG 407; for July 1931 to March 1938, see file no. AGO 702, RG 94, NA.

72. "Learns Plumbing Trade—Now Making Union Wages," *Recruiting News* 8, no. 11 (January 1, 1927): 7.

73. *Recruiting News* 9, no. 11 (June 1, 1927), and 9, no. 12 (June 15, 1927).

74. Harry G. Dowdall, "Air Corps Enlistment Problem," *Recruiting News* 10, no. 23 (December 1, 1928): 9.

75. Binder, no subject, beginning October 8, 1930, ending November 6, 1930, AGO 220.81, RG 407, NA.

76. Albert E. Brown, "Peacetime Enlistment Losses, Replacements and Methods," Memo for Commandant, Army War College, February 15, 1930, File 367-8, Military History Research Collection, MHI.

77. Harry G. Dowdall, "Modern Recruiting—A Problem," *Infantry Journal* 36, no. 6 (January 1930): 618, 619.

78. W. H. McKee, "Recruiting," *Infantry Journal* 37, no. 2 (August 1930): 139, 140.

79. Memo, G1 to CS, November 17, 1930, AGO 251.1, RG 94, NA.

80. Brown, "Peacetime Enlistment Losses, Replacements and Methods," p. 17.

81. Dowdall, "Modern Recruiting," pp. 616, 619, 625.

5

THE ARMY AND THE DEPRESSION

At the midpoint of the interwar years prospects for the volunteer army looked better than they had for a decade. The drastic reductions of both funds and personnel that characterized the first half of the 1920s had ended, and beginning in fiscal year 1927, Congress showed a willingness to grant modest increases for specific material improvements. By 1929, the General Staff felt confident enough to urge openly an expansion of the regular army.

The stock market crash of 1929 and the Great Depression that followed ended the army's brief period of recovery from the retrenchment of the 1920s. Once again economy-conscious critics of the military proposed cuts in the size of the standing force. Military leaders, arguing from Uptonian assumptions that the regular army served as an expandable core around which a larger emergency force could be built, steadfastly opposed any further reductions in personnel. Instead the War Department achieved savings by reducing research and development, deferring major capital projects, and postponing purchases of new weapons systems and mechanized equipment needed to build a more modern force.

When Herbert Hoover became president on March 4, 1929, few in America doubted that the next four years would be much different from the previous eight. Hoover's commitment to prosperity and efficiency was unquestioned. As Harding and Coolidge's secretary of commerce, Hoover had insisted on having a role in determining economic policies.[1] His retention of Andrew Mellon in the cabinet guaranteed, as well as it symbolized, that Hoover's administration would do nothing to disturb the ascendancy of business.

Interests concerned with reducing the size and capabilities of the military establishment looked forward to Hoover's presidency with anticipation. The peace groups, both conservative and radical, were already demanding new reductions of the army and navy following the signing of the Kellogg-Briand Pact, and they saw Herbert Hoover as an ally. Hoover was a Quaker and an ardent disciple of peace. As the director of relief for Belgium from 1914 to 1917 and postwar relief activities in Europe, Hoover witnessed the horror and destruction of war firsthand. During his campaign for the presidency Hoover remembered the war. "There is much that we must not forget,'' he said. ''Amid the afterglow of glory and legend, we forget the filth and the stench and the death of the trenches; we forget the dumb grief of mothers and of wives and of children; we forget the unending blight cast on the world by the sacrifice of the flower of every race.''[2]

When he accepted the Republican nomination, Hoover declared, ''We have been and we are particularly desirous of furthering the limitation of armament,'' and throughout his administration he never abandoned that goal. But at the same time he assured those elements of society concerned with maintaining the size and readiness of the military ''that in an armed world there is only one certain guarantee of freedom—and that is preparedness for defense.''[3]

Hoover's personal commitment to the pursuit of peace and disarmament was highly compatible with his devotion to business and the preservation of prosperity. Peace was essential to the domestic and overseas activities of American business. War, on the other hand, destabilized both domestic and foreign business enterprise. Disarmament would benefit business and the economy by releasing resources tied up in maintaining current levels of armament for more peaceful purposes. Not the least of these resources was capital diverted from private enterprise to the government in the form of taxes to finance the military establishment.

The ratification of the Kellogg-Briand Pact for the Renunciation of War gave Hoover the opportunity to combine his philosophy on armament reductions with economy in government. On the eve of proclaiming the pact in force, the president announced plans to reduce military expenditures. Hoover told a news conference, ''the American people should understand that the current expenditure for the Army and Navy constitutes the largest military budget of any nation in the world today, and at a time when there is less real danger of extensive disturbance of peace than at any time in more than half a century.'' The Kellogg-Briand Pact and concurrent efforts to resume naval disarmament talks, he said, modified the national situation. He reported that the secretary of war would shortly establish a commission ''to reconsider the whole of our Army program . . .'' and eliminate obsolete services and programs. ''The hope of a tax reduction,'' Hoover observed, ''lies very largely in the ability to economize military expenditure and still maintain an adequate defense.''[4]

The next day, July 24, 1929, at the ceremonial inauguration of the pact, Hoover declared ''the magnificent opportunity and compelling duty now open to us should spur us on to the fulfillment of every opportunity that is calculated to implement this treaty and to extend the policy which it so nobly sets forth.''[5] Later the same day the president took the opportunity to put his words into immediate action. Hoover and the new prime minister of Great Britain, Ramsey MacDonald, a man equally devoted to peace and disarmament, announced the suspension of cruiser construction in both countries as a gesture designed to get disarmament talks started again.[6]

Reaction to Hoover's arms reduction initiative was swift and predictable. Calling the suspension of cruiser production "the most significant action of the United States government during the past month," the historian Albert Bushnell Hart praised Hoover for "the most courageous act of [his] career as President so far. . . ."[7] The *Literary Digest,* surveying the editorial pages of the national press, found broad support for the move, but predicted that "a big disarmament fight looms in Washington." Hoover's decision to halt cruiser building attracted the most attention. Citing the *New York Times,* the *Digest* noted that some opponents claimed the reduction endangered the nation's defenses while certain labor unions complained that canceling the cruiser contracts would put hundreds of men out of work at the navy yards.[8] *The Nation* praised Hoover's decision but warned, "the Army and Navy and all their war-making allies in Congress and out of it will unquestionably gather their forces and fight for their life."[9]

Even before *The Nation* made its prediction, the *Army and Navy Journal* complained about Hoover's announced plans to reduce military spending. Taking issue with the president's statement that the United States spent more on purely military activities than any other nation, the *Journal* pointed out that in terms of national wealth, or on a per capita basis, the nation's military costs were far below those of other powers. "Considered purely as a matter of insurance for our national wealth," the *Journal* declared, "our expenditures . . . show quite pointedly that the United States is paying less for that insurance than any other power." The *Journal* conceded that the U.S. military outlay of over $600 million was the largest in the world. But, "our total cost for national defense is .14 percent of our national wealth" of $423 billion, the paper added. In those terms other nations paid far more than the United States. According to the *Journal* article the British Empire paid .40 percent; Japan, .55 percent; France, .67 percent; Italy, .72 percent; Russia, 1.33 percent. Even Germany, restricted by the Treaty of Versailles to an army of 100,000 and stripped of heavy armaments, spent a greater percentage of its national wealth (.30 percent) on defense than the United States.[10] The *Army and Navy Journal* scanned the pages of the nation's press and found "few were in favor of jeopardizing our national defense for any reason. . . ."[11]

The flurry of excitement and comment on arms reduction that followed Hoover's July announcement quickly subsided. The president assigned the task of reviewing military spending to the General Staff. Hoover directed the War Department "to reconsider our whole army program, to see what services and other outlays have become obsolete through advancement of science and war methods; and what development programs can be well spread over longer periods in view of the general world outlook and at the same time maintain complete adequate preparedness. . . ."[12] Secretary of War James Good and the chief of staff,

General Charles Summerall, realized that certain elements of public opinion would question the army's ability to review its own program. In his letter transmitting the study to the General Staff, Summerall noted that many public spokesmen had urged that the study be done by a civilian commission and emphasized, "It is therefore incumbent that reasons upon which reduction of expense can be based should be fully presented." Summerall wanted no whitewash. "The survey is not a defense of existing conditions but rather a prosecution to determine whether appropriations can be reduced."[13]

The General Staff presented its report, which included the personal views of all corps area commanders, the chief of each branch, and the commandants of the Command and General Staff School and War College, in November 1929. It represents the most comprehensive statement of the opinions of the army's leadership on the role and place of the military in national policy at the midpoint of the interwar era. If the president expected recommendations for major areas of reduction, he was surely disappointed. The report reflects, in the words of one student of the period, "a general reluctance to change the status quo and reduce military activities."[14]

Surveying the world situation, the General Staff concluded that "there does not appear in our present foreign relations any issue the foreseen development in connection with which can reasonably be considered a calling for immediate military preparation." But, the report added, "so long as wars are possible, adequate national defense demands a national military policy which will provide for the development of such part of its manpower and material resources as may be necessary to meet any given emergency up to its maximum strength, should the emergency require it."[15] With this point firmly established, and accepting totally the missions established for the army by the National Defense Act of 1920, the General Staff argued for a program (labeled Plan I) that proposed a peacetime strength of 14,063 officers and 171,500 enlisted men (including 6,500 Philippine Scouts) for the regular army as the minimum necessary to make "reasonable provision for carrying out the mandates contained in the National Defense Act."[16]

Plan I represented a compromise between the National Defense Act and the existing military establishment. Recognizing that the cost of Plan I was "greater than the establishment we now have" and acknowledging "that the establishment of military policy is not the function of the Army," the General Staff offered an alternative in the form of Plan II.[17] The staff assumed that "responsible authority . . . considered the present establishment adequate by reason of the fact that provision has been made for it." Arguing from that assumption, Plan II established $359 million, the original War Department estimate for fiscal year 1931, as the minimum amount necessary for maintaining the army. The alternate plan proposed to redistribute the $359 million in order to improve the existing army. Topping the list of improvements was the pay raise recommended by the Interdepartmental Pay Board in July. The pay raise, which would add an estimated $46 million to the military budget, was deemed necessary because "the most essential requirement for the military establishment is that it be properly maintained regardless ot its size." Plan II recommended that "the least essential military activities be curtailed in order to make possible the necessary raise in pay."[18]

Part of Plan II involved the transfer of appropriations for certain programs that the War Department considered nonmilitary in nature, such as retiree benefits, to that portion of the budget set aside for nonmilitary activities of the department (rivers and harbors, and so on) and as such represented only a paper savings. The General Staff offered real savings in the form of reductions in the existing establishment, including discontinuing certain categories of enlisted allowances, reduction of the Reserve Officers Training Corps and civilian military training camps, and reductions of both officer and enlisted strength. The report listed twenty-three reductions totaling $30 million. The staff cautioned the president that the reductions toward the end of the list might "seriously affect the size and state of training of the military establishment and, to that extent, actually jeopardize in some degree national defense."[19]

Not surprisingly the General Staff recommended Plan I to the president because it "provides the protection the nation ought to be afforded." Plan II, according to the staff, while providing "the same character of protection . . . slows up the time in which it could be put into operation to such a degree as to lay the nation liable to . . . dangers. . . ." The "dangers" associated with Plan II included "insufficient protection of our harbors, coasts, and frontiers," should the navy fail to "be completely successful in controlling the sea for a considerable period" after a war began.[20]

President Hoover received the report, classified "Secret," on November 7 and considered it to be for his personal use only. The report was never released or acted on as a packaged program. Copies went to some members of Congress, including the chairman of the House Subcommittee on War Department Appropriations. Some of the recommendations leaked out. Those involving strength reductions fueled press speculation briefly, but otherwise there was little interest in the report. In November 1929 attention was on the stock market panic.[21] Overtaken by the beginning of the Great Depression, the Survey of the Military Establishment was apparently forgotten, but many of the General Staff's twenty-three cost-saving recommendations, which were supposed to offset a pay increase, returned to haunt the army in the form of government economy schemes during the coming years.

Early in December President Hoover delivered his State of the Union message to Congress. Assessing national defense, he pronounced the army and navy fit but stated that he was "deeply concerned . . . at the growing expense." In an obvious reference to the requested pay increase Hoover observed that "the remuneration paid to our soldiers and sailors is justly at a higher rate than that of any other country in the world, and while the cost of subsistence is higher, yet the total of our expenditure is in excess of those of the most highly militarized nations in the world." Forgoing the pay increase would hold down costs. So would a reduction in the military budget, and in a reference to the Kellogg-Briand Pact the president implied that such a move might be considered.[22]

The next day, December 4, Hoover presented his administration's budget estimate for fiscal year 1931. The request totaled $3.8 billion, a slight decrease over 1930 appropriations. He also proposed an immediate tax reduction and demanded "a careful scrutiny of any . . . activities which would involve a material increase in expenditures in order that we may not jeopardize either the balanced . . . budget or . . . reduced taxation."[23]

After presenting his budget to Congress, Hoover held a news conference during which he released his "personal budget," a compilation of the federal budget that the president said would enable "the man in the street" to understand how his tax dollars were spent. Dubbed Hoover's "vest pocket" budget by the press, the document grouped government appropriations on a functional basis, according to four categories: fiscal affairs, social aids, machinery of government, and war. By consolidating appropriations for payments on the public debt, veterans, and national defense, the compilation showed that seventy-two cents of every tax dollar spent in fiscal 1930 was "devoted to payments for past wars and those that may occur in the future."[24]

Hoover's statements in December 1929 clearly indicated a desire to hold down government expenditures, especially military costs. The president enjoyed the support of some able allies in his effort to hold down military expenses. Hoover originally had appointed his 1928 campaign manager, James W. Good, an Iowa lawyer with many years of experience on the House Appropriations Committee, as his secretary of war. Good died in November 1929. He was replaced by Patrick J. Hurley, whom Hoover remembered as "a fighting Irishman with all the loyalties and the great personal charm of that inheritance. . . ."[25] Hurley was a wealthy Oklahoma oil lawyer. His military experience included service in the Oklahoma militia and as a legal officer on various staffs in France during the war. Hurley supposedly influenced Senator Charles Curtis's decision to run with Hoover in 1928, and he ran the Hoover-Curtis campaign in Oklahoma. This service earned him an appointment as assistant secretary of war under Good. But Hurley was ambitious. When Good died, Hurley actively sought the vacant office through Republican intermediaries.[26] As secretary of war, Hurley kept a close eye on army expenditures. One of his first official acts concerned the budget requests for fiscal year 1932, which were already being prepared by army planners. He ordered that the estimates be prepared with strict economy, that there be a "minimum of additional and continuing major projects," and that all departments present their estimates in order of priority.[27]

In seeking economy, Hoover could also count on the bipartisan support of the House Appropriations Committee. Republican William R. Wood of Indiana, who became committee chairman in 1929, was "in hearty accord" with Hoover's desire to reduce military spending. Speaking in August 1929, Wood declared, "We are further removed from war and the possibility of war than we have ever been since the foundation of the Republic. Yet we are better equipped to meet the eventualities of war than ever before. . . ." Wood directed most of his criticism toward obsolete programs and systems within the army. For example, he recommended abolishing the coast artillery. "The bombing planes have put the coast artillery out of business," he declared. He also proposed combining army departments such as finance with quartermaster and the Chemical Corps with ordnance to save money.[28]

Democrat Ross Collins of Mississippi also actively supported reductions in military spending. After 1930, when the Democrats gained control of Congress, Collins became chairman of the very important House Appropriations Subcommittee on Military Activities. Collins appreciated the army's desire to expand constantly, but he feared that Congress too frequently accepted military requests without question. He was concerned especially with finding "ways of eliminating useless expenditure. . . ." Collins believed that because "soldiering is a very old profession and has some very rigid traditions and attitudes, . . . officers are not always awake to changed conditions and often stick to old methods until forced to give them up." He singled out the cavalry as an "old method" especially resistant to change. "It is very easy for men who have ridden splendid horses all their lives to believe that in some way their learning to ride better will have some usefulness in wartime," he said. Collins was one of the first members of Congress to suggest that technology might be used as a substitute for manpower. Machines, he believed, were ultimately less costly than men or horses. Through mechanization he hoped to achieve not only a smaller, less expensive army but a more efficient one, too. Collins favored mechanization of ground warfare through the use of tanks. He also became an ardent supporter of army aviation, although here, too, he urged caution in procurement. Progress in aircraft design proceeded so rapidly, he said, that the army should avoid buying large numbers of planes that would become rapidly obsolete.[29]

None of those who supported economy in government through decreased defense costs could be considered antimilitary in the sense that the radical peace groups were. Men like Hoover and Collins did, however, differ with the army over what constituted an adequate military establishment and defense program. The army clearly had staked out its position in the Survey of the Military Establishment. Military strength was primarily a function of personnel. The army had learned to live with the reduction in strength of the 1920s, but was steadfastly opposed to any further manpower cuts. The General Staff was prepared to sacrifice virtually anything before it would give up another man, and in 1929 seemed to be making a more vigorous effort to recoup some of the losses of the past decade.

In the early months of 1930 the depression had not yet begun to grip the mind of the public or the government. The War Department's request of $367 million for strictly military activities for fiscal year 1931 aroused little attention. Congress approved $341 million for the army, the largest military budget since 1921.[30] The appropriation generally pleased the army, which was prepared to stabilize its spending at around $350 million according to the plan outlined in the Survey of the Military Establishment. But even before fiscal 1931 began in July 1930 the deepening depression doomed hopes for stabilization.

After the crash the stock market seemed to recover for a while. But the improved market was a chimera that belied more ominous indicators. Unemployment was rising. The Commerce Department's index of employment in manufacturing industries showed a steady decline from 101.9 in December 1929 to 97.0 by April 1930. By the end of 1930 the figure reached 83.8.[31] In human terms the index translated into 4.3 million unemployed, 8.7 percent of the work force in 1930. As if to confirm the other indicators, the stock market, where the Dow Jones industrial average had risen from 220.95 in November 1929 to 358.16 by April 1930, broke again and began a steady decline, closing the year with the Dow Jones industrial average at 209.23.[32]

The downward spiral had an immediate effect on the Hoover administration's efforts to balance the federal budget. Revenues declined. During fiscal 1931, receipts from income and profit taxes dropped 23 percent from approximately $2.4 to $1.8 billion.[33] The prospect of continuing decreased revenues forced Hoover to order spending by federal agencies held below 1931 appropriations. In September 1930, Hoover notified the army that it should limit its military and nonmilitary expenditures to $444 million, $65 million less than the amount appropriated. The president further specified that no expenditures be deferred from nonmilitary activities such as rivers and harbors projects.[34] The retrenchment order dashed plans for achieving a stabilized budget of $350 million.

The army reluctantly accepted the necessity of a reduced budget for fiscal 1932. Although it requested $351 million, the War Department made little objection when the Budget Bureau reduced the estimate to $340 million. Clearly, the military's leaders accepted their subordinate role in setting national priorities at this time of domestic crisis. Late in 1930,

Hurley and the new chief of staff, Douglas MacArthur, appeared before the House Subcommittee on Military Appropriations to testify on the revised budget request. Both acknowledged the requirement for the expenditure cuts. Hurley stated that the lower amount would permit the continuation of routine operations on an economical basis; MacArthur concurred.[35] Congress eventually pared the 1932 appropriation down to $336 million, and as the depression continued to worsen, the army, like the country, saw no relief in sight. As planning for fiscal 1933 began, Secretary of War Hurley notified the General Staff that he would not even present an estimate that exceeded $333 million.[36]

While planning for the 1933 budget went forward, another problem developed. By May 1931, it was obvious that reduced spending during the year had not been enough to stave off a budget deficit. To eliminate the impending deficit, President Hoover suggested a reduction in military personnel and the closing of some thirty bases. The army acquiesced to base closing but drew the line on personnel cuts.[37] The cumulative experience of strength reductions since the world war convinced army leaders that the absolute margin of safety had been reached. Any reduction below 12,000 officers and 118,750 enlisted men would make it impossible to carry out the multiple missions of the National Defense Act of 1920. The principal spokesman for the army's position was the chief of staff. Every chief since Payton C. March had warned of the dangers that would befall the nation if the army were reduced. When General Summerall retired on November 20, 1930, he was succeeded by an ardent defender of the cause of preserving manpower—General Douglas MacArthur.

MacArthur is one of the most complicated personalities in American military history. He was the son of Arthur MacArthur, a Civil War "boy colonel" who rose to be a lieutenant general. Douglas attended West Point and graduated first in his class in 1903. He was frustrated by some of his early assignments but in 1912 secured an assignment in the office of the chief of staff through the intervention of Leonard Wood, a friend of his parents. During the next five years in Washington in a variety of jobs, including working directly for Secretary of War Baker, MacArthur learned much about the inner workings of the War Department and made many important friends. When the United States entered World War I, he obtained a commission as a colonel of infantry in the national army. MacArthur emerged from the war a genuine hero and a brigadier general. During the 1920s, he served as superintendent of West Point, commander of the Third Corps Area, and president of the U.S. Olympic Committee during the Ninth Olympiad, and he served two tours of duty in the Philippines. In 1930 he was fifty years old and the youngest of the eleven major generals eligible to succeed Summerall as chief of staff. MacArthur received the recommendations of March, Summerall, and Hurley. Hoover announced his appointment to succeed Summerall on August 6, 1930.[38]

As commander of the Third Corps Area from 1925 to 1928, MacArthur had experienced firsthand the effects of appropriations and strength reductions on the army. Like many of his contemporaries he blamed the deterioration on pacifists and false economy.

In 1927 in an address to the annual convention of the Reserve Officers' Association, an ardent champion of preparedness, he lashed out at pacifist efforts toward continued disarmament declaring:

Pacific habits do not insure peace nor immunity from national insult and national aggression. Every nation that would preserve its tranquility, its riches, its independence, and its self-respect must keep alive its martial ardor and be at all times prepared to defend itself.

In a direct challenge to pacifist beliefs MacArthur asserted, "A warlike spirit, which alone can create and civilize a state, is absolutely essential to national defense and to national perpetuity." The Founding Fathers understood that principle, MacArthur continued.

Our first President . . . undertook to establish such military institutions as would not only secure the frontiers but insure [adequate preparedness]. . . . But even the influence of his great name was powerless to overcome the invincible prejudice against anything like an adequate military establishment.

In an obvious reference to the current state of the army MacArthur concluded, "What Washington failed to accomplish on behalf of an adequate military establishment has never been fully achieved by any of his successors."[39]

Shortly after he became chief of staff, MacArthur had another occasion to express his opinion on pacifism. Early in 1931 Henry Emerson Fosdick, pastor of the Riverside Church in New York City and a leading figure among Protestant pacifist clergymen in the United States, polled nearly 20,000 of his colleagues in all denominations concerning their views on war. The results, published in *The World Tomorrow,* revealed that 83 percent of the ministers opposed ROTC training, 80 percent favored further disarmament, 62 percent urged that their churches oppose any future participation of the United States in any war, and 54 percent refused to serve as combatants in any war. Kirby Page, editor of *The World Tomorrow,* asked MacArthur to comment on the poll. Characteristically MacArthur did so with vigor. He accused the ministers of exercising "privilege without assuming attendant responsibility and obligation. . . ." Jesus, the chief of staff asserted, required sacrifice of "certain priceless principles" of those who followed Him. Surely those principles included defense of national values. "History teaches us," MacArthur concluded, "that religion and patriotism have always gone hand in hand, while atheism has invariably been accompanied by radicalism, communism, bolshevism, and other enemies of free government."[40] Having thus stated his opinion on pacifism, the new chief of staff turned his attention to preserving what was left of the army until the opportunity for rebuilding it appeared.

The new chief of staff wholeheartedly supported the belief that the bottom had been reached in military reductions, whether for economic or pacifistic reasons. Above all, he concurred with the conventional wisdom that manpower levels were dangerously low. If forced to chose between men and materiel, MacArthur would, and did, sacrifice materiel. In the coming months this philosophy led to frequent clashes between MacArthur and those, like Ross Collins, who sought economy or increases in material readiness at the expense of personnel.[41]

Even after the depression increased the urgency for greater economy in government in the minds of those who sought reductions in military expenditures, MacArthur and the army found support for their efforts to preserve the military establishment from further cuts. The American Legion, for example, continued to oppose defense reductions even after the bonus incident of 1932 pitted regular army troops against veterans. Another influential lobby was the Reserve Officers' Association (ROA), composed of members of the Officers' Reserve Corps. Ross Collins considered the ROA "the most powerful political wing of the whole Army, . . . [because] these officers are in civil life scattered throughout the country, and in the various Government departments. . . ."[42] John C. O'Laughlin's *Army and Navy Journal* remained an ever vigilant watchdog over Congress and the administration and was quick to protest the merest suggestion of reductions affecting personnel. The *New York Times*, undoubtedly reflecting the views of assistant publisher Julius Ochs Adler, himself a member of the Officers' Reserve Corps, also opposed any further cuts in strength or appropriations that might affect the readiness of the army.

MacArthur apparently convinced Hoover in May 1931 to abandon the personnel cut proposed for the 1933 budget. But the issue of further personnel reductions for the sake of economy was far from dead.

In December 1931 the new Democratic Seventy-second Congress took up the 1933 military appropriations bill. The Hoover administration was already under Democratic fire for the 1931 deficit, and looking ahead to the 1932 elections, the congressmen on the Appropriations Committee could not have overlooked the political value of reducing military spending. The issue of strength reductions surfaced immediately. Nearly half of the $329 million requested was for pay and allowances. The obvious place to begin cost reductions was with personnel.

After public hearings during which Chairman Joseph W. Byrns of the House Appropriations Committee and Ross Collins, chairman of the Subcommittee on War Department Appropriations, both urged savings through troop reductions, the subcommittee went into closed executive session. The *Army and Navy Journal* gloomily predicted, "it is possible that the committee will work for the elimination of 1000 officers and 8750 enlisted men—or more if it can be achieved."[43] The subcommittee remained in closed session until May. Throughout the three-month period speculation on the bill ran high. Preparing for the worst, the army lobbied strenuously against any strength reduction. On January 30, Secretary Hurley made a personal plea to House Speaker John Nance Garner to oppose the reduction. Citing the recent developments in Manchuria, Hurley advised Garner that the world situation was too uncertain to permit such a move. Apparently Hurley's visit turned the tide. The following day the subcommittee announced that it no longer intended to drop 8,750 enlisted men from the ranks of the regular army.[44] Plans to eliminate up to 2,000 officers remained unchanged; the struggle continued.

As usual, the *Army and Navy Journal* waged the battle for the service. Army Day, April 6, 1932, the fifteenth anniversary of American entry in the world war, provided an opportunity for opponents of defense reductions to express their views. Surveying Army Day editorials, the *Journal* reported considerable opposition to further cuts. The *Indianapolis Star* told its readers:

The annual event serves to remind American citizens of the part the Regular Army plays in our national defense. . . . Due to the pounding of pacifist agitators and the need of utmost economy, the Regular Army already has been reduced to the point of imperiling the national security. . . . Efforts to cripple the efficiency of the meager establishment that remains should be stoutly resisted.

The Xenia, Ohio, *Gazette* declared, "We owe it to the Regular Army . . . to see that it is respected and not maligned and that it is maintained on a basis adequate to the duty it is expected to perform."[45]

Collins's subcommittee reported the bill on May 5, 1932. The bill proposed to appropriate $281 million for military expenses and provided for the reduction of the officer corps to 10,000. The bill also sought to achieve savings by eliminating funds for ROTC and organized reserve summer training and suspending civilian military training camps for a year.[46] Commenting on the cuts, the *New York Times* editorialized, "If adopted they would mean drastic reductions of personnel and of military activities in one form or another." The *Times,* no doubt reflecting Julius Ochs Adler's interest in the civilian components, felt the regular army could do with 2,000 fewer officers but deplored the cuts in civilian activities saying, "One reason we can have so small a standing army . . . is that provision was made for temporary training of officers ready to serve in a national emergency. . . . Abruptly to cut off this source of supply . . . would go counter to one of the purposes of the National Defense Act."[47]

Opposition to Collins's reductions surfaced immediately. Representative Henry Barbour of California, former Republican chairman of the War Department Appropriations Subcommittee, led the fight against Collins in the House. National Guard and organized reserve interests quickly and easily restored the cuts in funds for summer training of civilian components. Pay for organized reserve training was restored by a vote of 218 to 167. The House also overruled Collins on ROTC summer camps and the civilian military training camp program 236 to 151 and 243 to 141 respectively.[48] Summer training for civilians meant temporary "employment" for a substantial number of citizens in virtually every congressional district, and the congressmen were no doubt aware of the fact that for many of their constituents reserve pay would be the only money coming in during the summer before the elections of 1932.

Barbour was unable to move his colleagues on the matter of officer reductions. The House approved the proposed 2,000-man cut by a vote of 201 to 182 and sent the bill to the Senate.

The army launched a major campaign to defeat the provision. Hurley and MacArthur conducted a letter-writing campaign designed to convince both the Senate and the public of the necessity for a larger peacetime officer corps. In an open letter to Bertrand Snell, of Potsdam, New York, minority leader of the House, MacArthur indirectly accused Ross Collins of deceit for failing to mention his plans for an officer reduction during the hearings on the bill and thus depriving the army the opportunity to state its case properly. "Skilled officers," the chief of staff wrote, "are products of continuous and laborious study, training and experience. There is no short cut to the particular type of knowledge and ability they must possess." MacArthur reminded his readers that the army was already below the strength level the War Department considered "the minimum peace strength" of 14,000 officers and 165,000 enlisted men necessary to "carry out the missions assigned by the National Defense Act. . . . An army can live on short rations, it can even be poorly armed and equipped," MacArthur added, "but in action it is doomed to destruction without the trained and adequate leadership of officers." Driving home his point, the chief of staff concluded, "Further reductions would bring us to prostration—a condition not conducive to the promotion of a feeling of security at home nor to enhancing the respect with which our pacific counsels are received abroad."[49]

When it reached the Senate, the proposal to cut 2,000 officers from the regular army became the object of a vigorous lobbying effort. During hearings on the army appropriation bill contingents from the National Guard Association, the Reserve Officers' Association, and the American Legion opposed the reduction. The American Federation of Labor also objected to the proposed cut on the grounds that it would lead to the closing of the Philadelphia uniform factory. Spokesmen for the American Medical and Dental Association testified on behalf of army doctors and dentists who were included in the ranks of those officers to be eliminated. The *Army and Navy Journal* followed the hearings and supported the army with an editorial campaign that accused supporters of the reduction of pacifism, socialism, and communism.[50]

The Senate Committee on Appropriations unanimously restored the 2,000 officers. During the floor debate on the appropriation bill it became evident that few senators supported a reduction in strength of any sort. Senator Millard Tydings of Maryland argued briefly for economy and summarized the feelings of those who favored the reduction saying that the army could get along with 10,000 officers, and "if there is anything we could get along without now without serious impairment of our national defense, this is the time to adopt it. . . ." David Reed of Pennsylvania, chairman of the Military Affairs Committee pointed out persuasively that, because most of the 2,000 officers concerned would be retired at three-quarters pay, the savings would be minimal. Besides, he added, "we would be paying [them] hereafter 75 percent of what we are paying now, and getting nothing whatever in return for it." The Senate voted 51 to 16 to retain the 2,000 officers.[51]

In conference Ross Collins stubbornly refused to yield on the reductions, and the impasse kept the appropriations bill bottled up into July. But pressure from interests opposed to the cut continued to mount, and on July 12, the House reversed itself and voted against Collins 175 to 154.[52]

An analysis of the votes on the attempt to reduce army strength in 1932 suggests that the issue was largely a partisan one, but regional differences also influenced the decision. In the House 52 Republicans and 102 Democrats favored dropping 2,000 officers from the regular army's rolls; 118 Republicans and 57 Democrats opposed the measure. Nearly all of the Republicans who voted for the reduction came from rural, farm or mountain states. Democrats who voted to retain the officers represented northern, urban or industrial districts. In the Senate a similar pattern prevailed. All of the sixteen senators (eight from each party) who favored the cut were from rural midwestern, southern, or mountain states. They included William E. Borah of Idaho, Arthur Capper of Kansas, Robert LaFollette, Jr., of Wisconsin, and George Norris of Nebraska, men who had consistently voted for a small army since 1919.[53] Sentiment for the measure appeared strongest among representatives and senators from insular states where old populist or states' rights attitudes concerning big government and traditional antimilitary and isolationist views continued to prevail.

While the army successfully maintained its strength in 1932, it lost a significant round in terms of preserving pay and allowances. On June 23, 1932, the Senate passed the omnibus economy bill and sent it to the president for signature. The new law required officers and employees of the federal government to take a one-month furlough without pay during fiscal year 1933. Retired pay of officers and employees was reduced 8⅓ percent, and "automatic increases in compensation by reason of length of service or promotion" were suspended for the fiscal year.[54] Enlisted men were exempted from the provisions of the act.

The Economy Act of June 1932 evolved from a series of bills introduced in Congress during the first session of the Seventy-second Congress designed to reduce government deficit spending. One such bill, sponsored by Senator William E. Borah, proposed to reduce the salaries of government employees receiving between $3,000 and $10,000 annually by 10 percent; salaries over $10,000 would be reduced 20 percent.[55] Initially Congress seemed reluctant to reduce federal salaries, but in late January 1932, President Hoover reportedly informed House leaders that he was not opposed to a pay cut. The *Army and Navy Journal* reported that:

With the President inclining to salary cuts, conditions are favorable to a pay cut. The only hope of defeat lies in the fear of politicians that reduction in pay of federal employees will infuriate the rural free delivery carriers, city delivery carriers, agricultural department agents and the like, and cause them trouble in the forthcoming campaign.[56]

In its final form, however, the Economy Act of 1932 cut no one's pay directly. For the army the Economy Act affected only officers and those about to retire. But, like the renewed efforts for reductions in strength, the attempted pay cut profoundly affected the morale of the regular army. The air of uncertainty that had existed during the protracted debates over reorganization and strength reductions between 1919 and 1923 had returned. During the early part of 1932, for example, when it appeared likely that Congress would slash army appropriations and strength, Henry L. Stevens, national commander of the American Legion, publicly warned that the shaky world situation combined with an already understrength army and navy produced conditions "worse that they were in 1914 just prior to the outbreak of the World War. . . ." Stevens declared that the deterioration of the army resulting from low budgets in the 1920s had already reduced it to the point where the National Guard, not the regular army, was the first line of defense; the army, he said, consisted of nothing more than "highly trained technicians." Further reductions, Stevens concluded, would demoralize the guard as well as diminish what remained of the army.[57]

While the whole army suffered with the uncertainty of pay cuts and strength reductions in the early summer of 1932, units in Washington, D.C., participated in the dispersal of the Bonus Expeditionary Force, undoubtedly the most unfortunate incident of the Great Depression and one that brought little glory or cheer to the regular army. The army's role in breaking up the Bonus March was highly visible. While the incident served to discredit the Hoover administration further, it also besmirched the army through guilt by association.[58] As the depression continued to deepen, the army's participation in the dispersal of the Bonus Expeditionary Force was something it certainly could have done without. Many of the marchers were American Legionnaires, and the army could ill afford to lose the support of that organization. Secretary of War Hurley was

booed at the legion's national convention in September 1932 as he tried to
mend political fences for the administration, and there is little doubt that
the bonus incident cost Hoover dearly at the polls in terms of veteran
votes.[59]

In November the people ratified the failure of the Hoover administration. Franklin D. Roosevelt and his proffered "New Deal" represented an
ambiguous if not unknown quantity to the army. The Democratic platform
pledged to maintain "a Navy and an Army adequate for national defense,"
but also promised to examine the military establishment in an effort to
reduce costs which were "fast approaching a billion dollars annually."[60]
Roosevelt, declared the platform, "Honest to the core," and pledged to
cut the cost of government operations by one-quarter. But the *Army and
Navy Journal* pointed out that the combined costs of the army, navy, and
Marine Corps for fiscal year 1933 totaled only about $600 million and
accused the Democrats of being dishonest with the American people.[61]

During the interregnum the *Journal* suggested that the new president
would encounter difficulties in reducing army costs. "Mr. Roosevelt," it
observed, ". . . [is] confronted with the pledge to reduce all appropriations
25% and on the other hand with the political need of complying with the
current public opinion in favor of adequate support for the Army and the
Navy."[62] The *Journal* based its sanguine view of public opinion on the
response of the press to General MacArthur's recently released annual
report on the army in 1932. In that report, MacArthur summarized the
efforts to reduce the army during the previous fiscal year. Referring to the
"tense situation in the Far East" and the lack of progress toward disarmament at Geneva, MacArthur noted, "the United States has already
accomplished a degree of reduction in its land forces that stands as a
unique example among world powers." Further disarmament, he warned,
would have to wait for similar cuts by other nations. In view of the fact
that the United States Army ranked only sixteenth in size compared to
other armies, MacArthur felt that the nation had done enough. The chief
of staff did acknowledge that "the increased severity of the prolonged
economic depression, . . . a growing Treasury deficit . . . [and] . . . the
necessity for retrenchment has become so great as to constitute a dominant
factor in the shaping of national policy." But he repeated his opposition
to such measures as reductions in strength and curtailment of civilian
activities. "The inevitable effect of some of these proposals," he said,
"would be increased immediate and future expense for the United
States."[63]

At the same time pacifist and antimilitarist groups continued to demand
further reductions of American armaments and military forces and erro-
neously saw in Roosevelt support for their causes. The conservatives of
the peace movement, who were essentially Wilsonian internationalists,
pinned their hopes on the London Economic Conference and the World

Disarmament Conference at Geneva. Both Hoover and Roosevelt were associated with the internationalists. But during the 1932 campaign Roosevelt, in an effort to placate the strong isolationist wing in the Democratic party, played down his Wilsonian heritage. In February 1932, for example, Roosevelt told a New York farm organization that the League of Nations no longer reflected Wilson's vision and that he did not support U.S. membership in it. And during the interregnum between the 1932 election and Roosevelt's inauguration, the president-elect coolly rebuffed Hoover's overtures for a joint effort to get the stalled disarmament conference moving and establish the machinery for the economic conference at London.[64] Roosevelt's subsequent refusal to support international currency stabilization effectively wrecked the London conference in June 1933, and the when Hitler withdrew Germany from the League of Nations, the other hope of the internationalists, the Geneva Disarmament Conference, was doomed.

The more radical elements of the peace movement continued to demand unilateral arms and force reductions, and Roosevelt's denunciations of the Hoover deficits and promise to cut government spending appeared to offer indirect support for American disarmament. Militant pacifism was on the rise in the early 1930s in response to a deterioration of the world order evidenced by the Manchurian crisis and the rise of totalitarianism in Europe. Religious leaders and prominent pacifists proclaimed their refusal to sanction war and continued to attack vigorously symbols of militarism in America such as ROTC. College students pledged not to participate in war and staged annual campus demonstrations against war and preparedness.[65]

But as virile as antimilitarism was in the 1930s, it was not the dominant sentiment of the day. When Franklin D. Roosevelt became president, the state of the domestic economy overshadowed all other concerns. Americans wanted peace in order to give themselves the chance to rebuild the economy, and in their desire for peace most American shunned Wilsonian internationalism. But they stopped short of pacifism. Although pacifist groups continued to lobby hard for disarmament and rejection of war in the 1930s and enjoyed some triumphs in the Nye committee hearings, they received attention disproportionate to their influence, because, as Dorothy Detzer of the Women's International League for Peace and Freedom noted, "the newspapers loved it."[66] If pacifists and antimilitarists saw support for their cause in early New Deal economic policies, they were sadly mistaken, for Roosevelt was also a "big navy" supporter, and the trend in American isolationism was not toward peace at all costs but toward armed neutrality.

Pacifists, however, did discover an even bigger asset than fear of war: pressures for economy stemming from depression. Amid these pressures for economy in government it was perhaps inevitable that there was no "new deal" for the army. Fiscal year 1933 had already begun with reduced spending, when in December 1932 Hoover's lame-duck administration presented its budget proposals for fiscal year 1934. Under orders to reduce spending further, the Budget Bureau cut War Department requests for 1934 from $319 million to $278.6 million, some $27.1 million less than appropriated for fiscal 1933. As its final act the Seventy-second Congress approved $270 million for the army on March 3, 1933.[67] In another last-minute act the Seventy-second Congress continued the furlough pay-cut plan for another year and extended it to include enlisted men who earned more than $1,000 a year.[68] In both cases a clear desire to achieve a balanced budget through economy in government, not pacifism, motivated Congress. The floor debates in both houses reveal no antimilitary undertones.

This strong, bipartisan bloc for economy included conservatives as well as Democrats who would soon be loyal to the New Deal. Thus, Hamilton Fish, Jr., a conservative New York Republican, argued, "The Republicans and Democrats have a joint responsibility to try to restore confidence in the country, and we cannot restore business or industry unless the Budget is balanced, unless the credit of the United States is maintained above any question of suspicion." The military budget, Fish implied, was a good place to start. Ross Collins, who managed the bill in the House, reiterated his belief that modern armies required material, not masses of personnel. "The only way in the world . . . you can give to this country adequate military preparedness and not impoverish the people of the country by the levying of taxes that they cannot stand is to cut down on personnel and put your savings in effective machines which we call material," he said. In the present depression savings realized on personnel cuts could be deferred to balance the budget.[69]

The overwhelming desire to find solutions to the consequences of the depression even diverted the attention of such enthusiastic antimilitarists as Senators William E. Borah of Idaho and Robert LaFollette, Jr., of Wisconsin, both strenuous opponents of the "big army" bill of Peyton March and UMT in 1919 and 1920 and supporters of army reductions throughout the 1920s. When Senator James Couzens of Michigan proposed an amendment to the army appropriation bill that would have added $22 million for the purpose of augmenting the civilian military training camp program by providing space for 88,000 unemployed military-aged males, Borah supported the measure. LaFollette, who objected "to the method [Couzens] seeks to employ to meet the problem of the transient youth," also voted for the amendment because of his urgent desire to do something "to stop the spread of hunger, starvation, want, destitution, cold, and the breakdown of health in the United States."[70] The amendment failed to receive the support of the House in conference largely because of objections from the army that it was not equipped to handle the burden of the additional youths in the civilian military training summer camp program.[71]

The climax of the effort to find solutions to the depression through economy in government and a balanced federal budget came in 1933–1934. As if to outdo earlier congressional money-saving schemes, the new Roosevelt administration immediately stunned the army with three quick blows aimed at reducing costs. Three weeks after Congress approved the appropriation bill for 1934, Lewis Douglas, Roosevelt's budget chief, directed that $90 million be trimmed from the military budget. About the same time the furlough plan was scrapped in favor of a more comprehensive economy act, which reduced the pay of all federal employees by as much as 15 percent and froze all employees at their present pay levels. Both provisions included all enlisted men. Finally, in mid-April, Roosevelt asked Congress for authority to furlough officers on half pay, stating that he intended to order between 3,000 and 4,000 army officers off active duty. The *Army and Navy Journal* reported erroneously that FDR also intended to cancel enlistment contracts and reduce the regular army by between 13,000 and 25,000 men.[72]

For all its alleged concern about the welfare of its personnel, the War Department offered no resistance to the pay cut, which was swiftly approved by Congress. But it fought stiffly against the budget cut and officer furlough plan. MacArthur attributed the new officer furlough plan, which the administration included as part of the independent offices appropriation bill, to the work of a "pacifist element in Congress."[73] He lobbied against it with untiring determination. Speaking before the House Military Affairs Committee in late April, he said:

> If you have to cut everything out of the National Defense Act, the last element should be the Officer Corps. If you had to discharge every soldier, if you had to do away with everything else, I would still professionally advise you to keep these 12,000 officers. They are the mainspring of the whole mechanism, each one of them would be worth a thousand men at the beginnng of a war. They are the only ones who can take this heterogeneous mass and make of it a homogeneous fighting group.[74]

MacArthur's apparently callous reference to preferring enlisted cuts to officer reductions was clearly a reflection of Uptonian principles and reveals much about his and the army's attitude toward the relationship between manpower and military preparedness. The regular army officer corps embodied the collective military expertise of the profession of arms. It had to be preserved at all costs. Troops and materiel were important in peacetime, too, but only as vehicles for the continued progressive training and development of officers, who would provide the nucleus of an expanded citizen army in wartime.

MacArthur enjoyed some support within the Roosevelt administration. President Roosevelt's secretary of war was George Dern, former governor of Utah. Dern knew little of the army and suffered from poor health. These two conditions undoubtedly contributed to the ease with which the smooth MacArthur won the new secretary's confidence. Together they waged a tough inside fight against the proposed reduction.[75]

As usual, the *Army and Navy Journal* objected to the cuts. The journal charged the new administration with endangering the nation's security, pointing out, "with war talk in Europe, with popular indignation in Japan aroused against the United States, it is the solemn business of the President and the Congress at least to maintain the present insufficient strength."[76]

Unmoved and loyal to President Roosevelt, the House on May 12 passed the independent offices appropriation bill with the furlough provision by a vote of 249 to 118. MacArthur continued the fight with the aid of the *Army and Navy Journal,* which urged its readers to write to legislators and the president protesting the move. "The President should know that the country is for National Defense," the *Journal* cried.

Write him, telegraph him. Through organizations, patriotic, business, commercial, social, by petitions signed by individuals, by personal communications, demand that he abandon purposes which would make our protection hardly able to assist in the preservation of public order much less resist invasion, and wholly contemptible from the point of view of foreign nations which want to grind their axes at our expense.

Civic groups and patriotic organizations continued to deluge Washington with statements opposing the furlough plan. Even the Florida legislature protested, passing a resolution that declared:

. . . [T]he Legislature of the State of Florida believes . . . that the present officer personnel of the Regular Army is needed to properly train the National Guard, Reserve Officers' Training Corps, citizens' military training camps, and Officers' Reserve Corps. . . .[77]

Faced with such strenuous opposition, Congress and the administration backed down. On May 30, the Senate, without debate or roll call, dropped the furlough plan. The same day, after a five-hour conference with Budget Director Douglas, who was the principal supporter of the plan within the administration, General MacArthur jubilantly wired all major army headquarters: "There will be no cut in the strength of the Army either in officers or enlisted men. Inform all ranks." The *Army and Navy Journal* declared:

Across the black clouds which have hung threateningly over the Army, the Navy, and the Marine Corps has appeared a rainbow. . . . To all who responded to the appeals addressed to them to communicate their protests to the President and his advisors we express . . . sincere and appreciative gratitude. . . .[78]

While the strength of the army had been saved, the proposed $90 million budget cut remained. The administration plan to cut army appropriations for fiscal 1934 to around $196 million drastically reduced the activities of the civilian components of the army. During the infighting over the proposal MacArthur and Secretary Dern conferred directly with Roosevelt. Dern warned the president that such cuts, coming as Germany and Italy were rearming and as Japan was continuing its conquest of Manchuria and China, would dangerously weaken the nation's defense. The president was unmoved. MacArthur recalled:

I felt it my duty to take up the cudgels. The country's safety was at stake, and I said so bluntly. The President turned the full vials of his sarcasm upon me. He was a scorcher when aroused. The tension began to boil over. . . . In my emotional exhaustion I spoke recklessly and said something to the general effect that when we lost the next war, and an American boy, lying in the mud with an enemy bayonet through his belly and an enemy foot on his dying throat, spat out his last curse, I wanted the name not to be MacArthur, but Roosevelt. The President grew livid. "You must not talk that way to the President!" he roared. He was, of course, right, and I knew it almost before the words had left my mouth. I said that I was sorry and apologized. But I felt my career was at an end. I told him he had my resignation as Chief of Staff. As I reached the door his voice came with that cool detachment which so reflected his extraordinary self-control, "Don't be foolish Douglas; you and the budget must get together on this."
Dern had shortly reached my side and I could hear his gleeful tones, "You've saved the Army." But I just vomited on the steps of the White House.[79]

The army and budget got together as Roosevelt directed and on June 10, 1933, agreed upon a figure of $225 million, $75 million less than in fiscal 1933. The cuts resulted in the suspension of regular army field training for the year; National Guard field training remained at two weeks, but armory drills were cut from forty to between twelve and twenty nights a year. The reduction also eliminated ROTC and civilian military training camps summer activities. The *Army and Navy Journal* called the compromise "Another victory in the fight to maintain at least a semblance of the principles of the National Defense Act. . . ."[80]
Whether MacArthur had "saved the army" is debatable. He certainly did not think so at the time. On June 13 he addressed the graduating class at West Point. Undoubtedly comfortable in home territory, he took the occasion to lash out at "The unabashed and unsound propaganda of the peace cranks [which] leads to muddled thinking." Warming to his subject, the chief of staff continued, "as the necessity of National Defense is sacrificed in the name of economy, the United States presents a tempting spectacle" and predicted that the possibility for another war existed "if hard common sense is not substituted for petty provincial politics."[81]
It is also doubtful that MacArthur's intercession with FDR was decisive.

One student of the period speculates that the president changed his mind because "being a consummate pragmatist and political tactician, he undoubtedly realized that he would need the Army's support and willing cooperation to bring off the CCC [Civilian Conservation Corps] program successfully."[82] The summer of 1933 was upon the New Deal, and the army was already intimately involved with the CCC. Combined with the outcry against the furlough plan and other military cuts, the need for army cooperation is the most plausible explanation.

The Civilian Conservation Corps represented one of the New Deal's first efforts to provide work relief for large numbers of America's unemployed. The plan for the CCC combined Roosevelt's desire to relieve unemployment with a long-stated interest in conservation. Whether intended or not, the CCC also removed large numbers of able-bodied military-age men from the ranks of potential mobs in an hour of national desperation.

The original plan called for limited army involvement. As presidential adviser Louis Howe envisioned it, the army would enroll and process the recruits and put them through a two-week physical conditioning program and transport them to the camps, where the Forest Service would take over. FDR's goal was to have 250,000 enrollees in the camps by July 1. But organizational and administrative problems hampered the effort, and the army was asked to take over a greater share of the project. On May 10, the General Staff turned its full attention to the CCC and worked out a plan for mobilizing and running the entire program that would meet the president's deadline. Two days later the army's plan was approved.[83]

The army did not seek such a large role for itself in unemployment relief in general or the CCC in particular. During the Hoover administration the War Department had expressed reluctance even to assume a much smaller burden in the form of an expanded civilian military training camp program proposed in the Couzens bill. But MacArthur was no fool. As the New Deal began to take shape in March and April and as it became obvious that a mobilization effort such as only the army could manage would be required to make the CCC work, the chief of staff must have seen the opportunity to help the army by making it indispensable to the New Deal. Furthermore, MacArthur, who was deeply concerned about the strength of the army, could not have overlooked the potential of the CCC as a reserve force or recruiting pool for the regular army.

During the coming summer months the army diverted virtually every resource to the CCC. Service schools, ROTC and civilian military training summer camps, reserve and National Guard training camps, and regular army units within the United States were stripped of officers and noncommissioned officers. Supplies, vehicles, and other items of equipment were sent to the conditioning and work camps. But the tremendous effort paid off. By the July 1 target date nearly 220,000 enrollees were in some 1,315 work camps.[84] It is doubtful that the CCC could have succeeded without the army, and the army knew it. In his report of army activities during fiscal 1933 MacArthur reminded everyone that the army's role in mobilizing the CCC demonstrated

. . . the value of systematic preparation for emergency, including the maintenance of trained personnel and suitable supplies and the development of plans and policies applicable to a mobilization.[85]

Its role in mobilizing and operating the CCC did much to improve the army's image after the Bonus March. Indeed, the participation of the military in the CCC as a relief effort gave the army a peacetime visibility that it seldom had before the cold war.

As the operation of the CCC became routine, reserve officers were substituted for regulars. Not all army officers agreed, though, that regular officers should be completely phased out of the CCC. In late 1935, when Colonel Duncan Major, the army representative on the CCC Advisory Council, toured the corps's facilities, he found that the regular army officers and agencies involved with the CCC showed considerable interest in the project and felt that the army's role in it should be continued. Major recommended that every company-grade officer in the regular army spend at least six months on CCC duty because it presented an extraordinary peacetime opportunity for leadership and administrative training.[86] Command of a CCC camp gave junior officers experience in managing men and resources similar to that which they could expect commanding small military units. Since there were not enough units in the small regular army for every officer to get an opportunity at command, the CCC offered a possible alternative.

The army's interest in the CCC extended beyond its potential value as a training ground for officers. Although originally hostile to any role in relief activities, the General Staff quickly saw the corps as a possible source of an enlisted reserve if appropriately developed. But the idea proved troublesome for the army, which was especially concerned that it not lay itself open to charges of militarism that surely would follow the advocacy of such a plan. So sensitive was the army to this issue that when the National Rifle Association proposed to inaugurate recreational shooting at CCC camps and even offered to provide the arms and ammunition, the War Department felt obliged to disapprove of the offer. And in January 1934, when Assistant Secretary of War (later Secretary of War) Harry H. Woodring suggested in an article in *Liberty Magazine* that the CCC and the army's role in it be expanded to include giving the enrollees military training, a storm of protest arose. Liberals from around the country wrote to FDR demanding Woodring's resignation. Roosevelt declined to fire Woodring but did take the occasion to state his opposition to such a scheme.[87]

Despite the obvious pitfalls of suggesting a military role for the CCC and a general reluctance on the part of the War Department to raise the issue, MacArthur broached the subject in 1935. He proposed the CCC enrollees be given the option to volunteer for two months of military training upon the expiration of their six months of service in the corps. After such training the enrollee could join an auxiliary enlisted reserve. Introduced as a bill by John McSwain, chairman of the House Military Affairs Committee, MacArthur's plan drew severe criticism. The Committee on Militarism in Education, the antimilitary organization that opposed compulsory ROTC, vigorously opposed the idea and demanded the complete withdrawal of the army from all CCC activities. The bill quickly died in committee, and the army returned to its previous position of avoiding charges of militarizing the CCC.[88] In the late 1930s when preparedness groups began to suggest military training schemes for the CCC similar to MacArthur's, the War Department resisted the temptation to reenter the debate. By then military appropriations and strength were again on the rise, and the army could avoid getting involved in diversions from professional development.[89] But the army continued to share the task of mobilizing, training, and equipping enrollees and running the camps until the CCC's demise in 1942.

As the army tried to cope with the retrenchment of the fiscal 1934 budget and its expanded responsibilities with the CCC, work began on the fiscal 1935 budget. In the spring of 1933 the War Department Budget Advisory Committee submitted an estimate of $331 million to MacArthur as the minimum amount necessary for a "coordinated and well balanced military program" in the fiscal year beginning July 1, 1934.[90] By autumn the Bureau of the Budget whittled this estimate down to about $246 million and forwarded it to Congress. During hearings on the bill MacArthur observed that while "in view of the current economic situation . . . the estimates . . . provide for essentials, . . . little progress in developing the Military Establishment may be expected."[91] The chief of staff restated for Ross Collins's subcommittee the familiar minimum needs of the War Department, which began with an increase in strength to 165,000 enlisted men for the regular army, a strength of 210,000 for the National Guard, and 120,000 for the Officers' Reserve Corps, with adequate funds for training and equipment for all.[92]

Despite MacArthur's urging, Congress refused to question continued retrenchment in military spending. The final budget, approved in conference in April 1934, provided for about $316 million for military activities. The increase over the administration figure represented flood control projects of an essentially nonmilitary nature.[93]

Congress did not completely overlook MacArthur's renewed quest for a 165,000-man regular army in 1934. In April 1934 Representative Clark Thompson of Texas, introduced a bill to enlist 25,000 men annually for three years as an unemployment relief measure.[94] Testifying on the bill before the House Military Affairs Committee, MacArthur took the opportunity to air again his views on the strength of the army. Observing that the entire regular army could be crowded into Yankee Stadium, the chief of staff lamented, "With our present little Regular Army we would be relatively helpless in the event of an invasion by a major power." He added that "the difference between what we have now and what is proposed in this bill marks the difference between relative helplessness and a chance to accomplish our mission of defense." Concluding his testimony, MacArthur employed a tone frequently found in later addresses when he implored, "Pass this bill, Mr. Chairman, I beg of you, as an old soldier who has probably seen his last battlefield. Pass this bill and give the American Army a chance in the next battle it fights for the life of the country."[95] In later testimony before the Senate MacArthur gave Congress a good reason for expanding the army to combat unemployment. Bringing in unemployed men as privates would cost the government about a dollar a day per man. "There is no method that I know of which has been devised in the efforts the government has made to relieve unemployment that would do it so cheaply," he said.[96]

The Thompson bill received enthusiastic support from Secretary of War Dern, General Pershing, former Secretary of War Baker, and other prominent military figures even though the War Department opposed the one-year enlistment feature of the bill as expensive and inefficient. Content, for the present, with an army of 118,750 men, Roosevelt's administration showed no interest in the bill, and although it created a brief flurry of activity and comment in the press, the bill never emerged from committee.[97]

The army's interest in the Thompson bill is noteworthy. Prior to 1934 the War Department had expressly opposed schemes for using the army as an unemployment relief agency. The army had also scrupulously avoided proposals to militarize the CCC, MacArthur's interest in the corps notwithstanding. And even MacArthur saw voluntary military training for the CCC only as a means of improving the reserve system. He, too, as he stated many times, preferred an increase in the strength of the regular army. The Thompson bill represented the first proposal to raise the strength of the army to be considered by a congressional committee since the post–World War I reductions began. The army had been pleading for a 165,000-man enlisted force since 1928. Little wonder that the War Department jumped to support the bill despite its objections to the feature of one-year enlistments for unemployment relief. Although the Thompson bill never got out of committee, it marked a significant step on the road to reviving the military establishment. Congress had demonstrated its willingness to discuss a strength increase.

Apparently heartened by congressional disposal to consider an expanded force, the War Department prepared a request of $341 million for fiscal year 1936. Most of the increase over previous annual requests was earmarked to pay for a regular army enlisted force of 165,000 men. Predictably the Bureau of the Budget immediately reduced the request by eliminating $20 million projected for the strength increase.[98]

Roosevelt had just extended MacArthur's term as chief of staff through the first legislative session of the Seventy-fourth Congress (1935). The president did so over the objections of numerous liberals at the specific request of House and Senate leaders who believed that MacArthur's expertise in legislative procedure and views on military preparedness would be valuable in the coming session.[99] MacArthur could not have been unaware of the conflicting interests involved in his extension, and knowledge of the fact that this budget fight would be his last emboldened him.

In his appearance before the House Subcommittee on Military Appropriations in January 1935, MacArthur reviewed the strength and appropriations reductions that had emasculated the National Defense Act. In his testimony the chief of staff made it clear that the Bureau of the Budget's estimates did not represent army desires. In openly challenging the administration budget, MacArthur, in the opinion of one student of the period, bordered on insubordination.[100] While he indicated that all of the budgetary items were important to the army, the chief of staff stressed restoration of the strength increase.

By 1935 Congress and the nation were more willing to listen to military professionals like MacArthur who warned that the United States's defense system was inadequate. Germany had already left the League of Nations and repudiated the Treaty of Versailles. Japan had abrogated the Washington Naval Arms Treaty. Both nations were arming rapidly. Italy, too, was building up its armed forces and making plans to strike Ethiopia. Commenting on these developments, the *Philadelphia Inquirer* observed, "However little the United States may be inclined to intervene in international affairs, and however pacific its ideals, it cannot allow its defenses to be endangered and expect to be unmolested." In the same vein, the *Washington Herald* declared, "There is no substitute for adequate preparedness and to be adequate it must be equal to the strongest in all the essentials of defense."[101]

While the House Appropriations Committee worked on the army budget, the strength increase got a boost from the Military Affairs Committee. On January 31, 1935, that body approved a bill sponsored by Representative R. Ewing Thomason of Texas providing for an increase of 50,000 enlisted men in the strength of the regular army, to be spread over a five-year period.[102] MacArthur's bold defense of the 165,000-man figure, deteriorating world conditions, and the Military Affairs Committee approval of the Thomason bill moved the Appropriations Committee to disregard

Roosevelt's budget estimate for the army and recommend the largest appropriation bill since 1921. The committee voted $379 million for the War Department, $319 million of which was for strictly military purposes.[103]

The House approved the bill, which included the long-sought strength increase, but amended it to give the president discretionary authority to carry out the enlargement.[104] The amendment, sponsored by administration supporters, clearly threatened any expansion in personnel. MacArthur immediately turned his attention to the Senate to get the provision struck from the appropriation bill. MacArthur advised the Senate Appropriations Committee that the discretionary clause in the House bill "places a burden upon the Executive branch. . . . If the Congress should leave such a statement as this in the bill, we should have to go before the President and in effect have these hearings all over again." The chief of staff continued, "If you multiply such instances and continue to load on the President the technical details not only of our Department but of the other departments, you are going to break down government."[105] The Senate agreed with MacArthur that the president should not have such discretionary power and approved the funds necessary to expand the army to 165,000 men without discretion. House and Senate conferees agreed on the Senate version, and this decision reopened the debate on the real issue—the size of the army.[106]

During final debate in the House representatives from across the spectrum of political opinion bitterly opposed the increased strength and appropriations as imprudent and unnecessary. For example, Vito Marcantonio of New York, the only socialist in Congress, objected to grants to colleges and schools for military training, charging that it would lead to "goose-stepping in institutions of higher learning." Everett M. Dirksen of Illinois argued that increasing military expenditures would simply fuel an arms race. "An armed force as such is perfectly all right, and I am in accord with that sentiment; but as we do increase, what happens?" he asked. "Those folks on the other side of the earth in Japan, Germany, France, England, and elsewhere watch our expenditures so far as concerns our military forces, and they in turn say that they have got to build up their own defense forces." He was supported by Knute Hill of Washington, who declared that the increasing appropriations and manpower "simply puts the world on notice that we're preparing for war." Despite such opposition, the House approved the appropriations for a larger army on February 22 without a recorded vote.[107]

In the Senate the debate focused on the warlike intentions of European nations and Japan. J. Hamilton Lewis of Illinois warned that other nations were arming. While disarmament conferences took place, "we watched the army move out from Italy to the land of Ethiopia to the border of three countries, where a conflict may arise equal to that which brought on the

World War." Lewis asked his colleagues, does the Senate "really feel that the first great countries of the world that have now entered into programs for increasing their armies, for multiplying their navies, for the aggregation of every form of aircraft and every capability for assault, have done so without an object?" William King of Utah objected. He accused the Senate of militarism. "I see no foes disguised and masked . . . which threaten the peace and security of this Republic," he declared. "I am unable . . . to justify our military budgets, . . . and I regret exceedingly that the American people do not demand of Congress that there shall be a reduction in the military burdens imposed upon the people." Senator Borah supported King. "If the situation is at all as indicated by those who favor the increase," he said in an unintended prophecy, "then the additional number of men would be wholly inadequate." Looking at the world situation, the ardent isolationist spokesman said he saw no danger of war involving the United States in Europe or Asia. "Japan undoubtedly has a program with reference to the Orient," he conceded, but "could Japan seek a controversy with the United States? Her plans indicate no such suicidal program." Borah flatly opposed the increase as unnecessary and wasteful. But as in the House, the Senate supported raising the army to 165,000 men by a vote of 56 to 26. The same coalition of senators from rural southern, midwestern, and mountain states led by Borah, LaFollette, and Norris opposed the increase.[108]

The army expressed elation over the passage of the 1936 appropriations. In his final report as chief of staff, MacArthur observed, "For the first time since 1922, the Army enters a new fiscal year with a reasonable prospect of developing itself into a defense establishment commensurate in size and efficiency to the country's minimum needs."[109] The *Army and Navy Journal* felt that "the curve has begun to rise again," adding, "Impressed by the rumblings of war in Europe, aware that our riches are open to spoliation, the people are determined to avert war by possessing the strength which their expert advisers tell them will enable defense in case of attack and make foreign nations hesitate to force us to fight."[110]

Not everyone agreed with MacArthur and the *Army and Navy Journal.* Speaking for the pacifist community, Oswald Garrison Villard noted that "If a proposal of this nature had been presented at any time in the last dozen years, it would have provoked a veritable avalanche of protests from organized peace groups throughout the country." Villard lamented that "The apparent collapse of the peace movement is the more distressing because of the powerful weapon placed in its hand by the Senate munitions investigations."[111] The outspoken opponent of military expenditures was referring to the Nye committee, which was currently receiving considerable attention over its investigations into war profits.

The *New York Times,* which had supported a modest increase in the army in the past, also noted an ambiguity in the rise in military spending, pointing out that Congress approved the appropriations at the same time that Representative Louis Ludlow of Indiana introduced his constitutional amendment requiring a plebiscite on any United States entry into war.[112] Indeed, most observers of the 1930s consider that the years 1934–1937 mark the high tide of American isolationist sentiment. In addition to the Nye committee hearings and the introduction of the Ludlow amendment, 1935 witnessed passage of the First Neutrality Act (August 31, 1935) and the introduction of several antiwar profit bills in Congress.[113]

But in fact the modest strength increase approved in 1935 should not be confused with preparedness or rearmament. The objections of the peace advocates aside, the increase for fiscal 1936, as well as the one the following year, should be seen as part of an effort to enable minimal functioning of the army. The 165,000-man regular army represented, in the stated judgment of the War Department, a minimum peacetime strength for the military establishment. President Roosevelt reiterated this concept when he signed the appropriation bill on April 9 and noted that the increase merely restored existing units to "peace strength, fixed by the necessity for efficient training and for reasonable readiness. . . ."[114]

Roosevelt had apparently opposed a larger army in 1935. The Bureau of the Budget's reduction of the War Department's original proposal for augmentation and the administration's pursuit of presidential discretion over any additional troops in the appropriation bill suggest that FDR was not ready to expand the army. Why, then, did Roosevelt let the War Department press its case before Congress and in so doing permit the increase? There are two possible explanations. First, Roosevelt was about to embark on his "Second Hundred Days." He did not want his "must" legislation stalled by a fight over the army's strength. He sacrificed a much-desired discretionary clause in the Neutrality Act of 1935 for the same reason.[115] Second, Roosevelt may not have disapproved of the modest expansion at all. But by allowing Congress to provide for a larger army over his head, he could strengthen the nation's defense without personally affronting the considerable antiwar and isolationist sentiment then prevalent in both Congress and the country. In any case he still held a trump card on the increase. As the new fiscal year began, the Bureau of the Budget informed the War Department that $9 million of the $20 million appropriated to augment the regular army to 165,000 men would be withheld until January 1936. The deferment was allegedly intended to obviate the necessity of reducing the army's strength in 1937 should Congress fail to continue the appropriations for 165,000 men in fiscal 1937.[116] By withholding the funds, the Budget Bureau limited the army's size for fiscal 1936 to 147,000 men, a figure that the army quickly achieved through a massive recruiting campaign.

The War Department estimate for 1937 totaled about $467 million, a figure which, in addition to providing for 165,000 men, included $108 million for new aircraft. The Bureau of the Budget reduced the request to $383 million, eliminating almost all of the money for airplanes and providing for only 147,000 men.[117] Following MacArthur's precedent, the new chief of staff, General Malin Craig, forcefully argued for the army's estimate before Congress. Craig succeeded MacArthur in October 1935. He had served under Pershing during World War I and since the war as a corps area commander, an assistant chief of staff, and commandant of the War College. The new chief of staff shared MacArthur's concerns about the size of the army but sought to balance personnel increases with improvements in materiel as well. That he was able to obtain modest advances in both areas may have been due to the deteriorating world situation as much as to his own considerable skill and determination as a spokesman for preparedness.[118] For example, in February 1936 the House was unwilling to support the army's request for 165,000 men in fiscal 1937 despite Craig's efforts. On February 14, 1936, by voice vote, the House authorized $378 million for military expenditures including provisions for an enlisted strength of only 150,000 men.[119] But the Senate's consideration of the army bill coincided with the German reoccupation of the Rhineland in March. Perhaps that is why the Senate Appropriations Committee restored the 165,000-man strength level, a provision that the Senate approved on March 23. The conference bill preserved the increase but required the army to limit its growth to 1,500 men per month until the new figure was reached. President Roosevelt signed the measure on May 16, 1936.[120]

Most people who followed military affairs approved of the army budget for fiscal 1937. An early opinion poll commissioned by the *Washington Post* in December 1935 revealed that only 11 percent of the sample favored reducing army expenditures while 48 percent favored an increase. A United States Chamber of Commerce survey revealed strong support for an improved defense establishment among businessmen and firms polled.[121] Newspaper editors also supported the increase. The Providence, Rhode Island, *Journal* noted, for example, "However much one may regret the necessity for such huge expenditures, the fact remains that one nation cannot economize in this field when another insists on having more."[122]

Not everyone, of course, agreed. Oswald Garrison Villard's *The Nation* voiced the most damning opposition. In an editorial titled "America is Arming," the weekly charged that the increases were the combined result of "European war hysteria" and "bureaucratic pride, professional jealousies, narrowness of world outlook, and the sheer desire to play with toys you have gone to infinite trouble in making." *The Nation* warned that "a war prepared for . . . is a war whose coming is thereby facilitated," and concluded that involvement in war would plunge the United States into fascism.[123]

The appropriations for the War Department for fiscal 1937 did respond in some measure, as *The Nation* suggested, to "war hysteria" both in Europe and Asia. However, there is no suggestion in either the army estimates or testimony that anyone anticipated American involvement in a war. Indeed, many of the army's leaders shared the isolationist convictions of most Americans in the mid-1930s. According to a student of military thought, "one can read all the reports of the War Department, as well as the speeches and articles published by our military leaders clear up to Pearl Harbor and find little or no indication that we were prepared or wanted to do anything more than defend the western hemisphere from aggression in case of war."[124] In 1935, for example Major General Stanley D. Embick urged the War Department to abandon the Philippines and Guam and concentrate its efforts on defending the Alaska-Oahu-Panama triangle. Embick, who was the army's chief planner at the time, concluded that the army could not defend the Philippines even if existing forces there were beefed up, that U.S. interests in the area really did not warrant an increase, and that the obvious weakness of America's current military disposition in the area invited Japanese adventurism. In 1938 Embick and William C. Rivers, a retired general, openly supported the efforts of Frederick Libby's National Council for Prevention of War to ease tensions in Europe.[125] Charles Summerall, the former chief of staff, was another officer who urged neutrality. In November 1939, after the outbreak of war in Europe, Summerall told members of the Union League Club of Chicago that the United States should keep out of the war entirely. "[We] cannot settle their quarrels nor maintain the balance of power in Europe," he said. "America must not bleed to death over there."[126] Given these attitudes, the 1937 budget, like the increased appropriation for the previous year, should be seen as legislation in support of the Neutrality Acts. Further evidence of this view is found in the $8 million appropriated to improve coastal defenses in Hawaii, in Panama, and on the West Coast.[127] American military leaders had no visions of supporting allies in 1936 and 1937. The modest increase of the army was intended only to insulate the nation further from an increasingly hostile world.

For the second consecutive year Congress chose to disregard the administration's wishes concerning the strength of the army. Congressional commitment to a 165,000-man regular army fulfilled a War Department goal first formally stated in 1928. Since post–World War I retrenchment began, army leaders had stressed minimum manpower needs above all else. With these needs met for the foreseeable future the way was clear to press for materiel needs (new equipment, mechanization, and motorization) that had been sacrificed during the depression.

The little army of the interwar years was indeed deficient in terms of materiel readiness. The tendency of army leaders to view military strength largely in terms of numbers of men combined with the austerity budgets of the 1920's and 1930's to limit the development of new weapons systems. After World War I the army found itself with large stores of weapons, munitions, and other equipment. In 1935 MacArthur reported that the army was still equipped largely with surplus. The infantry continued to carry the 1903 Springfield rifle even though better weapons were available. The standard field artillery piece continued to be the "French 75 mm." Although a more accurate weapon existed (the 105 mm howitzer), only fourteen had been purchased by 1933. In the mid-1930s most of the army's trucks and motors were of World War I vintage. At a time when Germany was busy experimenting with combined armor and infantry formations the American army could muster only twelve tanks built since the war.[128]

The 1937 appropriation bill did provide for modest materiel improvements but hardly suggested that the United States was entering the arms race. Army spokesmen expressed optimism that the increased strength and appropriations would restore the United States to the defensive posture anticipated in the National Defense Act. Harry H. Woodring, who replaced George Dern as secretary of war on the latter's death in August 1936, commented in his first annual report, "With increased personnel in the combat units, it is possible to devote a greater amount of time to training both at garrison and in the field. The result has been a marked improvement in efficiency." With reference to materiel Woodring added, "the appropriations . . . have sufficed to permit a notable expansion in the number of aircraft and a beginning of the program of modernization of the ground troops." Malin Craig echoed the secretary's optimism but cautioned, "It is of the highest importance that this program be carried to completion and maintained. It is a program for defense—intended solely to ensure our national safety."[129]

During the first half of the 1930s the army reached the nadir of its interwar decline. At the beginning of the Hoover administration there was a brief period when it looked as if the army would be able to stabilize its level of spending and perhaps even begin a comeback. The depression ended those hopes, and the War Department spent five more years fighting for every cent it could get. Because personnel costs made up such a large proportion (about 55 percent) of the annual budget during the interwar years, reductions in strength offered tempting solutions to economy-minded congressmen and citizens. MacArthur took great pride in the knowledge that he had played an instrumental role in preserving the regular army from further reductions during his tenure as chief of staff. Mac-Arthur's successor, Malin Craig, and the civilians who supported him both in and out of government were equally heartened by the modest improvements in men and materiel provided for in the 1936 and 1937 appropriations. They believed that their efforts, begun in the early 1920s by Pershing and Weeks, Summerall and Good, to educate Congress and the nation about the needs for an adequate military system were finally coming to fruition. In fact, a growing recognition and fear of militarism abroad plus a decline after 1934 in the power of the idea that economy in government and a balanced budget were necessary to promote general recovery probably contributed more to congressional willingness to spend more for defense than the pleas of generals.

NOTES

1. Harris G. Warren, *Herbert Hoover and the Great Depression* (New York: Oxford University Press, 1959), p. 26.

2. Campaign speech by Herbert Hoover recorded on "Eleven Presidents Speak," a Columbia Transcriptions Production,© 1956 by General Electric. The date and place of the speech are not given.

3. Ray Lyman Wilber, *The Hoover Policies* (New York: Charles Scribner's Sons, 1937), p. 614.

4. Herbert Hoover, "The President's News Conference of July 23, 1929," in *Public Papers of the Presidents of the United States, Herbert Hoover,* (hereafter, *Hoover Papers*), 1929 (Washington, D.C.: GPO, 1974), pp. 229–30.

5. Herbert Hoover, "Remarks Upon Proclaiming the Treaty for the Renunciation of War, July 24, 1929," *Hoover Papers,* 1929, p. 235.

6. Herbert Hoover, "Statement on Cruiser Construction Suspension, July 24, 1929," *Hoover Papers,* 1929, p. 236; Arthur A. Ekirch, Jr., *The Civilian and the Military: A History of the American Antimilitarist Tradition* (Colorado Springs, Colo.: Ralph Myles, Publisher, 1972), p. 215.

7. Albert Bushnell Hart, "President Hoover Acts to Reduce Military Cost," *Current History* 30 (September 1929): 1130.

8. "A Big Disarmament Fight Looms in Washington," *The Literary Digest* 102, no. 6 (August 10, 1929): 5.

9. "Peace Pact and Disarmament," *The Nation* 129, no. 3344 (August 7, 1929): 132.

10. *Army and Navy Journal* (hereafter, *ANJ*), July 27, 1929, p. 977.

11. *ANJ,* August 3, 1929, p. 1002. Editorial excerpts include: *New York Sun, New York World, Washington Post, New Orleans Item,* and *Kansas City Journal Post.*

12. Summerall quoted Hoover's instructions in a memo to the Adjutant General in which he also dictated his guidance for the commission. Memo, CS to AG, August 29, 1929, AGO 333, RG 407, National Archives, Washington, D.C. Hereafter, NA.

13. Ibid.

14. John W. Killigrew, "The Impact of the Great Depression on the United States Army, 1929–1936" (Ph.D. diss., Indiana University, 1960), chapter 2, p. 6.

15. "Report of the Survey of the Military Establishment," (hereafter, "Survey"), November 1, 1929, AGO 333, RG 407, NA, pp. 32, 33.

16. "Survey," pp. 157, 158. Plan I also called for a 250,000-man National Guard, an organized reserve of 116,000 reserve officers, the annual production of 6,000 reserve officers through ROTC, and a civilian military training camp program

capable of training 37,500 men annually. Plan I was expected to cost about $450 million a year in 1929 dollars.

17. Ibid., p. 124.

18. Ibid., pp. 124–31.

19. Ibid., p. 182.

20. Ibid., p. 133.

21. *ANJ*, November 9, 1929, pp. 217, 219; *New York Times*, (hereafter, *NYT*), November 8, 1929, p. 8.

22. Herbert Hoover, Annual Message to the Congress on the State of the Union, December 3, 1929, *Hoover Papers*, 1929, pp. 407–8; *NYT*, December 4, 1929, pp. 1, 26.

23. Herbert Hoover, Annual Budget Message to the Congress, Fiscal Year 1931, December 4, 1929, *Hoover Papers*, 1929, pp. 436–38, 449–50; *NYT*, December 5, 1929, p. 24.

24. "Federal Government Appropriations Grouped Upon a Functional Basis," *Hoover Papers*, 1929, pp. 451–52; *NYT*, December 6, 1929, p. 3.

25. Herbert Hoover, *The Memoirs of Herbert Hoover*, 4 vols. (New York: Macmillan, 1952), 2: 191–92, 219.

26. Russell D. Buhite, *Patrick J. Hurley and American Foreign Policy* (Ithaca, N.Y.: Cornell University Press, 1973), pp. 39–40, 44–45.

27. Killigrew, "The Impact of the Great Depression on the U.S. Army," chapter 3, pp. 1–3. Apparently Hurley's *first* act as secretary was to block the transfer of the Field Artillery School from Fort Sill in his native Oklahoma to Fort Bragg, N.C. Buhite, *Patrick J. Hurley and American Foreign Policy*, pp. 45–46.

28. *ANJ*, August 24, 1929, p. 1075.

29. U.S. House, *Congressional Record*, 71st Cong., 2d sess., 72, pt. 2, pp. 1388–89.

30. Killigrew, "The Impact of the Depression on the U.S. Army," appendix 1, chapter 3, p. 8. See also appendix D.

31. U.S., Department of Commerce, Bureau of the Census, *Statistical Abstract of the United States, 1942,* (hereafter, *Statistical Abstract*), (Washington, D.C.: GPO, 1942), Table 412, p. 389.

32. U.S., Department of Commerce, Bureau of the Census, *Historical Statistics of the United States, Colonial Times to 1957* (Washington, D.C.: GPO, 1960), p. 73; *NYT*, January 1, 1931, p. 46.

33. Broadus Mitchell, *Depression Decade* (New York: Harper Torch Book, 1969), p. 35; *Statistical Abstract, 1940*, Table 177, p. 167.

34. Killigrew, "The Impact of the Great Depression on the U.S. Army," chapter 3, p. 9.

35. Ibid., chapter 3, pp. 19, 24.

36. Ibid., chapter 4, p. 1.

37. *ANJ*, May 16, 1931, pp. 873, 892, 896; D. Clayton James, *The Years of MacArthur*, Vol. 1, *1880–1941* (Boston: Houghton Mifflin, 1970), pp. 357–58; Killigrew, "The Impact of the Great Depression on the U.S. Army," chapter 4, p. 9.

38. James, *The Years of MacArthur*, 1: 1–344, passim.

39. Douglas MacArthur, "The Necessity for Military Forces," *Infantry Journal* 30, no. 3 (March 1927): 328, 330.

40. James, *The Years of MacArthur*, 1: 376–77.

41. Ibid., 1: 312–14, 355–57.

42. U.S. House, *Congressional Record*, 71st Cong., 2nd sess., 72, pt. 2, p. 1390.

43. *ANJ*, January 23, 1932, p. 481.

44. *NYT*, January 31, 1932, p. 7; February 1, p. 13.

45. *ANJ*, April 16, 1932, p. 770.

46. Summarized from Killigrew, "The Impact of the Great Depression on the U.S. Army," Chapter 5, pp. 2–5, 10–14.

47. *NYT*, May 7, 1932, p. 14.

48. *ANJ*, May 21, 1932, p. 889.

49. James, *The Years of MacArthur*, 1: 360–61.

50. *ANJ*, May 14, 1932, p. 866; May 21, pp. 890, 896; May 28, p. 914; June 4, p. 938; April 2, p. 721; June 11, pp. 962, 963.

51. U.S., Senate, *Congressional Record*, 72nd Cong., 1st sess., 75, pt. 11, pp. 12421–29.

52. *ANJ*, July 16, 1932, pp. 1165, 1167–68, 1172, 1174; U.S., House, *Congressional Record*, 72nd Cong., 1st sess., 75, pt. 14, pp. 15138–45.

53. U.S., House, *Congressional Record*, 72nd Cong., 1st sess., 75, pts. 11, 14, pp. 12429, 15145; *ANJ*, June 11, 1932, p. 983; July 16, p. 1074.

Senators for Reduction (16)

Bankland (D), Ark.	Dill (D), Wash.
Blaine (R), Wisc.	Fraizier (R), N.D.
Borah (R), Idaho	Harrison (D), Miss.
Bratton (D), N. Mex.	LaFollette (R), Wisc.
Brookhart (R), Iowa	Norris (R), Neb.
Capper (R), Kans.	Nye (R), N.D.
Careway (D), Ark.	Walsh (D), Mont.
Costigan (D), Colo.	Wheeler (D), Mont.

54. *ANJ*, June 25, 1932, p. 1005; July 2, p. 1035.

55. *ANJ*, January 2, 1932, p. 416, 420.

56. Ibid., January 23, 1932, pp. 481, 504.

57. *NYT*, January 30, 1932, p. 10; January 31, p. 21.

58. The army's role in the Bonus March incident of July 28, 1932, is detailed in Roger Daniels, *The Bonus March* (Westport, Conn.: Greenwood Press, 1971). The official army report on the incident is in the Military District of Washington File, No. A41–485, RG 98, NA. MacArthur expressed his views on the incident in his memoirs, *Reminiscences* (New York: McGraw Hill, 1964), pp. 92–97. For a critical appraisal of MacArthur's role, see James, *The Years of MacArthur*, 1: 382–414.

59. Buhite, *Patrick J. Hurley and American Foreign Policy*, pp. 58–59.

60. *ANJ*, July 2, 1932, p. 1027.

61. Ibid., August 6, 1932, p. 1132; James, *The MacArthur Years*, 1: 415.

62. *ANJ*, January 7, 1933, p. 376.

63. *War Department Annual Reports for 1932* (Washington, D.C.: GPO, 1932), pp. 53–57. Hereafter *Annual Report, 1932*.

64. Selig Adler, *The Isolationist Impulse*, 2d ed. (New York: The Free Press, 1966), pp. 229–30; F. D. Roosevelt, *The Public Papers and Addresses of Franklin D. Roosevelt*, 13 vols. (New York: Random House, 1938): 1: 877–84. Hereafter, *FDR Public Papers*.

65. Ekirch, *The Civilian and the Military*, pp. 234–36; Robert A. Divine, *Roosevelt and World War II* (Baltimore, Md.: Penguin Books, 1969), p. 7.

66. Detzer quoted in Ralph B. Leverling, *The Public and American Foreign Policy, 1918–1978* (New York: William Morrow and Company, 1978), p. 52.

67. Killigrew, "The Impact of the Great Depression on the U.S. Army," chapter 9, pp. 6, 21.

68. *ANJ*, March 4, 1933, p. 529.

69. U.S., House, *Congressional Record*, 72nd Cong., 2d sess., 76, pt. 2, pp. 1773–74, 1803–8.

70. U.S., Senate, *Congressional Record*, 72nd Cong., 2d sess., 76, pt. 4, pp. 3838–44, 3936–53.

71. See letters from Secretary of War Hurley in U.S., House, *Congressional Record*, 72nd Cong., 2nd sess., 76, pt. 4, pp. 3838–39; U.S., House, Ibid., 76, pt. 5, pp. 5379–80, 5382–87.

72. James, *The Years of MacArthur*, 1: 426–28; *ANJ*, March 18, 1932, pp. 569–70; April 22, pp. 669–70, 687.

73. MacArthur, *Reminiscences*, p. 100.

74. *ANJ*, May 6, 1933, p. 711.

75. For a fuller sketch of Dern, see Keith D. McFarland, *Harry H. Woodring: A Political Biography of FDR's Controversial Secretary of War* (Lawrence, Kans.: The University Press of Kansas, 1975), pp. 79, 82–83. MacArthur remembered that Dern "was in thorough agreement with Army plans and was a pillar of support for the Military." The inescapable impression is that MacArthur completely dominated his chief. MacArthur, *Reminiscences*, p. 100.

76. *ANJ*, April 8, 1933, p. 636.

77. Ibid., May 13, 1933, p. 730.

78. Ibid., June 3, 1933, pp. 789–90.

79. MacArthur, *Reminiscences*, p. 101. Roosevelt said nothing of this meeting. D. Clayton James, MacArthur's most critical biographer, repeats MacArthur's very self-serving version. See James, *Years of MacArthur*, 1: 428–29; see also Fraizer Hunt, *The Untold Story of Douglas MacArthur* (New York: The Devin-Adair Company, 1954), pp. 151–53. According to Hunt, a very sympathetic biographer, MacArthur threatened to resign over the proposed reduction and carry the fight to the public. Hunt implies that Roosevelt backed down in the face of this threat.

80. *ANJ*, June 17, 1933, pp. 829, 847.

81. Hunt, *The Untold Story of Douglas MacArthur*, pp. 153–54.

82. Killigrew, "The Impact of the Great Depression on the U.S. Army," chapter 10, p. 14.

83. James, *The Years of MacArthur*, pp. 418–19.

84. Ibid.; *Annual Report*, 1933, p. 6.

85. *Annual Report*, 1933, p. 8.

86. Killigrew, "The Impact of the Great Depression on the U.S. Army," chapter 13, p. 32.

87. Ibid., chapter 13, pp. 20, 24; McFarland, *Harry H. Woodring*, pp. 87–88.

88. James, *The Years of MacArthur*, pp. 424–25; Killigrew, "The Impact of the Great Depression on the U.S. Army," chapter 13, pp. 20–24.

89. Killigrew, "The Impact of the Great Depression on the U.S. Army," chapter 13, p. 40.

90. Ibid., chapter 14, p. 1.

91. U.S. Congress, House, *Hearings on the War Department Appropriations Bill,* 1935, 73d Cong., 2d Sess., January 25, 1934, p. 21. Hereafter House Appropriations Hearings, 1935.

92. Ibid., pp. 16–17.

93. Killigrew, "The Impact of the Great Depression on the U.S. Army," chapter 14, p. 6.

94. *ANJ,* April 21, 1934, p. 683; Killigrew, "The Impact of the Great Depression on the U.S. Army," chapter 14, pp. 7–8.

95. *ANJ,* April 21, 1934, p. 683.

96. U.S. Congress, Senate, *Hearings on the War Department Appropriations Bill,* 1935, 74th Cong., 1st Sess., February 27, 1935, p. 7. Hereafter Senate Appropriations Hearings, 1936.

97. *ANJ,* May 5, 1934, pp. 705, 723; May 19, p. 745; June 2, pp. 809, 811; June 16, pp. 849, 866; Killigrew, "The Impact of the Great Depression on the U.S. Army," chapter 14, p. 8.

98. Killigrew, "The Impact of the Great Depression on the U.S. Army," chapter 14, p. 27; James, *The Years of MacArthur,* p. 448.

99. James, *The Years of MacArthur,* pp. 443–47.

100. Killigrew, "The Impact of the Great Depression on the U.S. Army," chapter 14, pp. 29–30.

101. *ANJ,* February 16, 1935, p. 498.

102. Killigrew, "The Impact of the Great Depression on the U.S. Army," chapter 14, pp. 27–28; *NYT,* February 1, 1935, p. 28; *ANJ,* February 3, 1935, p. 459.

103. *NYT,* February 20, 1935, pp. 1, 13.

104. Ibid., February 23, 1935, pp. 1, 23.

105. Senate Appropriation Hearings, 1936, pp. 4–6; *NYT,* March 2, 1935, p. 13.

106. *NYT,* March 8, 1935, p. 1; March 24, p. 28.

107. U.S., House, *Congressional Record,* 74th Cong., 1st sess., 79, pt. 2, pp. 2408–19, 2485–87, 2492; *NYT,* February 23, 1935, p. 1.

108. U.S., Senate, *Congressional Record,* 74th Cong., 1st sess., 79, pt. 3, pp. 3084–105; *NYT,* March 8, 1935, pp. 1, 11; *ANJ,* March 9, 1935, pp. 561, 581.

Senators Voting Against the Increase (26)

Black (D), Ala.	Fraizer (R), N. Dak.
Bone (D), Wash.	Glass (D), Va.
Borah (R), Idaho	Hatch (D), N. Mex.
Brown (D), N.H.	King (D), Utah
Bulow (D), S. Dak.	LaFollette (Progressive), Wisc.
Byrd (D), Va.	McKellar (D), Tenn.
Byrnes (D), S.C.	Murphy (D), Iowa
Capper (R), Kans.	Neely (D), W. Va.
Clark (D), Mo.	Norris (R), Neb.
Costigan (D), Colo.	Nye (R), N. Dak.
Couzens (R), Mich.	Pope (D), Idaho
Cutting (R), N. Mex.	Shipstead (Farm-Labor), Minn.
Dickinson (R), Iowa	Vandenberg (R), Mich.

109. *Annual Report,* 1935, p. 41.

110. *ANJ,* March 30, 1935, p. 632.

111. Oswald Garrison Villard, "War Preparations and the Arms Inquiry," *The Nation* 140, no. 3635 (March 6, 1935): 265–66.

112. *NYT,* March 29, 1935, p. 20.

113. The antiwar profits bills were an outgrowth of the Nye committee hearings. The idea of limiting profits in war drew support from a wide spectrum of opinion. Antimilitarists, peace groups, and preparedness advocates all approved of the concept. See Adler, *Isolationist Impulse,* pp. 234–43, and Manfred Jonas, *Isolationism in America, 1935–1941* (Ithaca, N.Y.: Cornell University Press, 1966).

114. *NYT,* April 10, 1935, p. 4.

115. Most historians of the Second Hundred Days conclude that FDR gave up the fight for a discretionary embargo in order to save domestic legislation in the summer of 1935. See, for example, James M. Burns, *Roosevelt: The Lion and the Fox* (New York: Harcourt, Brace and Co., 1956), pp. 253–56, and William E. Leuchtenburg, *Franklin D. Roosevelt and the New Deal* (New York: Harper & Row, 1963), pp. 217–20.

116. Killigrew, "The Impact of the Great Depression on the U.S. Army," chapter 14, p. 36; *ANJ,* December 21, 1935, pp. 305–6.

117. Killigrew, "The Impact of the Great Depression on the U.S. Army," chapter 14, p. 39, Appendix I; U.S. Congress, House, *Hearings on the War Department Appropriations Bill, 1937,* 74th Cong., 2d Sess., December 18, 1935, pp. 6–8.

118. Russell F. Weigley, *History of the United States Army* (New York, Macmillan, 1967), p. 415.

119. *NYT,* February 15, 1935, p. 1.

120. *ANJ,* March 21, 1936, pp. 613, 614; March 28, p. 644; May 9, 1935, pp. 789, 808; May 23, p. 839.

121. *ANJ,* January 4, 1936, p. 354.

122. *ANJ,* January 18, 1936, p. 390; February 22, p. 514; May 30, p. 862.

123. *ANJ,* February 22, 1936, p. 514; *The Nation* 142, no. 3692 (April 8, 1936): 436, 437.

124. Richard C. Brown, "Social Attitudes of American Generals, 1898–1940" (Ph.D. diss., University of Wisconsin, 1941), p. 360.

125. Ronald Schaffer, "General Stanley D. Embick: Military Dissenter," *Military Affairs* 37, no. 3 (October 1973): 91, 92.

126. Brown, "Social Attitudes of American Generals," pp. 355–56.

127. *ANJ,* May 9, 1936, pp. 789, 808.

128. Weigley, *History of the U.S. Army,* pp. 413–15; *Annual Report,* 1935, pp. 51–54. For a more complete discussion of materiel planning and procurement between the wars, see Constance M. Green, Harry C. Thomson, and Peter C. Roots, *The Ordnance Department: Planning Munitions for War* (Washington, D.C.: Department of the Army, 1955), chapters 2 and 7.

129. *Annual Report,* 1936, pp. 2–4, 31.

6

MAINTAINING THE VOLUNTEER ARMY DURING THE DEPRESSION

The massive unemployment of the Great Depression represented a bonanza to the regular army. Until 1933 no recruiter had to look far to fill his quotas. The vexing problem of high losses encountered in the 1920s evaporated as well. Because of the depression the recruiting system worked, and the army responded to this blessing by attempting to improve the quality of its enlisted ranks.

Unemployment rose rapidly beginning in 1930. In 1929, 3.2 percent of the civilian labor force was out of work. A year later the figure was 8.7 percent, and by 1933 nearly 25 percent of the work force was unemployed.[1] The employment pool to which Major Brown had referred in his War College study was growing.

As civilian employment declined, army losses by desertion and purchase discharges also dropped. At the same time the number of soldiers reenlisting, which already had been high, increased further. Desertion dropped by two-thirds between 1929 and 1932 while the number of men who purchased discharges halved and those reenlisting increased by 50 percent.[2]

The decline in losses and rise in reenlistments were predictable. Woodbury's study of desertions, done in 1920 for the old Morale Branch of the General Staff, clearly established the relationship between civilian employment and army gains and losses. What is especially significant about the Great Depression is that with army strength fixed, the decline in losses and the rise in reenlistments combined to reduce the need for new enlistments while the pool of available recruits grew to tremendous proportions. Because high unemployment continued as long as it did, the army was able to inaugurate a systematic program to take advantage of the situation and recruit quality enlisted men. This situation remained until the summer of 1933 when New Deal programs began to compete with the army for men. In fiscal 1930 the adjutant general reported that "during the year [recruiting] was so prolific in results that it became necessary at times to limit the number of enlistments in order not to exceed the authorization. . . ."[3]

The Recruiting Service needed no prompting to take advantage of the situation. In April 1930 the editor of *Recruiting News* advised recruiters:

Now is the time when every application for service with the colors must be scrutinized with unusual care. . . . The good man should be shown every consideration. . . . But the army has no place for the individual who is merely seeking "three squares and a flop." The "quality not quantity" idea must be kept always in mind. . . .[4]

In fiscal 1931, the army accepted only 18,258 original enlistments and began to tighten up on standards. According to the adjutant general, "Men applying for original enlistment were required to furnish letters of recommendation as to character, and intelligence tests were applied to all such applicants, resulting in the rejection of many who were unsuited for military service."[5]

During fiscal 1932 the army reviewed its entire recruiting program and made some major changes in a dual effort to improve the quality of recruits and to cut down on expenses. As directed by the adjutant general, the Recruiting Service had already modified its practices, but in the summer of 1931 the initiative for further change came from a higher level.

A personal letter sent directly to General MacArthur by Captain James C. Anthony, commandant and professor of military science at John Marshall High School, Richmond, Virginia, stimulated the army's major effort to raise its recruiting standards in the early 1930s. Anthony related to MacArthur his observations of John Marshall students who enlisted in the army, navy, or marines during a six-year period. He concluded that of the recruits returning to school on visits those trained by the army were clearly an inferior lot. Anthony felt that part of the problem was, "the type of boy enlisting in the Army from here . . . has been of somewhat lower calibre than that enlisting . . ." in the other services. He defined "calibre" as "intelligence, character, and family background."[6]

MacArthur replied personally on August 22, 1932, saying, "I deeply appreciate your letter . . . and the suggestions it contains. . . . I am happy to tell you that I have the matter on my agenda for correction."[7] MacArthur directed the General Staff to conduct a thorough study of recruiting and recruit training procedures. After two months of study assistant chief of staff for personnel Andrew Moses presented his final recommendations to MacArthur. Moses proposed a twofold program of improvements. First, he suggested that corps area commanders review all officers and enlisted men on recruiting duty. Anyone "considered unsuited for the duty he is performing, due to any cause . . ." should be relieved. In order to assist corps area commanders in measuring the efficiency of recruiters, the adjutant general would furnish quarterly reports "showing the total number of recruits produced by each station . . . together with the total number of avoidable enlisted losses chargeable to each station during that time." Second, in an obvious effort to take advantage of the depression, Moses proposed that standards for both original enlistment and reenlistment be raised in order to improve the quality of enlisted men in the regular army. MacArthur approved the entire package on October 29.[8]

On November 2, 1931, the adjutant general notified the corps area commanders that "no man discharged from his first enlistment with character less than 'very good' will be reenlisted. . . ." He raised the minimum rating on the intelligence test acceptable for original enlistment from thirty-four to forty-four (a score "which corresponds to completion of the 8th grade in school") and withdrew the authority of corps area commanders to waive physical defects of applicants.[9]

A year later, in September 1932, the surgeon general of the army proposed an additional change in recruiting practices in an effort to reduce "the number of enlistments in which physical defects existing prior to enlistment are subsequently found. . . ." The surgeon general felt, "with the great number of men available to select from at the present time, there is no reason why the acceptance of physically or medically unfit men should not be materially reduced." He recommended greater care in the conduct of preliminary examinations, that new recruits receive a second examination at their unit of assignment, and that corps area commanders be notified of recruits found subsequently unfit. The surgeon general's recommendations received prompt approval. Letters advising corps area commanders of the additional changes were mailed on October 12, 1932.[10]

The higher physical and mental standards established by the War Department between 1930 and 1932 clearly indicated that the General Staff had taken the criticisms of "poor quality" recruits made by commanders in the "line" army during the 1920s to heart. The necessity for more intelligent and reliable soldiers was well stated by Major Albert E. Brown in his War College study of peacetime recruiting problems:

Warfare is constantly increasing its requirements on the individual soldier as well as on the training, maneuverability and fighting efficiency of the infantry platoon. The more scientific the weapons of warfare, the more exact the methods of its prosecution become, the more efficient must be its units of conduct. . . .[11]

That the advancing technology of war dictated the need for more intelligent soldiers, men capable of learning and performing more complicated jobs, was perhaps self-evident. But the army was also coming to realize that more selective recruiting could also eliminate the misfits who subsequently deserted or became disciplinary problems. By creating an enlarged recruiting pool, the depression thus gave the army an opportunity to accelerate its program to reduce losses and improve enlisted quality that it had begun in the late 1920s.

On January 6, 1932, only two months after most of the higher standards went into effect, general recruiting halted indefinitely. According to the adjutant general, "Employment conditions throughout the country were such that recruiting resolved itself into a matter of selection." Qualified applicants poured in at such a high rate there was a danger of exceeding authorized strength. After January 1932, "enlistments were confined almost entirely to men who applied for reentry into the service within 3 months from the date of their latest honorable discharges."[12] General recruiting did not resume until November 10, 1932. But this discontinuation of general recruiting did not signify any decrease in applications for enlistment. Civilians caught in the grip of the depression continued to seek entry. For example, in September 1932 the commandant of the Air Corps Training Center at Chanute Field, Illinois, wrote to the chief of the Army Air Corps requesting special authorization to enlist "200 exceptionally qualified applicants. . . ." He reported that he had "a waiting list of applicants now numbering 850. . . ," and went on to say, "these are all high school graduates, many with some additional technical education, and all . . . exceptionally qualified as to character, intelligence and general fitness."[13]

During the suspension of active recruiting the War Department, responding to pressures from the Hoover administration, took steps to save money in the fiscal year beginning July 1, 1932, by reducing the General Recruiting Service of 89 officers and 309 enlisted men to 33 and 250 respectively. The cut resulted in a savings of $450 per day in rental and subsistence allowances alone. The army achieved additional savings in the amount needed for transportation and subsistence of recruits for overseas commands by prohibiting the enlistment or reenlistment of men for foreign service except in designated corps areas close to ports of embarkation. Applicants for foreign service assignments had to enlist within 200 miles of the port of embarkation or pay the cost of travel to the port themselves. Soldiers could reenlist only for their own vacancy or a vacancy on the same post, and the army would accept new enlistments only for the post nearest the place of enlistment and only for existing vacancies.[14]

When general recruiting resumed in November 1932 to make up losses sustained during the summer months, the War Department found much to be pleased with. Reports from all corps areas indicated widespread satisfaction that the higher standards indeed had improved the quality of recruits. Furthermore, the steps taken to reduce costs did not appear to hinder the recruiting effort. The commanding general of the Second Corps Area in New York reported that in the "opinion of the Commanding Officers in this Corps Area . . . a much higher type of recruit is being obtained at present, both physically and mentally."[15] The commander of the Fourth Corps Area with headquarters in Charleston, South Carolina, added that the recruits procured in his region were "well above average," and went on to report that "each district in this Corps Area maintains a live waiting list of from 200 to 500 men and that it is possible to secure a large majority of original enlistments of high school graduates and some men of college experience."[16]

The concurrent successful cutting of recruiting costs without impairing the efficiency of the recruiting service added to the good news. Recruiting costs prior to the fiscal 1933 reductions ranged from between $3 to $3.5 million annually. The cost per recruit between 1927 and 1932 averaged $55.87. Economy measures begun during fiscal 1933 reduced the total expenses of recruiting to $1,721,165.10. The cost per recruit dropped to $35.22.[17] Not only was the army getting better recruits, it was getting them at two-thirds the price! Brigadier General Andrew Moses, the assistant chief of staff for personnel, was so pleased that he recommended the further curtailment of recruiting activities, observing that:

The effect of the present period of depression has been to increase the facility with which men of capability and good character can be obtained for the Army, and as recovery from this economic situation cannot help but be a process covering several years, it hardly seems logical to maintain the Recruiting Service at a capacity beyond that necessary to meet the estimated needs of the Army.

Moses proposed the elimination of all leased recruiting stations, a reduction of the number of recruiting districts and stations, a further reduction of enlisted men on recruiting duty, and accepting enlistments only when and where a vacancy existed except for overseas duty and special assignments. The chief of staff approved the recommendations, which went into effect July 1, 1933.[18]

By 1933 the army had fully recognized the effect of the depression on enlistments and recruiting and the implications of that effect. But in its exuberance over the improved caliber of recruits, rising reenlistments, and declining losses, the army overreacted. War Department plans to ride the crest of the wave of improved enlistments, fostered by the depression, soon foundered. New Deal legislation, aimed at stimulating recovery and providing relief, resulted in conditions both inside and outside of the army that partially reduced the appeal of the military as a haven from the depression. The Economy Act of 1933 and many of the New Deal relief programs combined to pull the rug out from under the army recruiters.

Before the New Deal the economy measures of the government hardly touched army enlisted men. True, joint service efforts for a pay increase in 1929 and 1930 failed as a result of the depression. But the declining cost of living after 1929 effectively put more money into the soldier's pocket. The consumer price index dropped from 73.3 in 1929 to 55.3 in 1933.[19] Most soldiers lived in barracks and ate their meals at the mess hall and thus had the basic necessities of life provided. Enlisted men detached from their units and living away from posts received monthly rental and subsistence allowances. The system of reenlistment bonuses and specialty pay established by the Pay Readjustment Act of June 1922 continued in effect. The Hoover administration's efforts to economize, which required officers to take a month's furlough without pay and reduced officers' pay, travel, and rental and subsistence allowances, did not affect enlisted men. It was left to Franklin D. Roosevelt to bring the depression home to the soldier.

Hoover's economy measures were extended into 1933 as part of the post office and treasury appropriations for fiscal 1934, but on assuming office, Roosevelt asked for greater cuts. On March 11, 1933, the *Army and Navy Journal* reported "the spectre of a more drastic cut in pay for the military as well as the civilian personnel of the government loomed yesterday, when President Roosevelt sent to Congress a message asking that the furlough plan be repealed and that he be given authority to cut pay."[20] Congress approved the economy bill, designed "to maintain the credit of the United States Government," despite hastily organized opposition by the American Legion and a brief revolt by about ninety Democrats in the House.[21] On March 28, 1933, FDR took full advantage of the new law. Pay cuts of 15 percent began on April 1. For a private the reduction amounted to $3.15 per month (from $21 to $17.85). In addition, Roosevelt imposed a freeze on longevity pay increases, suspended reenlistment bonuses beginning July 1, and reduced rental and subsistence allowances 15 percent below 1928 levels except during travel between assignments.[22]

It is difficult to establish the real impact of these economizing measures. Most casual observers conclude that because he had a job, a place to live, and something to eat, the soldier managed well even after the cuts. Most unmarried soldiers in the barracks probably did. The career "noncom" with a family to support was another matter. How did this group manage? Most suffered their pay cut and struggled to make ends meet in silence. But when the General Staff sent questionnaires to officers (not enlisted men) seeking to determine the effects of the depression on the army, a few hundred noncommissioned officers obtained the forms and responded, too. Their answers provide a few clues to depression conditions in the army.

Master Sergeant William Lepski, assigned to the Service Company of the Eighteenth Infantry at Governor's Island, New York, found, "although the cost of living is somewhat lesser in 1933 that due to [the] growth of my dependents the cost of their maintenance is approximately [the] same as obtained in 1928." To Lepski, who received $138.52 a month plus government quarters, the 15 percent pay cut meant, "I am forced to exercise considerably more care in keeping my expenses within the limit of my income," to support a wife and three children.[23] To Technical Sergeant Allen Spencer, who lived in government quarters in the Southwest, the reduction brought greater hardship. Spencer reported that his monthly income dropped $1.59 to $95.41 between 1928 and 1933 despite a promotion from staff sergeant and a longevity pay increase in the interim. Adding to his burden was "the support of my wife's father and mother . . . since May 1933 due to his failure after 20 years in business, a result of the depression."[24]

Staff Sergeant Raymond Conner, on duty in New England, computed his pay as follows:

Authorized Pay and allowances 30 day month for Staff Sergt., Over 20 yrs service	$153.45
Monthly share of Savings of Clothing Allowance	3.33
Monthly share of Reenlistment Bonus	4.17
	$160.95
Present Pay and Allowances	$126.22

Sergeant Conner wryly concluded that the $34.73 reduction "is a monthly contribution to the public welfare."[25]

Married enlisted men below noncommissioned officer rank constituted a class of soldier that always lived on the edge of poverty. The army did not like the idea of married enlisted men. Although the War Department regulations officially discouraged the practice, they left the decision to enlist or reenlist a married man to the local commander. During the relative prosperity of the 1920s, when every applicant was needed, few commanders resisted the enlistment or reenlistment of married men. Raymond G. Alvord, who retired as a first sergeant in 1955, remembered, "When I got married I had no trouble getting permission; the catch was you had to live within your means. If the company commander got one letter from a collection agency that was it; you couldn't reenlist." In the 1930s Alvord supplemented his income of $50 a month with "a job down town." He lived in government quarters consisting of a living room, bedroom, shared bath, and a community kitchen "three floors down."[26] Sergeant Alvord was lucky. Most others were not so fortunate, and the army, which never considered itself a relief agency, was not sympathetic.

In March 1931, Brigadier General William P. Jackson, commanding general of Madison Barracks at Sackett Harbor, New York, in a report on married enlisted men complained:

They *exist* in squalid surroundings, in dingy dark, overcrowded rooms where the simplest rules of sanitation and hygiene are difficult if not impossible of accomplishment. Their health, morale, vitality and efficiency is [sic] bound to suffer. Undernourishment is frequently observed, resulting in at least one instance at this station in hospitalization due to weakness. . . . Some become objects of charity—an unjust liability on the garrison. Recently a donation of nineteen dollars was made by officers to provide fuel and milk for a new mother and her baby.[27]

General Jackson proposed to remedy this situation by modifying regulations governing the enlistment and reenlistment of married men.

An investigation then found that 1,219 of the 8,958 enlisted men assigned to the Second Corps Area (which included Madison Barracks) were married. Of these married men 862 were below grade 3 (staff sergeant), and 489 were unable to support their families properly. The report concluded that the situation probably reflected conditions throughout the army and added, "remedial action should be taken by the War Department."[28]

The condition of married enlisted men and their families was not a product of the depression but the result of low pay, poor housing, ignorance, and lack of official concern. Indeed, as prices fell during the 1930s the situation facing this wretched class of people in the army probably improved as their limited resources went further. The army's sudden interest in married enlisted men arose as the society in general became more conscious of poverty and the effects of unemployment in its midst.

No one in the Second Corps Area or the General Staff suggested that the army take action to relieve the distressed enlisted men or their families. In the extensive staff study that followed, the assistant chief of staff for personnel stressed two points. The situation had reached the point where "the large number of married enlisted men below the first three grades is today a serious detriment to the efficiency, morale and readiness for field service of the many organizations in the Army." However, the army would have to exercise caution in seeking a solution to the problem because, "The present economic situation makes this an inopportune time for the War Department to take action which might be construed as forcing married men out of the service."[29]

The adjutant general believed that the problem was due to the failure of local commanders to follow existing regulations but agreed that stricter guidelines should be adopted. In December 1931 General Douglas MacArthur, who in 1920 had urged greater efforts to eliminate "misfits," approved the new regulations. Corps area commanders were notified that:

No married man or any man with dependents will be enlisted or reenlisted who cannot maintain his dependents on his pay as an enlisted man. . . . No man below grade three will be reenlisted who after receipt of these regulations, marries without the consent of his organization and post commanders.[30]

The War Department's views on the subject of married enlisted men reflected the detached, efficiency-conscious perspective of administrators far from the daily concerns of peacetime army life. No wholesale discharges or barring of reenlistments followed the change in regulations. There is no evidence that local commanders threw married enlisted men and their families out into the cold.

Some commanders did all they could to ease the distress of enlisted men and their families. Major General Johnson Hagood, the outspoken commander of the Seventh Corps Area, demonstrated special concern for those married enlisted men released from detached duty with the Recruiting Service, ROTC, and reserve units when their jobs were eliminated due to "false economy." Most of "these splendid soldiers" returned to duty at posts without sufficient quarters even for those senior noncommissioned officers who were authorized to have them. Wherever he could find them on the posts in his corps area, Hagood turned over "abandoned wartime structures, one story affairs that had been used as barracks, hospital wards, warehouses, etc.," to the men and their families. He also provided salvaged building material and ordered local commanders to detail post plumbers and electricians to help make the places habitable. "They made a fine job of it as soldiers always will if given a chance." Hagood recalled. He took great pride in his philanthropy, and showed off some of the quarters to Secretary of War Dern during an inspection visit. One stop on the tour produced unexpected results:

[When] I showed the layout at Omaha to Mr. Dern, we found a woman weeping. She said that in all her twenty five years in the army as a soldier's daughter and as a soldier's wife, never had she known of a corporal's being provided with such a home; and that she knew when the Secretary of War came into her kitchen, it could only mean that it was going to be taken away from her and given to someone else with much more rank in the army.[31]

Hagood's philanthropic attitude was probably unusual. Still, the impact of the depression on enlisted men and their families was undoubtedly not as acute as it was on the ranks of the unemployed. Despite War Department interest in relieving itself of the "inefficiency" of married enlisted men and the "burden" of their dependents, there is no evidence that the tougher regulations governing reenlistment of married men worked. Later reports, indeed, indicate that the number of enlisted men with families increased during the depression and that these married men managed to cope. The Economy Act of 1933 added to the distress of many soldiers, but they still had jobs and a steady if diminished income.

On balance the married enlisted man during the depression fared about the same as a regularly employed blue-color worker. A staff sergeant (grade 3) with twenty years of service made about $1,000 a year, including base pay, longevity pay, and a rations allowance paid to men who did not use the mess hall. Men occupying government quarters paid no rent and did not have to pay for heat or electricity. Housing, fuel, and light expenses averaged $309 a year for civilians in the same income range. The soldiers also saved on expenses for clothing and medical care. In other areas such as food, household operations, transportation, and recreation, the soldier and civilian were about equal. Thus, the sergeant who earned $1,000 in 1933 enjoyed the purchasing power of a civilian worker with an income of around $1,400 a year.[32]

The New Deal did more than cut pay, however; it created jobs and brought some measure of recovery. The establishment of the Civilian Conservation Corps (CCC) signaled a significant, if temporary, change for the volunteer army.

Congress approved Roosevelt's plan for the CCC on March 31, 1933. The War Department was already intimately involved in planning and preparing for mobilizing the CCC when President Roosevelt signed it into law and ordered it into operation.[33] As noted earlier, the organization and mobilization of the corps consumed much of the regular army's available manpower during the summer of 1933. An average of three officers and four enlisted men were required at each of the 1,315 camps.[34]

The army's relationship with the CCC did more than sidetrack regular officers from troop duty, professional schooling, and reserve or National Guard training and inspection assignments. While War Department spokesmen took pride in the army's crucial role in making the CCC work, they soon began to identify some problems arising from the close association of the regular army with relief work. The success of the CCC and the modest benefits of the New Deal relief and recovery efforts temporarily undermined the army's ability to attract and retain good enlisted men for the rest of the depression.

It did not take enlisted men long to find out that while the new administration cut their pay by 15 percent to reduce government spending, it simultaneously created the CCC and effectively hired 250,000 government employees at a higher rate of pay than privates received. The *Army and Navy Journal* frequently reminded its readers that army privates received $17.85 a month while CCC enrollees were paid $30 a month.[35]

The results of New Deal relief and economy measures began to affect the army as early as the summer of 1933. Between April and May the enlisted strength of the regular army dropped from 117,224 to 116,214. The decline continued until August when it reached 113,694. Reenlistments, which averaged over 3,000 a month for much of the fiscal year, also began to decline. Desertions, which had not been above 300 a month since September 1931, jumped above 400 in April.[36]

By August genuine concern over declining enlistments and reenlistments prompted Lieutenant Colonel Robert S. Bamberger, the adjutant general's assistant for recruiting, to fire off a letter of complaint to the corps area commanders. Replies were not long in coming. "My Dear Bamberger," began the letter from Colonel Harvey W. Miller, replying for the Second Corps Area commander, "the bulk of prospective applicants for original enlistment appear to be more interested in the CCC which offers $30 per month whereas the pay of a private is $17.85. . . ." In addition, Miller continued, "the great amount of publicity given the NRA [National Recovery Act] has placed renewed hopes for employment in the minds of many young men. . . ."[37] Major General Edwin B. Winans, commander of the

Eighth Corps Area, replied personally. He reported that reenlistments in his command decreased approximately 30 percent from May to July. Based on reports from post commanders Winans concluded "this was due to causes such as discontinuance of [the] reenlistment bonus, 15% reduction in pay, reduction in clothing allowance, and [the] possibility of obtaining more remunerative employment in civil pursuits as a result of [the] NRA." Concerning the decline in original enlistments, Winans noted, "City recruiting stations report that prospective recruits are delaying [their] decision to enlist in view of probable civilian employment under NRA and Public Works programs and that their most available prospects have been reduced by over 25,000 young men entering the CCC."[38] Every reply cited the pay reduction and competition from the CCC as factors discouraging new enlistments. The discontinuance of the reenlistment bonus, the pay cut, distaste for duty with the CCC or discontent because CCC enrollees got higher pay than army privates, and brighter civilian job prospects were the most frequently offered explanations for the decline in reenlistments. In addition, the replies from the First and Ninth Corps Areas, encompassing the Northeast and West Coast respectively, blamed the poor results on economy measures recently imposed on the General Recruiting Service. The commanding general of the First Corps Area wrote a terse reply to Bamberger blaming the shortages in his area on the closing of substations and reduction of recruiting districts in accordance with War Department orders.[39]

The War Department quickly went to work to remedy the situation. First, the army requested that enlisted men at CCC camps who received less pay than CCC enrollees be relieved from such duty as soon as possible. This goal was achieved by the end of 1933.[40] The task of restoring the pay cut proved more formidable. The *Army and Navy Journal* put restoration of the 15 percent reduction in pay and other benefits such as the reenlistment bonus and rental and subsistence allowances on the top of its priority list. In an editorial printed July 22, 1933, the *Journal* observed:

It is difficult . . . to reconcile the words and deeds of the Administration in connection with the Industrial situation. On the one hand it is applauding the Steel and other private businesses which have announced an increase in wages, and on the other it is persisting in continuing the 15 percent cut in government pay. . . .

The *Journal* further noted that the cost of living was on the rise and pointed to Department of Labor statistics to substantiate the claim.[41]

Employment did improve in 1933. The index of employment in manufacturing industries rose steadily from a low of 62.2 in March to 82.9 in October, the high for the year. But living costs in major cities also rose from 74.5 to 77.2 between June and December 1933.[42] The *Journal* kept up a steady barrage of articles and editorials reminding its readers of the inequity of the pay cuts. *Journal* articles on the effects of the pay cut frequently appeared with articles on army-CCC activities, a not so subtle reminder that CCC enrollees were paid more than most soldiers.

In September 1933, Lewis Douglas, director of the Bureau of the Budget, instructed the War Department to prepare its budget request for fiscal 1935 on the basis of 100 percent pay and allowances but to plan on continuing the longevity pay freeze. The Economy Act, Douglas said, applied only to fiscal 1934 and might not be continued.[43]

While Douglas' message inspired hope for pay restoration, later statements by members of Congress presaged a fight over the issue. In November, House Speaker Harry T. Rainey declared that restoration would have to await general recovery. "I haven't got much sympathy for the Army and Navy fellows," Rainey said. "Their jobs are sure." The Democratic floor leader of the House, Joseph Byrns, supported Rainey, but an American Federation of Government Employees poll showed more than eighty senators and congressmen in favor of restoration.[44]

In January 1934 Congress received the budget estimate. The Bureau of the Budget recommended restoration of one-third of the pay cut and continuation of the pay freeze. The *Army and Navy Journal* demanded full restoration of the pay cut and reenlistment bonus and an end to the freeze.[45] During House committee hearings War Department spokesmen argued for restoration at every opportunity. Major General James F. McKinley, the adjutant general, told the committee that intimate contact between regular army soldiers and CCC enrollees had produced considerable discontent among the former due to the pay differential. McKinley presented a CCC inspection report that stated in part:

The enlisted men have generally displayed a commendatory loyalty and a willingness to work long hours at difficult tasks, and great credit is due to them. There is, however, an undercurrent of dissatisfaction, due to the unfavorable comparison of their pay with that of the enrollees and the greater solicitude shown for the Civilian Conservation Corps members. There is some indication that desertions have increased and reenlistments have fallen off.

McKinley substantiated the rise in desertions and the drop in reenlistments and further pointed out the effect of the pay cut on recruiting.[46]

General MacArthur, although more concerned with the overall readiness of the army and raising its strength, also pressed for an end to the 15 percent pay reduction. Speaking of the general morale of the army, the chief of staff noted, "Only morale will carry a soldier into the dangers and hardships of modern war, and only morale will build up a military organization capable of sustaining the shock of present-day battle." Morale was intangible, MacArthur said, but it was essential and could be easily shattered. "Morale is born of just treatment, efficient leadership, thorough training, and pride in self, in organization, and in country." The pay cut

and freeze "worked peculiar hardship on military . . . personnel,"
MacArthur observed, and he urged complete restoration.[47]

In mid-January 1934, President Roosevelt, after reviewing cost of living
figures, continued the 15 percent pay cut for the remainder of the fiscal
year. The same week the House defeated an attempt to end the freeze on
longevity pay increases. The President insisted that, under the provisions
of the Economy Act, he was required to continue the pay cut until the
cost of living again rose to 1929 levels.[48]

Supporters of pay restoration were furious. The American Federation
of Government Employees attacked the validity of Roosevelt's cost of
living figures, charging, "The President's decision not to restore any part
of the salary reduction shows the fallacy of the cost of living method of
setting salaries. It is a matter of common knowledge that prices have
increased very appreciably." The National Legislative Council of Federal
Employees Organizations and the American Federation of Labor also
issued statements condemning the continuation of the reduction and
pledged to make every effort to overturn the action.[49] Not to be outdone,
the *Army and Navy Journal* declared:

> The American people have the right and power to see that their servants are
> treated equitably and justly. To use the latter as a football of politics, to make
> savings at their expense while hundreds of millions are being scattered broadcast
> with no return to the government or very slight return . . . are not measures
> conducive to efficient and contented service.

The *Journal* accused President Roosevelt and Congress of duplicity noting,
"as the President and the House Appropriations Committee are talking
about the splendid men who make up the armed forces, the 15% pay cut
is directed to continue in application."[50]

Apparently responding to pressure from government employee groups,
Congress agreed to restore the pay cut in three 5 percent increments
beginning February 1, 1934. Roosevelt, again claiming that the increase
was unjustified, vetoed the bill but was overridden almost immediately by
sizable majorities in both houses. Commenting on the outcome, the *Army
and Navy Journal* crowed:

> What has been won as a result of Congressional action is not only a partial
> restoration of pay and amelioration of the pay freeze, but recognition of the soldier
> and sailor and marine, commissioned and enlisted, as subjects of governmental
> consideration.[51]

Complete restoration of pay came in July 1935. The ban on the reenlistment bonus remained in effect and was the object of annual debates in
both the House and Senate until it was restored in 1939.[52] After restoration
of pay the War Department renewed efforts, terminated earlier by the

onset of the depression, to raise army pay across the board. Congress heard testimony on the subject in 1936, and in 1938 a new Interdepartmental Pay Board was created to study the situation and prepare a joint services proposal.[53] Little real progress occurred, however, before 1940 when events overtook the army, Congress, and the country. By the end of the year pay was increased, but not because the War Department finally convinced Congress of the necessity of such an increase. The pay raise came as part of the Selective Training and Service Act, presumably because the elected representatives of the people declined to pay draftees from their constituencies what they had been paying volunteers for years.[54]

But this pay increase of 1940 was a long way off in mid-1933 when the army faced up to the competition that the New Deal meant in terms of maintaining enlisted strength. Recruiters, who undoubtedly enjoyed a relatively easy couple of years because of the depression, went back to work on a full-time basis. Despite the handicaps caused by the pay cut, CCC pay differential, and reduced operating funds, the Recruiting Service rallied to secure enough men to balance losses and maintain the regular army at its average strength of 118,750 throughout fiscal years 1934 and 1935. After the decline in early 1933, applications for original enlistment during both years exceeded the army's needs. Between July 1933 and June 1934, for example, 47,589 men applied for original enlistment. Losses during that fiscal year totaled 48,101. The army accepted 23,788 original enlistments in fiscal 1934, about 50 percent of the applicants, but if all applicants had met enlistment standards, the army theoretically could practically have maintained its strength with recruits alone.[55]

Undoubtedly much of the credit for the success of the recruiting effort should go to the continuing depression. The optimistic talk of the summer of 1933 waned by winter as Americans grimly realized that they still had a long way to go toward complete recovery. In the harsh winter of 1933–1934 the Civil Works Administration employed more than 4.25 million men. In the same period the Federal Emergency Relief Administration reported almost 2.5 million families and some 450,000 single persons on relief, and the CCC reported an enrollment of nearly 300,000 in January 1934. The Bureau of Labor Statistics estimated unemployment in the United States at 10,968,000 in 1934, only a slight improvement over the peak of 12,634,000 of the year before. The number of unemployed remained around 10 million through 1935, dropping to 8.5 million in 1936.[56] Little wonder that despite competition from the CCC, recruiters continued to enjoy success.

Late in 1935 the situation facing the Recruiting Service changed. Congress, in appropriating funds for the army for fiscal year 1936, provided enough money to raise the enlisted strength of the regular army to 165,000. In April 1935 the adjutant general's office made plans to achieve the new strength level. The War Department hoped to accomplish the increase quickly and without adding to recruiting expenditures. To accomplish this general plan, the adjutant general directed that each corps area recruit 25 percent of its new authorization per month beginning in July. In order to hold costs at their present level, corps area commanders were directed to mount intensive local recruiting efforts using soldiers from units and post personnel. The plan was similar in scope to the 1923 campaign. Specially organized recruiting parties provided by every post, camp, and station in each corps area were to "conduct an intensive campaign in [its] immediate vicinity." The adjutant general anticipated no lowering of existing standards for enlistment.[57] *Recruiting News,* the official organ of the General Recruiting Service, published the new quotas and reminded recruiters, "The slogan, 'Quality not Quantity' will continue to be the watchword as canvassers and post recruiting parties seek the finest type of young Americans only."[58]

The drive began on July 1, 1935. Reporting on the commencement of stepped-up recruiting, the *New York Times* noted that the White House had put the CCC off limits to recruiters stating that President Roosevelt "made it clear that he did not want the CCC used as a 'feeder' for the military services."[59] Still, recruiting moved along at a brisk pace during the summer of 1935. In the first month of the drive more than 10,000 enlisted. By September enlisted strength stood at 133,727, a postwar peak. In order to remain within its recruiting budget, the War Department terminated the drive early in October. Limited recruiting designed to offset losses continued through the winter, maintaining enlisted strength at around 139,000. In March the drive resumed and quickly raised enlisted strength to 147,000 where it remained until the beginning of fiscal 1937.[60]

That recruiters made their quotas and raised enlisted strength to the newly authorized level in fiscal 1936 suggests that the task was simple. But raw procurement figures do not tell the whole story. Recruiters worked harder in the summer of 1935 than they had since 1929. A letter from a recruiting sergeant in Indiana shows that competition was keen. Sergeant Frank Scott, commanding the substation at South Bend, complained of encroachment on his territory by recruiters from Selfridge Field, Michigan. According to Scott, officials from the Sixth Corps Area placed advertisements in the Elkhart, Indiana, post office and ran ads in the local newspaper resulting in the enlistment of four men. The adjutant general ordered the Sixth Corps Area recruiting officer to end the alleged encroachment if it existed.[61]

Late in July the adjutant general restored the authority of local recruiters to grant waivers permitting applicants with minor physical defects such as flat feet to enlist. Restrictions on such waivers had been imposed in 1931 when "very few such cases were involved because recruiting was no problem. . . ." Now, the adjutant general argued in justifying decentralization, "this situation no longer exists. . . ." Obviously the army was granting more waivers in order to meet the higher quotas.[62]

Further evidence that some drop in quality occurred in fiscal 1936 is the ratio of original enlistment to applications for original enlistment. In 1934 and 1935 the army accepted one original enlistment for every two applicants. In 1936 the ratio dropped to one enlistment for every 1.24 applicants.

Table 6.1 *Ratio of Applicants for Original Enlistment to Original Enlistments, 1934–1937*

YEAR	APPLICANTS	ENLISTMENTS	RATIO
1934	47,589	23,788	2:1
1935	43,947	21,494	2:1
1936	58,043	46,906	1.24:1
1937	55,797	45,533	1.23:1

Sources: Annual Reports, 1934–1937, and "Report on Results Connection Intelligence Tests for Applicants for Enlistments." (See note 55.)

Clearly recruiters cast their nets farther in 1936; they also took more of the applicants than previously.

Moreover, the increase was not accomplished by the General Recruiting Service alone. Budgetary constraints prohibited an increase in the number of men assigned to recruiting duty. In 1935, 43 officers and 428 enlisted men manned the Recruiting Service to maintain enlisted strength at 118,-775. In 1936, when the average strength jumped to 147,000, the Recruiting Service gained six enlisted men.[63] Local recruiting by unit or post canvassing parties accounted for the army's ability to raise its strength by 28,225 during fiscal 1936 without increasing the size or budget of the General Recruiting Service. In New York the Sixteenth Infantry obtained through its own efforts most of the 361 men authorized to augment its ranks. The Eighteenth Infantry, also stationed in New York, secured 210 replacements in the summer of 1935 with unit recruiters.[64]

In California the commander of the Thirteenth Infantry, Colonel Irving J. Phillipson, announced in August 1935 that, "until further notice, recruiting would be the primary mission of the regiment." Phillipson was no stranger to recruiting. In 1921 he had prepared the extensive study of the regular army's recruiting experience during the immediate postwar years. Later in the twenties he served as the chief of the Recruiting Section in the adjutant general's office.[65] Phillipson sent recruiting parties out from every company in the regiment. Regimental trucks bedecked with special Thirteenth Infantry posters and banners toured San Francisco, officers gave radio talks, enlisted men set up exhibits at the Sacramento, San Jose, and Fresno fairs, recruiting announcements were made at baseball games, and with the permission of state officials, recruiters canvassed the relief camps in central California. From September 1 to October 4, when the

War Department called off the drive, the Thirteenth Infantry added 250 men to its rolls.[66]

The army that these men entered differed little from that of the pre-depression years. After they were sworn in, new recruits went straight to their units; recruit training depots, equivalent to today's basic training and advanced individual training centers, had been abolished in 1922 as an economy measure. Recruit training took place the unit level, where three or four newly assigned soldiers received basic instruction in military skills and customs from a noncommissioned officer. The length and quality of such training varied according to the devotion of the instructor and the needs of the unit. Usually recruits were integrated into the organization quickly and were soon performing housekeeping chores, such as post police and barracks repairs, and guard duty with the rest of the privates. They acquired their military skills "on the job."[67]

Training was decentralized. At the beginning of each yearly training cycle the War Department issued a training directive that listed broad guidelines to be followed by local commanders. The War Department training directive for fiscal year 1935 is a typical example. For soldiers in combat units the emphasis was on marksmanship and battle drill. Infantry and cavalry units were told to stress machine-gun training "within the limits of ammunition authorized." All units had to conduct a two-week march every year and, "funds permitting, the mobile troops of each Corps Area . . . will be assembled once during the year in one or more concentration camps for a period of not less than two weeks for combined field exercises." The War Department specifically enjoined commanders "to reduce the demands of routine administration and . . . emphasize the importance of training."[68]

In 1934 MacArthur ordered a thorough study of army training procedures. A board of officers, chaired by Major General Edward Croft, chief of infantry, found little fault with the system.[69] But not all officers agreed with Croft's analysis, especially on the subject of decentralized recruit training. As early as 1928, thoughtful students at the War College suggested a return to the recruit depot system. Under a more centralized program, suggested one report, the recruits would be "classified, weeded out, given five weeks of training and forwarded to units . . . according to the needs of the army."[70] Another War College study suggested that centralized recruit training would give the army more time to identify and "insure the rejection of any man who has mental or physical characteristics which would make him unsuitable as a soldier," before he arrived at a unit.[71]

In 1935, as the army began to expand, Major LeRoy Lutes of the coast artillery suggested that the time was right to overhaul the recruit training system. Speaking of the 46,000 new men who would enter the army during the coming year, he asked, "Are we going to train them into alert, active young soldiers or are we going to make them into hedge clippers, lawn trimmers, garbage haulers, etc. with soldiering as a sideline."[72] Lutes' article did not attract any letters or editorial comment. Local recruit training remained the norm until late 1940 when the rapid expansion of the army through selective service led to the establishment of reception centers, which gave draftees thirteen weeks of basic training before assigning them to units.[73] The modest strength increase of the mid-1930s did not tax the decentralized training system; besides, the troop augmentation for the coming year would raise an even more basic question.

Garrison life in the mid-1930s followed an easy routine. Officers still found more than enough time to mix polo with training and administration. Second Lieutenant William C. Westmoreland, assigned to the Eighteenth Field Artillery at Fort Sill, Oklahoma, in 1936, spent his first summer of active duty "supervising horses while they grazed, . . . breaking remounts, . . . [and] firing demonstrations for the Artillery School. . . ." Westmoreland remembered later that social life was sometimes as demanding as the military duties.[74]

As in the 1920s enlisted men in garrison performed military duties and training in the morning and devoted their afternoons to athletics and recreational activities. Some posts called a "training holiday" one afternoon a week in order to observe the scheduled competition between unit athletic teams. Even the post schools closed so the children could cheer on their favorites.[75]

The effects of the depression altered but did not completely disrupt the easygoing pace of peacetime army life. Colonel George C. Marshall, commander of the Eighth Infantry Regiment at Fort Moultrie near Charleston in 1933, for example, had the additional responsibility of supervising the CCC camps in South Carolina. Marshall thus witnessed the effects of the depression on both the army and society. In her memoirs, Katherine Tupper Marshall remembered both the "rather frail, anemic-looking youths . . ." who entered the CCC camps and the measures Colonel Marshall took to alleviate the distress of his own soldiers:

In order that the men could manage to feed their families on their small pay, my husband personally supervised the building of chicken yards, vegetable gardens, and hog pens. He started a lunch pail system whereby the men could get a good hot dinner, cooked at the mess, to take home to their families at a very small cost. We ate this mid-day dinner ourselves until the custom was well established—so that he might know what the men were getting.[76]

Soldiers complained, as they always do, of the low pay, but were well aware that they were better off than many. Men enlisted for a number of reasons, but few who gave their personal reasons for joining failed to mention job security. Joseph Zafrano of Brooklyn signed up "because enlistment in the Army is a much better proposition for any young man. You have a chance to be something after a few years, and you can always reenlist." John Foy, of New York City, tried to join the CCC before enlisting in the army. "It is difficult to enroll in the CCC because you must be on home relief," he said. "I've tried to do that and have given it up as hopeless." Foy enlisted because, "all necessities are given you in the Army, in addition to the pay, and there are retirement provisions."[77]

The army appreciated the value of job security and its retirement system to the recruiting program and stressed them during the lean years of the depression. Under the provision of the Pay Readjustment Act of 1922 a soldier could retire at three-fourths pay (including longevity pay) plus a monthly allowance of $15.75 for housing expenses. Thus a master sergeant (grade 2) who retired after thirty years service could expect $120.75 a month. The army's retirement plan was better than most private plans then in operation. A railroad worker who retired after thirty years of work in 1934, for example, received an average of $90 a month beginning at age sixty-five. The average amount paid by private pensions in 1933 was $58 a month.[78]

An example of the army's retirement-security "pitch" was an article directed at new recruits that first appeared in 1929 and was reprinted periodically in *Recruiting News*. Major Richard P. Rifenbrick advised new soldiers to begin their enlisted careers by saving five dollars a month and all reenlistment bonuses they would receive. At the end of a thirty-year career, he said, "you will have saved $10,000. [sic] You can go to any town in the United States, buy the best business there is in the trade you have learned, and still have that $100 a month [retirement pay] coming in on the side."[79]

In 1936 when Congress again authorized an enlisted strength of 165,000 for the regular army, the adjutant general responded by announcing new quotas. He advised each corps area that the army required an additional 1,500 men a month in order to raise the army to its new strength. The First Corps Area, which had been recruiting men at an average of 206 a month, was directed to enlist an additional 71 soldiers monthly.[80] For the first time since the depression began, recruiters balked at the order. Colonel Harvey W. Miller, adjutant general of the First Corps Area, informed Washington, "it is not believed that this corps area will be able to fill the requisitions set forth. . . ."[81] In August, Miller wrote to his friend Lieutenant Colonel Victor B. Taylor in the adjutant general's office to explain the magnitude of the problem in New England. Miller cited the efforts of Major Charles G. Hutchinson, district recruiting officer at Springfield, Massachusetts, to obtain recruits. Hutchinson sent letters to 970 postmasters in his area asking for the names of young men who might be favorable recruiting prospects. He received 280 replies furnishing 1,040 names. Of the 1,040 prospects not one enlisted.[82]

Colonel Miller was not alone in complaining. In the Second Corps Area, Colonel Robert S. Bamberger, recently transferred from Washington to

New York, suddenly found the shoe was on the other foot. In August 1936, he wrote to Washington to explain why his recruiters were failing to meet their quotas. Bamberger listed the familiar reasons: improved economic conditions, competition from the CCC and other state and federal agencies, and added two of his own: "the inclination of parents . . . to discourage enlistment because of frequent press news on the European situation . . . , and the communistic character of a considerable portion of the population of New York City."[83]

Continuation of unit and post recruiting cut deeply into training. While local recruiting efforts continued at a less hectic pace in fiscal 1937, the War Department turned to other means to combat slumping production of recruits by augmenting the General Recruiting Service by fifty-five enlisted men and increasing its budget nearly 10 percent. Cost per recruit in fiscal 1937 increased from $23.89 to $26.58.[84] Not even the new minimum intelligence test score was inviolate. In December Major General William E. Cole, commanding the Fifth Corps Area, urged reduction of the minimum test score from forty-four to thirty-six. Cole argued:

This reduced rating will be used in the case of applicants from the mountain section . . . where the educational facilities are not up to the standards maintained in the other sections of the corps area. This type of applicant with a small amount of education makes a very good soldier.

The request was approved for the Fifth Corps Area only.[85] Cole's views and request were exceptional to the prevailing attitude. Most commanders, as previously indicated, approved of the higher standards and applauded the results. Cole's request for a reduction in educational standards was the only one received by the adjutant general. While it was willing to make exception, clearly the War Department had no intention of returning to predepression standards, particularly in terms of minimum intelligence levels. The army was mechanizing on a greater and greater scale and could no longer afford men with strong backs alone.

Despite prodigious efforts, the army failed to raise enlisted strength to the new level by the end of fiscal year 1937. The regular army finished the year understrength. Captain Harris F. Scherer, acting adjutant general of the First Corps Area, believed "present improved economic conditions throughout New England doubtless is a factor," despite a Works Progress Administration (WPA) report of 212,800 unemployed in Massachusetts. He argued strenuously for an end to travel pay restrictions designed to encourage applicants to enlist for assignments close to home, an immediate restoration of the reenlistment bonus, and an additional twenty recruiting sergeants for the corps area's General Recruiting Service.[86] Similar complaints and explanations arrived from recruiting officers in the other corps areas.

In July 1936, Major General E. T. Conley, the adjutant general, wrote to all corps area commanders concerning the recruiting situation. Conley noted that the regular army was some 6,000 men understrength, and he urged the commanders to make full use of available resources to eliminate quickly the shortage and then maintain the 165,000-man level. Failure to do so, the adjutant general suggested, might lead Congress to reduce strength again. Conley acknowledged that avoidable losses such as desertions and purchase discharges were on the increase again and promised that the General Staff would do its part to combat the situation. But he offered little in the way of additional funds. Economy measures such as reduced travel expenses would continue.[87]

Clearly, the depression no longer assisted recruiting after 1936. Despite continued widespread unemployment and a sharp recession in 1937–1938, recruiting again became a full-time job. Competition from New Deal relief programs and a moderately improved economy cut into the army's ability to attract recruits. Ironically the long-sought strength increase also added to the recruiting problem. Increasing the size of the army strained the recruiting system. Unable or unwilling to spend more in search of replacements, the War Department again began to examine the causes of losses. In the coming years the General Staff renewed studies of purchase discharge policies, the conditions of married enlisted men, and the relationship of pay to enlistment and reenlistment. All of these areas had been studied in the past when maintaining enlisted strength and efficiency proved vexing problems. By the beginning of fiscal 1938 it was clear that these problems had returned, and the programs established during the depression to improve enlisted quality and recruiting efficiency now compounded the situation. Once again the volunteer army was in trouble.

NOTES

1. U.S., Department of Commerce, Bureau of the Census, *Historical Statistics of the U.S.,* (Washington, D.C.: GPO, 1960), Table D46–47, "Unemployment, 1900 to 1957," p. 73.

2. Exact figures for the period are found in the Report of the Secretary of War in U.S. War Department, *Annual Report, 1929,* and *Annual Report, 1932* (Washington, D.C.: GPO, 1929, 1932). Hereafter *Annual Report* for the respective years noted. Nineteen-twenty-nine, losses, Table B, p. 188; enlistments, p. 230; 1932, losses, Table B, p. 199; enlistments, p. 238. Desertions dropped from 9,691 to 3,101 between 1929 and 1932. Purchased discharges declined from 8,538 to 3,547, and reenlistments rose from 18,473 to 28,161 during the same period.

3. *Annual Report,* 1930, pp. 354–56.

4. "Parting the Sheep from the Goats," *U.S. Army Recruiting News,* (hereafter, *Recruiting News*) 12, No. 8 (April 15, 1930): 2.

5. *Annual Report,* 1931, pp. 213–15.

6. Letter, J. C. Anthony to Chief of Staff, August 18, 1931, in Central Files of the Adjutant General's Office, file 341, Record Group 94, Box 14, National Archives, Washington, D.C. (hereafter AGO 341, RG 94, Box 14,NA).

7. Letter, MacArthur to Anthony, August 22, 1931, AGO 341, RG 94, Box 14, NA.

8. Memo, Assistant Chief of Staff for Personnel (ACS, G1) to CS, October 23, 1931, AGO 341, RG 94, Box 14, NA.

9. Letter, Adjutant General (AG) to Commanding General, VI Corps Area (CG, VI CA), AGO 341, RG 94, Box 14, NA.

10. Surgeon General to AG, September 20, 1932; Letter, AG to all Corps Area Commanders, October 12, 1932, AGO 342.15, RG 94, Box 1798, NA.

11. Maj. Albert E. Brown, "Peacetime Enlisted Losses, Replacements and Methods," Memo for the Commandant, Army War College, February 15, 1930, file 367-8, Military History Institute, Carlisle Barracks, Pa. Hereafter, MHI.

12. *Annual Report*, 1932, p. 237.

13. Letter, Headquarters, Chanute Field, Ill., to Chief of Air Corps, September 17, 1932, AGO 341, RG 94, Box 1793, NA.

14. Memo, ACS G1 to CS, May 28, 1932, AGO 341, RG 94, Box 1793, NA; Memo, ACS G1 to CS, July 18, 1932; Letter, AG to CG's all Corps Areas, September 1, 1932.

15. Letter, CG II CA to AG, February 21, 1933, AGO 341, RG 94, Box 1793, NA.

16. Letter, CG IV CA to AG, February 10, 1933, AGO 341, RG 94, Box 1793, NA.

17. These figures are extracted from a series of special reports prepared by the Statistics Branch of the General Staff. The reports are located at the Military History Research Collection, Carlisle Barracks, Pa. They appear to be a statistical summary of War Department activities for each fiscal year, 1924–1940; 1925 and 1932 are missing. See file 198-Am, MHI.

18. Memo, ACS G1 to CS, March 23, 1933, AGO 341, RG 94, Box 1793, NA.

19. U.S. Bureau of the Census, *The Statistical History of the United States from Colonial Times to the Present,* (New York: Basic Books, 1976), p. 702.

20. *Army and Navy Journal* (hereafter *ANJ*), March 11, 1933, p. 549.

21. James M. Burns, *Roosevelt: The Lion and the Fox* (New York: Harcourt, Brace and Co., 1956), pp. 167, 168; William E. Leuchtenburg, *Franklin D. Roosevelt and the New Deal, 1931–1940* (New York: Harper & Row, 1963), pp. 45, 46.

22. *ANJ*, April 1, 1933, pp. 608, 619.

23. In October 1933, the Statistics Branch of the General Staff began a study of the effects of the depression and the Economy Act of 1933 on commissioned officers. The chief of the Statistics Branch reported the results to the chief of staff in December 1934. The report summarized the results of a questionnaire and suggested that it be used to justify reopening the pay question. The study did not include a section on enlisted men, but several hundred enlisted men had filled out questionnaires. These enlisted responses were not tabulated but were filed with the report. The report, Memo, Chief, Statistics Branch, General Staff to CS, December 27, 1934, is filed in AGO 240, RG 94, Box 1175, NA. The unprocessed

NCO questionnaires are filed under the same number in a separate package listed AGO 240 Bulky.

24. Ibid.

25. Ibid.

26. Interview with Raymond G. Alvord, West Point, N.Y., February 6, 1975.

27. Memo, G1 to CS, August 10, 1931. This is part of a large bound study titled "Marriage of Enlisted Men," filed under AGO 220.81, RG 94, Box 1100, NA.

28. The report is summarized in Memo, G-11 to CS, August 10, 1931, AGO 220.81, RG 94, Box 1100, NA.

29. Memo, G1 to CS, September 21, 1931; Memo, G1 to CS, December 11, 1931, AGO 220.81, RG 94, Box 1100, NA.

30. Memo, G1 to CS, December 11, 1931, AGO 220.81, NA. MacArthur's signature approving the changes is dated December 29, 1931.

31. Johnson Hagood, "Down the Big Road," unpublished manuscript of memoirs, chapter 40, p. 392, the Hagood Family Papers, MHI.

32. Based on a comparison of the army pay system (see Appendix C) and "Consumption Expenditures of Families of City Wage and Clerical Workers, 1934–36," *Historical Statistics of the U.S.*, Table G 244–330, p. 180.

33. John W. Killigrew, "The Impact of the Great Depression on the U.S. Army, 1929–1936," (Ph.D. diss., Indiana University, 1960), chapter 12, p. 9.

34. *Annual Report,* 1933, p. 6.

35. *ANJ,* April 1, 1933, p. 616.

36. *Annual Report,* 1933, pp. 152, 186; 1934, p. 192.

37. Letter, HQ II CA to AG, September 22, 1933, AGO 341, RG 94, Box 1792, NA.

38. Letter, HQ VIII CA to AG, September 21, 1933, AGO 341, RG 94, Box 1792, NA.

39. Letter, HQ I CA to AG, September 22, 1933; Letter, HQ IX CA to AG, September 22, 1933, AGO 341, RG 94, Box 1792, NA.

40. Killigrew, "The Impact of the Great Depression on the U.S. Army," chapter 13, pp. 8–10.

41. *ANJ,* July 22, 1933, p. 936.

42. U.S. Department of Commerce *Statistical Abstract of the U.S.* (Washington, D.C.: GPO, 1938), pp. 313, 324.

43. *ANJ,* September 9, 1933, p. 21.

44. Ibid., November 4, 1933, p. 190.

45. Ibid., January 6, 1934, pp. 365, 366, 372.

46. House Appropriation Hearings, 1935, p. 109.

47. Ibid., p. 19.

48. *ANJ,* January 13, 1934, pp. 383, 389, 395, 397.

49. Ibid., pp. 389, 397.

50. Ibid., p. 392.

51. Ibid., March 31, 1934, pp. 605, 606, 612.

52. Ibid., March 18, 1939, p. 654. Between 1935 and 1939 the House consistently voted to eliminate the ban on reenlistment bonuses from the independent offices bill and the Senate consistently voted to retain it. In conference the House always backed down until 1939. Senator James F. Byrnes expressed the Senate's position

(and undoubtedly the administration's) in March 1939 when he observed that the bonus was not needed to stimulate reenlistments. Strenuous House opposition that year forced Byrnes to yield. *ANJ,* March 11, 1939, pp. 629, 649; March 18, p. 654.

53. Extract, "Report of the Interdepartmental Pay Committee, 1938," in vol. 1, G1, *Guide Book on Readjustment of Service Pay and Allowances* (no date), AGO 240, RG 94, Box 1182, NA.

54. *ANJ,* August 17, 1940, pp. 1245, 1247. During the Senate debate on the selective service bill both sides on the draft agreed that soldiers should be paid at least the same as CCC enrollees. *ANJ,* August 10, 1940, pp. 1217, 1234.

55. Figures on applicants are compiled from two sources. Data for November 1927 to June 1931 are contained in quarterly reports from each corps area titled "Report on Results Connection Intelligence Tests for Applicants for Enlistment," filed under AGO 319.12, RG 407, Box 1343, NA. Beginning with fiscal 1932 the file number was changed. Data for July 1931 through March 1938, when the reports were terminated, are filed under AGO 702, RG 94, Box 3170, NA. These reports were instituted in 1927 when the army began regular testing of applicants for original enlistment. See Chapter 4, pp. 102–3. Figures on losses are compiled from *Annual Report,* 1934, p. 164.

56. Broadus Mitchell, *Depression Decade* (New York: Harper & Row, 1969), p. 316 and appendix, p. 453; *Statistical Abstract of the U.S.,* 1935, Table 361, p. 326; Table 363, p. 327.

57. Letter, AG to All Corps Area Commanders, April 26, 1935, AGO 341, RG 94, Box 1790, NA.

58. "Army to Enlist 31,700," *Recruiting News* 17, no. 12 (June 15, 1935): 7.

59. *New York Times* (hereafter, *NYT*), July 1, 1935, p. 3.

60. *Annual Report,* 1936, p. 90; *NYT,* September 22, 1935, p. 7; summarized from testimony of Brig. Gen. E. T. Conley, acting AG, before House Appropriations Committee, U.S., Congress, House, Committee on Appropriations, *Hearings on War Department Appropriations Bill, 1937,* 74th Cong., 2d Sess., December 19, 1935, p. 65; *Annual Report,* 1936, p. 89.

61. Letter, Sergeant Frank Scott to District Commander, Indianapolis, July 2, 1935; Letter, AG to VI CA Recruiting Officer, no date, AGO 341, RG 94, Box 1790, NA.

62. Memo, AG to ACS G1, July 26, 1935, AGO 341, RG 94, Box 1790, NA.

63. *Hearings, War Department Bill, 1937,* p. 91.

64. *Recruiting News* 18, no. 1 (January 1, 1936): 10.

65. Ibid. 6, no. (July 1, 1924): 8.

66. *ANJ,* November 9, 1935, p. 186.

67. Major LeRoy Lutes, "The New Recruit Class," *Infantry Journal* 42, no. 3 (May-June, 1935): 264–65.

68. War Department Training Directive, Fiscal Year 1935, as quoted in *ANJ,* March 31, 1934, pp. 607, 608.

69. *ANJ,* July 14, 1934, pp. 929, 932; October 20, p. 166.

70. "Recruitment in Peace for Regular Army and National Guard," Supplement No. 1 to Report of Committee No. 2, AWC Class 1928–1929, G1 Course, File 350-2, MHI.

71. Major C. C. Stokely, "Improvement of the Enlisted Personnel of the Regular Army," Memo for the Asst. Cmdt., AWC, March 31, 1930, File 367-75, MHI.

72. Lutes, "The New Recruit Class," pp. 264–65.

73. Leonard L. Lerwill, *The Personnel Replacement System in the United States Army* (Washington, D.C.: Department of the Army, 1954), pp. 248, 249.

74. William C. Westmoreland, *A Soldier Reports* (Garden City, N.Y.: Doubleday, 1976), pp. 15–16.

75. Based on interview with Raymond G. Alvord, West Point, N.Y., February 6, 1975.

76. Katherine Tupper Marshall, *Together: Annals of an Army Wife* (New York: Tupper and Love, Inc., 1946), p. 5.

77. "Why They Enlisted," *Recruiting News* 17, no. 16 (August 15, 1935): 5.

78. The army's retirement program is outlined in "The United States Army as a Career" (Washington, D.C.: The Adjutant General of the Army, 1929), pp. 31, 32. For private pension plans during the period, see Paul H. Douglas, *Social Security in the United States* (New York: McGraw Hill, 1936), pp. 172–76, 271–91.

79. Richard P. Rifenbrick, "A Talk to Recruits," *Recruiting News* 12, no. 5 (March 1, 1930): 7.

80. Letter, AG to CG, I CA, June 2, 1936, AGO 341, RG 94, Box 1791, NA.

81. Letter, HQ I CA to AG, June 8, 1936, AGO 341, RG 94, Box 1791, NA.

82. Letter, Harvey W. Miller to Victor B. Taylor, August 21, 1936, AGO 341, RG 94, Box 1791, NA.

83. Letter, Office of the Corps Area Commander, II CA to AG, August 11, 1936, AGO 341, RG 94, Box 1791, NA.

84. Figures derived from cost of recruiting tables in Special Reports 243 and 252 for fiscal years 1936 and 1937 respectively, file 198-A, MHI.

85. Letter CG, V CA to AG, December 17, 1936, AGO 702, RG 94, Box 3170, NA.

86. Letter, Captain H. F. Scherer to AG, March 9, 1937, AGO 341, RG 94, Box 1791, NA.

87. Letter, Major General E. T. Conley to CG, I CA, July 6, 1937, AGO 341, RG 94, Box 1790, NA.

7

PREPARATIONS FOR WAR

In 1936 the already shaky world order established by the Treaty of Versailles began to collapse. News from abroad became increasingly grim. Germany remilitarized the Rhineland in March and moved rapidly ahead with its rearmament program. In the summer Germany and Italy intervened in the Spanish Civil War, thereby elevating that conflict to one of international concern. In 1937 Japan began its undeclared war in China, and as a result of the *Panay* incident, momentarily involved the United States in a war scare.

For the most part, however, Americans continued to be concerned primarily with domestic issues. Franklin D. Roosevelt, beginning his second term as president in 1937, also worried mainly about domestic affairs. Following his disastrously abortive attempt to reorganize the Supreme Court, he struggled with an increasingly hostile Congress and tried to deal with a sharp recession that continued into 1938 and interrupted gradual business recovery.

By the end of 1937, however, world events began to intrude on America's preoccupation with problems at home, and on January 28, 1938, there began the first important steps toward American rearmament.[1] On that date President Roosevelt told Congress, "As Commander in Chief . . . it is my constitutional duty to report . . . that our national defense is, in the light of the increasing armaments of other nations, inadequate for purposes of national security and requires increase for that reason." Emphasizing naval rearmament, the chief executive recommended a 20 percent increase in the existing naval building program, two additional battleships and cruisers, and the "construction of a number of new types of smaller vessels. . . ." The cost of the program for fiscal 1939 came to about $28 million. Roosevelt also recommended a 14 percent increase in army appropriations of about $17 million, primarily for improvements in antiaircraft facilities.[2]

Reaction to Roosevelt's message developed along predictable lines. Many pacifists and liberals led the assault on his plan. Testifying before the Senate Committee on Military Affairs, Louise Bransten of the American League Against War and Fascism opposed rearmament, arguing that instead, "The United States, in cooperation with the peace forces of the world, could effectively stop war in any part of the world without resorting to armed conflict." She advocated collective action "through instruments such as the Kellogg-Briand Pact . . . The Washington Treaty and the Treaty of Buenos Aires . . . that express the sentiments of the people and prevent war.'' Charles A. Beard, a noted historian known for his opposition to armaments, urged the House Committee on Naval Affairs to reject the president's requests. Beard called predictions of fascist interest in South America a ''new racket created to herd the American people into President Roosevelt's quarantine camp.'' Even a navy twice the size proposed, he declared, could not challenge Japan in her own waters. Beard told the committee that before it voted any funds for rearmament, ''it must inquire into the foreign policy represented by the general and specific demands made upon it by the Executive.''[3]

The opponents of rearmament, though vehement, received little support for their position. Most newspapers saw Roosevelt's proposals as prudent efforts toward defensive, not offensive, protection. The *San Francisco Chronicle,* for example, called FDR's message ''a sad answer to have to make, but it is a sorrowful truth . . . that the world today is an unsafe place for our country in the present state of its defenses.''[4]

Congress wrote Roosevelt's recommendations into the War and Navy Departments' appropriation bills for the fiscal year beginning July 1938, and for the most part, approved them with little significant delay. For the army the appropriation amounted to about $612 million, an increase of $97 million over the previous budget. Almost all of the increase over previous fiscal years went for improvement of coast and air defenses. Authorized enlisted strength remained unchanged.[5]

President Roosevelt remained publicly silent on the subject of rearmament for the remainder of 1938. But world developments, notably Germany's takeover of Austria and the dismemberment of Czechoslovakia at Munich, compelled him to plan for further increases in defense spending. On November 14, 1938, at a meeting with his civilian and military advisors, Roosevelt laid the groundwork for a further increase in the nation's air and ground forces.[6] According to Major General Henry H. Arnold, who took notes for the chief of staff, the president did most of the talking. The emphasis was entirely on airplanes, and Roosevelt directed the army to prepare a two-year plan for the production of 10,000 planes.[7]

The following day Louis Johnson, acting secretary of war, directed the General Staff to prepare the plan. What emerged was something far different from what the president desired. Under the direction of Brigadier General George C. Marshall the War Plans Division (WPD) developed a plan for the balanced expansion of the entire military establishment. In addition to addressing the president's desire for more airplanes WPD urged an expansion of the regular army based within the United States in order to furnish an expeditionary force capable of limited operations in South America, further improvements of the defenses in Alaska, Panama, and the Caribbean, and an increase in the National Guard.[8]

The chief of staff, General Malin Craig, realized that WPD was exceeding the president's directive but supported his planners' views. Craig, who served as chief of staff from October 1935 to August 1939, has not received proper attention from historians. He was a transitional figure between MacArthur, the Uptonian who placed preservation of personnel strength before all other considerations, and Marshall, who under Palmer's influence sought to develop a balanced force in being. When Craig became chief of staff, the struggle to preserve army strength had been won, and a modest increase was already under way. Thus, Craig devoted his attention to improving the training and material readiness of the small peacetime force.

In December Craig presented the "Two-Year Army Augmentation Plan" to the secretary of war arguing that such an increase was necessary in view of the apparent Nazi and Fascist penetration of Latin America.[9] By this time Roosevelt was aware that his military planners were far afield of his original intentions, and he called another meeting of his military advisers. According to James H. Burns, an assistant to the secretary of war, Roosevelt told the assembled group that he intended to ask Congress for $500 million in new armaments for fiscal 1940. By new armaments the president meant airplanes, but he now found the army and navy asking for everything but airplanes. FDR wanted $500 million worth of fighter planes to intimidate Hitler. The army and navy argued that aircraft without crews and modern support facilities would not convince anyone that the United States meant to defent itself. Roosevelt acknowledged the logic of the argument and relented. He agreed to a balanced expansion but was still not ready to increase army manpower.[10]

In his annual message to Congress on January 4, 1939, the president, alluding to Munich, reported, "A war which threatened to envelop the world in flames has been averted; but it has become increasingly clear that world peace is not assured." Declaring the necessity "of putting our own house in order in the face of storm signals from across the seas," Roosevelt told the lawmakers and the country, "we must have armed forces and defenses strong enough to ward off sudden attacks against strategic positions and key facilities essential to sustain resistance and ultimate victory."[11] Ten days later he spelled out his intentions in a message that requested an additional $525 million for the army and navy.[12] Routine army requests for fiscal 1940 appropriations already totaled $456 million for military activities. Nearly the entire supplement of $525 million was also earmarked for the army; $300 million for new aircraft, $110 million for equipment for regular army and National Guard units, $32 million for educational orders to prepare industry for emergency production, $27 million to strengthen the forces in Panama, and $8 million for improved coastal defenses in Panama, Hawaii, and the United States.[13] Neither the original request nor President Roosevelt's supplement called for increasing the manpower strength of the army.

Response to the president's requested defense increases followed about the same lines as the year before. Idaho Senator William E. Borah, a veteran isolationist, said that rearmament would lead to American involvement in foreign wars. "What will happen to this Republic?" he asked. Warning that participation in war abroad would mean an end to democracy at home, Borah predicted, "There would be no free speech, no free press, no liberty, except such liberty as would be essential to serve the cause of war."[14] Senator Burton K. Wheeler of Montana agreed. "I do not feel that the United States should again attempt to be the guardian of all the people of the world," he said. Deploring fascist dictatorship, Wheeler nevertheless charged that American rearmament was "provocative" and would mislead British and French leaders into believing that the United States might indeed support them. This would not happen, he said: "the intelligence of the American people must and will prevent our entry into another world war."[15]

Advocates of preparedness countered heatedly. In an emotional address before the American Forum of the Air, Senate Foreign Relations Committee Chairman Key Pittman of Nevada defended the requested increases, declaring that the treaties and bodies designed to preserve peace "have utterly failed to accomplish their purposes." To claims that the United States was not in danger Pittman responded, "Those who make this argument are thinking only of the present. . . . The trend of events should be sufficient answer to impel the President and Congress to start preparations for successful defense."[16] From Paris, Roy Howard of the Scripps-Howard newspapers reported that only Adolf Hitler knew whether Europe would be at war by the end of the year and added that in his opinion only a miracle could prevent American involvement. "We should begin to base our judgments on hard-boiled reason and common sense," Howard said and urged, "For once we should be smart enough before the fact . . ." and begin to arm.[17]

Public opinion concerning the proposed increases is difficult to measure. The *Army and Navy Journal* found the editors of daily newspapers throughout the nation generally in favor of the increase.[18] Similarly, a Gallup poll in December 1938 revealed that while 95 percent of the sample opposed American involvement in another war, 82 percent favored a larger army and 90 percent supported increases in the air force. But in another poll taken the same month only 37 percent favored mandatory peacetime military training and service for twenty-year-olds.[19] Public ambivalence on preparedness suggests that most people viewed the increases as necessary for the preservation of American neutrality but not for actual use in war.

Congressional actions during 1939 lend credence to this view of national ambivalence toward rearmament. In early 1939 Congress approved army and navy appropriations for fiscal year 1940 and the president's January requests for some $500 million in additional expenditures. The army thus received a total of $989 million in fiscal 1940.[20] During the same period that Congress approved larger appropriations for defense, Roosevelt tried and failed to repeal the arms embargo in order to allow Britain and France to purchase arms and ammunition from the United States once war began.[21] America was rearming for its own defense and for no one else.

The army's leadership generally shared the notion that it was rearming for defense. As previously noted, several of the army's more eloquent spokesmen expressed the opinion that Europe's problems were not the business of the United States. When in 1936 Stanley Embick submitted his views to the president on abandoning the Philippines in favor of a shorter defensive line in the Pacific, he indicated that the proposal had the unqualified support of most of the General Staff. Embick remained a key figure in the War Department planning process throughout the buildup. He consistently urged his superiors, including the president, to avoid getting too close to the British whose interests differed from ours. Until the fall of France in 1940 few in the army disagreed with Embick's sentiments.[22]

Regular appropriations for the army approved in April 1939 had already provided for a continuation of the average enlisted strength of 165,000 men, the strength the army had finally achieved in mid-1938. During hearings on the appropriation bill army spokesmen had advised Congress that the expansion of the air force required an additional 4,633 officers and enlisted men. Furthermore, the garrison in Panama needed 180 officers and 5,285 enlisted men. Taking these men from the existing base of 12,000 officers and 165,000 enlisted men would be counterproductive, the army argued.[23] Unlike previous augmentations of the air corps when Congress ordered an expansion of that branch while maintaining a fixed strength overall, thereby effectively reducing the rest of the army, in 1939 Congress willingly authorized an increase in the strength of the army to accommodate the latest expansion of the air corps. Then in a broader authorization, which removed the specific limitation on average strength, Congress in May 1939 permitted the regular army to increase to approximately 13,000 officers and 210,000 enlisted men by June 30, 1940, and voted the additional funds necessary to pay the new men.[24] Recruiting to achieve the new strength began at once and proceeded with moderate success, but events moved so rapidly in 1939 and 1940 that additional increases in authorized strength eventually overwhelmed the limited peacetime recruiting effort.

These increases, however, still left the army in a weakened state. The National Defense Act of 1920 had envisioned a regular army of 280,000 men backed up by a 450,000-man National Guard. On July 1, 1939, when George Marshall became acting chief of staff the actual strength of the regular army was about 174,000 enlisted men. The strength of the National Guard was about 200,000.[25] The War Department's plan for mobilization, which Marshall had helped prepare while chief of War Plans Division, called for the creation of an initial protective force of 730,000 men through recruitment of the regular army and National Guard to full strength.[26] Active army units overseas were at full strength, but in the United States the military establishment was a mere skeleton. Of nine authorized infantry divisions the regular army could field but three and one-half at approximately 50 percent strength. Each of the two cavalry divisions was 1,200 men understrength. Corps and general headquarters troops, necessary to provide reserve forces for the infantry divisions, existed virtually on paper only. The eighteen infantry divisions of the National Guard, two per corps area, were all about half-strength.

The state of army equipment was equally unsuited for large-scale war. Both the National Guard and the regular army were equipped with World War I–vintage equipment. The field artillery still used the French 75 mm gun, infantrymen still carried the Springfield rifle and used the inaccurate Stokes three-inch mortar. Superior weapons existed in every category but were available only in small quantities. For example, in February 1939, the army had on hand but one 37 mm rifle, the proposed replacement for the existing antitank weapon. Although mechanizing, the army still depended to a large degree on horses. The field artillery and infantry machine-gun units were horse drawn. There were no tank divisions, and the few tank companies that had survived the retrenchment of the early 1930s operated in support of the infantry. The army still contained a large number of cavalry regiments (fourteen), and only two of these were mechanized.[27] In May 1939 the army estimated that $1 billion would be needed to provide essential items of equipment for the initial protective force.[28]

Germany invaded Poland on September 1, 1939, the day that George Marshall officially became chief of staff. Marshall had served as an operations officer during World War I. His skill attracted Pershing's attention, and the general of the armies brought Marshall to his staff where he became acquainted with John McAuley Palmer. During the reorganization of the army after the war Marshall and Palmer worked together with Pershing as he prepared to support the citizen army concept.[29] Marshall expected that a European war would bring an immediate increase in the regular army and National Guard to full authorized strength. But President Roosevelt, fearing that public opinion was not prepared for such a momentous increase, declined to do so. On September 8 he declared a "limited national emergency" for the purpose of preserving neutrality and strengthening the nation's defense "within the limits of peacetime authorizations."[30] Under the authority of the proclamation Roosevelt increased the strength ceiling of the regular army from 210,000 to 227,000 and the National Guard to 235,000 men and released contingency funds necessary to pay for the expansion.[31]

Though disappointed, the General Staff used the 17,000-man increment to the regular army to flesh out units for the purpose of testing a new type of infantry division. The old World War I "square" division of 28,000 men each consisting of four infantry regiments and various supporting units, was replaced by a "triangular" division made up of three infantry-artillery combat teams that could operate separately or as a mass. Using the strength increase, the army created five effective new divisions of 7,800 men each, which were trained and tested during the spring of 1940. The War Department could field more of the new divisions because they required fewer men and thus give the impression that the army was growing more rapidly than it actually was. But the 1940 maneuvers also revealed that the new combat organizations were indeed more flexible, faster moving, and independent than the old divisions. Eventually all regular army and National Guard divisions were reorganized in this manner.[32]

Meanwhile planning went ahead on other contingencies. During the winter of 1939–1940, the War Department presented its budget estimates of $879 million for fiscal 1941. The amount was not all the army wanted. The request did not include $150 million for planes and critical material for the initial protective force because Marshall doubted that Congress would approve the additional items. The estimate provided for the attainment of a balanced regular army–National Guard of 600,000 men by the end of the year. The Bureau of the Budget, responding to continued administration fears that the public was not yet prepared for such a high figure, pared the request to $853 million.[33]

Marshall defended the request before the War Department subcommittee of the House Appropriations Committee in February 1940. Referring to the situation abroad, he told the members it was time to "face facts." Changes for the worse in Europe required "added precautions in this country." In an often quoted remark he prophetically declared, "If Europe blazes in the late spring or summer we must put our house in order before the sparks reach the Western Hemisphere." If the situation deteriorated further, Marshall said, further increases in the regular army and National Guard would be necessary. In the opinion of the General Staff an additional 15,000 men were already needed for the regular army, "until it is apparent that the world is assuredly embarked on a period of prolonged peace."

But, Marshall added, the army needed materiel before men. He urged a continuation of balanced increases, stating flatly, "I am opposed to plunging into a sudden expansion of personnel to the limit of present authorizations, and I am equally opposed to the policy of waiting until the last moment and then attempting the impossible. . . ."[34] It was not that Marshall opposed more manpower. Quite the contrary, the chief of staff was dismayed in September 1939 when Roosevelt had ordered an increase of only 17,000 men for the regular army. Marshall had recommended a 40,000-man expansion. His concern about the size and rate of the personnel buildup was twofold. First, he appreciated Roosevelt's fears that the public was not ready for a more rapid expansion. Second, and of more immediate concern to the army, the chief of staff doubted the wisdom of bringing in more recruits than the existing establishment was able to house, equip, or train.[35]

Many remained skeptical during the winter of the "phony war" that even further balanced increases in men, materiel, and appropriations were necessary. Representative D. Lane Powers of New Jersey reflected this feeling as he questioned Marshall on the need for men and new weapons. "Year after year it is the same," Powers complained. "I sat here in 1933 and heard General MacArthur say, 'if we had 165,000 enlisted men in the Army, we would not fear anything that might happen.' " "The present world situation has changed conditions," replied Marshall. Powers was not convinced. He pressed Marshall to explain why the army now needed 5,500 planes when the year before General Arnold had said 3,300 would do. He also worried about the cost of defense. Pointing to the national debt of $45 billion, Powers said that the country was headed for ruin if it spent $2 billion annually on the army and navy. "[If] through some unfortunate circumstances we are forced into this present war," he lamented, "frankly, I cannot see what the outcome is going to be."[36] Reflecting the power of this economizing argument, the committee reported the bill on April 3, after cutting approximately $64 million from the request. The House approved the measure as reported on April 4.[37]

Before the Senate took up the War Department requests for fiscal 1941, Europe "blazed" as Marshall warned. The rapid turn of events in the spring of 1940, especially the fall of the Low Countries, deeply shocked the American people and galvanized them into action. A preparedness mania swept the country. Near Pittsburgh a local gun club formed a "civilian anti-parachutist legion" designed to shoot down enemy paratroopers directed at Pittsburgh's industrial plants. Congress was deluged with "suggestions" from would-be inventors hoping to aid in the home defense effort. Among the more exotic suggestions were Magic Grease, designed to increase the speed of bullets; and Liquid Cement, which when sprayed on advancing troops would harden, stopping the enemy in his tracks.[38]

Responding to the debacle in Europe, Marshall immediately requested $25 million for additional critical items. Mania for preparedness affected the government as well. On May 16 at the Senate's request, President Roosevelt appeared before Congress and personally asked for additional defense appropriations of $1 billion, $734 million of it for the immediate needs of the army, and an increase of the regular army to 280,000 men. On May 31, Roosevelt submitted an additional request for $1 billion more. Congress quickly added $50 million to the first request to provide for a troop strength of 255,000 men and then added $322 million to the second request and raised the authorized strength of the regular army to 375,000 enlisted men. Thus, in less than a month Congress had almost doubled the size of the army.[39]

The rapid increases in authorized troop strength left in a shambles General Staff plans for gradual balanced increases as envisioned by the Protective Mobilization Plan. Based on a thorough reevaluation of the nation's ability to mobilize ordered by General Craig's insistence, the Protective Mobilization Plan, approved in 1938, provided for the creation of a 400,000-man initial protective force composed of full-strength regular army and National Guard divisions on M-Day (Mobilization-Day). In the first month following the decision to mobilize the planners expected enough volunteers to increase the initial protective force to 1 million men. Thereafter volunteers were expected to decline and conscription, which was to begin on M-1, would provide enough men to raise the force to a strength of 1.5 million trained men by M+ 60. In situations short of war only the first increment of 400,000 needed to be mobilized.[40] The Protective Mobilization Plan had assumed that peacetime mobilization would not exceed the strength ceilings established by the National Defense Act of 1920. But under the new authorization the regular army alone surpassed the planning figure by 95,000 men. The army could not procure equipment fast enough to outfit the new men. Furthermore, the new troops themselves could not be obtained overnight. Indeed, every time Congress had increased the strength ceiling between 1935 and early 1940, the army had taken a long time to reach it. In July 1940 when Congress authorized the increase to 375,000 men, the army had just reached the strength level ordered the previous September.[41]

Table 7.1 *Summary of Strength Increases, 1935–1940*

DATE OF INCREASE	STRENGTH AUTHORIZED	DATE ACHIEVED
Average strength, 1923–1935	118,750	—
April 9, 1935	147,000	March 1936
May 15, 1936	165,000	July 1938
May 2, 1939	210,000	December 1939
September 8, 1939	227,000	June 1940

Source: Compiled from Annual Reports, 1936–1941.

The harsh reality of the British evacuation of Dunkirk and the collapse of France prompted William Knudsen, recently appointed to head the Advisory Commision to the Council of National Defense, to ask the War Department for specific goals of army growth so that he could properly plan production. On June 13 Marshall informed Knudsen that a rate of production capable of supporting an army of 1 million by October 1, 1941, 2 million by January 1, 1942, and 4 million by April 1, 1942 was "imperative."[42]

The General Staff assumed that the 4-million-man army would be raised after general mobilization. Concerned that continued expansion of both the regular army and the National Guard prior to actual mobilization would deprive one or the other of needed equipment, War Plans Division considered expanding the regular army to 530,000 for the purpose of providing the entire initial protective force. The rest of the General Staff, while still thinking of a volunteer army and not of selective serivce, doubted that such a force could be raised by voluntary enlistment. The WPD then accepted a revised figure of 400,000, to be raised by a high-pressure civilian volunteer effort. The secretary of war presented this proposal to Roosevelt on June 4.[43] The civilian volunteer effort, designed to raise 90,000 men in thirty days, anticipated augmenting the General Recruiting Service with 400 officers and 500 enlisted men and creating special task forces in each state. Under the direction of state adjutants general voluntary committees of "patriotic citizens in every community [would] assist in canvassing for men."[44] By this time, however, public concern over events in Europe moved to the point that even intensive recruiting such as envisioned by the civilian volunteer effort began to seem obsolete to many.

Meanwhile, other experienced spokesmen for the army took steps to jettison primary reliance on a volunteer army. On May 8, 1940, members of the Executive Committee of the Military Training Camps Association of the United States for the Second Corps Area met in New York City to discuss plans for a reunion of the veterans of the World War I Plattsburg camps. The group had supported universal military training after World War I and had remained an active advocate of civilian military training ever since. At the meeting Grenville Clark, a prominent New York attorney, expressed concern over the direction of American rearmament. At Clark's suggestion a larger gathering was called for May 22 to discuss the question of compulsory military training and service.[45] More than one hundred members from all parts of the country attended, including John McAuley Palmer, the acknowledged architect of the National Defense Act of 1920. Meeting at the Harvard Club, the MTCA adopted a resolution calling for the immediate enactment of peacetime military training and selective service.[46]

On May 25 Palmer presented the views of the MTCA to Marshall, an old friend, to solicit his support. Marshall refused to back the proposal, citing the president's unwillingness to seek conscription in peacetime, but he did release three members of a joint services committee then considering options for wartime selective service to go to New York and discuss plans with the MTCA. Among the three was Major Lewis B. Hershey, who later became the director of selective service and remained so until he retired in 1970.[47] Undaunted by Marshall's rebuff, Clark and Julius Ochs Adler, vice-president and general manager of the *New York Times,* visited Marshall on May 31 to urge his support. Marshall again refused to do so, repeating the political objection to the idea and adding two more. He feared the introduction of a selective service bill might jeopardize the large appropriations soon to go before Congress. Furthermore, Marshall was on record as opposing swift, massive expansion of the army, a move that would require stripping regular army units of trained men to furnish cadre and dilute already limited stocks of critical supplies.[48] Marshall preferred to hold the regular army at 400,000 men through the end of the fiscal year and, after a vigorous period of training, use it as the core of a rapidly expanding citizen army in a fashion similar to Emory Upton's expandable army schemes. Firmly committed to gradual, controlled expansion, the chief of staff supported the civilian volunteer effort as the best means for raising additional troops in peacetime.[49] Though sympathetic to the concept of a citizen army, Marshall felt that the deterioration of the standing force between the wars left him with no alternative but to proceed with the schemes advanced by his Uptonian predecessors.

It was not that Marshall opposed the principle of conscription. On the contrary, since the mid-1920s a Joint Army-Navy Selective Service Committee had been studying the manpower needs of the services in the event of a major war. Both the committee and manpower mobilization planners in the office of the deputy chief of staff for personnel assumed from the start of the interwar period that general mobilization implied conscription. The joint committee prepared several selective service bills during the interwar years. These bills were not, as one critic suggested at the time, intended to impose a peacetime draft on an unsuspecting public or even require peacetime registration. Neither service presumed to make national policy. The bills were prepared and held in reserve until such time as needed. In early 1940 Marshall, a model of military subordination to civil authority, heard no such call for conscription, least of all peacetime conscription.[50]

Clark and his associates doubted that there was enough time for a gradual buildup. They decided to move on their own. Clark formed a National Emergency Committee (NEC) consisting of 1,000 prominent members of the MTCA, and prepared a bill for compulsory selective service and training. The bill was drafted largely by Palmer and Representative James W. Wadsworth, Jr., of New York. Wadsworth, who sponsored the bill in the House, had led the fight for UMT in the Senate after World War I. The bill, sponsored in the Senate by Edward R. Burke, was introduced on June 20, 1940.[51] Debate on it raged even as others pressed for the civilian volunteer effort to add 90,000 volunteers in thirty days. Seldom if ever had the major alternatives for military strength—Uptonian and Palmerian—been so clearly and dramatically opposed.

Because of the resources of the NEC the bill received widespread publicity and editorial support including that of Adler's *New York Times,* which on June 7 declared:

We have no possible alternative but to take advantage of such time as is given us to strengthen our defenses. Congress has taken the first necessary step by appropriating funds for the acquisition of materiel; but materiel is of no value without men who are trained to use it. . . . We should proceed at once to establish a genuinely democratic system of military service which will give us an adequate defense force and give the men who constitute that force adequate training.[52]

The introduction of the Burke-Wadsworth bill coincided with the nomination of Henry L. Stimson and Robert P. Patterson as secretary and assistant secretary of war. Both were members of the NEC; both had been suggested to Roosevelt by Grenville Clark.[53] Stimson advised the president that he vigorously supported selective service and accepted the nomination with the understanding that Roosevelt did, too.[54]

Stimson's nomination did much to end George Marshall's opposition to a peacetime draft. Marshall must have reasoned that since Stimson's views on selective service were well known and since Roosevelt had nominated Stimson as secretary of war, the political climate regarding conscription had changed. Other forces contributed to Marshall's shift on the peacetime draft issue. War Department planners were beginning to doubt that the volunteer system could provide enough men for the growing army.[55] Furthermore, Stimson, at Grenville Clark's urging, advised the president to reject the proposed civilian volunteer effort, and Roosevelt did so immediately.[56] Finally, it appeared that the National Guard would have to be called into federal service.

By mid-June the complete collapse of France and Italy's entry into the war rekindled fears of an attempted Axis penetration into Latin America necessitating the dispatch of an American expeditionary force into that region. Such a force could come only from the regular army and would then require the activation of the National Guard. The president already had requested standby authority to call up the guard on May 31. Now, faced with a possible threat in South America and the prospect of having to train and equip draftees, Marshall urged an immediate mobilization of the guard. An activated National Guard could not only back up the regular army if it had to leave the United States but also serve with the regulars as the training nucleus for a citizen army.[57] Thus, in July with the civilian volunteer effort dead, the chief of staff threw his support behind the selective service bill.

Hearings on the Burke-Wadsworth bill began in July. Grenville Clark, representing the MTCA, led the long line of supporters. The arguments in favor of selective service, he said, were simple. The United States was "gravely threatened," Clark declared. The armed forces needed trained men as well as modern equipment to preserve and protect "the integrity and the institutions" of the nation. Voluntary enlistments alone were insufficient to raise "any adequate force" in the short time left before the United States must surely become involved in the widening world conflict.

The only solution was selective service. Clark pronounced a draft both fair and efficient. It was fair because "in a free society it is just and right that the obligations and risks of military training and service be shared by all." Selective service was efficient because it would "create a balanced adequate force without disrupting the whole life of the country."[58]

A variety of supporters then elaborated on different aspects of the bill's philosophy. John McAuley Palmer proffered a history lesson. He reminded the senators of the army's efforts to obtain UMT in 1920 and of the failure to adhere to the spirit of the National Defense Act during the previous two decades. "If [Senator Wadsworth and his associates] had succeeded in getting [UMT] through we would be prepared for war today," Palmer chided. The passage of the selective service bill, he said, would rectify the situation "in a minimum of time and with a maximum of economy and efficiency." Palmer declared the draft consistent with American historical tradition. President Washington, he observed, proposed a form of universal military service "long before the modern nation in arms was thought of in France or Germany."[59] Palmer and others would later again advocate peacetime universal military training, but in 1940 he concerned himself with the immediate needs of the army.

All supporters of the MTCA bill accepted the proposal's first premise, that the United States was under immediate threat of war, as given. After Palmer the supporters fell into two groups: those who emphasized the need for rapid manpower procurement in the existing crisis, and those who justified compulsory selective service as the best way consistent with American democratic ideals. Spokesmen from the National Guard and organized reserve stressed the immediate need for men. Colonel William J. Donovan, a New York lawyer who had commanded the famed "Fighting Sixty-ninth" Infantry Regiment during World War I and would head the OSS in World War II, for example, urged compulsory training before war began because soldiers "are entitled to a fair chance by their country to go into war with some kind of a reasonable opportunity to live while they do their duty." He suggested that heavy American losses early in the last war were due to "our inadequacy of training and preparation."[60] Julius Ochs Adler, a colonel in the reserves and a prominent member of both the MTCA and Reserve Officers' Association, lent his prestige as general manager of the *New York Times* to the bill. Adler's main point in his justification of the immediate need for peacetime conscription was that while the nation probably had enough officers, counting both regulars and National Guard and organized reserve officers, "many of these officers have never been in command of troops; do not know how they behave; their qualities of leadership have not yet been demonstrated."[61]

The other group of supporters of the Burke-Wadsworth bill, those who argued that conscription was the most efficient means of defending the United States consistent with the principles of democracy, came largely from the nation's academic community. James B. Conant, president of Harvard University, best expressed the views of this group. Conant accepted the necessity for an expanded national defense. "The threat against us is not only physical," he stated flatly. "The threat is against our entire way of life." Given the nature and magnitude of the danger, he added, "I can see no method of building an army in a free democracy more efficient and more just than that of compulsory selective service."[62]

Antimilitarists, isolationists, and peace groups joined together in a vigorous effort to defeat the Burke-Wadsworth bill in committee. Opponents questioned both the ends and the means of the proposal; they disagreed with the MTCA's view "that the integrity and institutions of the United States are gravely threatened," and they challenged the assumption that compulsory selective military training and service "in a free society . . . is just and right. . . ." Dorothy Day, editor and publisher of the *Catholic Worker,* insisted, "We still think the 3,000 miles of water between us and Europe [is] a great protection," and added, "If we are thinking in terms of South America, I would say then that we are thinking in terms of our markets rather than our home, our own land." Norman Thomas warned, "Conscription jeopardizes the rights to labor. It gives reaction an instrument of repression."[63] Edwin C. Johnson, secretary of the Committee on Militarism in Education, perhaps best summarized the opposition to conscription by reading a statement on behalf of over 300 leading educators, writers, and clergymen:

In our judgment military conscription in peacetime smacks of totalitarianism, and we are convinced that its adoption would be highly dangerous to the spirit and traditions of American democracy. The reasons upon which we support this conviction are as follows:

First, the essential idea underlying military conscription is the major premise of every dictatorship and all totalitarianism. It is the assumption that the individual citizen is but a pawn in the hands of unlimited state power.

Second, we consider that peacetime conscription is in itself a flagrant negation of democracy.

Third, the adoption of military conscription in peacetime would be a radical departure from heroic American tradition.

Finally, we oppose conscription because of the disruption it will cause in our American way of life, and also because we question its necessity and wisdom as a defense measure.[64]

After hearing from the civilians who proposed peacetime conscription and from those groups in the society opposed to it, the Senate Committee on Military Affairs turned to the nation's military leaders. By midsummer both the army and the navy supported selective service. Marshall testified first. The chief of staff told the lawmakers that under existing legislation the War Department had the authority and funds to raise the regular army to a strength of 375,000 men. He acknowledged that such a figure could probably be achieved with voluntary enlistments, but he added, "we will be procuring them at much too slow a rate in view of the present international situation. . . ."

According to Marshall the United States faced an imminent threat. "We must carry our regular army organizations now up to full strength, and we must immediately bring the National Guard up to its full peace strength, and then as rapidly as possible to full war strength."[65] Rear Admiral Chester W. Nimitz, chief of the Bureau of Navigation, the office responsible for naval manpower procurement, spoke for the chief of naval operations. Nimitz indicated that at its present strength of 170,000 men the navy was not experiencing any difficulty in securing sufficient voluntary enlistments. But he told the senators that if the navy were ordered to increase from 85 to 100 percent strength "and to man the ships that we hope to have in commission the next fiscal year, 1942, . . . and to man the completed aviation program, [it] would take in the neighborhood of 400,000 men." Under those circumstances, Nimitz said, he could not say whether or not the navy could depend on volunteers alone, "and for that reason I would like to see this bill go through."[66]

A larger public debate paralleled the congressional inquiry as advocates for and against selective service sought to win support. The Military Training Camps Association conducted an extensive campaign designed to educate the public to the necessity for speedy approval of the bill. Clark's group compiled a file of editorials supporting passage in an effort to demonstrate that informed opinion throughout the nation overwhelmingly favored peacetime selective service. The MTCA reported that " 'inland' editors as well as coast publishers, are 87 percent united in urging immediate action by Congress."[67] Patriotic organizations and other preparedness groups traditionally interested in military readiness naturally supported a draft. "Let us have all the machinery of national defense we need for any emergency," proclaimed the American Legion, a longtime supporter of a standby draft in peacetime.[68]

Businessmen's associations and publications also endorsed the Burke-Wadsworth bill. A special committee of the United States Chamber of Commerce studied the issue and reported that "one of the weaknesses of America's present defense is the absence of a large reservoir of trained men, from which, in time of attack . . . adequate forces might be drawn to expand America's protecting army and navy." The committee recommended a permanent policy of universal military training. W. H. Prentis, president of the National Association of Manufacturers, supported conscription. *Business Week* said it "would be murder" to send untrained men into battle with modern equipment.[69]

Opponents of the draft organized a vigorous public campaign to defeat the Burke-Wadsworth bill. The most outspoken criticism came from the antimilitarist groups that made up the more radical wing of the American peace movement. Leaders of several pacifist or noninterventionist organizations coordinated the lobby effort against both the draft and aid to the allies through a coalition called the Keep America Out of War Congress (KAOWC). Throughout the summer the KAOWC ensured that a steady flow of critics kept the message of the opponents of conscription before the American people. The Youth Committee Against War, for example, pledged "mass resistance if conscription becomes law" at its annual convention. Antiwar leaders like Frederick Libby, Dorothy Detzer, Oswald G. Villard, and Norman Thomas made speeches and attended rallies throughout the country and repeated the argument they had made during the Senate hearings: The United States was not threatened, increases in military strength were not necessary, and conscription was diametrically opposed to American tradition and values.[70]

Many religious and labor organizations joined in opposing the draft. Harry Emerson Fosdick, pastor of the Riverside Church in New York City, coordinated the efforts of pacifists in the Protestant churches. Fosdick, representatives from other Protestant denominations, and leaders from the Mennonite and Quaker sects lobbied, with limited success, for a broad definition of conscientious objection in the Burke-Wadsworth bill. *The Commonweal,* a liberal publication of the American Catholic church, expressed skepticism that the nation was indeed threatened by events in Asia and Europe and called sponsors of the Burke-Wadsworth bill "hysterical." Furthermore, the publication argued, "this scheme would drag the nation toward war. It would arouse the national military consciousness." *The Commonweal* also suggested that supporters of the bill were, through their control of the press, denying both sides of the argument to the public, and lamented "the temper of the day leads most people to refuse to admit that this question is open."[71]

Both the AFL and CIO opposed conscription. The *American Federationist* declared, "It would be sheer folly to denude industry of workers essential to production of defense equipment and bring them into the army ranks before we are ready to provide them with the necessary training and equipment." Modern war dictated that "maximum efficiency, plus mechanical superiority, are the qualities of victory. . . . We cannot hope to achieve these qualities within one year of compulsory training of 2,000,000 conscripts," concluded that AFL organ. John L. Lewis agreed. "In the excitement of a period of crisis measures are sometimes advanced so fundamentally in opposition to our national democratic traditions that their proponents would not dare propose them at any other time," he said. Lewis argued that voluntary enlistments could meet the army's needs if the enlistment period were reduced to one year and Congress raised soldier's pay "at least to compare with that of the self-respecting workman." He also demanded that laborers who enlisted be guaranteed their civilian jobs; called for social security protection for soldiers; and recommended more commissions from the enlisted ranks.[72] Farm labor organizations joined the unions in opposing the draft. Robert Handschin, representing serveral state farmers' unions and the National Junior Department of the National Farmers Union, told the House Committee on Military Affairs that farmers believed that the burden of conscription would fall on "unemployed young men in the cities and farm boys . . . who have no cause for deferment because of vital jobs, dependents, or health. . . ." The result, Handschin argued, would be that the lower-income youth of the nation would be selected for combat service. He charged the supporters of the Burke-Wadsworth bill with seeking to " 'solve' our unemployment problem by drafting these men for purposes of war."[73] All of these groups stressed their support for an adequate national defense but urged the continuation of the volunteer principle as the best means for raising manpower.

Roosevelt remained publicly silent on the issue, obviously waiting to see how the people responded. Polls showed a small margin in favor of conscription. A Gallup poll of military-age men in July, for example, found 52 percent in favor of the draft.[74] Finally, after prodding from Stimson and others, the president openly supported the measure. He did so dramatically, as he accepted nomination for a third term on July 19. Reminding the convention that he had not sought renomination, he said, "Because of the millions of citizens involved in the conduct of defense, most right thinking persons are agreed that some form of selection by draft is as necessary and fair today as it was in 1917 and 1918." I accept the nomination, he said, because:

Lying awake, as I have, on many nights, I have asked myself whether I have the right, as Commander-in-Chief . . . to call on men and women to serve their country or to train themselves to serve and, at the same time, to decline to serve my country in my own personal capacity, if I am called upon to do so by the people of my country.[75]

After the president publicly endorsed the bill, Wadsworth ensured that the issue did not enter the arena of politics by urging Wendell Willkie to support the measure, too. Willkie agreed and went on record in support of conscription on August 17.[76]

Even with both candidates behind the bill final passage was delayed until September. House hearings, a repetition of those in the Senate and the nation at large, lasted through most of August. Finally, on September 14, the Senate voted 47 to 25 to approve a conference report. Forty Democrats and seven Republicans supported the bill in the Senate. The measure received support from every region of the country. Areas of strongest support included the northeastern industrial states, the South, and Southwest. Regional opposition to conscription came largely from the Midwest, mountain, and West Coast states. The strong support of the southerners for conscription represented a clear break from the alignment they had maintained with midwestern and mountain states' congressmen on issues of army size and composition since 1919. Partisanship surely accounted for part of the shift. In an election year few Democrats were willing to break with the party on an issue involving military preparedness. Geography and tradition were also factors. In 1940 the war in Europe seemed far more remote to midwesterners and westerners than it did in the East and the South. The desire to remain aloof from the war found its greatest expression in the inland regions of the country. The South, on the other hand, would be more directly affected by Axis activities in the Atlantic and by the perceived threat to Latin America. Finally, despite their often stated objections to large and expensive standing armies under federal control, southerners cherished a tradition of martial spirit and a willingness to "answer the call" when threatened. An hour later the House approved the bill 232 to 124. As in the Senate vote, House Democrats favored the draft by a wide margin, 186 to 32; Republicans opposed the measure two to one (88 to 46). The regional breakdown of the vote was similar to that in the Senate. Opponents of selective service included in their ranks many who had voted against UMT, large army appropriations, and expansion of army strength during the previous two decades.[77]

The Selective Training and Service Act of 1940 required registration of all male citizens between the ages of twenty-one and thirty-six. Men selected for training and service in peacetime would serve for twelve months and be transferred to the reserves for a period of ten years. The act included a revision of the enlisted pay system, something the services, especially the army, had been seeking since the mid-1920s. Privates, for example, received a raise from $21 to $30 a month. Unlike in the World War I draft, voluntary enlistments for all services continued. One-year enlistments, never popular with the army, ended when registration began. Men could still volunteer for the standard three-year enlistment. Only selectees served for one year.[78]

Congress had already authorized the president to call the National Guard into federal service. Roosevelt issued the first call-up on September 16, the same day he signed the Selective Service Act. The combined forces authorized between May and September 1940 provided for an army of 1,400,000 by June 30, 1941: 500,000 in the regular army, 270,000 in the National Guard, and 630,000 selectees. Actual strength on that date totaled 1,351,666; 479,880 in the regular army, 262,722 in the guard, 2,149 in the enlisted reserves, and 606,915 selectees. This represented a threefold increase in the number of men on active duty or available for service in July 1940, and a fivefold increase over July 1939, two months prior to the outbreak of the war in Europe.[79]

Passage of the first peacetime draft in the nation's history depended greatly on organized pressure groups, which shrewdly used the crisis in world affairs. Prior to June 1940 the army had assumed that peacetime conscription was a political impossibility and was preparing to implement the civilian volunteer effort. The navy admitted to Congress that it did not need selective service in peacetime. The speed with which the German armies overran the Low Countries and France in the spring of 1940 certainly influenced the public climate in which the decision to implement the draft was made. Americans were genuinely shocked by the rapidity of events that summer. But to understand properly the swiftness of the legislative action leading to passage of the Burke-Wadsworth bill, one should not underestimate the role of the National Emergency Committee of the Military Training Camps Association. Grenville Clark and his associates, many of whom had supported preparedness schemes before and after World War I, wrote the Burke-Wadsworth bill and lobbied for it without rest until its passage was assured. Henry L. Stimson and Frank Knox, Roosevelt's bipartisan secretaries of war and the navy, were members of the NEC and supporters of the draft. The ties of the MTCA to the army, the government and the business community were indeed impressive. Besides Stimson and Knox the inner circle of the NEC included Adler of the *New York Times,* Allen L. Lindley, vice-president of the New York Stock Exchange, Major General (Ret.) James G. Harbord, a director of the National Broadcasting System, and leading executives from numerous banks, industrial firms, and investment houses. At one point during the congressional hearings on conscription, Lindley wrote to every member of the New York Stock Exchange requesting contributions "to help enact the Burke-Wadsworth bill into legislation."[80]

Opponents of the draft did not overlook the "old boy network" of the MTCA. During the floor debate on the bill Senator Rush D. Holt of West Virginia asked, "Does anyone suppose that the Military Training Camps Association was organized among poor people?" Holt suggested that the MTCA really wanted to get the United States into the war to save England and protect the investments of its members. Holt's rhetoric was overdrawn, and he admitted that "some of the finest and most patriotic men I know are for the draft," but the fears that he expressed were real.[81] The traditional concern for the dangers conscription and a large standing army posed to a democracy and the widely held belief that monied interests had led the United States into World War I convinced many Americans that the draft was but the first stage of a conspiracy to bring the nation into the latest European war.

A year later these fears were revealed. At that time, in the summer of 1941, war had still not come to America. England had survived the Battle of Britain and Germany was embroiled in a new war with the Soviet Union. America continued to arm, but the immediacy of the crisis that had accompanied the passage of the Burke-Wadsworth bill seemed to have passed. In this context when the War Department and the administration sought to extend national guardsmen, reserve officers, and selectees beyond the one-year service limit imposed by the acts of August 27 and September 16, 1940, they faced a bitter opposition. The House approved extension by only one vote on August 12, 1941, and it remained in force for thirty years.[82]

Selective service was thus a reality. But was it necessary? Had selective service not been proposed or approved in 1940, the army would probably have continued to prepare for war on the basis of the civilian volunteer effort and the Protective Mobilization Plan. According to those plans, General Staff analysts in June 1940 estimated that the United States could have a standing army of approximately 500,000 enlisted men backed up by a 320,000-man National Guard on July 1, 1941, or approximately one-half of the forces actually available on that date.[83] Whether the United States would have been as well prepared when war actually came without the peacetime draft is impossible to determine; on the basis of numbers alone the conclusion must be that it would not have been. But even with the additional trained forces provided by selective service the nation was not capable of conducting an effective defense against the Japanese attack in December 1941 or of mounting offensive operations in the Pacific until the summer of 1942; offensive operations involving United States forces in the European theater did not begin until November 1942. The best that can be said is that the enactment of peacetime selective service gave the United States a larger base upon which to build after Pearl Harbor brought the country into the war. Complete mobilization after the war began for the United States surely was less frantic as a result of the buildup in 1940 and 1941.

Enactment of the peacetime draft did not end the army's mobilization problems in 1940; it merely assured the army the number of men it thought it needed and eliminated the uncertainty associated with volunteerism. In the months after September 1940 the War Department struggled to organize, house, equip, and train the rapidly growing force. Even these preparations paled in significance when compared to the expansion following December 7, 1941. The prewar plans and preparations of the United States were unprecedented in American history. But after the war began, critics considered those preparations inadequate. The subsequent massive mobilization of the nation's resources and the total victory that followed further obscured the prewar effort. Supporters of UMT or a continuation of selective service after World War II were quick to point to the events of 1940–1941 as evidence that the United States could never again afford to be unprepared for war in time of peace.[84] The small peacetime volunteer army thus became a casualty of World War II.

NOTES

1. See, for example, C. Joseph Bernardo and Eugene H. Bacon, *American Military Policy,* 2d ed. (Harrisburg, Pa.: Stackpole Books, 1961), p. 405; Mark S. Watson, *Chief of Staff: Prewar Plans and Preparations* (Washington, D.C.: GPO, 1950), p. 126ff; Russell F. Weigley, *History of the United States Army* (New York: Macmillan Co., 1967), p. 417.

2. Franklin D. Roosevelt, *The Public Papers and Addresses of Franklin D. Roosevelt,* 13 vols., ed. Samuel I. Rosenman (New York: Macmillan Co. 1941), 7: 68–71. FDR refers to this message as "but the beginning of a vast program of rearmament." Roosevelt, *Public Papers of FDR,* 7: 71.

3. These and other arguments against the rearmament program are found in the *Congressional Digest* 17, no. 3 (March 1938); 67–92.

4. *Army and Navy Journal* (hereafter, *ANJ*) February 12, 1938, p. 494.

5. Elias Huzar, *The Purse and the Sword* (Ithaca, N.Y.: Cornell University Press, 1950), p. 141; *ANJ,* June 4, 1938, pp. 877, 878.

6. Watson, *Chief of Staff,* p. 126.

7. Ibid., pp. 128–39.

8. Ibid., pp. 139–40.

9. Ibid., pp. 141–42.

10. Ibid., pp. 142–43.

11. Roosevelt, *Public Papers of FDR,* 8: 1, 4.

12. Ibid., pp. 70–74.

13. *ANJ,* January 7, 1939, p. 411; January 14, p. 433.

14. Radio address by Senator Borah, March 25, 1939, reprinted in *Vital Speeches* 5, no. 13 (April 15, 1939): 397–99.

15. Speech by Senator Wheeler before the American Forum of the Air, April 9, 1939, reprinted in *Vital Speeches,* 5, no. 13 (April 15, 1939): 406–7.

16. Speech by Senator Pittman on January 22, 1939, reprinted in *Vital Speeches* 5, no. 13 (April 15, 1939): 404–6.

17. Radio report by Roy Howard, Paris, April 5, 1939, reprinted in *Vital Speeches* 5, no. 13 (April 15, 1939): 401–2.

18. *ANJ,* January 14, 1939, p. 434; January 28, p. 482; March 11, p. 630; April 22, p. 778.

19. As reported in *ANJ,* December 31, 1938, p. 396. The American Institute of Public Opinion did not break down the results of the polls cited. See George H. Gallup, *The Gallup Poll: Public Opinion, 1935–1971,* 3 vols. (New York: Random House, 1972), 1: 129, 131, 132.

20. Huzar, *The Purse and the Sword,* p. 141.

21. For details of FDR's efforts to repeal the arms embargo prior to September 1939 see for example, William L. Langer and S. Everett Gleason, *The Challenge to Isolation, 1937–1940* (New York: Harper & Brothers, 1952), pp. 136–47; Donald Drummond, *The Passing of American Neutrality, 1937–1941* (Ann Arbor, Mich.: University of Michigan Press, 1955), pp. 87–89; and Robert Divine, *The Illusion of Neutrality* (Chicago: University of Chicago Press, 1926), pp. 229–85.

22. Fred Green, "The Military View of American National Policy, 1904–1940," *American Historical Review* 66, no. 2 (January 1961): 354–58; Ronald Schaffer,

"General Stanley D. Embick: Military Dissenter," *Military Affairs* 38, no. 3 (October 1973): 92–94.

23. Testimony of Brig. Gen. Lorenzo D. Gaser, ACS, G-1, before the House Military Affairs Committee on January 26, 1939, as reported in *ANJ,* January 28, 1939, pp. 481, 483.

24. U.S. War Department, *Annual Report for the Year Ending June 30, 1939* (Washington, D.C.: GPO, 1939), p. 26, (hereafter *Annual Report, 1939)*; Watson, *Chief of Staff,* 154–55.

25. Biennial Report of the Chief of Staff, July 1, 1941, in *Annual Report, 1941,* p. 47; Watson, *Chief of Staff,* p. 157.

26. Marvin A. Kreidberg and Merton G. Henry, *History of Military Mobilization in the United States Army, 1775–1945* (Washington, D.C.: GPO, 1955), pp. 548–50.

27. Weigley, *History of the U.S. Army* p. 418; U.S. War Department, *The Army of the United States* (Washington, D.C.: War Department, 1939), pp. 57–73; for a detailed description of mobilization plans and planning, see Kreidberg and Henry, *History of Military Mobilization,* pp. 476–91.

28. Kreidberg and Henry, *History of Military Mobilization,* pp. 552–53.

29. Russell F. Weigley, *Towards an American Army: Military thought from Washington to Marshall* (New York: Columbia University Press, 1962), pp. 242–43.

30. Roosevelt, *Public Papers of FDR,* 8: 482–83.

31. Weigley, *History of the U.S. Army,* p. 424; Watson, *Chief of Staff,* pp. 156–57.

32. Watson, *Chief of Staff,* p. 158.

33. Ibid., pp. 161–63.

34. Ibid., p. 165; U.S., Congress, House, Committee on Appropriations, *Hearings on Military Establishment Appropriations Bill for 1941,* p. 3.

35. Watson, *Chief of Staff,* pp. 157–58.

36. House Appropriations Committee, *Military Establishment Appropriations Bill for 1941,* pp. 37–41.

37. *ANJ,* April 6, 1940, p. 737.

38. *New York Times* (hereafter, *NYT*), May 17, 1940, p. 24; May 26, p. 6.

39. *Annual Report,* 1941, p. 50.

40. For a detailed examination of the Protective Mobilization Plan, see Kreidberg and Henry, *History of Military Mobilization,* pp. 476–92.

41. *Annual Report,* 1940, Table A, facing p. 31. Details of the recruiting situation during this period are discussed in chapter 8.

42. Watson, *Chief of Staff,* pp. 174–75; Weigley, *History of the U.S. Army,* p. 425.

43. Kreidberg and Henry, *History of Military Mobilization,* pp. 573–76.

44. Memo, ACS, G-1 to CS, June 3, 1940; Letter, Louis Johnson to the President, June 25, 1940; Memo G-1 to CS, July 3, 1940, AGO 341, RG 94, Box 1787, National Archives, Washington D.C. (hereafter, NA).

45. John M. Palmer, *America in Arms* (New Haven, Conn.: Yale University Press, 1941), pp. 197, 198.

46. *NYT,* May 23, 1940, pp. 1, 13.

47. Watson, *Chief of Staff,* p. 190.

48. Ibid.

49. For a detailed examination of interwar plans for conscription, see Kreidberg and Henry, *History of Military Mobilization,* pp. 463–92 and 451–58. Marshall's views on peacetime selective service are found in Watson, *Chief of Staff,* pp. 184–89.

50. Selective Service System, *The Selective Service Act,* Special Monograph No. 2, Vol. 1 (Washington, D.C.: GPO, 1954), pp. 58–68; Duff Gilford, "The New Conscription," *The New Republic* 40, no. 773 (September 25, 1939): 149–51.

51. Watson, *Chief of Staff,* pp. 190–91. For a good account of Wadsworth's role, see Martin L. Faushold, *James W. Wadsworth, Jr., The Gentleman from New York* (Syracuse, N.Y.: Syracuse University Press, 1975), pp. 311–19.

52. *NYT,* June 7, 1940, p. 22.

53. Faushold, *James W. Wadsworth, Jr.,* p. 311; Watson, *Chief of Staff,* p. 191.

54. Henry L. Stimson and McGeorge Bundy, *On Active Service in Peace and War* (New York: Harper & Brothers, 1948), pp. 323–24.

55. Watson, *Chief of Staff,* pp. 191–92. Marshall's biographer argues that the chief of staff never opposed the principle of the peacetime draft, only the practicality of it. See Forrest C. Pogue, *George C. Marshall, Ordeal and Hope, 1939–1942* (New York: The Viking Press, 1956), pp. 57–58.

56. Watson, *Chief of Staff,* p. 191.

57. Ibid., pp. 193–94.

58. U.S., Congress, Senate, Senate Committee on Military Affairs, *Hearings on S. 4164,* 76th Cong., 3d sess., July 3, 1940, pp. 26–33.

59. Ibid., pp. 19–21, 44–47.

60. Ibid., July 5, pp. 67–68.

61. Ibid., July 3, pp. 22–25.

62. Ibid., pp. 152–53.

63. Ibid., pp. 255–60.

64. Ibid., pp. 201–8.

65. Ibid., July 12, pp. 327–30.

66. Ibid., pp. 360–65.

67. Ibid., July 10, p. 217. The MTCA presented a digest of editorials to Senator Burke, who entered them into the record of the testimony.

68. National Publicity Division, American Legion, Mimeographed releases, April 1940, reprinted in Julia E. Johnson, ed., *Compulsory Military Training* (New York: H. W. Wilson Co., 1941), pp. 138–41.

69. Johnson, *Compulsory Military Training,* pp. 101–3, 127, 128.

70. Proceedings of the National Youth Anti-War Congress, 1940, reprinted in Johnson, *Compulsory Military Training,* pp. 220–21; Selective Service System, *The Selective Service Act,* p. 77.

71. Charles Chatfield, *For Peace and Justice: Pacifism in America, 1914–1941* (Knoxville, Tenn.: University of Tennessee Press, 1971), pp. 302–6.

72. "Labor Weighs Conscription," *American Federationist* 48, nos. 3–4 (September 1940): 3–4, 31–32, Lewis's views were expressed in a letter to all members of Congress, August 14, 1940, reprinted in *Congressional Record,* 76th Cong., 3d sess., 86, pt. 10, pp. 10722–23.

73. U.S., Congress, House, House Committee on Military Affairs, *Hearings on H.R. 10132,* 76th Cong., 3d sess., July 26, 1940, pp. 278–84.

74. *NYT,* July 10, 1940, p. 17.

75. Roosevelt, *Public Papers of FDR*, 9: 295–96.

76. Faushold, *James W. Wadsworth, Jr.*, pp. 316–17.

77. *NYT*, September 15, 1940, p. 1; U.S., House, *Congressional Record*, 76th Cong., 3d sess., 86, pt. 11, pp. 12160, 12161, 12227.

Senators Opposing Selective Service (25)

Brown (D), Mich.	McCarran (D), Nev.
Bulow (D), S.D.	Murray (D), Mont.
Capper (R), Kans.	Norris (Ind), Neb.
Clark (D), Idaho	Reed (R), Kans.
Clark (D), Mo.	Wheeler (D), Mont.
Danaher (R), Conn.	Schwellenbach (D), Wash.
Downey (D), Ohio	Taft (R), Ohio
Frazier (R), N.D.	Thomas (R), Idaho
Walsh (D), Mass.	Townsend (R), Del.
Holt (D), W. Va.	Vandenberg (R), Mich.
Johnson (R), Calif.	Van Nuys (D), Ind.
Johnson (D), Colo.	Wiley (R), Wisc.
LaFollette	
(Progressive), Wisc.	

78. The Selective Training and Service Act of 1940, Public Law no. 783, 76th Cong., 3d sess.

79. *Annual Report, 1939*, p. 56; *1940*, p. 31; *1941*, p. 95; U.S. Department of Commerce, *Statistical Abstract of the United States 1943*, (Washington, D.C., GPO, 1942), p. 162.

80. U.S., Senate, *Congressional Record*, 76th Cong., 3d sess., 86, pt. 10, pp. 10718–22.

81. Ibid.

82. For a summary of the proposal and debate over the extension of National Guard and selective service men on active duty in 1941, see Watson, *Chief of Staff*, pp. 214–31.

83. Kreidberg and Henry, *History of Military Mobilization*, pp. 468–575.

84. See James M. Gerhardt, *The Draft and Public Policy: Issues in Military Manpower Procurement, 1945–1970* (Columbus, Ohio: Ohio State University Press, 1971), chapters 1 and 2, for a discussion of the postwar continuation of selective service.

8

THE LAST YEARS OF THE VOLUNTEER ARMY, 1936–1940

Though recruiting for the volunteer army differed according to the economic situation—difficult in the relatively prosperous 1920s, somewhat easier from 1930 to 1935—it had operated within a constant set of restraints imposed by a consensus opposing high levels of strength. Dealing with relatively small numbers, slightly above 100,000, the army usually managed to reach its quotas, even if the quality of recruits—as in the 1920s—left something to be desired. From 1935 to 1939 the army struggled to improve this quality by making the service more attractive and by weeding out misfits. As the threat of fascism increased after 1938, however, the problem changed from one of assuring decent quality to one of security large numbers of volunteers in short order. The task all but overwhelmed the Recruiting Service after 1939 and convinced contemporaries of the disadvantages of a volunteer army.

Before mid-1939 the army handled the problems associated with augmenting enlisted strength in a routine manner. Modest increases in the number of enlisted men on recruiting duty and in the amounts spent in support of recruiting accompanied the rises in the troop ceiling. By the end of 1938, when the 165,000-man level was finally achieved, the army found it possible to cut back on the number of men in the General Recruiting Service. Because enlisted strength had stabilized at the new level, maintenance of the enlisted force required fewer recruiters.

Table 8.1 *Recruiting Expenditures and Personnel, 1935–1939*

| | | | GENERAL RECRUITING SERVICE | |
YEAR	*AUTHORIZED STRENGTH*	*EXPENDITURES FOR RECRUITING*	*Officers*	*Enlisted*
1935	118,750	$1,566,843.44	72	884
1936	147,000	1,787,050.90	74	889
1937	165,000	1,949,545.95	74	937
1938	165,000	1,831,738.07	75	957
1939	165,000	1,845,504.31	74	687

Source: Personnel: *Annual Reports, 1935–1939*; Expenditures: Special Reports, Statistical Branch, General Staff, 1935–1939

While recruiters worked to increase strength, the War Department took a renewed interest in improving enlisted efficiency and morale. These efforts fell into two categories. First, the army continued to try to improve service attractiveness in order to retain good soldiers. To War Department analysts "service attractiveness" equaled higher pay. Thus the major effort in the area of improving enlisted morale and retention was to seek a pay increase and restoration of the reenlistment bonus suspended as part of the New Deal efforts to reduce government spending in 1933.

The army's philosophy with regard to the role of pay, allowances, and bonuses in manpower procurement was stated simply: "Pay of the soldier . . . should be sufficient to induce original enlistment and to hold in the service an adequate number of trained enlisted leaders and technicians."[1] The army viewed the reenlistment bonus as an incentive to encourage soldiers to "re-up" at the end of each enlistment term. The bonus, as authorized by the Pay Readjustment Act of 1922, amounted to $150 for soldiers reenlisting in the top three grades and $75 for those in the remaining grades.[2] President Roosevelt suspended the bonus in 1933 when, under the authority of the Economy Act, he reduced government pay 15 percent. Congress restored the pay cut in 1935, but refused to reestablish a reenlistment bonus. From 1936 to 1939 Senate opponents of restoration successfully inserted a rider continuing the ban on payment of the reenlistment bonus in the annual independent offices appropriation bill. During the same period reenlistments declined from an average of 77 percent of honorably discharged soldiers between 1931 and 1936 to 66.3 percent in 1938 and 69.03 percent in 1939. The army argued that the "somewhat improved economic conditions during the past few years [sic]" were clearly related to "a definite trend . . . toward a reduction in the reenlistment rate," and urged Congress to restore the bonus. Finally, in March 1939 at the insistence of House conferees, the bonus was restored. Reenlistments rose to 77 percent again in 1940, but the effect of restoration of the bonus on soldiers' decisions to stay in the army is hard to measure.[3]

Although anxious to restore the reenlistment bonus, the army was more interested in obtaining a general pay increase. As soon as the worst of the depression seemed to be over, the War Department renewed efforts to obtain such a raise. In his testimony before the House Appropriations Committee in February 1935, General James F. McKinley, the adjutant general, warned that low pay, at the level established by the Pay Readjustment Act of 1922 with base pay for a private, for example, at $21,[4] threatened to weaken morale and urged an enlisted pay increase along the lines of that proposed in 1930. McKinley's testimony was but the opening gun in a struggle that continued until August 1940. War Department studies pointed to improved economic conditions, the higher pay received by CCC enrollees, and a gradually declining reenlistment rate after 1936 to justify the pay raise. In 1939, for example, the Personnel Division's brief for officers testifying before Congress on behalf of a pay increase concluded:

The present trend indicates that with improved economic conditions reenlistments are falling off and that should the nation experience an era of general prosperity, the Army might be faced with a serious problem of retaining in the service the proper proportion of career men. It is likewise probable that maintenance of existing strength will create a serious problem.[5]

No amount of arguing about the relationship between pay and morale moved Congress. The army finally got its pay raise as part of the Selective Service Act. Originally the Burke-Wadsworth bill proposed paying selectees $5 a month. During hearings on the bill several members of the Senate Military Affairs Committee objected to such low pay for draftees and further criticized the low pay of soldiers in general. Senator Maloney urged a pay increase for all services:

Unless and until their pay is increased, they are suffering from discrimination. No one intended a discrimination; but it has been pointed out that those enrolled in the Civilian Conservation Corps are now receiving a greater remuneration than are the young men of the army. . . . This is obviously unfair, and a definite effort to rectify the mistake has been too long delayed.[6]

In the summer of 1940, when a mania for preparedness gripped the nation, few opposed a pay raise for servicemen. When the Selective Service Act became law, the army got its long-sought pay increase. Privates, for example, received a boost of $9 a month ($21 to $30). Other benefits and allowances remained unchanged.[7]

In addition to seeking positive means to improve service attractiveness, enlisted efficiency, and morale, the army considered some negative ways either to hold skilled soldiers or to get rid of men who were deemed inefficient. About the same time as it began to press for a pay raise, for example, the General Staff also reviewed its policy on permitting enlisted men to purchase their discharges prior to expiration of enlistment. A War College study prepared in 1938 by Major J. C. Daly revealed that between 1934 and 1938, 30,360 soldiers had purchased their discharges. Approximately 15 percent were army technical school graduates. The Signal Corps, Quartermaster Corps, and Air Corps lost 19.8, 19.3, and 16.4 percent of their technical school graduates respectively. Purchased discharges had declined during the darkest days of the depression but rose sharply at the first hint of recovery. Daly believed that the continued high number of skilled soldiers buying their way out of the army during the "Roosevelt recession" of 1937–1938 was partly due to the army's "Learn while you serve" recruiting slogan. Men were joining the army, acquiring skills in these areas, and then purchasing their discharges.

The agencies affected offered several solutions. The chief of the Air Corps, for example, wanted to raise the purchase price from $120 to a higher fixed price plus the cost of any technical training received. The chief of the Signal Corps proposed that men sent to technical schools be prohibited, as a condition of entry, from purchasing their discharges. But the adjutant general objected to any change in the policy on the grounds that the purchase discharge rate, though vexing, (at less than 5 percent of total losses) was not high. Summarizing earlier policy reviews, the adjutant general noted that any modification of the policy allowing enlisted men to purchase their discharges after one year of service would clearly conflict with the intent of the provision as established by Congress in 1890. Another objection to tampering with the purchased discharge came from the Personnel Division of the General Staff. Men leaving the service after acquiring a marketable skill were a good advertisement for the army. "[A] young man who goes back to his home town and spreads the word that a few years in the Army Air Corps have fitted him for an excellent job in civil life is most beneficial and puts the Army in a different light to what antimilitary organizations would have the public believe." This view was not a throwback to the altruism of UMT advocates who justified military training for all for the alleged social benefits it would have; it just recognized good public relations. Finally, the adjutant general observed, a partial solution lay in increasing the pay of enlisted men to induce them to remain in the service. He recommended no change in the regulation governing purchased discharges but urged continuation of the effort to raise pay. The chief of staff concurred, and the data on purchased discharges was used to justify further a general pay raise in 1939 and 1940.[8]

Another problem that continued to trouble the army was that of married enlisted men below the rank of staff sergeant (grade 3). In the army's official view, soldiers with families that they could not support constituted a burden to the service. The more stringent regulations governing the enlistment and reenlistment of married men issued in 1932 did not seem to have reduced the number of men with families.[9] In 1937, the problem had reached such a magnitude that the chief of staff reopened the subject for study in a letter to the corps area commanders saying, "The situation which confronts the Army is serious and is increasing in seriousness." The situation to which General Craig referred was that one-fifth of the enlisted men in the army were married, and of that number only one-quarter were authorized quarters. The remaining men—approximately 18,000—did not receive the quarters, quarters allowance, or subsistence allowance authorized to married enlisted men in the top three grades. The families of these men numbered about 45,000 unwanted dependents. They lived "in buildings on military reservations not built for assignment as quarters," taxed the medical, dental, and hospitalization facilities of the army, and constituted a potential "black eye" for the War Department. Craig expressed especial concern over the disposition of unauthorized dependents "in the event of an emergency requiring extensive movement. . . ." He ordered a thorough review of the problem.[10]

The study revealed that since the revision of regulations governing married enlisted men in 1932, the problem had grown still worse. Furthermore, reports from the field indicated that many of the families of grades 7 to 4 soldiers lived in conditions "deplorable in the extreme." The commanding general of the Eighth Corps Area, Major General Herbert J. Brees, reported that as of March 1, 1938, "of the total garrison at Fort Sam Houston, Texas, . . . nine hundred twenty-two, or 15%, known members of the command below grade 3, with 899 dependent children, were married." Most of these families experienced "want and suffering . . . due to lack of proper clothing, housing, food and sanitary conditions." General Brees added that it was commonplace for married enlisted men to obtain divorces shortly before their enlistment expired in order to reenlist. Brees concluded:

The economic welfare of these people is distinctly a responsibility of the Army, as opposed to the community of the city of San Antonio. Yet, if at any time the troops of the Fort Sam Houston garrison should be removed for a considerable period, provisions for the destitution that would result from the withdrawal of such support as is now afforded by the soldiers' pay and allowances and the Community Chest of San Antonio would fall on the civilian community; and it cannot be supposed that such an occurance would be without discredit to the Army.[11]

Brigadier General L. D. Gasser, assistant chief of staff for personnel, advised Craig "that the situation at Fort Sam Houston . . . is neither better nor worse than that to be found at most army posts." Gasser urged "immediate corrective action, . . ." because:

The Regular Army *must* be highly mobile in order to carry out its missions. It cannot be mobile if a large number of its enlisted personnel are married, without entailing great hardship upon the dependents of these enlisted men. In fact, it is quite possible that the War Department might encounter resistance to permanent change of station of large garrisons in any situation, short of actual war, due to political pressure and other civilian influence brought to bear as a result of the present situation of married enlisted men and their dependents.

The Personnel Division of the General Staff concluded that the regulation in effect since 1932 left too much discretion to the local commander with regard to permitting the reenlistment of married enlisted men under grade 3 who had married without permission or had families they could not support properly on their army pay. These enlisted men with their "burdensome" dependents were not being eliminated from the service.[12]

In preparing its recommendations, the Personnel Division relied heavily on the views of commanders in the field. Most commanders agreed that no restriction on marriage should be imposed on the senior enlisted grades and that enlisted men in the lowest three grades should not be married or have dependents. Differences developed over the marital status of grade 4 sergeants, the junior noncommissioned rank. Some commanders felt that grade 4 sergeants, who averaged nine years of service, should be permitted to marry because attainment of that rank generally indicated a commitment on the soldier's part to a career in the army. Others demurred, arguing that the pay of a sergeant was insufficient to support a family.

The chief of staff made his decision on June 7, 1939, and ordered the adjutant general to amend the regulation as follows:

Enlisted men except in grades 1, 2, or 3, who marry without the written permission of the Corps Area or Department Commander after June 30, 1939 will be discharged without delay for the convenience of the Government and will not be reenlisted.

Permission to marry could be granted only to grade 4 enlisted men who completed eight or more years service and then "only in worthy cases. . . ."[13] The new ruling was harsh. Men so discharged received no severance pay or other benefits.

The War Department immediately applied the new provisions regulating the marriage of junior enlisted men. During fiscal year 1940, the army discharged 3,382 men at the "convenience of the Government for marriage without permission of [the] commanding officer."[14] The army did not report the number of men barred from reenlistment under the tighter regulation.

But even as the new policy went into effect, expansion of the army was already under way. Preparations for war soon negated the desire of a peacetime army to purge itself of the unwanted burden of married enlisted men. In the spring of 1940, as the expansion became more frantic, the commander of the Eighth Corps Area, General Brees, whose detailed report on the status of married enlisted men in the San Antonio area had significantly influenced the existing policy, requested an exception to that policy. Brees wanted permission "to reenlist, during the present emergency, married men who have been discharged with excellent character and whose dependents are capable of supporting themselves." The adjutant general agreed, saying, "every trained man that can be obtained is needed in the present expansion and formation of new units." On July 17, 1940, the chief of staff approved the change. Henceforth, during the "limited national emergency" corps area commanders were authorized to reenlist "deserving" former enlisted men with dependents provided they had served at least six years, been discharged with an "excellent" character rating, were in grade 5 (corporal) or higher, and that their dependents could furnish proof of their ability to support themselves financially.[15] The revised policy virtually ended the army's efforts to improve enlisted efficiency by barring unauthorized marriages. The army discharged only two soldiers for marrying without permission between July 1, 1940, and June 30, 1941.[16]

By 1939 War Department efforts to reduce losses and improve enlisted morale and efficiency were overshadowed by the army's increasing difficulty with filling its expanding ranks. Quantity—not quality—became the overriding concern. Before 1939 the General Recruiting Service had blamed its frequent inability to meet quotas on low recruiting budgets, competition from the CCC, and rising employment. In fiscal 1940 the Recruiting Service got the chance to prove what it could do if given more money when its budget was tripled. The General Recruiting Service spent over $4 million between July 1939 and June 1940, almost twice as much as in fiscal 1939.[17] The number of enlisted men assigned to the General Recruiting Service also doubled, from 687 to 1,184.[18]

The Recruiting Service welcomed the additional funds and personnel, for it faced a monumental task at the beginning of fiscal year 1940. The actual enlisted strength of the regular army at the beginning of fiscal 1940 (July 1, 1939) was 174,079. War Department appropriations and special legislation designed to augment the Air Corps and increase the size of the garrison in Panama required an expansion to 210,000 enlisted men. Additionally, the Recruiting Service received the task of obtaining former servicemen for the newly established regular army reserve. The adjutant general estimated that the army needed approximately 115,000 enlistments and reenlistments during the year to replace losses and raise the army to its new authorization. Total enlistments and reenlistments in fiscal 1939 had numbered 74,861.[19]

So it was that in July 1939 the biggest recruiting campaign since World War I began. There was no talk of readying the nation for war. Recruiters continued to emphasize the needs of an increasingly technical army and stress the opportunities that military service held to men seeking self-improvement. In October, for example, Secretary of War Harry Woodring declared, "there are plenty of responsible young men in America, well qualified physically, who have some education and want more, who have some technical training and want to develop it further, and who have a native-born curiosity and desire to see and do other things. This is the type the army needs and wants right now."[20] By any previous peacetime standard this drive was highly successful. In September the War Department processed an average of 750 enlistments daily.[21] The "earn while you learn" inducement seemed especially popular. According to Colonel L. R. Magruder of the Second Corps Area, seven out of every ten recruits "joined primarily to learn a trade and not to find adventure."[22] Recruiters also continued to sell the army's travel opportunities. Qualified applicants for original enlistment could still pick their branch, unit, and place of assignment from the list of vacancies at recruiting stations. If the army had no immediate vacancies for recruits where an applicant wanted to go, he could still enlist for a distant post or overseas area provided he agreed to waive return travel pay upon discharge.[23]

When President Roosevelt proclaimed the "limited national emergency" in September and raised army strength to 227,000, the army tried some new recruiting techniques. In October the Recruiting Service pressed into service eighteen mobile recruiting stations, two for each corps area. In December four flying recruiting stations were added to the effort.[24] Despite the obvious relationship between the expansion of the army and the war in Europe, the Recruiting Service continued to advertise the peacetime opportunities offered by the army. "Rarely have young men of this country been afforded the chance that is theirs, now that the Regular Army is expanding to a larger peacetime strength," proclaimed *Recruiting News,* whose monthly articles suggested potential lures to recruiting sergeants with quotas to fill. "Consider just a few of the many opportunities now open to forward looking, ambitious, young Americans who desire to 'earn, learn, and travel' with the Regular Army," added the *News.* "Analytical-minded youth" interested in mathematics could find jobs calling for "precise gunnery and plotting figures" in the coast artillery. The field artillery needed mechanics; so did the infantry, "now that the day of the foot-slogging doughboy has given way to the modern 'streamlined' idea with Infantry riding in motor cars instead of hiking along that 'last long mile.' " Every enlisted job, it seemed, could be linked to a real skill that would serve as an entry ticket to better civilian employment and higher pay in the future. Men who sought travel and adventure were offered "vacancies in Hawaii, Panama Canal Zone and the Philippines for those who desire to see the world while still young." This was the opportunity of a lifetime![25] A national advertising program further boosted the campaign. The increased budget enabled the Recruiting Publicity Bureau to erect 15,000 ten-by-twenty-foot billboards and display 25,000 car cards in trolleys, subways, and buses throughout the country.[26]

The stepped-up recruiting continued to produce results. On December 11, War Department officials announced that the army had reached its highest strength since 1921—205,800.[27] Recruiters set new peacetime records almost weekly. The Second Corps Area, for example, doubled its normal average recruit production, and in July 1939 exceeded all monthly records since fiscal year 1925.[28] But thanks to ever-increasing needs the drive was only a partial success. After President Roosevelt raised the strength of the army to 227,000 in conjunction with his "limited emergency" declaration on September 8, 1939, the adjutant general notified recruiters that the army intended to achieve the new manpower level by December 31. To accomplish this goal the adjutant general told recruiters they would have to secure over 14,000 new recruits a month.[29]

Almost immediately some local recruiters began to inform Washington that they could not meet the goal. On September 21, the commanding general of the Second Corps Area centered in New York advised the adjutant general that his recruiters could not meet the quota imposed after the limited emergency proclamation unless "additional personnel . . . be placed on recruiting duty at once and . . . additional funds necessary for this purpose be supplied at the earliest possible date. . . ." The adjutant general replied that no additional resources were available.[30] In October the adjutant general queried the Second Corps Area concerning its continued inability to meet quotas. In a personal reply the corps area commander, Major General Hugh A. Drum, pointed out that enlistments in his region for September exceeded all records since 1924 and offered the following explanation for his difficulties.

[The] very large foreign born and recently emigrated population in this Corps Area is peculiarly susceptible to wars, rumors of wars, and crises in Europe. The average immigrant mother simply will not give her consent to the enlistment of a minor when conditions are unsettled. This reaction has been seriously felt even in the CCC. Furthermore, there has been a marked increase in employment in the industrial areas of this command since September 1, 1939.[31]

The First Corps Area also lagged behind its quotas. A report prepared by the Adjutant General's Office in November ranked that corps area, encompassing all of New England, last in total recruit production for the first quarter of fiscal year 1940.[32] Commenting on the report, War Department officials observed that the Eighth and Fourth corps areas, both located in rural and southern areas of the country, led in production of recruits. This development represented a distinct change over previous years when urban centers outstripped rural regions in the total number of men enlisting. Army recruiting analysts attributed the change to the effectiveness of "country recruiting methods" and "to the fact that the reservoir of possible new recruits is naturally greater in the country than in urban districts, where young men without dependents are comparatively few."[33]

The analysts missed the point. The increased productivity in the more rural corps areas resulted from a reorientation of the recruiting system itself. Throughout the 1920s and early 1930s, when regular army strength was stable and recruiting budgets low, emphasis was on maintaining strength. Recruiters concentrated their activities in urban areas where a few canvassers could effectively come into contact with a large number of prospects. When the recruiting drives began and more money and men for recruiting duty became available, effective penetration of previously untapped rural regions became possible. But the increased productivity of the rural recruiting districts was not enough. On December 26, 1939, the adjutant general announced that the goal of 227,000 men in the regular army by January 1 could not be met.[34]

Recruiters finally achieved the objective over a month late on February 7, 1940. They did so by signing up 106,549 men, a new record for enlistments during a seven-month period. But the ultimate success of the drive obscured the fact that the recruiting system had been strained to its limit. Furthermore, the recruiters could not rest on their laurels. They still had to maintain the new higher strength, and the adjutant general wanted 75,000 men enlisted in the regular army reserve as soon as possible. Finally, Congress was already considering another strength increase.[35]

In May, as a result of the German blitzkrieg in France and the Low Countries, President Roosevelt called for another troop increase. Without waiting for final congressional action on the request, the War Department announced its most ambitious drive yet: 15,000 men by June 30.[36] In the Second Corps Area, encompassing New York, New Jersey, and Delaware, which was supposed to supply 2,100 of the new recruits as well as 1,300 others in the same amount of time to maintain its own strength,[37] problems developed immediately. The corps area, which traditionally recruited most of the army's replacements for Panama, quickly reported that it could not meet the higher quota. Colonel R. M. Brambila, recruiting officer for the Northern New Jersey district, reported, "the number of applications for enlistment appear to be increasing, but physical disqualifications and cases of 'consent refused,' also appear to be increasing." Major C. A. Pivirotto of the New York City district added that recruits "are reluctant to go to Panama because of the general belief that climatic conditions are not good." Pivirotto also observed that the lack of motorized units in Panama discouraged technically inclined applicants from going there.[38] Appraised of the dilemma, Major General E. S. Adams, the adjutant general, tersely informed the commander of the corps area, "The solution appears to be in positive action in the approach to the situation."[39]

By mid-June only 6,033 of the desired 15,000 had enlisted. Results through June 11 revealed that the rural southern Corps Areas, the Fourth based in Atlanta and the Eighth centered in San Antonio, led in new recruits with 1,026 and 1,414 respectively. The First and Second Corps Areas, headquartered in New York City and Boston, trailed in production with less than 500 men combined.[40] Though recruiting analysts offered no explanation for the situation, the new upward trend in rural southern and southwestern recruiting districts merely perpetuated that of late 1939. But although the First and Second corps areas lagged behind the other areas in the drive, total monthly enlistments and reenlistments for the northeastern areas still were more than double the rates of similar periods before the drive began.

Throughout the summer of 1940, as Congress and public advocates debated calling up the National Guard and peacetime conscription, the War Department exhorted recruiters to keep on the job. Recruiters worked harder than ever, with impressive results. The War Department announced 8,605 new enlistments for the week of August 11 to 18, a new peacetime record.[41] But even with such impressive results the army continued to fall behind quotas. In New York only 315 enlisted during the record-breaking week. Instead of enlisting, young men, spurred by news reports that married men would not be drafted, rushed to the altar. In Brooklyn couples waited in rain for over an hour on Saturday, August 17, to apply for marriage licenses. License bureaus in the five boroughs of New York City issued 784 permits, a new record for a Saturday.[42]

After passage of the Selective Training and Service bill voluntary enlistments continued and remained high. Figures for the week of September 15 through 22 show that 8,464 enlisted. In New York enlistments skyrocketed. In mid-September the Second Corps Area recruiting office reported 3,185 enlistments since September 1. On Tuesday, September 24, an estimated crowd of 700 young men lined up four abreast on the sidewalk outside the main office in New York City. Military police had to be called to assist city police in handling the crush.[43] In October another rush to the recruiting stations occurred.

The reasons for the army's popularity in the last days before selective service are easy to detect. During the summer, when the draft remained in question, the War Department had begun to accept more one-year enlistments. The one-year option, unpopular with the army since its establishment by Congress in the 1920s, did not require a discharged soldier to serve in the reserves, as would the Selective Service Act. Between passage of the draft and the beginning of registration many prospective candidates for the draft chose to enlist for one year rather than wait for selection. After passage of the conscription bill the army announced that one-year enlistments would end October 15, the day before registration. In New York nearly 500 youths rushed to enlist for one year on the last day of the option. Recruiters worked until 11 P.M. the evening of October 15 processing the applicants, closing the doors on one hundred latecomers.[44] Altogether 1,793 volunteered in September and October for one year.[45]

Voluntary enlistments, for three years only, continued after selective service began in October. Surmising that public opinion expected volunteers to reduce draft quotas, the army adopted a policy of accepting all physically able volunteers to avoid being "placed in the embarrassing position of turning away volunteers at the time when large numbers are being selected for involuntary service."[46] There was no dearth of volunteers. Although monthly enlistments dropped from the record-breaking highs of September and October 1940, a total of 123,919 men enlisted for three years during the remainder of fiscal 1941.[47] The army assigned draftees where it needed them. Again, desire to avoid the draft played a part: Volunteers for the regular army could still enlist for the unit, branch, or location of their choice and thus exercise some control over their fate.

Expansion of the regular army, federalization of the National Guard, and the beginning of selective service transformed the army. At the beginning of fiscal 1941, Marshall reported that the military establishment had grown eightfold to 1.5 million men. The ground forces now consisted of four field armies organized in nine corps, twenty-nine infantry divisions, and four armored divisions. The air force consisted of fifty-four combat groups. The rapid expansion, creation, and training of new units was made possible, Marshall said, by "the continuous formation of training cadres" of experienced officers and noncommissioned officers drawn from regular army units. The success of the expansion "proved the soundness of the [mobilization] plans laboriously prepared throughout the years by the General Staff. . . ."[48]

The influx of approximately 400,000 selectees during late 1940 and early 1941 dictated the abandonment of many peacetime practices, notably local recruit training. The army established twenty-nine reception centers and twenty-one replacement training camps throughout the United States. Upon induction selectees reported to the reception centers where the army tested and classified the new men and issued them uniforms. From the reception centers the selectees went to the training camps for thirteen weeks of basic training. Only then did they receive assignment to units. Marshall expressed high praise for the new training system. "From now on our regiments and divisions can steadily advance with their combat training," he said, "unburdened by the necessity of training recruits or delaying their work in order to conduct individual instruction in weapons or similar matters."[49]

To provide for the welfare of the growing army the War Department reestablished the Morale Branch, relegated to a minor office under the adjutant general since World War I, and placed it under direct control of the chief of staff. Headed by a general officer, the Morale Branch coordinated athletic programs, provided motion pictures at 185 bases in the United States, and by the end of June 1941 built 113 service clubs and 95 guest houses and for soldiers stationed far from civilian communities, established twenty-six tent cities adjacent to towns with recreational facilities.[50]

Rapid expansion forced the army to examine and reaffirm one of its long-standing policies, separation of soldiers by race. Throughout the two decades since World War I, the army adhered to its policy of assigning blacks only to the infantry or cavalry and to the quartermaster and medical service units in direct support of the black regiments. Four "Colored" regiments, the Twenty-fourth and Twenty-fifth Infantry and the Ninth and Tenth Cavalry, remained on the active rolls of the regular army. During the 1920s and 1930s any black citizen who wanted to join the army had to enlist in one of those units. A typical information pamphlet of the period advised:

To avoid any unnecessary delays or misunderstandings, colored applicants should in every case include a statement as to their race in making any written application for enlistment or for any information regarding enlistment.[51]

The regular army units in which blacks could enlist had a combined war strength on paper of 10,436 men.[52] But the peacetime reductions that had affected the whole army since 1921 reduced the black units to skeletons. By 1925 the army counted only 3,896 blacks among its total enlisted strength of 115,177. The black regiments enjoyed extremely high reenlistment rates. In 1930, 703 blacks reenlisted; total losses among blacks that year numbered 943, leaving only 240 vacancies. All black units had waiting lists.[53] Still, young blacks tried to enlist. During the highly publicized recruiting campaign of 1939–1940, Brigadier General Clement A. Trott, the commanding general of the Fifth Corps Area, which included Indiana, Michigan, and Ohio, advised the adjutant general that the recruiting stations in his area had turned away hundreds of blacks. Trott warned, "Their disappointment and dissatisfaction after having met with failure in their efforts to get into the Army, makes them fertile ground for the activities of subversive agents. . . ."[54]

Black organizations had questioned army policies regulating the enlistment of blacks since the early 1930s. The Air Corps, which excluded all blacks, was a prime target. The army refused to accept black pilots on the grounds that "there are no [aviation] units composed of colored men." Using twisted logic, the Air Corps then refused to create black squadrons on the grounds that there were not enough black pilots to warrant such a move.[55]

In August 1940, Chester C. Davis, a member of the Advisory Commission to the Council of National Defense, asked the adjutant general to clarify the policy on enlistment of blacks. Davis quoted a letter from a friend who, traveling in the Southwest, found "a substantial number of young Negro men who have tried without success to enlist. . . ." The adjutant general, Major General E. S. Adams, informed Davis that blacks could serve only in "Colored organizations." Because, the adjutant general continued, "A large proportion of colored men who enlist in the Army make the service a lifetime career," there were relatively few vacancies for new enlistments.[56] In September General Marshall further clarified the policy in a letter to Senator Henry Cabot Lodge, Jr. "It is the policy of the War Department," the chief of staff wrote, "not to intermingle colored and white enlisted personnel in the same regimental organization. The condition which has made this policy necessary is not the responsibility of the Department, but to ignore it would produce situations destructive of morale and therefore definitely detrimental to the preparations for national defense in this emergency." Marshall expressed concern over "evidence of an extensive campaign . . . to force a change in this policy," and counseled against such a change, saying, "The present exceedingly difficult period . . . is not the time for critical experiments, which would inevitably have a highly destructive effect on morale—meaning military efficiency."[57]

The expansion of the army after 1939, and especially after the passage of the Selective Service Act, created more openings for blacks. The initial strength increase allowed the army to recruit existing units up to war strength. Then the call-up of the National Guard in August 1940 and the activation of new units in September 1940 and thereafter to receive draftees as well as volunteers brought the total black strength of the army to 97,725 by November 1941. Of that number over 10,000 were volunteers in the regular army.[58] Black spokesmen, hopes abetted, continued to demand a larger role in the defense effort. In October 1940, the War Department, under pressure from the White House, acquiesced to pressures to form black organizations in every branch of the army including the Air Corps.[59] But "separate but equal" remained the norm throughout the war and thereafter until 1948, when President Truman began desegregation of the armed forces by executive order.[60]

The army housed black units separately from whites. In many cases barracks or tent cities for blacks were located some distance from the main section of posts. At the beginning of the buildup black units did not exceed brigade strength. This policy ensured that relatively small numbers of blacks would be assigned to any division-size post. Since the army constructed troop housing in divisional-size units, quarters for black troops were frequently built last at new posts. These housing policies affected training. Under the new training guidelines all troops received instruction as a unit. Black units waiting for housing filled up slowly and thus fell behind other troops in the training cycle.

Another policy delayed the effective development of black units. Adhering to "separate but equal," the army sought black noncommissioned officers from the regular army black regiments to act as cadre for the new formations. There were not enough black regulars to provide an effective training nucleus. Furthermore, the black NCOs were mostly infantrymen and cavalry troopers and did not have the expertise necessary to develop troops in other branches. The result, again, was delayed or inferior training.[61]

Separation of races extended beyond blacks and whites. In addition to the black regiments, the army maintained a Puerto Rican regiment and the Philippine Scouts. The army refused to accept enlistments by Filipinos and mestizos except for service in the Philippine Scouts or units stationed in the Philippines that would accept them.[62]

The clause in the Selective Training and Service Act (Section 4a) prohibiting discrimination presented no problem with respect to blacks, Puerto Ricans, and Filipinos. They were inducted and assigned to existing or newly created segregated units. Oriental selectees, by contrast, threatened the segregation policy. Prior to 1940 the army simply refused to enlist the handful of qualified applicants of Oriental background who sought entry, out of a stated concern for "the doubtful loyalty to the United States of this class of personnel in case of a war with [Japan]." In November 1940 the General Staff decided to accept Oriental inductees rather than create special units. The staff based its decision on several factors. First, refusal to induce Oriental selectees might create resentment. Second, the staff believed that "much better use can be made of those whose loyalty is unquestioned, and more effective control be had over others, if only a few . . . are assigned to any unit." Oriental selectees were inducted, but the army refused to assign them to air force units or overseas.[63] After the United States entered the war, the War Department created separate Oriental combat units, which fought in Europe.

What about "quality not quantity"? What did the rapid voluntary expansion of the regular army before October 1940 and the introduction of selectees after that date do to the army's long-term effort to improve the caliber of its enlisted men? During the depression the army had raised minimum intelligence test standards for enlistment from thirty-four to forty-four. This higher standard remained in effect for the rest of the decade. It appears that, in terms of intelligence as measured by the Simon-Binet test, the caliber of enlisted men in the army permanently improved. Beyond the subjective comments and qualitative evidence there is not much to go on. A survey conducted in 1938 by the Adjutant General's office of 220 recruits showed fifty-seven high school graduates, including eight with college experience. An additional ninety-four completed some high school, but sixty-nine, or 31 percent of the sample, did not go beyond the eighth grade. Most of the group, about 42 percent, came from skilled trades; 27 percent listed their civilian occupations as "ordinary laborer," 18 percent were students, and 13 percent were farmers.[64]

During the early stages of expansion following the outbreak of war in Europe the War Department announced that the average recruit was "21, native born and has a small town background. He has a high school education, some mechanical or clerical training and is inclined to take part in sports." A *New York Times* feature article on the army, prepared about the same time, quoted officers as saying that the education and intelligence of recruits was "the best they ever had except in wartime." The article also reported that "older non-commissioned officers," were appalled by the "deplorable tendency among the present recruits to draw to 18 in Black Jack and to pass their evenings in violent jitterbug sessions."[65] Clearly officers and noncommissioned officers differed in their definitions of "quality." Officers wanted recruits capable of learning new skills. NCOs sought youths who accepted discipline.

Most comprehensive studies of army enlisted men began just after Pearl Harbor. In 1941 the War Department created the Research Branch within the Information and Education Division of the General Staff. One of the functions of the Research Branch was to determine soldiers' attitudes. The branch conducted its first survey on December 8, 1941.[66] After gathering data on recent recruits and inductees, the Research Branch compared

them with existing information on World War I soldiers. The results
showed dramatic improvement in educational levels. The study also
revealed a significant difference between selectees, who represented a
cross section, and volunteers, who as always were drawn disproportionately from lower socioeconomic families.

Table 8.2 *Educational Level of White Enlisted Men, World War I and World War II*

YEARS OF EDUCATION	WORLD WAR I DRAFTEES	REGULAR ARMY VOLUNTEERS*	WORLD WAR II SELECTEES**
College	5%	4%	11%
High school graduate	4	21	30
Some high school	12	34	28
Grade school	79	41	31

Source: Stouffer, et al., *The American Soldier: Adjustment During Army Life,* p. 59.

*Volunteers serving December 31, 1941, who enlisted prior to July 1, 1940.
**Selectees in the army on December 31, 1941.

Although there is a significant difference between regulars and selectees
in 1941, the change in both groups over World War I draftees suggests that
the improvement during the 1930s may have simply followed a more
general trend in improving educational levels nationally.

Table 8.3 *High School Graduates and College Attendance, 1910–1940*

(percentage of population)

	1910	1920	1930	1940
High school graduates over 17	8.8%	16.8%	29.0%	50.8%
College attendance, 18–21	5.0	8.0	12.4	15.7

Source: Historical Statistics of the United States, Table H 223–33, p. 207; Table H 316–26,
pp. 210–11.

The differences in educational levels between selectees and regulars
affected the swelling army in some fundamental ways. The Research
Branch survey of an infantry division in December 1941 revealed that 96
percent of the sergeants and 66 percent of the corporals were regulars.
Nearly 60 percent of the privates, on the other hand, were selectees. Not
surprisingly, the study also found that in terms of educational levels, "the

top enlisted leadership [was] in the hands of men who, on the average, had less education than the men they were trying to lead." Almost 80 percent of the sergeants, for example, lacked a high school diploma, and 47 percent had not gone beyond grade school. Clearly, the "higher caliber" men allegedly attracted to the army during the depression had not remained in the service or were not in the infantry. Among the selectees in the division 48 percent were high school graduates.[67]

The implications of these educational differences between selectees and regulars were predictable. Selectees tended to question the ability of their noncommissioned officers, preferred to wear civilian clothes rather than uniforms when off duty (until United States entry into the war, wearing the uniform off duty was optional), criticize the authoritarian structure of the army, and express frustration over their low status. The result of these differences was a tension between selectees and regulars that challenged the "old army" customs and traditional practices to the point of breaking them forever by the end of the war.[68]

By July 1941 the peacetime volunteer regular army had ceased to exist. The volunteer principle never received the chance to demonstrate its worth in 1940. It was lost in the rush for preparedness. Swelled by selectees, training at full strength with new equipment, the units of the new army bore little resemblance to the skeletonized force that had existed between 1921 and 1939. The center of national attention, the military was again at full strength, well equipped, and better paid. For a little longer they prepared for war. Then, almost as an afterthought following Pearl Harbor, the War Department announced that "all enlisted men now in the Army of the United States will be held for the duration."[69]

NOTES

1. G1 Guide Book on Readjustment of Service Pay and Allowances, 5 vols. (hereafter, G1 Guidebook), 3: 6, AGO 240, RG 94, Box 1182, National Archives, Washington, D.C. (hereafter, NA).

2. War Department Bulletin No. 9, June 10, 1922, in *General Orders and Bulletins, 1922* (Washington, D.C.: GPO, 1922).

3. *Army and Navy Journal* (hereafter, *ANJ*), March 18, 1939, p. 654; U.S. War Department, *Annual Report for the Year Ending June 30, 1940* (Washington, D.C.: GPO, 1940) pp. 31, 58, Table A, facing p. 31 (hereafter *Annual Report, 1940*); G1 Guide Book, 4–5.

4. *ANJ*, February 23, 1935, p. 519. See appendix C for pay scales.

5. G-1 Guide Book, 3: 6.

6. Selective Service System, *The Selective Service Act*, 5 vols., Special Monograph No. 2, (Washington, D.C.: GPO, 1954), 2: 685–89.

7. Ibid., pp. 690–709. See appendix C.

8. Memo, AG to CS, June 8, 1938, AGO 220.814, RG 94, Box 1103, NA; Memo, Major J. C. Daly to Asst. Commandant, Army War College, November 5, 1938,

File 7-1939-23, Military History Institute, Carlisle Barracks, Pa. (hereafter, MHI); G1 Guide Book, p. 6.

9. The 1932 policy directed commanders to bar from reenlistment soldiers who could not support their families on their pay as enlisted men, and directed the discharge of men below grade 3 who married without permission. See chapter 6. 155–57.

10. Letter, CS to all Corps Area and Department Commanders, March 26, 1931, AGO 342.1, RG 94, Box 1798, NA.

11. Quoted in Memo ACS-G1 to CS, November 7, 1938, AGO 341, RG 94, Box 1789, NA.

12. Ibid.

13. Ibid. The cited memo was extensively revised between November 7, 1938, and June 1939 when Craig formally approved it.

14. *Annual Report,* 1940, Table A, facing p. 31.

15. Memo, ACS-G1 to CS, July 17, 1940, AGO 341, RG 34, Box 1789, NA.

16. *Annual Report,* 1941, Table A, p. 104.

17. Special Report, Statistics Branch, General Staff, 1939, 1940, File 198-A, MHI.

18. *Annual Report,* 1939, p. 64; 1940, p. 40.

19. *Recruiting News,* 21, no. 7 (July 1939), p. 14; *Annual Report,* 1939, 84.

20. *New York Times* (hereafter, *NYT*), October 2, 1939, p. 10.

21. Ibid., October 6, 1939, p. 3.

22. Ibid., November 5, 1939, p. 22.

23. Army Regulation 600-750, "Personnel-Recruiting for the Regular Army and the Regular Army Reserve," April 10, 1939, Section II, paragraphs 8–16. At the USMA Library, West Point, N.Y.

24. *ANJ,* October 21, 1939, p. 158; *NYT,* December 28, 1939, p. 24.

25. *Recruiting News* 21, no. 11 (November 1939), p. 7.

26. *Recruiting News* 22, no. 1 (January 1940), pp. 10–11.

27. *NYT,* December 12, 1939, p. 6.

28. Letter, CG, 2d CA to AG, October 13, 1939, AGO 341, RG 94, NA.

29. Memo, G1 to AG, September 18, 1939, AGO 341, RG 94, NA.

30. Memo, CG II CA to AG, September 21, 1939; 1st Indorsement, AG to CG, II CA, September 27, 1939, AGO 341, RG 94, Box 1789, NA.

31. Letter, CG, II CA to AG, October 13, 1939, AGO 341, RG 94, Box 1789, NA.

32. Letter, CG, I CA to AG, November 15, 1939, AGO 341, RG 94, Box 1786, NA.

33. *NYT,* December 3, 1939, p. 38.

34. Ibid., December 27, 1939, p. 8.

35. Ibid., February 17, 1940, p. 6; Letter, AG to CG, I CA, February 6, 1940, AGO 341, RG 94, NA.

36. *NYT,* May 19, 1940, p. 24.

37. Ibid.

38. Letter, R. M. Brambila to CG, II CA, June 14, 1940; Letter, C. A. Pivirotto to CG, II CA, June 14, 1940, AGO 341, RG 94, Box 1786, NA.

39. Letter, E. S. Adams to CG, II CA, July 2, 1940, AGO 341, RG 94, Box 1786, NA.

40. *NYT,* June 12, 1940, p. 15.

41. Ibid., August 20, 1940, p. 1.

42. Ibid., August 18, 1940, p. 2.

43. Ibid., September 25, 1940, p. 24.

44. Ibid., October 13, 1940, p. 6; October 16, p. 10.

45. *Annual Report,* 1941, p. 132.

46. Memo, ACS, G1 to CS, October 9, 1940, AGO 341, RG 94, Box 1787, NA.

47. *Annual Report,* 1941, p. 134.

48. Ibid., pp. 53, 56.

49. Ibid., pp. 53–54.

50. Ibid., pp. 75–77.

51. The Adjutant General of the Army, *The United States Army as a Career* (Washington, D.C.: GPO, 1929), p. 16.

52. Ulysses Lee, *The Employment of Negro Troops,* The United States Army in World War II Special Studies (Washington, D.C.: GPO, 1966), p. 43.

53. Ibid., p. 24; *Annual Report of the Surgeon General* (Washington, D.C.: GPO, 1925), pp. 18–19; 1931, pp. 18, 20.

54. Lee, *Employment of Negro Troops,* p. 67.

55. Ibid., pp. 55–64.

56. Letter, Chester C. Davis to AG, August 29, 1940; Reply, September 4, 1940, AGO 341, RG 94, NA.

57. Letter, CS to Henry Cabot Lodge, Jr., September 27, 1940, AGO 341, RG 94, NA.

58. Lee, *Employment of Negro Troops,* pp. 69–70, 88; *Annual Report,* 1941. p. 131.

59. Lee, *Employment of Negro Troops,* pp. 75–76.

60. Richard M. Dalfiume, *Desegregation of the U.S. Armed Forces: Fighting on Two Fronts, 1939–1953* (Columbia, Mo.: University of Missouri Press, 1969), p. 4.

61. Lee, *Employment of Negro Troops,* pp. 97–110.

62. Memo, G1 to CG, September 8, 1933, AGO 341, RG 94, NA.

63. Memo, G1 to CS, November 5, 1940, AGO 341, Classified, RG 94, NA.

64. Memo, AG to CS, May 4, 1938 in G1 Guide Book, vol. 3, AGO 240, RG 94, NA.

65. *NYT,* December 3, 1939, p. 9; Kenneth Campbell, "Join the Army and—" *New York Times Magazine,* November 26, 1939, p. 12.

66. Samuel A. Stouffer, et al., *Studies in Social Psychology in World War II,* vol. 1, *The American Soldier, Adjustment During Army Life* (Princeton, N.J.: Princeton University Press, 1949), p. 54.

67. Ibid., pp. 61–63.

68. Ibid., pp. 71–81.

69. *ANJ,* December 13, 1941, p. 399.

9

EPILOGUE AND CONCLUSIONS

Selective service continued after World War II while the nation debated whether to institute some form of universal military training. In March 1947, before a decision on UMT was reached, the Selective Service and Training Act expired. While advocates for UMT debated with traditional opponents of the plan, the developing cold war brought a resumption of the draft in 1948. Despite widespread opposition to both selective service and UMT, the draft continued into the 1950s. After the Korean War opposition to the draft muted. Congress renewed the Selective Service Act with little debate every four years beginning in 1951. Throughout the decade support for the program remained high. As late as 1965 a Harris poll revealed that 90 percent of those surveyed favored selective service.[1]

In the late 1960s growing opposition to American participation in the Vietnam conflict quickly engulfed the draft as well. Resistance to the draft mounted with increased monthly calls. Inductions from 1954 to 1964 averaged 100,000 a year. In 1966, 400,000 were called. As American involvement in Vietnam escalated, casualties increased. Casualties among draftees were especially high. Draftees, who constituted only 16 percent of the armed forces but 88 percent of infantry soldiers in Vietnam, accounted for over 50 percent of combat deaths in 1969.[2] The draft was a natural casualty of the longest, most unpopular war in American history.

Responding to public opposition to the war, Richard Nixon, perhaps to demonstrate his sincerity to end the war, promised in October 1968 to return to the volunteer concept after the war. Shortly after his election Nixon appointed a presidential commission chaired by Thomas S. Gates "to develop a comprehensive plan for eliminating conscription and moving toward an all-volunteer armed force."[3]

The Gates Commission presented its report in February 1970. As if paraphrasing opponents of compulsory service in 1920, the members of the study group unanimously agreed:

That the nation's interests will be better served by an all-volunteer force, supported by an effective standby draft, than by a mixed force of volunteers and conscripts; and that steps should be taken promptly to move in this direction. . . .[4]

The commission viewed the decision to volunteer in peacetime largely from an economic perspective and argued, "Reasonable improvements in pay and benefits in the early years of service should increase the number of volunteers" necessary to maintain a stable voluntary force of about 2.5 million men. Thus, a major recommendation of the commission was an immediate increase in pay for first-term volunteers. The report also proposed "comprehensive improvements in the conditions of military service. . . ."[5]

The peacetime draft ended on June 30, 1973. Anticipating the shift to all-voluntary recruiting, Congress doubled the pay of junior enlisted men in November 1971. The monthly pay of a private, for example, jumped from $134 to $269.[6] In 1972, at Pentagon urging, Congress approved payment of a $1,500 bonus to volunteers for combat branches once the draft expired. The bonus was raised to $2,500 in 1973.[7]

In addition to paying better, the armed forces, especially the army, went to considerable lengths to make service life more attractive to potential recruits. Civilians replaced privates in traditionally obnoxious jobs such as KP, post maintenance, and in many administrative areas. The army spent $3.2 billion dollars on barracks improvements in 1973 alone. Reveille formations disappeared, and commanders were ordered to maintain a forty-hour, five-day workweek in garrison.[8]

When draft calls ended in January 1973, 6,000 army recruiters went to work seeking enough high school graduates to maintain an active army strength of over 800,000 men. This was 10 percent of men aged twenty to twenty-four, compared to 2.2 percent of the same age group needed to fill the 118,750-man army of the interwar years.[9] The army wanted high school graduates. According to an official report, "The high school diploma has proven to be one of the most important predicters of success in the Army." Compared to high school graduates, dropouts had more disciplinary problems and "less potential for long-term professional development." Initially, the army hoped to enlist up to 70 percent high school graduates.[10]

From the start, the volunteer army experienced difficulty attracting recruits. In Fall River, Massachusetts, a city with 7.2 percent unemployed in 1973, an army recruiter advertised the $1,500 bonus for volunteers for the infantry, armor, or artillery. Because of a typographical error the ad offered $15,000; no one responded.[11] By October, 101,793 men and women had volunteered, but the army was already short of its goal of 120,770 by 16 percent. Army Secretary Howard Callaway declared, "the alternative to an all-volunteer army is failure," and vowed, "We are going to make the all-volunteer army work."[12]

In April 1974, after fourteen months without selectees to back up or stimulate volunteers, army enlistments (all for three years) totaled 186,720, still 13 percent short of the desired figure for that time. Furthermore, only 47 percent of all army enlistees in 1974 possessed high school diplomas. The shortage was all the more vexing because strength declined during the

same period as Congress reduced the size of the postwar armed forces by
nearly 100,000 men.[13]

Faced with this inability to meet minimum strength goals, the army
compromised its stated desire for 70 percent high school graduates and
began accepting more dropouts almost immediately. The armed forces as
a whole also found it necessary to increase recruiting personnel 75 percent
after the end of conscription. Total recruiting and advertising costs after
1973 averaged $500 million annually, compared to $3.2 million between
1924 and 1931.[14]

The situation facing the all-volunteer armed forces changed dramatically
between 1974 and 1975. As in the depression, rising unemployment made
the volunteer force concept work.

Table 9.1 *Percent Unemployed, 1973–1976*

GROUP	1973	1974	1975	1976 (Jan.–April)
All	4.9	5.6	8.5	8.3
White males	3.7	4.3	7.2	7.3
Black males	7.6	9.1	13.7	13.8
Teenagers	14.5	16.0	19.9	20.1

Source: Statistical Abstract of the United States, 1976, p. 361.

Recruiters reported that they achieved 101 percent of their quotas in
January 1975. Captain Joe Bellard of the Detroit Recruiting District said,
"Now we go after the quality market. Where we used to want quantity
and quality, we now want quality and quantity." Bellard merely echoed
what earlier observers of the relationship between the economy and voluntary military service had said: "Industry's extremity thus becomes the
Army's opportunity."[15] In February 1975, William K. Brehm, assistant
secretary of defense for manpower and reserve affairs, declared the volunteer concept a success. Brehm pointed out that 66 percent of the volunteers were high school graduates and that 92 percent were classified
above average or average mentally. Conceding that high unemployment
"allowed the services to be more selective," Brehm nevertheless pronounced the volunteer system fit, concluding: "We now believe we can
maintain our planned peacetime force levels on a voluntary basis."[16]

The recession proved to be a temporary windfall to the army. By April
1975 enlistments by high school graduates exceeded 75 percent. Even
Vietnam veterans were signing up. Between autumn 1974 and June 1975
the enlistments of prior-service men with Vietnam combat experience
doubled. Most cited difficulty finding jobs and higher army pay, the bonus

for combat branches, and other increased benefits as reasons for reentering the service.[17]

Enlistments in 1975 improved so much that the army discontinued or lowered bonuses for the hard-to-fill combat branches. High school graduates continued to join in large numbers: 62.2 percent of all enlistments in 1975. But the success was short-lived. In 1976 the recession seemed to level off and unemployment declined slightly. So, too, did the educational level of army enlistees. In October and November 1976, only 54.5 percent of the 31,078 new enlistees were high school graduates. Some critics of the volunteer system also pointed out that blacks made up 21.9 percent of the total strength of the army, while representing only 10.9 percent of the U.S. population, according to 1970 statistics. In January 1977 Army Secretary Martin Hoffman acknowledged some difficulties but insisted that the army "is not doing badly."[18]

In February 1977, Senator Sam Nunn of Georgia, a member of the Senate Armed Services Committee, held subcommittee hearings on the future of the all-volunteer system. Nunn pointed to the $500 million spent annually on recruiting and the 150 percent increase in military pay since 1967 and called the volunteer force "a luxury which we may no longer be able to afford."[19] In a study prepared for Nunn's subcommittee Professor William R. King of the University of Pittsburgh warned that if unemployment declined further and civilian pay continued to increase, the armed forces, especially the army and Marine Corps, would find it increasingly difficult to attract recruits from the declining pool of high school graduates. King estimated that an attempt to increase strength to Vietnam War levels through the all-volunteer concept would cost $29 billion. He recommended instead a form of universal national service.[20]

Despite talk in Congress and reports in the media of the alleged failure of the all-volunteer system, there seemed little likelihood that the United States would soon return to the draft or adopt some form of universal service. The same week that Senator Nunn held his hearings on the problems of the volunteer program President Carter told a Pentagon audience that while he was concerned about the inability of the army to fill its needs under the all-volunteer system, he did not contemplate a return to the draft.[21]

Carter's disclaimer did little to stifle the debate over the adequacy of the concept of an all-volunteer force. As the armed services entered their fifth year of dependency on the volunteers principle, the record of the all-volunteer force revealed that while the ranks were being filled, many problems persisted. In fiscal year 1978, 70 percent of the non-prior-service males entering the army possessed high school diplomas, but while education levels of recruits rose, aptitude test scores declined. The army reported that 60 percent of the enlistees in fiscal 1978 were "considered below average'' in mental ability. Furthermore, the army continued to report difficulty in filling vacancies in the combat arms, particularly armor. In fiscal 1978 recruiters delivered 9,200 recruits to armor units, 2,200 men short of the tankers' needs. To compensate, the army lowered vision standards for armor enlistees, thereby raising the specter of sending men into combat who were unable to see enemy forces clearly.[22]

Critics of the all-volunteer force pointed to shortfalls in combat arms recruiting and to declining mental test scores as indicators of the bankruptcy of the volunteer principle. Professor Charles C. Moskos, Jr., a sociologist at Northwestern University, told Senator Nunn's Armed Services Manpower and Personnel Subcommittee ''that earlier studies showing the AVF to be a success were 'flat wrong.' '' Moskos acknowledged that reviving the draft was ''politically impossible'' and supported, as an alternative, two-year enlistments for the combat arms coupled with increased postservice benefits such as a guaranteed college education.[23]

The Defense Department countered by insisting on the ''continuing success'' of the all-volunteer force. Secretary of Defense Harold Brown pronounced the volunteer system ''more equitable than the system of conscription it superseded,'' and ''billions of dollars cheaper than universal military training or some form of national service. . . .'' John P. White, assistant secretary of defense for manpower, reserve affairs and logistics, suggested that higher pay would cure the services' ills. ''If pay goes up, quality goes up,'' White argued.[24] Nevertheless, in December 1978 the army announced plans to test a two-year enlistment for volunteers for the combat arms, offering a $2,000 education fund to those who completed the two-year hitch as an incentive. The Pentagon designed the plan to attract ''high school graduates and young persons in upper mental categories'' to hard-to-fill jobs in the infantry and other combat branches.[25]

The effort was to no avail. Fiscal year 1979 turned out to be the worst yet for the volunteer army. Army recruiters fell short of their goal by more than 16,000 men in 1979; only 64 percent of the enlistees were high school graduates (the army wanted 70 percent) and nearly half of the recruits accepted in 1979 scored in the lowest mental category accepted for enlistment.[26] Furthermore, according to a report in the *Wall Street Journal,* ''Droves of career people, both in the noncommissioned and officer ranks, are leaving the services because of dissatisfaction with their pay and the morale problems resulting from low-quality recruits.''[27] Clearly, the new all-volunteer force has failed to live up to expectations.

The seizure of the American embassy in Iran in November 1979 and the Soviet invasion of Afghanistan late the following December focused public attention on the personnel problems of the all-volunteer force. Concerned about the apparent unreadiness of the armed forces as evidenced by their inability to rescue the hostages in Iran or deter Soviet adventurism, Americans began to give more attention to those spokesmen who argued that adequate preparedness required a return to the draft.[28] In March 1979, 45 percent of adult Americans favored a return to peacetime conscription; 76 percent favored peacetime registration. By February 1980, 59 percent supported a renewed draft, and 83 percent wanted immediate registration of young men.[29]

In January 1980, President Carter ordered the registration of twenty- and twenty-one-year-old males as a gesture of American determination to oppose further Soviet aggression. Congress provided the enabling legis- lation by June, and registration began in July. Although opposition to peacetime draft registration came from church groups, antiwar activists, and libertarians, all of whom restated arguments reaching back to 1917,[30] the issue aroused little debate in either Congress or public forums. None of the presidential candidates in 1980 favored a return to peacetime con- scription. But registration was enough to alert traditional opponents of the draft, and their modest efforts against even standby selective service should serve as a warning to preparedness advocates that the issue will be contested if it arises in the future.

Looking at the contemporary debate over the all-volunteer armed forces concept from the perspective of America's experience with a volunteer army between the world wars, one is struck with a profound sense of *déjà vu*. Although the armed forces are bigger, are more complicated, and play a much larger and more visible role in the affairs of the nation than in the 1920s and 1930s, their manpower problems and the solutions the Defense Department has applied to those problems are hauntingly familiar.

A comparison of the two volunteer systems suggests several conclu- sions. First, the volunteer principle does work in peacetime insofar as gross numbers are concerned. Rarely in either period did the army fail to meet its modest overall strength objectives. On those occasions during the interwar years when the army ended a fiscal year considerably under- strength the source of the failure lay more in recruiting policy than with the volunteer principle. In 1923 and 1937, for example, the army tried to secure recruits "on the cheap" through intensive local recruiting cam- paigns instead of bolstering the professional General Recruiting Service. Other manpower shortages in the 1920s and 1930s can also be traced to underfunded recruiting programs.

In the 1970s, on the other hand, both Congress and the Defense Depart- ment have recognized that maintaining an all-volunteer force is an expen- sive proposition and have provided ample funds and personnel in support of the recruiting effort. In 1978 the Defense Department spent about $1,400 for every recruit obtained. Even if one takes the declining purchasing power of the dollar into account, this expense far exceeds the $56.98 per recruit spent by the army in 1929.[31] Increased recruiting expenditures since 1973 unquestionably have been instrumental in the military's success in maintaining current strength levels. Indeed, the pre–World War II army showed that it, too, could raise large numbers of men when, in fiscal year 1940, it was given sufficient resources and recruited over 100,000 new soldiers.

The willingness of the people, through their elected representatives, to spend more for the volunteer armed force extends to the pay of service members and leads to a second conclusion. Higher pay and improved service benefits, as army spokesmen of the interwar years claimed, attract volunteers. Base pay for privates has more than tripled since the draft years. The precise role that pay raises play in the decision to enlist is difficult to measure, because the advent of the all-volunteer force also brought enlistment bonuses and increased recruiting expenditures with the pay increases. But it cannot be denied that the $501 paid to recruits beginning in October 1980 with a guaranteed promotion and raise to $559 a month after six months is considerably more attractive than the $21 a month authorized to privates between 1922 and 1940.[32]

In addition to pay, volunteers in the contemporary army are entitled to veterans' benefits such as education assistance and housing loans. All men and women entering the army after January 1, 1977, can, for example, establish "participatory" funds for their postdischarge education. Soldiers may save a maximum of $2,700 during their period of service and receive a matching grant of $2 for $1 from the government for use in approved educational programs. Post–Vietnam War veterans also are qualified for Veterans Administration home loans. No such programs existed during the interwar years.[33]

Service attractiveness has also improved considerably compared to the "old army." Except in basic training, soldiers no longer bunk in forty-man platoon-size barracks. Single enlisted soldiers share a two- or three-person dormitory-type room. The armed forces no longer prohibit low-ranking enlisted persons from marrying and extends most benefits such as medical care, commissary and exchange privileges, and housing to all ranks. Enlisted people also enjoy greater freedom in their use of personal and off-duty time. In short, the quality of life of today's enlisted soldier has dramatically improved over that of his pre–World War II counterpart.

But despite its ability to outspend the interwar army in every capacity, the contemporary volunteer force suffers from the same problems: concerns that not enough "quality" recruits are being obtained and high losses of men to civilian life. There is obviously a limit to what money can buy in the military manpower market.

Losses and reenlistments may provide some clues to whether or not the volunteer army is, in fact, effectively attracting and retaining enlisted men.

Desertions from the wartime draft army reached a peak of 6.2 per hundred in 1972.

Table 9.2 *Regular Army Losses and Reenlistments, 1964–1978 (Selected Years)*

YEAR	LOSSES		REENLISTMENTS	
	Attrition (% first term)	Desertion (per hundred)	First Term (% eligible)	Total (% eligible)
1964	. . .	1.34	22.5	50.1
1968	. . .	2.91	. . .	. . .
1971	25	. . .	. . .	30.1
1972	28	6.20	. . .	22.2
Average 1968–73	. . .	. . .	19.3	34.0
1974	40	4.12	28.8	47.4
1975	39	. . .	36.7	50.2
1976	40	1.77	32.1	48.3
1977	36	1.33	34.1	51.9
1978	33	. . .	32.6	51.4
Average 1974–78	37.6	. . .	33.0	49.8

Sources: Annual Report, 1979, pp. 330, 338; Sabrosky, *Defense Manpower Policy,* pp. 17, 18; Reenlistment and rates by service, Department of Defense Directorate of Information.

In 1974, the first year of the all-volunteer army, about four men in one hundred deserted. Since 1974 the desertion rate has declined until, in 1977, it approximated the pre–Vietnam War rate of the mixed draftee-volunteer army. While the desertion rate has returned to peacetime levels, the number of men failing to complete their first enlistment has increased. During the first five years of the contemporary all-volunteer army over 37 percent of first-term enlistees failed to complete a full three-year assignment. In 1971 only 25 percent of all selectees or volunteers left the army early.[34] The high attrition rate for first term soldiers is, in part, the result of a conscious decision on the army's part to let misfits and malcontents out before they become disciplinary problems. But the increase in early departure from the service also clearly indicates that many volunteers do not find military life to their liking.

Reenlistments in the modern volunteer force, on the other hand, suggest that many volunteers do like the army. In 1964, before the war in Southeast Asia became an issue, about 50 percent of all eligible regular army enlisted men reenlisted. But only 22.5 percent of eligible first-term enlisted men chose to remain in the army. During Vietnam reenlistments dropped off. After five peaceful years of the volunteer army 50 percent of all soldiers are again making the army a career. Furthermore, 33 percent of first-term volunteers between 1974 and 1978 elected to stay in the army beyond their initial three-year obligation.[35] Thus, while fewer volunteers complete their first enlistment, more of those who do reenlist. If one focuses on losses, the modern volunteer force must be deemed a failure in terms of service attractiveness; reenlistment figures, however, point to success.

Once again, the "quality" of men (and women) enlisting and reenlisting in the army must be considered. In terms of quality the results do not look good for the volunteer army. Department of Defense (DOD) studies reveal that "recruits at the highest educational and mental levels are more likely than other recruits to leave the military after a single term of service." Furthermore, DOD expects "the number of male volunteers with high school diplomas to decline over the next several years." If fewer high school graduates are attracted to military service and fewer still remain in uniform, then the quality of the enlisted force will surely decline.[36]

In an effort to overcome shortages of male high school graduates the services have increasingly opened their ranks to women. In 1964, for example, 8,000 enlisted women served in the army (0.1 percent of enlisted strength). With the advent of the volunteer force the army opened a number of military occupations previously closed to women. In 1977, the army reported 46,000 women (6 percent enlisted strength) in uniform and estimated that it would have jobs for 80,000 by 1983.[37]

The services have expressed general satisfaction with the job that women are doing. But the increased number of women in uniform has created new issues even as it has helped solve the "man"power shortage problem. In 1977 the pregnancy rate among women soldiers jumped to 15 percent, up 3 percent over the previous year. Pregnancy, which used to be grounds for immediate discharge, is tolerated. But the services are concerned about the effect that motherhood will have on the efficiency of enlisted women. As one general put it, "If a bugle is blown they (military mothers) can't be baby-sitting." The number of single parents in uniform (male or female) also concerns the army. Starting in January 1979, the army began to enforce stiff new regulations that could result in the discharge of single-parent soldiers "when parenthood causes repeated absence from work, nonavailability for worldwide assignment or poor duty performance. . . ."[38] As in the interwar years, the army is finding that it must regulate the personal affairs of its soldiers in order to preserve enlisted efficiency. But policies that seek to influence sexual or familial behavior may be counterproductive. Prospective recruits or soldiers who perceive that the military is interfering with their lives unnecessarily may decline to enlist or reenlist and add to the overall manpower shortage problem. Thus, the army, as it learned in the 1930s, must find ways to balance its need for quantity and quality with its requirements for efficiency.

The personnel policy makers and managers of the modern volunteer force must also relearn and accept a lesson that recruiters of the "old" volunteer army learned well: The volunteer armed forces will remain somewhat at the mercy of conditions beyond their ability to influence in their constant search for manpower. In terms of recruiting and retention of enlisted people, the record of the interwar years reinforces more recent experience. No matter how much money is spent on recruiting, military pay, and service benefits, and no matter how extensively the quality of service life is improved, the decision to enlist seems to be more a function of conditions in the society at large than of the attractiveness of the armed forces per se. The health of the economy is the single most important factor in the decision to enlist. During periods of recession and high unemployment, as was the case during the Great Depression and during the 1974–1976 recession, the army filled its ranks with relative ease and was well pleased with the quality of recruits obtained. High unemployment among Detroit auto workers and factory workers in other industrial areas during the slump in 1980 proved once again to be a windfall for recruiters. The Detroit recruitment center reported that 33,000 men and women enlisted between June 1, 1979, and May 31, 1980, twice as many as during the previous year.[39] Once the economy improved and unemployment declined after 1976, the army again experienced difficulty maintaining strength. There is no reason to assume the same pattern will not repeat itself after the current recession abates. But the conclusion that the military institutions of the United States exercise little real control over the forces that influence military manpower extends to military policies beyond those concerned with the specifics of manpower procurement and retention. During most of the interwar years military leaders found themselves powerless to influence the size of the appropriations for the army's maintenance and operations. Indeed, most uniformed professionals in 1930 agreed "that the establishment of military policy is not a function of the Army."[40] The reductions in army strength and appropriations in the 1920s resulted from the failure of legislators to perceive a real need for a large peacetime armed force—there was no such need—and a desire to curb government expenditures. During the early 1930s domestic economic imperatives again threatened to reduce the size of the army and resulted in further cuts in military spending. Throughout the interwar years, a broad spectrum of opinion, including pacifists, preparedness advocates, antimilitarists, isolationists, and political economists, conducted the debate that ultimately shaped the military establishment. Uniformed military professionals were generally absent from the debate.

After World War II military leaders enjoyed a far greater role in formulating defense policy than they had ever experienced before. The crusade against fascism had silenced most of the opponents of a large military establishment. During the cold war, too, there was little real debate over either the ends or the means of defense.

Vietnam ended an era of bipartisan agreement on foreign and defense policy. As Americans began to question the assumptions behind their foreign policy, they also began to examine the means by which those policies were achieved. In the 1970s voices long muted on defense policy again began to be heard. Advocates of arms control and reduction stridently argue that "We waste billions on military overkill, when our country—and the world—need to relieve poverty, hunger, and disease." Furthermore, critics charge that America's role in the arms race is leading the nation toward another war, that because of the momentum of weapons development "it will be inevitable that nuclear weapons will be used someplace at some time." New York City's Riverside Church, a prominent center of pacifist and antimilitary activity during the interwar years, has, under the leadership of the Reverend William Sloane Coffin, a veteran of the 1960s antiwar movement, committed itself to a program "seeking to create a national awareness of arms proliferation."[41]

The revival of special interest groups specifically concerned with defense spending and arms reduction in the 1970s coincided with a growing concern over government spending in general. As Americans once again demand reductions in government spending and taxes, Congress may be encouraged to take a new look at costly military programs. Manpower expenditures have accounted for over 50 percent of all defense budgets since the mid-1960s.[42] Forced to choose between men and machines, America's lawmakers may conclude, as did Ross Collins in the 1930s, that a smaller, highly technical army is preferable to one that is both large and technical. If so, the expensive economic incentives designed to lure and hold volunteers may be among the first programs to be eliminated, and recruiters will once again have to scour the earth in search of both quality and quantity.

The American people value their personal freedom as much as their collective independence. The antimilitary tradition in America is older than the republic itself. A return to the draft may appear to be a beguiling solution to some of the current problems of the all-volunteer force (it will not solve the problems associated with retention of skilled midcareer personnel). But for the armed forces to support such a move in the absence of "clear and present danger" may place them at odds with other American institutions and values. Here again the experience of the army of the interwar years may prove useful. In 1920 the army strenuously lobbied for UMT without a clear understanding of the depth of American hostility to what amounted to peacetime conscription. The subsequent defeat of the scheme along with the traditional American desire to return to a small peacetime establishment cast a pall over army efforts to maintain even a modest force in readiness for the next twenty years. When the crisis of 1940 revived the issue of a large standing army supported by conscription, the army avoided the temptation to lead the debate. The decision to abandon the volunteer army rested with the people in 1940 as it should always.

If, on the other hand, the continuing instability in the Near East and western Asia and renewed Soviet adventurism, as exemplified by the invasion of Afghanistan, leads Americans to conclude that they must have both a large and technical army, peacetime conscription may prove attractive once again.

NOTES

1. John W. Chambers, *Draftees or Volunteers: A Documentary History of the Debate Over Military Conscription in the United States, 1783–1973* (New York: Garland Publishing, 1975), pp. 359–71, passim. For an analysis of the debate over UMT versus a return to a voluntary system after World War II, see James M. Gerhardt, *The Draft and Public Policy: Issue in Military Manpower Procurement, 1945–1970* (Columbus, Ohio: Ohio State University Press, 1971), pp. 3–141.

2. Chambers, *Draftees or Volunteers,* pp. 428, 430–31.

3. Statement by the President Announcing the Creation of the Commission, March 27, 1969, in *Report of the President's Commission on an All-Volunteer Armed Force* (New York: Macmillan Co., 1970), n.p.

4. *Report of the President's Commission on an All-Volunteer Armed Force,* p. 5.

5. Ibid., p. 10.

6. *Army Times,* May 10, 1976, p. 18.

7. Chambers, *Draftees or Volunteers,* p. 454.

8. Worcester (Mass.) *Sunday Telegram,* February 4, 1973, p. 35A; *U.S. News & World Report,* April 2, 1973, pp. 51–53. For a detailed study of the changes made in enlisted training and life during the early years of the volunteer army project, see Harold C. Moore and Jeff M. Tuten, *Building a Volunteer Army: The Fort Ord Contribution* (Washington, D.C.: Department of the Army, 1975).

9. U.S. Bureau of the Census, *Historical Statistics of the U.S. from Colonial Times to the Present* (Washington, D.C.: GPO, 1976), Table A, p. 15.

10. "Maintaining a Quality Force," *Commanders Call,* DA Pamphlet 360–832 (March–April 1977), pp. 6–9.

11. *The Stars & Stripes,* August 20, 1973, p. 14.

12. *U.S. News & World Report,* October 15, 1973, pp. 63–66.

13. Ibid., April 1, 1976, pp. 47–48; Alan N. Sabrosky, *Defense Manpower Policy: A Critical Reappraisal,* Monograph No. 22 (Philadelphia, Pa.: Foreign Policy Research Institute, 1978), p. 11.

14. *Report of Secretary of Defense James R. Schlesinger, FY 197T,* February 5, 1975, p. IV-20; Averaged from "Cost of Recruiting FY 1929–1931" Special Reports, Statistics Branch, General Staff, Military History Institute, Carlisle Barracks, Pa. (hereafter, MHI).

15. *Washington Post,* January 6, 1975, p. A20; *U.S. News & World Report,*

March 24, 1975, pp. 43–44; Maj. C. W. Harlow to AG, December 13, 1920, AG 251.1 (10-12-20) Bulky, RG 407, Box 1709, NA.

16. *New York Times* (hereafter, *NYT*), February 14, 1975, p. 9.

17. Ibid., June 8, 1975, p. 1.

18. Ibid., January 11, 1977, p. 9.

19. Ibid., March 6, 1977, p. E3; April 10, p. E3.

20. Ibid., March 3, 1977, p. 18.

21. Ibid., March 6, 1977, p. E3.

22. *Army Times,* June 19, 1978, p. 8; November 20, p. 24.

23. Ibid., July 3, 1978, pp. 1, 23.

24. Warren Rogers, "Volunteer Army—Is It Working?," Boston *Sunday Globe,* July 27, 1978, pp. A1, A4; *Army Times,* July 3, 1978, p. 23.

25. As reported in Worcester (Mass.) *Telegram,* December 29, 1978, p. 17.

26. *Army Times,* October 22, 1979, p. 11; July 28, 1980, pp. 1, 45.

27. Norman C. Miller, "A Military Disgrace," *The Wall Street Journal,* July 3, 1980, p. 16.

28. See, for example, articles in popular magazines such as James Webb, "The Draft: Why the Army Needs It," and James Fallows, "The Draft: Why the Country Needs It," *Atlantic Monthly* 245, no. 4 (April 1980): 33–37, and "Who'll Fight for America?" *Time,* June 9, 1980, pp. 24–36.

29. *The Gallup Opinion Index,* August 1979, pp. 4–18; February 1980, pp. 3–8.

30. See, for example, Mary McGory, "Student Firestorm over Registration a Surprise to Carter," *The Kansas City Star,* February 20, 1980, p. A11; "Proposal to Ready America for War," letter to editor, *NYT,* February 27, 1980, p. A26; "Dangerous Mood Produces the Draft," letter to editor, *Kansas City Star,* March 3, 1980, p. A12; "Carter's State of the Union Address: A Libertarian Response," paid political ad by Libertarian party, *NYT,* February 10, 1980, p. 22E; Richard Halloran, "All the Old Arguments Revived on the Draft," *NYT,* February 10, 1980, p. 3E; Richard Halloran, "Draft Registration Beginning Amid Controversy," *NYT,* July 21, 1980, pp. A1, 13.

31. Drew Middleton, "The Volunteer Army: Is It Enough?," *NYT,* August 2, 1978, p. A8; "Cost of Recruiting—FY 1929," Special Report No. 209, Statistics Branch, General Staff, October 15, 1929, File 198-A-209, MHI.

32. The figures for pay are found in *Army Times,* September 22, 1980, p. 16. Even at this writing, a pay raise of 5.3 percent is before Congress. Furthermore, military pay is subject to annual cost-of-living increases keyed to the rate of inflation.

33. Supplement to Compilation of Veterans Laws, 94th and 95th Congress (Washington, D.C.: GPO, 1978), pp. 85–88; U.S. Veteans Administration, *Annual Report, Administrator of Veterans Affairs, 1977* (Washington, D.C.: GPO, 1977), pp. 5, 69–70, 73–77.

34. U.S. Department of Defense, *Annual Report, 1979,* (Washington, D.C.: GPO, 1979), pp. 330, 338; Sabrosky, *Defense Manpower Policy,* pp. 17–18; Department of Defense Directorate of Information.

35. U.S. Department of Defense, *Annual Report, 1979;* Sabrosky, *Defense Manpower Policy;* Department of Defense Directorate of Information.

36. *Annual Report, 1979,* pp. 327, 331.

37. Ibid., pp. 327–29.

38. *Army Times,* December 11, 1978, pp. 1, 18.

39. "Recession Helps Armed Forces Meet Enlistment Goals," *NYT,* August 2, 1980, pp. 1, 9.

40. War Plans Division, *Report on the Survey of the Military Establishment,* Washington, D.C., November 1, 1929. AGO 333 E.P., RG 407, NA, p. 124.

41. "Cause For Alarm," *New York Sunday Times,* November 5, 1978; "The Pentagon's Secret First Strike Plans," *New York Sunday Times,* February 4, 1979. These two advertisements were paid for by Promote Enduring Peace, Inc. See also *NYT,* December 10, 1978, p. 77.

42. *New York Sunday Times,* April 10, 1977, p. E3; *Annual Report,* 1978, pp. 322–23.

APPENDIX A
Regular Army Enlisted Strength, Gains and Losses, and Recruiting Costs, 1920–1940

FY	STRENGTH	TOTAL LOSSES	ETS	DESERTED	REEN-LISTMENT	ORIGINAL	APPLICANTS FOR ORIGINAL ENLISTMENT	RECRUITING COSTS (MILLIONS)
1920	177,974	718,346	659,216	12,422	82,452	69,061		
1921	N/A	104,595	67,105	14,548	50,994	90,233		
1922	125,272	134,273	47,541	8,769	25,884	20,654		
1923	111,341	68,071	34,326	12,423	12,867	27,122		
1924	121,108	75,868	36,538	14,406	17,555	42,545		$4.34
1925	115,177	62,551	22,886	13,752	12,696	26,499		
1926	112,901	64,490	24,459	13,752	15,785	32,990		3.17
1927	113,066	69,811	32,781	11,580	21,015	35,659		3.57
1928	114,785	57,517	22,209	10,467	15,469	30,895	65,092	
1929	117,725	59,094	24,074	9,691	18,473	33,335	60,230	3.32
1930	117,821	62,714	31,314	8,632	23,544	29,411	43,779	3.27
1931	119,034	48,424	26,986	5,075	22,690	18,258	27,809	2.99
1932	113,441	50,684	31,341	3,010	28,161	7,381	27,077	
1933	115,390	50,519	31,456	3,018	32,829	14,998	47,947	1.72
1934	117,517	48,101	26,159	3,857	22,412	23,531	43,947	1.36
1935	118,727	48,948	22,375	3,076	24,747	21,314	58,043	1.56
1936	146,826	49,665	26,704	3,556	26,249	46,607	55,797	1.78
1937	158,626	63,393	26,769	5,414	26,486	45,134		1.95
1938	163,800	61,572	24,053	5,686	26,336	34,979		1.83
1939	167,712	72,196	35,446	3,861	36,699	32,871		1.84
1940	243,095	83,968	34,436	5,661	45,283	108,114		4.07

Sources: Compiled from Annual Reports, 1920–1941, Adjutant General Files, and Statistics Branch Reports.

*ETS = Expiration Term of Service. Refers to soldiers leaving service at the end of their enlistment.

APPENDIX B
Corps Areas Organized by the National Defense Act

Enlisted Strength of Corps Areas and Overseas Departments

CORPS AREAS	STRENGTH AS OF JUNE 30, FISCAL YEAR				
	1920 [a]	1925	1930	1935	1940
I	4,163	4,302	4,165	4,045	6,865
II		10,992	11,368	12,920	20,303
III	20,776	12,687	13,316	10,853	19,847
IV	24,294	10,545	9,993	11,638	34,429
V	Included	3,600	3,218	4,210	13,110
VI	in II & III	5,272	5,469	5,161	9,883
VII		6,249	7,707	7,228	11,625
VIII	29,659	20,534	20,762	20,419	30,495
IX		11,509	11,225	11,733	38,857
TOTAL Continental U.S.	78,892	85,690	87,223	88,207	185,414

Enlisted Strength of Corps Areas and Overseas Departments

DEPARTMENT	STRENGTH AS OF JUNE 30, FISCAL YEAR				
	1920	1925	1930	1935	1940 [b]
Hawaii	4,292	13,902	14,380	14,033	np
Panama	4,272	8,629	8,870	10,115	np
Alaska	864	322	305	275	np
Puerto Rico	5	1,083	1,030	1,030	np
Philippines					
Regulars	11,776	4,103	4,111	4,560	np
Native [c]	6,930	6,585	6,480	6,371	np
China [d]	1,437	917	948	704	np
Europe	15,068				np
Other [e]	38,653	531	954	41	np
Total Overseas	106,012	36,072	37,078	36,891	64,027
GRAND TOTAL	184,904	121,762	124,301	125,098	249,441

Sources: Map, Kreidberg and Henry, *History of Military Mobilization in the United States Army,* p. 386; Strengths, compiled from *Annual Reports,* 1920, 1925, 1930, 1935, 1940.

[a] Strengths given are for old territorial departments abolished by the National Defense Act.

[b] Overseas strengths were not reported beginning in 1940.

[c] Refers to Philippine Scouts, Filipinos recruited and trained under their own officers as part of United States Constabulary.

[d] Refers to the Fifteenth Infantry Regiment stationed at Tientsin until 1938.

[e] In 1920 included troops in Russia and enroute to the United States. Thereafter refers to military attachés, students abroad, and personnel on leave or enroute to and from overseas assignments.

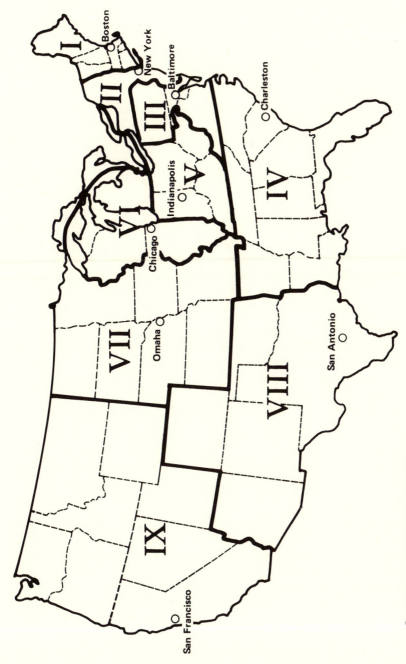

○ CORPS AREA HEADQUARTERS

APPENDIX C

Enlisted Pay Systems, 1908–1940

GRADE	BASE PAY PER MONTH						
	1	2	3	4	5	6	7
1908–1916	$ 45	$40	$36	$30	$24	$21	$15
1917–1919	51	48	44	38	36	35	30
1920–1921	74	53	45	45	37	35	30
1922–1939	126	84	72	54	42	30	21
1940	126	84	72	60	54	36	30*

*$21 per month for recruits.

LONGEVITY PAY

1908–1917   Longevity pay was linked to grade and number of enlistments. Soldiers in the top three grades received an additional four dollars a month for each enlistment up to seven. Soldiers in grades four, five, and six received three dollars a month for each enlistment. Privates received three dollars a month for the second and third enlistment and one dollar monthly thereafter to the seventh. Each enlistment represented three years service.

1920–1921   Ten percent of base pay for each five years of service up to 40 percent.

1922–1939   Five percent of base pay for each four years of service up to 25 percent.

1940   Ten percent of base pay and specialty pay after the first four years of service and a 5 percent additional increase for each four years thereafter to a maximum of 25 percent.

SPECIALTY PAY

1908–1917   Before 1920 specialty pay was linked to rank and job. The Pay Act of 1908 listed hundreds of specific specialty-rank-job combinations with a separate base pay for each.

1920–1940   In 1920 specialty pay was separated from base pay. Only soldiers in grades six and seven received specialist designations. The National Defense Act established six specialty classes and pay rates as follows: First Class, $25; second class, $20; third class, $15; fourth class, $12; fifth class, $8; sixth class, $3. The number of men in each specialty class was established each year and based on a percentage of the total number of soldiers in grades six and seven. A soldier lost his specialty rating when transferred.

1922   The Pay Readjustment Act increased specialty pay as follows: First
                Class, $30; second class, $25; third class, $20; fourth class, $15; fifth
                class, $6; sixth class, $3. The Selective Service Act did not make any
                changes in the specialty pay system.

REENLISTMENT BONUS

1908–1920   Three months' pay at the rate received at the time of last enlistment.

1922–1940   Grades 1 to 3 received $50 times the number of years served in their
                last enlistment. Grades 4 to 7 received $25 times the number of years
                served in the last enlistment. A normal enlistment was three years.
                The Selective Service Act did not alter the reenlistment bonus com-
                putation.

MARKSMANSHIP BONUS

1908–1940   Bonuses for weaponry skills established in 1908 remained unchanged
                throughout the interwar period. Only soldiers assigned to combat
                units could receive the bonus. The number of soldiers who could
                receive the bonus was determined as a precentage of the total enlisted
                strength of the army. Bonuses were paid in the following categories:

                Marksmen, second class gunners $2/month
                Sharpshooters, first class gunners $3/month
                Expert riflemen $5/month
                Gun pointers, gun commanders, observers
                    second class, chief loaders $7/month
                Plotters, observers first class,
                    casemate electricians $9/month

Sources: 1908, General Order No. 80, May 15, 1908; 1917, Bulletin No. 32, May 24, 1917;
1920, General Order No. 44, July 20, 1920; 1922, Bulletin No. 9, June 10, 1922; 1940, Bulletin
No. 25, October 14, 1940, in *War Department General Orders and Bulletins* (Washington,
D.C.: GPO, respective years).

APPENDIX D

Military Estimates Requested by the War Department, Amounts Allowed by the Bureau of the Budget, and Amounts Appropriated by Congress for Military Activities, 1921–1940

FISCAL YEAR	ARMY REQUEST	ALLOWED BY BUDGET BUREAU	APPROPRIATED BY CONGRESS
1921	$982,800,020	N/A	$394,700,577
1922	699,275,502	N/A	328,113,530
1923	np	$293,333,027	270,563,264
1924	np	264,284,200	257,274,768
1925	np	259,024,006	256,515,279
1926	np	259,685,274	260,757,250
1927	np	261,116,650	269,339,246
1928	np	281,616,286	282,118,885
1929	334,368,880	310,902,655	311,167,468
1930	349,986,426	329,366,607	332,404,342
1931	362,382,069	340,802,365	341,050,664
1932	351,304,294	340,301,759	336,081,865
1933	331,243,723	302,106,542	299,993,920
1934	320,900,513	273,366,338	277,126,281
1935	305,271,154	287,703,033	250,846,736
1936	361,351,154	312,235,811	345,861,022
1937	467,022,915	369,586,298	382,787,267
1938		410,936,294	406,398,954
1939		427,060,318	449,931,374
1940		461,710,990	660,167,878

Sources: Appropriations and amounts allowed by the Bureau of the Budget, from *Message of the President of the United States Transmitting the Budget for the Service of the Fiscal Year Ending June 30, 1923–1941,* inclusive. Estimates for 1921 and 1922 are from *ANJ,* December 6, 1919, p. 424, and *ANJ,* December 11, 1920, p. 426. Estimates for 1923–1928 were not published. A statement by the Secretary of War, published in *ANJ,* October 21, 1922, p. 178, suggests that the army's estimates for those years conformed to limits established by the Bureau of the Budget and did not truly reflect any requests. Estimates for 1929–1937 are from the *Cater Files,* "1941 Folder," Center of Military History, as quoted in John Killigrew, "The Impact of the Great Depression on the Army, 1929–1936," Appendix I.

SELECTED BIBLIOGRAPHY

UNPUBLISHED MATERIALS

In reconstructing the army's efforts to recruit and maintain enlisted strength between 1919 and 1940, I concentrated my primary research effort on official army documents found in the Central File of the Adjutant General's Office (AGO) and other material found in the National Archives in Washington, D.C. The other major source of primary documents used in this study was the Military History Research Collection of the Military History Institute (MHI), Carlisle Barracks, Pennsylvania. I found personal papers of key figures discouragingly meager on the subject of military manpower policy. Some of the more important documents used in this study from these collections are listed below. The rest are cited in chapter notes.

National Archives

Adjutant General's Office. *Proposed Plan for Resumption of Active Recruiting.* Memorandum for Chief of Staff. Washington, D.C., July 18, 1921. AGO 341.1 (7-18-21), RG 407.

———. *Recruiting Situation.* Memorandum for Chief of Staff on Recruiting from 1919 to 1926. Washington, D.C., April 26, 1926. AGO 341.1 (4-26-26), RG 94.

———. *Report on Results Connection Intelligence Tests for Applicants for Enlistment.* Quarterly reports from each corps area. October 1927 to June 1931. AGO 319.12, RG 407. July 1931 to March 1938. AGO 702, RG 94.

Dowdall, Lt. H. G. *Excerpts of the Report of . . .* (Confidential) December 13, 1920. AGO 341.1, RG 407.

Office of the Chief of Staff. *Financial Status of Officers.* Binder on . . . during the Depression. AGO 240 (12-27-34), RG 94.

Personnel Division, G-1. G-1 Guide Book on *Readjustment of Service Pay and Allowances,* vol. 3. AGO 241 (1-1-26), RG 94.

———. *Marriage of Enlisted Men.* Binder containing reports on. . . . AGO 220.81 (11-2-28) (1), RG 94.

———. *Recruiting. Improvement in Calibre of Recruits.* Binder on . . . Washington, D.C. AGO 341 (8-18-31) (1), RG 94.

Phillipson, Major I. J. *Report on Recruiting.* A Report to the Adjutant General on Procurement Conditions from July 1, 1916, to January 31, 1921. n.d. AGO 341.1, RG 407.

War Plans Division. Report of the Survey of the Military Establishment by the War Department General Staff. Washington, D.C., November 1, 1929. AGO 333 E.P., RG 407.

Woodbury, Major E. N. *Review of Comments on "Study of Desertions."* A Report to the Chief of Morale Branch. War Plans Division, General Staff, Washington, D.C., April 13, 1921. AGO 251.1 (10-12-20) Bulky, RG 407.

Military History Research Collection

Benson, Colonel C. C. *A Study of Voluntary Enlistments, Army of the United States (1775–1945).* History Section, Army War College, Washington, D.C. September 1945.

Brown, Major Albert E. *Peace Time Enlisted Loses, Replacements and Methods.* Memorandum for the Commandant, Army War College, Washington, D.C. February 15, 1920.

Daly, Major J. C. *Purchase of Discharge by Enlisted Men.* Memorandum for the Assistant Commandant, Army War College, Fort Humphres, D.C. November 5, 1938.

Statistics Branch, General Staff. *Cost of Recruiting, 1924–1940.* Collection of Special Reports prepared by the . . . , War Department, Washington, D.C., 1924–1940 (1925, 1928, 1932 missing).

Woodbury, Major E. N. *A Study of Desertion in the Army.* Mimeograph ed. Morale Branch, War Plans Division, General Staff, Washington, D.C. September 15, 1920.

———. *Morale: Improving the Standard of Enlisted Men.* Memorandum for the Assistant Commandant of the Army War College, Washington, D.C. February 28, 1931.

Government Publications and Documents

Hoover, Herbert. *Public Papers and Proclamations of the Presidents of the United States, Herbert Hoover.* Washington, D.C.: GPO, 1974.

Roosevelt, Franklin D. *The Public Papers and Addresses of Franklin D. Roosevelt.* Edited by Samuel I. Rosenman. vols. 1, 2. New York: Random House, 1938, vols. 8, 9. New York: The Macmillan Co., 1941.

U.S., War Department, Adjutant General's Office. *Army List and Directory, 1918–1941* (bimonthly publication). Washington, D.C.: GPO, 1918–1941.

United States Congress. Supplement to Compilation of Veterans Laws, 94th and 95th Congress. Washington: GPO, 1978.

U.S. *Congressional Directory.*

U.S. *Congressional Record.*

U.S. Congress, House, Committee on Appropriations. *Hearings Before the . . . on Army Appropriation Bill, 1919–1941.*

———. Committee on Military Affairs. *Army Reorganization: Hearings Before the . . .* 66th Congress, 1st Sess., September 3, 1919.

———. Committee on Military Affairs. *General Douglas MacArthur on National Defense: Hearings Before the . . .* 73rd Congress, 1st Sess., April 26, 1933.

———. Committee on Military Affairs. *An Adequate National Defense: Hearings Before the . . .* 76th Congress, 1st Sess., January 17, 1939.

———. Committee on Military Affairs. *Selective Compulsory Military Training and Service: Hearings Before the . . .* 76th Congress, 3rd Sess., July 10, 1940.

U.S. Congress, Senate, Committee on Appropriations. *Hearings Before the . . . on Army Appropriations Bill, 1919–1941.*

———. Committee on Military Affairs. *Reorganization of the Army: Hearings Before the . . .* 66th Congress, 1st Sess., August 7, 1919.

U.S. Congress, Committee on Military Affairs. *Compulsory Military Training and Service: Hearings* Before the . . . 76th Congress, 3d Sess., July 3, 1940.

U.S., President, Commission on an All-Volunteer Armed Force. *The Report of the Commission.* Washington, D.C.: GPO, 1970.

_____. *Studies Prepared for the President's Commission on an All-Volunteer Force.* 2 vols. Washington, D.C.: GPO, 1970.

U.S., Department Selective Service System. *The Selective Service Act, Its Legislative History, Amendments, Appropriations, Cognates, and Prior Instruments of Security.* Special Monograph No. 2, Vols I-V. Washington: GPO, 1954.

U.S., *Statutes at Large.*

U.S., Veterans Administration. *Annual Report,* Administrator of Veterans Affairs, 1977.

U.S., War Department. *Annual Reports,* War Department, 1919–1941.

_____. *Army Regulations,* No. 600-750, "Personnel: Recruiting for the Regular Army," 1925, 1931, 1932, 1934, 1935, 1939. Washington, D.C.: GPO, 1925, 1931, 1932, 1934, 1935, 1939.

_____. *Compilation of General Orders, Bulletins, Circulars, and General Recruiting Service Circular Letters Relating to Recruiting (October 1, 1918 to June 30, 1919).* Washington, D.C.: GPO, 1919.

_____. *General Orders, Special Orders, Bulletins and Circulars,* 1919–1940. Washington, D.C.: GPO, 1919–1940.

_____. *Regulations for the Army of the United States, 1913.* Washington, D.C.: GPO, 1913.

_____. *Regulations for the Army of the United States, 1913,* corrected to April 15, 1917. Washington, D.C.: GPO, 1918.

_____. *Statement of a Proper Military Policy for the United States.* Washington, D.C.: GPO, 1915.

_____. *The Army of the United States.* Washington, D.C.: GPO, 1940.

U.S., War Department, Adjutant General's Office. *Army List and Directory,* 1918–1941 (bimonthly publication). Washington, D.C.: GPO, 1918–1941.

_____. *Official Army Register,* 1918–1941 (annual publication). Washington, D.C.: GPO, 1918–1941.

_____. *The United States Army as a Career.* Washington, D.C.: GPO, 1929.

NEWSPAPERS AND CONTEMPORARY PERIODICALS

I made extensive use of the *New York Times* and the *Army and Navy Journal* in preparing this study. The *Times,* because of its exhaustive index, proved to be an invaluable tool for filling in gaps between official documents and public events. The *Army and Navy Journal,* unfortunately not indexed, is especially valuable because of the close attention it paid to the progress of legislation, events, and opinions that affected the army. One must, however, be always mindful of the bias of this source. Periodicals used include:

American Mercury
The Arbitrator

Atlantic Monthly
The Cavalry Journal
Century Magazine
Coast Artillery Journal
Current History
Current Opinion
Fortune
Infantry Journal
Literary Digest
The Nation
New Republic
Newsweek
North American Review
The Quartermaster Review
Scientific American
Saturday Evening Post
The Survey
Time
U.S. Army Recruiting News
Vital Speeches

Significant articles from these periodicals are listed below. Others are cited as appropriate in the chapter notes.

"American Militarism Waning," *The Nation* 108, no. 2816 (June 21, 1919): 973.

"Arming for What?" *The Nation* 147, no. 17 (October 22, 1938): 396, 397.

Baker, Newton D. "A Permanent Military Policy for the United States," *Saturday Evening Post,* May 31, 1919, pp. 29–30.

Buel, Walker S. "The Army Under the New Deal." *Literary Digest* 116, no. 9 (August 26, 1933): 3.

Carter, Major General William H. "Tinkering With the Army," *North American Review* 217 (February 1923): 181–86.

"The Churches' Wrath at 'Defense Day,' " *Literary Digest* 82, no. 6 (August 9, 1924): 30, 31.

Connor, Major General Fox. "The National Defense," *North American Review* 225, no. 889 (January 1928): 1–11.

"Conscription?" *Newsweek,* June 17, 1940, 34.

Dowdall, Lieutenant Harry G. "Modern Recruiting—A Problem," *Infantry Journal* 36, no. 6 (January 1930), 616–25.

"Is It Dangerous to Slash Our Army?" *Literary Digest* 115, no. 18 (May 6, 1933): 8.

Johns, E. B. "The Housing of the Regular Army," *Infantry Journal* 27, no. 6 (December 1925), 687–722.

Marshall, Captain Otto. "Recruiting, and How," *Coast Artillery Journal* 72, no. 1 (January 1930): 62–66.

MacArthur, Douglas. "The Necessity for Military Forces." *Infantry Journal* 30, no. 3 (March 1927): pp. 327–31.

Miles, Sherman. "The Problem of the Pacifist." *North American Review* 217, no. 3 (March 1923): 313–26.

"No More 'Y'?" *Time,* September 30, 1940, pp. 19–20.

"Our Disappearing Army," *Literary Digest* 72, no. 11 (March 18, 1922): 10.

"Our Militaristic Peril," *Literary Digest* 62, no. 13 (September 27, 1919): 9, 10.

"Our Military System as it Appeared to America's Citizen Soldiers," *Infantry Journal* 15, no. 10 (April 1919): 771–87.

"Our Preparations for War," *The Nation* 118, no. 3066 (April 9, 1924): 387.

Pershing, General John J. "Our National Military Policy," *Scientific American* 127, (August, 1922): 83.

Phillipson, Captain Irving. "The Infantry's Recruiting Problem," *Infantry Journal* 16, no. 11 (May 1920): 967–71.

"Recruiting, 1940-Style," *Time* August 19, 1940, p. 19.

Reilly, Henry J. "Our Crumbling National Defense," (in four parts) *Century Magazine* 113, no. 3 (January 1927); 113, no. 5 (March 1927); 113, no. 6 (April 1927); 114, no. 2 (June 1927).

Stockton, Major Richard, Jr. "The Army We Need," *North American Review* 210 (November 1919): 645–55.

Summerall, Major General C. P. "Distinguishing Features of the Army," *Infantry Journal* 30, no. 2 (February 1927): 117–22.

Villard, Oswald Garrison. "The Army and Navy Forever," *The Nation* 136, no. 3527 (February 8, 1933): 139.

_____. "We Militarize," *Atlantic Monthly* 157, no. 2 (February 1936), 138–49.

"What Enlisted Men Think of Our Military System," *Current Opinion* 66, no. 6 (June 1919): 319–400.

Whittlesey, Charles. "Military Preparedness," *The New Republic* 22, no. 94 (March 17, 1920): 94.

INTERVIEWS, PRIVATE PAPERS, MEMOIRS, AUTOBIOGRAPHIES, AND BIOGRAPHIES

Alvord, Raymond G. Personal interview with 1st Sgt. Raymond G. Alvord (Ret). West Point, New York, February 6, 1975.

Baker, Newton. The Newton Baker Papers. General Correspondence, 1916–1921. Library of Congress, Washington, D.C.

Buhite, Russel D. *Patrick J. Hurley and American Foreign Policy.* Ithaca, N.Y.: Cornell University Press, 1973.

Chynoweth, Bradford, G. The Bradford Chynoweth Papers: Recollections of his Army Career. Letter to Col. Pappas. Military History Institute, Carlisle Barracks, Pennsylvania.

Coffman, Edward M. *The Hilt of the Sword: The Career of Peyton C. March.* Madison, Wisc.: The University of Wisconsin Press, 1966.

Cole, Wayne S. *Senator Gerald P. Nye and American Foreign Relations.* Minneapolis, Minn.: University of Minnesota Press, 1962.

Cramer, Clarence H. *Newton D. Baker, A Biography.* New York: The World Publishing Co., 1961.

Fausold, Martin L. *James W. Wadsowrth, Jr., The Gentleman from New York.* Syracuse, N.Y.: Syracuse University Press, 1975.

Hagood, Johnson, II. *Down the Big Road.* Manuscript of memoirs, unpublished. The Hagood Family Papers. Military History Institute, Carlisle Barracks, Pennsylvania.

Hoover, Herbert. *The Memoirs of Herbert Hoover,* Vol. 2. New York: The Macmillan Co., 1952.

Hunt, Frazier. *The Untold Story of Douglas MacArthur.* New York: The Devin-Adair Co., 1954.

James, D. Clayton. *The Years of MacArthur,* Vol. 1, *1880–1941.* Boston: Houghton Mifflin, 1970.

Johnson, Gerald W. *An Honorable Titan: A Biographical Study of Adolph Simon Ochs.* New York: Harper & Brothers, 1946.

Kelleher, Jerome. Personal Interview with WO3 Jerome Kelleher (Ret). West Point, New York, January 30, 1975.

Lane, Jack C. *Armed Progressive: General Leonard Wood.* San Rafael, Calif.: Presidio Press, 1978.

MacArthur, Douglas. *Reminiscences.* New York: McGraw-Hill Book Co., 1964.

Magruder, Carter B. The Carter B. Magruder Papers: Recollections and Reflections. Transcript of the Debriefing of Geneal Magruder by Col. Tucker, 1972. Military History Institute, Carlisle Barracks, Pennsylvania.

Marshall, Katherine Tupper. *Together: Annals of an Army Wife.* New York: Tupper and Love, Inc., 1946.

McFarland, Keith D. *Harry H. Woodring: A Political Biography of FDR's Controversial Secretary of War.* Lawrence, Kans.: The University Press of Kansas, 1975.

Pogue, Forrest C. *George C. Marshall: Education of a General, 1880–1939.* New York: The Viking Press, 1963.

Polk, James H. Recollections and Reflections. Transcript of the Debriefing of General Polk by Col. Tausch, 1971–1972. Military History Institute, Carlisle Barracks, Pennsylvania.

Porter, Robert. Personal interview with Gen. Robert Porter (Ret). West Point, New York, January 1979.

Seamon, Jonathan O. Recollections and Reflections. Transcript of the Debriefing of General Seamon by Cols. Clyde Patterson and Nicholas Psaki, 1971. Military History Institute, Carlisle Barracks, Pennsylvania.

Stimson, Henry L., and McGeorge Bundy. *On Active Service in Peace and War.* New York: Harper & Brothers, 1948.

Villard, Oswald Garrison. *Fighting Years: Memoirs of a Liberal Editor.* New York: Harcourt, Brace and Co., 1939.

Vinson, John Chambers. *William E. Borah and the Outlawry of War.* Athens, Ga.: University of Georgia Press, 1957.

Westmoreland, William C. *A Soldier Reports.* Garden City, N.Y.: Doubleday, 1976.

Wreszin, Michael. *Oswald Garrison Villard: Pacifist at War.* Bloomington, Ind.: Indiana University Press, 1965.

BOOKS, DISSERTATIONS, AND SCHOLARLY ARTICLES

Adler, Selig. *The Isolationist Impulse.* New York: The Macmillan Company, 1957.

Allen, Frederick Lewis. *Since Yesterday: The 1930's in America.* 1939, Reprint. New York: Harper & Row, 1968.

Baker, Roscoe. *The American Legion and American Foreign Policy*. 1954, Reprint.
Westport, Conn.: Greenwood Press, 1974.

Beard, Robin. "The All-Volunteer Army: Hard Facts and Hard Choices." *Strategic Review* 7, no. 3 (Summer 1979): 42–46.

Bernardo, C. Joseph, and Eugene H. Bacon. *American Military Policy: Its Development Since 1775*, 2d ed. Harrisburg, Pa.: The Stackpole Co., 1961.

Bernstein, Irving. *The Lean Years: A History of the American Worker, 1920–1933*.
Boston: Houghton Mifflin Co., 1970.

———. *Turbulent Years: A History of the American Worker, 1933–1941*. Boston:
Houghton Mifflin Co., 1970.

Bigelow, Donald N. *William Conant Church and the Army and Navy Journal*.
New York: Columbia University Press, 1952.

Brown, Richard C. "Social Attitudes of American Generals, 1898–1940." Ph.D.
dissertation, University of Wisconsin, 1941.

Chambers, John Whiteclay, II. "Conscripting for Colossus: The Adoption of the
Draft in the United States in World War I." Ph.D. dissertation, Columbia
University, 1973.

———. "Conscription for Colossus: The Progressive Era and the Origin of the
Modern Military Draft in the United States in World War I." In *The Military
in America: Essays and Documents*, edited by Peter Karsten. New York:
Macmillan, The Free Press, 1980.

———, ed. *Draftees or Volunteers: A Documentary History of the Debate Over
Military Conscription in the United States, 1787–1973*. New York; Garland
Publishing, Inc., 1975.

Chatfield, Charles. *For Peace and Justice: Pacifism in America, 1914–1941*. Knoxville, Tenn.: University of Tennessee Press, 1971.

———, ed. *Peace Movements in America*. New York: Schocken Books, 1973.

Clifford, John Garry. *The Citizen Soldiers: The Plattsburg Training Camp Movement, 1913–1920*. Lexington, Ky.: The University Press of Kentucky, 1972.

Coffman, Edward M., and Peter F. Herrly. "The American Regular Army Officer
Corps Between World Wars, A Collective Biography." *Armed Forces and
Society* 4, no. 1 (November 1977): 55–73.

Cole, Wayne S. *America First: The Battle Against Intervention, 1940–1941*. Madison, Wisc.: The University of Wisconsin Press, 1973.

Cooper, Richard V. L. "The All-Volunteer Force: Five Years Later." *International Security* 2, no. 4 (Spring 1978): 101–31.

Craven, Wesley Frank, and James L. Cate, eds. *The Army Air Forces in World
War II*, Vol. 1: *Plans and Early Operations, January 1939 to August 1942*.
Chicago: University of Chicago Press, 1948.

Curti, Merle Eugene. *Peace or War: The American Struggle, 1636–1936*. New
York: Garland Publishing, Inc., 1972.

Dalfiume, Richard M. *Desegregation of the U.S. Armed Forces: Fighting on Two
Fronts, 1939–1953*. Columbia, Mo.: University of Missouri Press, 1969.

Daniels, Roger. *The Bonus March*. Westport, Conn.: Greenwood Press, 1971.

Derthick, Martha. *The National Guard in Politics*. Cambridge, Mass.: Harvard
University Press, 1965.

Dickinson, John. *The Building of an Army*. New York: The Century Co., 1922.

Divine, Robert A. *The Illusion of Neutrality*. Chicago: University of Chicago
Press, 1962.

———. *The Reluctant Belligerent: American Entry into World War II*. New York: John Wiley and Sons, 1965.

Donovan, John C. "Congressional Isolationists and the Roosevelt Foreign Policy," *World Politics,* April 1951, pp. 299–316.

Douglas, Paul H. *Social Security in the United States*. New York: McGraw-Hill, 1936.

Ekirch, Arthur A., Jr. *The Civilian and the Military: A History of the American Antimilitarist Tradition*. Colorado Springs, Colo.: Ralph Myles, Publisher, 1972.

Etzold, Thomas H. "Our Diminishing Manpower Resources." *Army* 30, no. 1 (January 1980): 10–14.

Ferrell, Robert H. *Peace in Their Time, The Origins of the Kellogg-Briand Pact*. New York: W. W. Norton & Co., 1969.

Fenno, Richard F. *Congressmen in Committees*. Boston: Little, Brown and Co., 1973.

Finnegan, John Patrick. *Against the Specter of a Dragon: The Campaign for American Military Preparedness, 1914–1917*. Westport, Conn.: Greenwood Press, 1974.

Gallup, George H. *The Gallup Poll: Public Opinion, 1935–1971*. New York: Random House, 1972.

Ganoe, William Addleman. *The History of the United States Army*, rev. ed. Ashton, Md.: Eric Lundberg, 1964.

Gerhardt, James M. *The Draft and Public Policy: Issues in Military Manpower Procurement, 1945–1970*. Columbus, Ohio: Ohio State University Press, 1971.

Green, Constance McLaughlin, Harry C. Thomson, and Peter C. Roots. *United States Army in World War II, The Technical Services,* vol. 3, pt. 1: *The Ordnance Department: Planning Munitions for War*. Washington, D.C.: Department of the Army, 1955.

Green, Fred. "The Military View of American National Policy, 1904–1940." *American Historical Review* 66, no. 2, (January 1961): 354–77.

Greenfield, Kent Roberts, ed. *Command Decisions*. Washington, D.C.: Department of the Army, 1960.

Hicks, John D. *Republican Ascendancy, 1921–1933*. New York: Harper & Row, 1960.

Huzar, Elias. *The Purse and the Sword: Control of the Army by Congress Through Military Appropriations, 1933–1950*. Ithaca, N.Y.: Cornell University Press, 1950.

Janowitz, Morris. "The All-Volunteer Military as a 'Sociopolitical' Problem." *Social Problems* 22 (1975): 432–49.

Jensen, Joan M. "The Army and Domestic Surveillance On Campus." Paper presented at the 19th Annual National Archives Conference, May 17–18, 1979, Washington, D.C.

———. "Military Surveillance of Civilians in America." University Programs Modular Series. Morristown, N.J.: General Learning Press, 1975.

Johnson, Julia E. *Compulsory Military Training*. New York: H. W. Wilson, Co., 1941.

———, ed. *Peace and Rearmament*. New York: H. W. Wilson, Co., 1938.

_____. *The United States and War*. New York: H. W. Wilson, Co., 1939.

Jonas, Manfred. *Isolationism in America, 1935–1941*. Ithaca, N.Y.: Cornell University Press, 1966.

Killigrew, John W. "The Impact of the Great Depression on the United States Army, 1929–1936." Ph.D. dissertation, Indiana University, 1960.

Kreidberg, Marvin A., and Merton G. Henry. *History of Military Mobilization in the United States Army, 1775–1945*. Washington, D.C.: Department of the Army, 1955.

Langer, William L., and S. Everett Gleason. *The Challenge to Isolation, 1937–1940*. New York: Harper & Brothers, 1952.

Lee, Ulysses. *United States Army in World War II*, Special Studies, vol. 8: *The Employment of Negro Troops*. Washington, D.C.: Department of the Army, 1966.

Lerwill, Leonard L, *The Personnel Replacement System in the United States Army*. Washington, D.C.: Department of the Army, 1954.

Leuchtenburg, William E. *Franklin D. Roosevelt and the New Deal, 1931–1940*. New York; Harper & Row, 1963.

_____. *The Perils of Prosperity, 1914–1932*. Chicago: The University of Chicago Press, 1958.

Levering, Ralph B. *The Public and American Foreign Policy, 1918–1978*. New York: William Mrrow and Co., 1978.

Mellon, Andrew W. *Taxation: The People's Business*. New York: The Macmillan Co., 1924.

Miller, James C., III, ed. *Why The Draft? The Case for a Volunteer Army*. Baltimore, Md.: Penguin Books, Inc., 1968.

Mitchell, Broadus. *Depression Decade: From New Era Through New Deal, 1929–1941*. New York: Harper & Row, 1969.

Moley, Raymond, Jr. *The American Legion Story*. New York: Duell, Sloan and Pearce, 1966.

Mooney, Chase C., and Martha E. Laymen. "Some Phases of the Compulsory Military Training Movement, 1914–1920." *Mississippi Valley Historical Review* 38, no. 4 (March 1952): 633–56.

Moore, Harold G., and Jeff M. Tuten. *Building A Volunteer Army: The Fort Ord Contribution*. Washington, D.C.: Department of the Army, 1975.

Moskos, Charles C., Jr. "The All-Volunteer Military: Calling, Profession, or Occupation?" *Parameters* 7, no. 1 (January 1977): 2–9.

Munson, Edward L. *The Management of Men*. New York: Henry Holt and Co., 1921.

Olson, Keith W. *The G.I. Bill, the Veterans, and the Colleges*. Lexington, Ky.: University Press of Kentucky, 1974.

Palmer, John McAuley. *America in Arms: The Experiences of the United States with Military Organization*. New Haven, Conn.: Yale University Press, 1941.

_____. *Statesmanship or War*. New York: Doubleday, Page & Co., 1927.

Potter, Jim. *The American Economy Between the World Wars*. New York: John Wiley & Sons, 1974.

Prothro, James Warren. *The Dollar Decade: Business Ideas in the 1920's*. 1954, Reprint. Westport, Conn.: Greenwood Press, 1969.

Reddick, L. D. "The Negro Policy of the United States Army, 1775–1945." *The Journal of Negro History* 34, no. 1 (January 1949): 9–29.

Reely, Mary K., ed. *Selected Articles on Disarmament*. New York: H. W. Wilson, Co., 1921.

Ross, Davis R. B. *Preparing For Ulysses: Politics and Veterans During World War II*. New York: Columbia University Press, 1969.

Russell, Francis. *The Shadow of Blooming Grove: Warren G. Harding in His Times*. New York: McGraw-Hill Book Co., 1968.

Sabrosky, Alan Ned. *Defense Manpower Policy: A Critical Reappraisal*. Philadelphia, Pa.: Foreign Policy Research Institute, 1978.

Schaffer, Ronald. "General Stanley D. Embick: Military Dissenter." *Military Affairs* 37, no. 3 (October 1973): 89–95.

———. "The War Department's Defense of ROTC, 1920–1940." *Wisconsin Magazine of History* 53, no. 2 (Winter, 1969–1970): 108–20.

Schlesinger, Arthur M., Jr. *The Crisis of the Old Order, 1919–1933*. Boston: Houghton Mifflin Co., 1957.

Shannon, David A. *Between the Wars: America, 1919–1941*. Boston: Houghton Mifflin Co., 1965.

Slonaker, John. *The Voluntary Army: A Military History Research Collection Bibliography*. Carlisle Barracks, Pa.: U.S. Military History Research Collection, 1972.

Smith, Daniel M. *War and Depression: America, 1914 to 1939*. St. Louis, Mo.: Forum Press, 1972.

Soule, George H. *Prosperity Decade: From War to Depression, 1917–1929*. New York: Rinehart & Co., 1947.

Spencer, Samuel R., Jr. "A History of the Selective Training and Service Act of 1940 from Inception to Enactment." Ph.D. dissertation, Harvard University, 1951.

Starr, Paul. *The Discarded Army: Veterans After Vietnam*. New York: Charterhouse, 1973.

Stern, Frederick Martin. *The Citizen Army: Key to Defense in the Atomic Age*. New York: St. Martin's Press, 1957.

Stouffer, Samuel A., et al. *Studies in Social Psychology in World War II*, Vol. 1: *The American Soldier: Adjustment During Army Life*. Princeton, N.J.: Princeton University Press, 1949.

Sullivan, Mark. *Our Times, The United States, 1900–1925*, Vol. 6, *The Twenties*. New York: Charles Scribner's Sons, 1935.

Summers, Robert E., and Harrison B. Summers, eds. *Universal Military Service*. New York: H. W. Wilson, Co., 1941.

Syrett, David, and Richard H. Kohn. "The Dangers of an All-Volunteer Army." *Military Review* 52, no. 6 (June 1972): 70–79.

The Officer's Guide. Washington, D.C.: National Service Publishing Co., 1930.

Upton, Emory. *The Military Policy of the United States*. Washington, D.C.: GPO, 1912.

Waldron, William H. *The Old Sergeant's Conferences*. Washington, D.C.: The National Service Publishing Co., 1930.

Warren, Harris G. *Herbert Hoover and the Great Depression*. New York: Oxford University Press, 1959.

Watson, Mark S. *United States Army in World War II, The War Department,* Vol. 1: *Chief of Staff: Prewar Plans and Preparations.* Washington, D.C.: Department of the Army, 1950.

Weigley, Russell F. *History of the United States Army.* New York: Macmillan, 1967.

_____. *Towards an American Army: Military Thought from Washington to Marshall.* New York: Columbia University Press, 1962.

Wilbur, Ray L., and Arthur M. Hyde. *The Hoover Policies.* New York: Charles Scribner's Sons, 1937.

INDEX

About the Author

ROBERT K. GRIFFITH, JR. is a Major in the United States Army. Currently he is a Federal Fellow in the 1981–1982 Congressional Fellowship Program. He has served in Armored and Armored Cavalry Units in the United States, Germany, and Vietnam, and is a decorated combat veteran. Since completing advanced studies in history at Brown University, Major Griffith has served on the faculties of the United States Military Academy and the United States Army Command and General Staff College. His articles have appeared in the journals *Military Affairs* and *Parameters*.